*Decent Incomes for All*

# International Policy Exchange Series

*Published in collaboration with the
Center for International Policy Exchanges
University of Maryland*

## Series Editors
Douglas J. Besharov
Neil Gilbert

*United in Diversity?
Comparing Social Models in Europe and America*
Edited by Jens Alber and Neil Gilbert

*The Korean State and Social Policy:
How South Korea Lifted Itself from Poverty and
Dictatorship to Affluence and Democracy*
Stein Ringen, Huck-ju Kwon, Ilcheong Yi,
Taekyoon Kim, and Jooha Lee

*Child Protection Systems:
International Trends and Orientations*
Edited by Neil Gilbert, Nigel Parton,
and Marit Skivenes

*The Age of Dualization:
The Changing Face of Inequality in
Deindustrializing Societies*
Edited by Patrick Emmenegger, Silja
Häusermann, Bruno Palier,
and Martin Seeleib-Kaiser

*Counting the Poor:
New Thinking About European Poverty Measures
and Lessons for the United States*
Edited by Douglas J. Besharov
and Kenneth A. Couch

*Social Policy and Citizenship:
The Changing Landscape*
Edited by Adalbert Evers
and Anne-Marie Guillemard

*Chinese Policy in a Time of Transition*
Edited by Douglas J. Besharov and Karen Baehler

*Reconciling Work and Poverty Reduction:
How Successful Are European Welfare States?*
Edited by Bea Cantillon and Frank
Vandenbroucke

*University Adaptation in Difficult Economic Times*
Edited by Paola Mattei

*Activation or Workfare? Governance and the
Neo-Liberal Convergence*
Edited by Ivar Lødemel and Amílcar Moreira

*Child Welfare Systems and Migrant Children:
A Cross Country Study of Policies and Practice*
Edited by Marit Skivenes, Ravinder Barn,
Katrin Kriz, and Tarja Pösö

*Adjusting to a World in Motion:
Trends in Global Migration and Migration Policy*
Edited by Douglas J. Besharov and Mark H. Lopez

*Caring for a Living:
Migrant Women, Aging Citizens,
and Italian Families*
Francesca Degiuli

*Child Welfare Removals by the State:
A Cross-Country Analysis of Decision-Making
Systems*
Edited by Kenneth Burns, Tarja Pösö,
and Marit Skivenes

*Improving Public Services:
International Experiences in Using Evaluation
Tools to Measure Program Performance*
Edited by Douglas J. Besharov, Karen J. Baehler,
and Jacob Alex Klerman

*Welfare, Work, and Poverty:
Social Assistance in China*
Qin Gao

*Youth Labor in Transition:
Inequalities, Mobility, and Policies in Europe*
Edited by Jacqueline O'Reilly, Janine Leschke, Renate
Ortlieb, Martin Seeleib-Kaiser, and Paola Villa

*Decent Incomes for All:
Improving Policies in Europe*
Edited by Bea Cantillon, Tim Goedemé,
and John Hills

# SCHOOL of
# PUBLIC POLICY

# DECENT INCOMES FOR ALL

## *Improving Policies in Europe*

Edited by

BEA CANTILLON
TIM GOEDEMÉ
JOHN HILLS

OXFORD
UNIVERSITY PRESS

# OXFORD
UNIVERSITY PRESS

Oxford University Press is a department of the University of Oxford. It furthers
the University's objective of excellence in research, scholarship, and education
by publishing worldwide. Oxford is a registered trade mark of Oxford University
Press in the UK and certain other countries.

Published in the United States of America by Oxford University Press
198 Madison Avenue, New York, NY 10016, United States of America.

© Oxford University Press 2019

Library of Congress Cataloging-in-Publication Data
Names: Cantillon, Bea, editor. | Goedemé, Tim, editor. |
Hills, John, 1954– editor.
Title: Decent incomes for all : improving policies in Europe /
edited by Bea Cantillon, Tim Goedemé and John Hills.
Description: New York, NY : Oxford University Press, [2019] |
Series: International policy exchange series |
Includes bibliographical references and index.
Identifiers: LCCN 2018030322 (print) | LCCN 2018033091 (ebook) |
ISBN 9780190849702 (updf) | ISBN 9780190849719 (epub) |
ISBN 9780190849726 (Online Component) | ISBN 9780190849696 (hbk : alk. paper)
Subjects: LCSH: Poverty—Government policy—Europe. | Public welfare—Europe. |
Europe—Social policy.
Classification: LCC HC240.9.P6 (ebook) | LCC HC240.9.P6 .D43 2019 (print) |
DDC 362.5/82—dc23
LC record available at https://lccn.loc.gov/2018030322

9 8 7 6 5 4 3 2 1

Printed by Sheridan Books, Inc., United States of America

# CONTENTS

# FOREWORD

## A SELF-CRITICAL FLASHBACK ON THE EUROPEAN UNION'S ANTI-POVERTY PROMISE

### Franck Vandenbroucke

This book focuses on a question that has exercised policymakers and policy analysts for at least 10 years: why did European governments fail to deliver on their promise—proclaimed with so much emphasis at the turn of the century— to reduce poverty among European citizens? It constitutes an important sequel in a line of research marked by three earlier books, to which I return later. And this book cannot be read—at least not by me—without a self-critical flashback and some soul searching about the solemn promises made 18 years ago.

Therefore, I have to start with a relatively well-known story. For those concerned with poverty, expectations ran high at the turn of the century. Social policy was explicitly introduced as a distinct focus of attention for European cooperation at the special European Summit in Lisbon in March 2000. The Lisbon Council concluded that, "Steps must be taken to make a decisive impact on the eradication of poverty by setting adequate targets to be agreed by the Council by the end of the year." Objectives to fight against poverty and social exclusion were then agreed upon at the European Council in Nice in December 2000. Since it is impossible to monitor progress in the European Union (EU) Member States with regard to social inclusion in the absence of comparable, quantitative indicators, the Belgian government decided to make the establishment of common European social indicators a priority for its presidency of the Council of the EU during the second half of 2001. Indeed, the Council agreed on a set of common social indicators at the Laeken Summit. A crucial factor in this political success was the preparatory scientific work by the late Anthony Atkinson and his team, published in the book *Social Indicators* (Atkinson, Cantillon, Marlier, & Nolan, 2002). That seminal book is the first in the sequel of publications to which I referred in my introductory sentences.

Although the story is relatively well known, we may have forgotten about part of the inspiration. Why did we focus so single-mindedly on poverty in 2000? Many welfare-state scholars would emphasize that fighting poverty is but one dimension of the much broader mission state of welfare states, and I would not quarrel with them. However, apart from the idea that a litmus test for social justice is how well a society caters for its most vulnerable members, there was another, broader motivation as well as a "tactical" consideration. The underlying tactical consideration was that a call to fight poverty would have strong political traction and would inevitably imply a much broader concern with the quality of the welfare state at large. For sure, national political actors would be wary of a comprehensive debate about the architecture of their national welfare states and all the hardware applied in it; however, engaging them in a debate on poverty outcomes (which they could not refuse, so we thought), would also engage them in a much broader debate on policy inputs, needed to safeguard and modernize Europe's welfare states at large. This motivation was implicit in our campaign for the social chapter at the Lisbon Summit; one might even say that the broader agenda was introduced by stealth.[1] In the foreword to the *Social Indicators* book, it was formulated cautiously, but clearly: "The indicators are not a vehicle for defining any pecking order among Europe's nations, but are a tool to preserve and rejuvenate Europe's hallmark of social protection for all its citizens. Indeed, a credible commitment to combat poverty and social exclusion presupposes a firm commitment to the establishment of an efficient and productive welfare state, and its continuous adaptation to new social needs and risks" (Vandenbroucke, 2002a, p. viii).

The objectives set in the subsequent "Open Coordination on Social Inclusion" were thought to be ambitious but realistic. "Realism" was seen as a feature of the new process, in part because we were at pains to respect the policy sovereignty of Member States, in a spirit of subsidiarity and respect for diversity. "Our objectives should be realistic yet ambitious. What Europe needs is an exercise in ambition in the social policy area, the establishment of 'standards of excellence' rather than standards of mediocrity. . . . But there is not a single best practice: there are different ways to reach excellence, and there is no end in sight for this process, since we can always do better." Hence, the Open Method of Coordination put a strong emphasis not only on common objectives and guidance, rather than on hard legislation, but also on subsidiarity: "The Open Method of Coordination is designed to help member states develop their own policies, reflecting their individual national situations, to share their experience, and to review the outcomes in a transparent and comparable environment" (Vandenbroucke, 2002a, pp. v–vi).

In the same year, another book commissioned by the Belgian government was published. The brief of Gosta Esping-Andersen and his co-authors of *Why We Need a New Welfare State* (Esping-Andersen, Gallie, Hemerijck, & Myles, 2002) was "to reflect upon the *Gestalt* of social policy at the beginning of the new century, . . . from the point of view of both desirability and feasibility" (Vandenbroucke, 2002b, p. ix). The book called for social investment policies, but it also stressed that social investment is not a substitute for social spending, as is correctly recalled by Cronert and Palme in Chapter 9 of this volume. "The idea that the 'social investment state' can replace much of the traditional welfare state is unrealistic, especially given that we live in an ageing society, with ever more people dependent on benefits and social spending because of age" (Vandenbroucke, 2002b, p. x). Such carefully balanced ideas had to inform the further development of the Open Method of Coordination, which would become both a cognitive and a normative tool: European policymakers would learn from each other's practices, but the methodology would also allow them to define the objectives of "social Europe" in more specific terms, on the basis of substantive views on social justice. It was, therefore, also an exercise in consensus-building.

Nearly two decades later, there can be no denying that poverty, as defined in the Laeken indicators, has increased, and that bitter divisions on the policies to be pursued by EU welfare states, rather than consensus, emerged during the crisis of the Eurozone. What went wrong?

The softness of EU social governance is the usual suspect in these discussions. Yet, it is too easy to say that the essential problem was the "nonbinding" nature of the social objectives of the Lisbon Strategy and the antipoverty targets of its successor strategy, Europe 2020. A recent review of the EU's antipoverty strategy again illustrates this point (Jessoula & Madama, 2018). There is no denying that the nonbinding nature of the processes launched in the 2000s makes them weak. However, even within national welfare states, instruments against poverty sensu stricto are to a significant extent decentralized qua implementation and even qua design. Subsidiarity is a salient and sensitive principle when it comes to minimum income protection. Hence, the nonbinding nature of guidelines with regard to minimum income can also be seen as a precondition to getting a process off the ground at the EU level. Therefore, the actual governance challenge is different and multifaceted: it cannot be reduced to opposition between binding and nonbinding. In part, in the realm of policy coordination, the challenge is to move from "outcome indicators" to "policy input indicators," which can critically question the existing policy mix of member states without enforcing a uniform "one size fits all" ideal policy mix.[2] The need for consistent policy packages, tailored to national situations, is well identified by various contributions in this volume; Chapter 12 by Cantillon, Marchal, and Luigjes also suggests an operational way to pursue this. In part, the challenge is also to combine all the instruments the EU disposes of in an optimal way, that is, to combine benchmarking and "soft" policy coordination with EU funding instruments and with EU "hard" legislation in specific domains, and to steadily enhance the salience of social objectives in the fiscal and economic surveillance organized by the EU. If the European Pillar of Social Rights, solemnly proclaimed in 2017, is now translated into a comprehensive work program in which all the instruments at hand are indeed combined in this spirit, the Pillar may be a crucial turning point in the right direction. Importantly, the promise of the Pillar is that it formulates an agenda for social policy at large, that is, for the whole welfare edifice. (Below, I return to the observation that antipoverty success requires a well-functioning welfare state across the board.)

Rather than focusing on governance, Bea Cantillon launched a book that tried to understand why, before the financial crisis of 2008, improving employment records and worsening poverty records (for the non-elderly population) went hand in hand in a number of mature welfare states (Cantillon & Vandenbroucke, 2014). The book's title, *Reconciling Work and Poverty Reduction*, implicitly asked why the task had been so difficult. A key observation was that success in employment policies was neutralized by the fact that those left behind—non-elderly people living in households with little or no attachment to the labor market—were confronted with considerable and increasing poverty risks. The present book, edited by Cantillon, Goedemé, and Hills, adds important insights to the 2014 work. I will not try to summarize them, since that would not do justice to the richness of the material; also, sometimes, the emerging picture is still contradictory or triggers new questions. Instead, I can formulate what I consider to be the main take-home messages, in terms of social indicators, analysis, and policy.

In terms of indicators, this book firmly positions itself in a tradition that sees AROP, the European at-risk-of-poverty indicator formally endorsed in Laeken, as a legitimate key benchmark for the quality of mature welfare states. The AROP indicator measures risks of exclusion in our societies that we must not tolerate, although its metric is about inequality at the bottom end of the income distribution rather than poverty in an 'absolute' sense. Simultaneously, this new book adds two qualifications. The first qualification is that the reality of living below the national poverty threshold is very different in a poor country than in a rich country; Chapter 1, on reference budgets, shows this clearly. This does not diminish the relevance of a poverty threshold set at 60% of national median income (Chapter 1 corroborates this, too)[3], but it underscores the importance of convergence in prosperity across Europe as fundamental to the idea of "a European social model." Since 2008, inequality and poverty in Europe are very much a story of economic growth versus economic decline within the same "union," as Chapter 3, on the pan-European income distribution, sadly illustrates. My first take-home message is that upward convergence in prosperity is part and parcel of the European social model. Achieving upward convergence across Europe is a matter of economic policy, but it is not simply a matter of economic policy: it also depends on social policy.[4]

The second qualification with regard to the AROP indicator underscores the importance of the welfare state as a stabilizer of citizen's incomes. In Chapter 6 of this volume, Matsaganis and Leventi rightly use the AROP indicator anchored in time to assess the role of policies: indeed, that is the correct metric to gauge the impact of economic shocks. When an economic shock occurs, the actual experience of poverty for citizens is to lose out in terms of a standard of living that was once seen as essential to enjoying a minimally decent living. To put this in a somewhat broader perspective: the 2014 book, *Reconciling Work and Poverty Reduction,* was about creeping trends in poverty, with poverty risks for the non-elderly increasing slowly but steadily in mature welfare states with growing median incomes; in that context, relative income poverty with a "floating threshold" is a relevant benchmark. In contrast, this new book had to engage with both trends and shocks. To understand and judge the impact of shocks, also from a normative point of view, one needs both relative income poverty anchored in time and relative poverty with a floating income threshold.

This seemingly technical point about indicators leads to my take-home messages about the analysis of our welfare states' trajectories. Both slow trends and sudden shocks are at play. Let me first elaborate on the trends. An insight that emerges in this new book is that public policies were not necessarily the culprit in adverse trends in poverty among the non-elderly, at least not in a direct "active" sense. In six of the seven countries examined by Hills, Paulus, Sutherland, and Tasseva in Chapter 5, the Lisbon decade was not entirely a "lost decade" for poverty reduction: changes in the tax and benefit policy were actually poverty reducing. In these countries, it seems that "welfare states had to work harder to stand still." Hence, it is important to understand what exactly changed in the fabric of our societies and now forces welfare states to work harder for the same result. The usual suspect in these discussions is exogenous: it is globalization and technological change. Sweeping generalizations about globalization and its detrimental impact on welfare states abound; however, such generalizations are rarely underpinned by comprehensive empirical observations about the causalities at play. It is surprising how little attention is paid, in ongoing public debates, to trends that are endogenous to welfare states but not necessarily in a uniform way across all welfare states.

One such endogenous trend is the improving relative income position of the elderly population: poverty risks among the elderly are diminishing in a number of welfare states (not in all of them!), while poverty risks among the non-elderly increase. The former trend is a result of the maturation of pension systems and the gradual improvement of women's labor market participation, more than a result of policies. But it shows a change in the fabric of society, to the advantage of the elderly, that may force governments to work harder for the relative income position of the non-elderly, notably the non-elderly who are not economically active. (I write "may force," because the reason why welfare states have to work harder is not examined in this volume, and I dare not affirm my conjecture; the data available for the microsimulation exercises nevertheless make such examination possible, and this should be higher on the research agenda.) The reader is cautioned not to misinterpret the example I've given here. I don't presume a clash between generations, let alone a zero-sum game between the elderly and the non-elderly: for instance, adequate pension provision is an important macroeconomic stabilizer because it indirectly supports the younger population in times of crisis. However, improving pensions may contribute to some extent to a shift in the actual distribution of income.

Another slow trend is the development of dual earnership: in a society where households with two earners set the benchmark for a decent standard of living, single earners will inevitably tend to lose out. It may even be the case that, for complicated sociological reasons, incomes of dual earners increase more rapidly than incomes of single earners, as Salverda and Thewissen showed for the Netherlands (Salverda & Thewissen, 2018). Hence, it may not be the case that public policies change for the worse, but even a standstill in policies may lead to growing inadequacy of the existing policy mix. The extent to which that is the case will differ from country to country: in some countries, the rise of dual earnership cannot explain developments in the 2000s, because it dates back to earlier periods; in other countries, it might still be part of the story.

The analysis of shocks leads to a different focus, including the risks taken in the banking sector, the fragility of housing booms, the lack of automatic stabilizers at the Eurozone level, the lack of trust and consensus among Eurozone governments, the belief in austerity. In the beginning of the 2000s, the latent problem of stability was vastly underestimated, not only in the economic literature but also in much of our social policy literature, including in *Why We Need a New Welfare State* (except for the chapter on pension policy). In the run-up to monetary unification, the emphasis was put on the necessary "flexibility" of labor markets, often without much questioning. With the financial crisis, we learned a hard lesson: a well-functioning monetary union needs a consensus on labor market institutions that support both flexibility and stability. Flexibility was associated with "enabling" policies: equipping people with adequate skills would empower them and thus recreate individual security. "Social investment" can be seen as an enabling policy par excellence, but it cannot cater to stability. To achieve stability, one needs collective action: collective bargaining as well as the organization of collective insurance devices. Stability requires instruments that typically protect vulnerable individuals: unemployment insurance stabilizes the economy because it protects the purchasing power of the unemployed. In other words, stability is intrinsically associated with collective action and "protective" policies. Enabling and protective policies can be mutually reinforcing in creating resilient welfare states.

How could we have prevented the shocks that led to sharp increases in poverty "anchored in time"? The answer largely surpasses antipoverty policy sensu stricto. Avoiding the deep shocks would have required quite different economic and fiscal policies; we should have allowed Eurozone welfare states to function as welfare states must function in times of crisis, that is, as stabilizers. Partly, this was a matter of policy choices and belief systems, notably the belief in austerity. Partly, it was a matter of design flaws in the monetary union. Repairing the design flaws implies that the European Monetary Union becomes a true "insurance union," and, more generally, that the EU becomes a European *Social* Union. The latter expression is not happenstance: the aim should not be a European welfare state, but a union that supports national welfare states in some of their key systemic functions, such as stabilization. This entails a broad agenda, in which "social insurance," "labor market standards," and "social investment" are interwoven (Vandenbroucke, Barnard, & De Baere, 2017). We need to think in terms of a gestalt, to reiterate the term used in the introduction to *Why We Need a New Welfare State,* and we need to reconnect critically with issues broached in that book (see Chapter 9 by Cronert and Palme in this volume and this volume's conclusion in Chapter 13, as well as Hemerijck, 2017). I need not elaborate on this broad agenda here. However, there is a general take-home message that also emerges from this book. It may have been a mistake to think, in the year 2000, that antipoverty policies, understood as minimum income protection sensu stricto, could take the lead in the debate on social Europe and that the rest of welfare-state policy would inevitably follow suit. What seemed a clever and expedient strategy at that time turned out to be very incomplete. The policy failure was much broader than simply a failure in terms of adequate minimum income protection. To avoid a repetition of this dismal experience, antipoverty policies have to be embedded explicitly in a broad set of realistic social, employment, and economic policy objectives, both at the level of the Eurozone and the EU and at the level of individual countries.[5] This is what a European Social Union is about: it inevitably implies a broad, slow, and piecemeal process, but it is the only process that has at least the potential to avoid broken promises. The pages that follow contribute importantly to understanding the nature of that challenge.

## NOTES

The author thanks John Hills, Tim Goedemé, and Jonathan Zeitlin for comments.

1 The fact that separate processes of open coordination were introduced with respect to pensions and health care does not contradict this. In the beginning of the 2000s, the processes were much less center stage (and less developed) than the Open Method of Coordination on Social Inclusion.

2 At the moment of writing, this challenge is taken up by the Social Protection Committee and the Employment Committee, which are now jointly developing benchmarking frameworks for minimum income benefits and unemployment benefits.

3 However, one should be aware that AROP only reflects monetary incomes and thus neglects the role of social services in supporting low-income families and preventing deprivation. This creates a serious problem with analyses that focus only on AROP, which space forbids to pursue here. One of the reasons why reference budgets are interesting, is that they are influenced by the availability and affordability of social services.

4 With regard to the interplay between upward convergence in prosperity and welfare-state policy, the role of welfare states as developers of human capital, and, hence, the debate on the merits and caveats of social investment are important. Therefore, Hemerijck's work (2017) might be seen as a fifth book to be added to the sequel of books revisited in this foreword.

5 One might also say, conversely, that social, employment, and economic policies have to be embedded explicitly in a set of realistic antipoverty objectives. What is needed is a recognition of the complex interdependence of socioeconomic policies at large and poverty reduction sensu stricto, as well as a consequent implementation of that insight. This is what "mainstreaming" should be about.

## REFERENCES

Atkinson, A. B., Cantillon, B., Marlier, E., & Nolan, B. (2002). *Social indicators: The EU and social inclusion*. Oxford, England: Oxford University Press.

Cantillon, B., & Vandenbroucke, F. (2014). *Reconciling work and poverty reduction: How successful are European welfare states?* Oxford, England: Oxford University Press.

Esping-Andersen, G., Gallie, D., Hemerijck, A., & Myles, J. (Eds.). (2002). *Why we need a new welfare state*. New York, NY: Oxford University Press.

Hemerijck, A. (2017). *The uses of social investment*. New York, NY: Oxford University Press.

Jessoula, M., & Madama, I. (2018). *Fighting poverty and social exclusion in the EU: A chance in Europe 2020*. EUI Studies in the Political Economy of Welfare. Abingdon, England: Routledge.

Salverda, W., & Thewissen, S. (2018). How has the middle fared in the Netherlands? A tale of stagnation and population shifts. In B. Nolan (Ed.), *Inequality and inclusive growth in rich countries: Shared challenges and contrasting fortunes* (pp. 221–249). New York, NY: Oxford University Press.

Vandenbroucke, F. (2002a). Foreword. In A. B. Atkinson, B. Cantillon, F. Marlier, & B. Nolan, *Social indicators: The EU and social inclusion* (pp. v–xi). Oxford, England: Oxford University Press.

Vandenbroucke, F. (2002b). Foreword: Sustainable social justice and "open co-ordination in Europe." In G. Esping-Andersen, D. Gallie, A. Hemerijck, & J. Myles (Eds.), *Why we need a new welfare state* (pp. viii–xxiv). New York, NY: Oxford University Press.

Vandenbroucke, F., Barnard, C., & De Baere, G. (Eds.). (2017). *A European Social Union after the crisis.* Cambridge, England: Cambridge University Press.

# PREFACE

This book project originated in 2012 with the start of the ImPRovE project, a four-year project on poverty and social policy in the European Union (EU), financed by the European Commission's 7th Framework Programme (Grant Agreement N. 290613), to which all members of the team are very grateful. The project brought researchers together from 12 research groups and benefited from the advice of an academic advisory board and a societal stakeholder board. The project also built on the input of more than 20 internationally recognized academic leaders in the field of poverty and social policy who were associated members of the consortium. Furthermore, on several occasions, we had the opportunity to exchange ideas and to discuss work in progress, as well as policy implications, with members of the European Commission, and in particular Directorate-General Employment and Social Affairs. During three international conferences, preliminary research findings were presented, and we received generous feedback from all discussants and participants. We are very grateful to all those involved in the ImPRovE project, directly or indirectly, as these exchanges have forced us to look further, to improve the analyses, and to reflect more thoroughly on the policy implications of our findings.

Putting this book together has been a challenge, and we are very grateful to all contributors for having made it work, even when project resources were depleted. The team at the Herman Deleeck Centre for Social Policy provided excellent support in reviewing the chapters and harmonizing the layout of the manuscript, and we are very grateful to them. We would also like to thank the people at Oxford University Press and the editors of this book series, who supported the book project and took care of the copyediting work.

Finally, it is worth stressing that the success and quality of an empirical research project on poverty and social policy hinges critically upon high-quality, timely, and accessible microdata as well as high-quality simulation models of taxes and benefits. Several chapters in the book make use of the EU microsimulation model EUROMOD. We thank the past and current members of the EUROMOD consortium who make EUROMOD the indispensable research instrument that it is today. Undoubtedly, the EU Statistics on Income and Living Conditions (EU-SILC), coordinated by Eurostat but provided by the National Statistical Institutes of all participating countries, have been an important leap forward in our ability to quantify poverty and to assess the poverty impact of social and fiscal policies. EU-SILC is the source to which we have turned the most in this book project, apart from several other data sources. We hope data providers will continue their efforts to keep on increasing the quality and comparability of these much-needed data, without which this book would not have been possible.

Bea Cantillon, Tim Goedemé, and John Hills
April 2018

# CONTRIBUTORS

MARCO ARLOTTI, Researcher, Department of Architecture and Urban Studies, Politecnico di Milano, Milan, Italy

ANIKÓ BERNÁT, Researcher, TÁRKI Social Research Institute, Budapest, Hungary

BARBARA BINDER, Research Assistant, Institute of Sociology, Karlsruhe Institute of Technology, Karlsruhe, Germany

RÉKA BRANYICZKI, Researcher, TÁRKI Social Research Institute, Budapest, Hungary

BEA CANTILLON, Director, Herman Deleeck Centre for Social Policy, University of Antwerp, Antwerp, Belgium

ELENA CARILLO ÁLVAREZ, Associate Professor and Principal Investigator, Global Research on Wellbeing Research Group, Blanquerna School of Health Sciences, Universitat Ramon Llull, Barcelona, Spain

DIEGO COLLADO, Researcher, Herman Deleeck Centre for Social Policy, University of Antwerp, Antwerp, Belgium

PIETER COOLS, Senior Researcher, OASeS, Department of Sociology, University of Antwerp, Antwerp, Belgium

AXEL CRONERT, Researcher, Department of Government, Uppsala University, Uppsala, Sweden

IRENE CUSSÓ PARCERISAS, Researcher, PSITIC Research Group (Pedagogia, Societat i Innovació amb el suport de les Tecnologies de la Informació i la Comunicació), Faculty of Psychology, Education and Sport Sciences, Blanquerna-Ramon Llull University, Barcelona, Spain

ANNE FRANZISKUS, Researcher, National Institute of Statistics and Economic Studies of the Grand Duchy of Luxembourg (STATEC), Luxembourg, Grand-Duchy of Luxembourg

ANDRÁS GÁBOS, Senior Researcher, TÁRKI Social Research Institute, Budapest, Hungary

TIM GOEDEMÉ, Research Coordinator, Herman Deleeck Centre for Social Policy, University of Antwerp, Antwerp, Belgium, and Senior Research Officer, Institute for New Economic Thinking at the Oxford Martin School, University of Oxford, Oxford, United Kingdom

Anne-Catherine Guio, Senior Researcher, Living Conditions, Luxembourg Institute of Socio-Economic Research (LISER), Esch-sur-Alzette, Grand-Duchy of Luxembourg

John Hills, Richard Titmuss Professor of Social Policy, Department of Social Policy, London School of Economics and Political Science, London, United Kingdom

Tine Hufkens, Researcher, Herman Deleeck Centre for Social Policy, University of Antwerp, Antwerp, Belgium

Eleni Kanavitsa, Researcher, Athens University of Economics and Business, Athens, Greece

Alexandros Karakitsios, Economic Analyst, Council of Economic Advisors, Ministry of Finance, Athens University of Economics and Business, Athens, Greece

Yuri Kazepov, Professor of International Urban Sociology and Comparative Social Policy, Department of Sociology, Universität Wien, Vienna, Austria

Lane Kenworthy, Professor of Sociology and Yankelovich Chair in Social Thought, University of California-San Diego, San Diego, California, United States

Marianna Kopasz, Research Fellow, Institute for Political Science, Hungarian Academy of Sciences, Budapest, Hungary

Bernhard Leubolt, Social Scientist, Catholic Social Academy of Austria, Vienna, Austria, and Researcher, Department of Architecture, KU Leuven, Leuven, Belgium

Chrysa Leventi, Research Fellow, Institute for Social and Economic Research, University of Essex, Colchester, United Kingdom

Chris Luigjes, Researcher, Political Economy and Transnational Governance, University of Amsterdam, Amsterdam, The Netherlands

Lauri Mäkinen, Researcher, University of Turku, Turku, Finland

Sarah Marchal, Senior Researcher, Herman Deleeck Centre for Social Policy, University of Antwerp, Antwerp, Belgium

Manos Matsaganis, Associate Professor, Department of Architecture and Urban Studies, Politecnico di Milano, Milan, Italy

Geranda Notten, Associate Professor, Graduate School of Public and International Affairs, University of Ottawa, Ottawa, Canada

Andreas Novy, Professor, Institute of Multi-Level Governance and Development, Vienna University of Economics and Business, Vienna, Austria

Stijn Oosterlynck, Associate Professor, OASeS, Department of Sociology, University of Antwerp, Antwerp, Belgium

Joakim Palme, Professor, Department of Government, Uppsala University, Uppsala, Sweden

Alari Paulus, Research Fellow, Institute for Social and Economic Research, University of Essex, Colchester, United Kingdom, and Senior Analyst, PRAXIS Centre for Policy Studies, Tallinn, Estonia

Tess Penne, Researcher, Research Foundation–Flanders, and Herman Deleeck Centre for Social Policy, University of Antwerp, Antwerp, Belgium

Jordi Riera Romaní, Principal Investigator, PSITIC Research Group (Pedagogia, Societat i Innovació amb el suport de les Tecnologies de la Informació i la Comunicació), Faculty of Psychology, Education and Sport Sciences, Blanquerna-Ramon Llull University, Barcelona, Spain

Veli-Matti Ritakallio, Professor, University of Turku, Turku, Finland

Tatiana Saruis, Researcher, University of Modena and Reggio Emilia, Modena, Italy

Bori Simonovits, Senior Researcher, TÁRKI Social Research Institute, Budapest, Hungary

Bérénice Storms, Senior Researcher, Herman Deleeck Centre for Social Policy, University of Antwerp, Antwerp, Belgium

HOLLY SUTHERLAND, Professor and Director of EUROMOD, Institute for Social and Economic Research, University of Essex, Colchester, United Kingdom

PÉTER SZIVÓS, Managing Director, TÁRKI Social Research Institute, Budapest, Hungary

IVA TASSEVA, Senior Research Officer, Institute for Social and Economic Research, University of Essex, Colchester, United Kingdom

ISTVÁN GYÖRGY TÓTH, Director, TÁRKI Social Research Institute, Budapest, Hungary

KAREL VAN DEN BOSCH, Senior Researcher, Herman Deleeck Centre for Social Policy, University of Antwerp, Antwerp, Belgium, and Expert, Federal Planning Bureau, Brussels, Belgium

DIETER VANDELANNOOTE, Researcher, University of Antwerp, Antwerp, Belgium, and Researcher, Federal Planning Bureau, Brussels, Belgium

FRANK VANDENBROUCKE, Professor, University of Amsterdam, Amsterdam, The Netherlands; Professor, Herman Deleeck Centre for Social Policy, University of Antwerp, Antwerp, Belgium

GERLINDE VERBIST, Research Coordinator, Herman Deleeck Centre for Social Policy, University of Antwerp, Antwerp, Belgium

FLORIAN WUKOVITSCH, Researcher, Wirtschaftsuniversität Wien, Vienna, Austria

LORENA ZARDO TRINDADE, Researcher, Herman Deleeck Centre for Social Policy, University of Antwerp, Antwerp, Belgium

# INTRODUCTION

## Bea Cantillon, Tim Goedemé, and John Hills

For more than a decade, organizations like the International Monetary Fund (IMF), the Organisation for Economic Co-operation and Development (OECD), and the International Labor Organization (ILO) have issued concerns about the trend of increased inequality in rich welfare states. The influential works of globally leading experts, such as the late Sir Anthony Barnes Atkinson, Nobel Laureates Paul Krugman and Joseph Stiglitz, Thomas Piketty, and, more recently, Branko Milanovic, converge on one point: globalization and technological progress are making the currents of social market economies more unequal. In Europe, despite high social spending and work-related welfare reforms, poverty remains a largely intractable problem for policymakers (Cantillon & Vandenbroucke, 2014). In 2015, about 17% of the European Union (EU) population lived on an income below the threshold of financial poverty most commonly used in the EU, and there are no signs that the number is going down. On the contrary, over the past 10 years, on average, income poverty has increased.

Growing inequalities and the failure to make any progress in the fight against income poverty[1] stand in contrast to the progress achieved during the "Golden Age" of the flourishing welfare state in the 1960s and 1970s. This explains Piketty's and Milanovic's references to "waves." Although Atkinson tends to refer more to "episodes" rather than to waves, he identifies "the welfare state and the expansion of transfers, the rising share of wages, the reduced concentration of personal wealth, and the reduced dispersion of wages" as candidate explanations for the period of falling European income inequality while "the main reason that equalization came to an end appears to be . . . that these factors have gone into reverse (welfare-state cutbacks, declining share of wages, and rising earnings dispersion) or come to an end (the redistribution of wealth)" (Atkinson, 2015, p. 75).

1

In *Divided We Stand* (2011) and *In It Together* (2015), the OECD has made an attempt to show how technological changes, globalization, polarization between two-earner and workless households, individualization, and the associated policies have often sparked inegalitarian forces through complex, inextricable interplays.

The prevalence of these trends across the world of rich welfare states—albeit with big differences in both levels and pace of changes—fuels the idea of the existence of strong and ineluctable deterministic forces leading to increasing inequalities and mounting pressures on the most vulnerable in society. In *Global Inequality*, Branko Milanovic (2016) put forward the notion that technology, openness, and policy—the three "TOP elements"—"are dependent upon each other and impossible to separate from each other in any meaningful way" (Milanovic, 2016, p. 110). He considers that policy is *endogenous*, meaning that it is necessarily imposed by economic preconditions. His pessimistic assumption is that, in the current era, this is likely to further enhance poverty and inequality. Although Milanovic hopes that the benign forces will triumph, he seems to lean toward the malign forces: "It is doubtful whether this . . . decline (of inequality) will be accomplished by the same mechanisms as those that reduced inequality in the twentieth century: increased taxation and social transfers, hyperinflation, nationalization of property, and wars" (Milanovic, 2016, p. 217). However, although welfare states clearly face a myriad of challenges, for policymakers, the maneuvering space may well be greater than suggested by Milanovic. As Tony Atkinson (2015, p. 308) wrote in his latest book: "[t]he solutions . . . lie in our own hands. If we are willing to use today's greater wealth to address these challenges, and accept that resources should be shared less unequally, there are indeed grounds for optimism."

This book aims to shed new light on how European welfare states reacted to the inequality wave, and how progress can be made in the future. The contributions largely focus on poverty among children and the population at working age, given the complexity, the magnitude, and the range of the poverty issues at stake. This is not to say that poverty in old age is a less challenging problem for European welfare states, especially in the context of an aging population and rising debt levels. Also, poverty among the elderly population is clearly linked to living standards and distributive policies that affect both old and young. However, tackling poverty in old age requires a distinct set of policies (notably pension systems) that fall outside the scope of this book.

The book's intended coverage is pan-European, and where appropriate and possible, analysis covers all member states of the EU (at time of writing). For detailed analysis, particular chapters narrow the focus to smaller groups of countries (or single-country case studies), while some chapters (notably Chapter 7) widen the focus to include lessons for Europe drawn from elsewhere.

To what extent are the disappointing poverty trends among children and the working age population a consequence of lack of effective political will to protect the most vulnerable, the result of failures in the prevailing policy paradigm, or the reflection of systemic limits, structural constraints, and functional pressures on social protection? By analyzing the effect of policies before, during, and after the crisis in EU Member States and by studying the impact of alternative policy packages, the authors link the hypotheses stemming from the meta-analysis of long-term trends in inequality on the one hand with real changes in national social policies on the other. In doing so, they contribute to a better understanding of the policies required for progress in individual countries and in the EU as a whole.

There are reasons for both optimism and pessimism. The book argues that there are indeed structural constraints on the increase of the social floor and difficult trade-offs involved in the reconciliation of work and poverty reduction. Differences across countries are, however, enormous. This suggests that there is ample maneuvering space for policymakers. There is also no evidence of a universal decrease in the generosity of social protection. Instead, throughout the past decade, many European welfare states were "working harder." However, it appears that increasing financial work incentives was often prioritized, while in many cases additional efforts were not used to raise minimum income packages for jobless households. The story behind the data is that the persistent and almost general inadequacy of minimum income protection for jobless households is structural in nature—that is, related to low gross wages. Although most welfare states effectively started to work harder, efforts to raise wages and the social floor need to be increased significantly almost everywhere.

The book builds on the "social indicator movement"[2] that was embraced in the Lisbon Strategy, in the subsequent Europe 2020 social agenda, and in the underlying social governance known as the Open Method of Coordination (OMC). The introduction of a set of social indicators to underpin the European social coordination can be considered a major step forward in European social history (Atkinson, Cantillon, Marlier, & Nolan, 2002). The hope was that the indicators would enable policymakers to define and to monitor the substance of the European Social Model (Vandenbroucke, 2002, p. v). In the aftermath, a stronger emphasis on social rights and solidarity was incorporated into the Lisbon Treaty. Subsequently, the indicators and the underlying data that have become available via the European Statistical System became more sophisticated and accurate, while the bold but rather vague "eradication of poverty" as a strategic social policy goal of the Lisbon Strategy was replaced by the more concrete Europe 2020 targets aiming for a reduction of the number of persons living in poverty, jobless households, or material deprivation by 20 million. Concurrently, economic governance has been partially but progressively "socialized" through the inclusion of so-called auxiliary social indicators in the macroeconomic imbalance procedure (Zeitlin & Vanhercke, 2014). The social indicators have also increasingly been used by researchers, the European Commission, and Eurostat to assess policies and to "map" changes in poverty, employment, and social spending (Cantillon & Vandenbroucke, 2014).

Regrettably, however, this approach has so far failed to make real progress for the poor, either at the national or at the European level. On the contrary, the EU's social fabric is under major stress: convergence in national living standards has halted or reversed, while progress in terms of poverty reduction in the last decades has been disappointing in most EU Member States, to say the least. Undoubtedly, external and largely inegalitarian forces—such as globalization, technological progress, and migration—internal economic and political tensions, the problems besetting the monetary union, and the prioritization of economic and budgetary goals largely account for these failures. However, the deficiency of the OMC is also related to the fact that the link between "goals"—as measured by the portfolio of social indicators—and "policies" has remained vague and unarticulated; difficult trade-offs have not been made sufficiently explicit, while for many policymakers the implications for households of living on an income below the at-risk-of-poverty threshold, the threshold most commonly used in the EU, has remained largely elusive. As a consequence, in Europe, social coordination risks collapsing into mostly technical work programs, unachievable benchmarks, ineffective "targetology", and, ultimately, a total loss of legitimacy.

With a view to strengthening the social dimension of the EU, the aim of this book is to elucidate what it means for households to live on an income below the at-risk-of-poverty threshold and to link social goals with policies. The contributions point to policy packages to meet the European social targets and signal the difficult trade-offs involved. The book presents innovative methods to identify coherent policy menus capable of improving the living conditions of those at the bottom and tools to construct output indicators to monitor progress in a concrete way.

The book brings together some of the main outcomes of the ImPRovE project, Poverty reduction in Europe: Social Policy and Innovation, financed under the 7th Framework Programme of the European Commission.[3] The book contributes to a better understanding of how social progress can be achieved and how the EU and its Member States can tackle the persistent problem of poverty.

The ImPRovE project started from the observation that, before the crisis, despite higher employment rates and economic growth, only a few countries had made substantial progress in combating relative financial poverty. Since the crisis, the picture has become truly negative, not in the least due to strong diverging trends within the EU. This stands in stark contrast with the ambitious policy goals formulated by the EU ever since the Lisbon Strategy was adopted in 2000. While the deteriorating position after the onset of the crisis may be unsurprising, it is the lack of progress in the pre-crisis years that suggests the existence of structural constraints against which national welfare states and EU social governance seemed to be powerless.

Since the crisis, in many countries, the most important drivers of increasing poverty among the working-age population have been the increase in the share of jobless households and a marked increase in their poverty risk. In *Reconciling*

*Work and Poverty Reduction,* Cantillon and Vandenbroucke (2014) showed that these trends were already observable before the crisis: at that time, in many countries work-poor households benefited less from job growth while the poverty-reducing capacity of social protection decreased, to the detriment of these households especially.

Today, even in the most generous settings, minimum income protection for jobless households falls short of the at-risk-of-poverty thresholds, in particular for families with children. Moreover, in a large majority of the EU Member States, the wage floor is also inadequate for families with children, although large variations exist. If Europe wants to reduce income poverty, unemployment traps should be tackled while minimum income protection packages for working and nonworking families with children should simultaneously be increased. How can this be achieved, given the expenditures necessitated by aging, increasing health care costs, social investment, and the creation of quality jobs? How can a further deterioration of the compensation for social risks that are strongly correlated with poverty (most notably unemployment and household low work-intensity) be stopped while increasing work incentives? How can a more successful European social policy agenda be envisaged that accommodates national diversity and autonomy?

The central question we and our co-authors, together with other contributors to the ImPRovE research program, ask in this book is how we can realize decent incomes for all in Europe. To answer this question, the book reflects upon the most prominent measure of income poverty in the EU (the at-risk-of-poverty indicator) and describes past trends in poverty and inequality in Europe. It evaluates the impact of the economic crisis and austerity measures on poverty and inequality and assesses the effectiveness of detailed policy packages as well as the impact of social innovation and social investment. Finally, the book looks at the future by analyzing concrete policy packages that could contribute to meeting the EU 2020 social inclusion target in a more distant future.

The first part of the book reflects upon the meaning and implications of the at-risk-of-poverty indicator and describes trends in poverty and inequality in Europe before and after the onset of the economic and financial crisis in the EU. First, Chapter 1 explores what lessons can be drawn from comparing the EU at-risk-of-poverty threshold with "reference budgets for adequate social participation." In the ImPRovE project, researchers from seven European countries undertook a unique effort to develop for the first time comparable reference budgets—that is, illustrative priced baskets of goods and services that represent in a concrete way the minimum required for adequate social participation. In this chapter, they use these budgets to show that, especially in the poorest EU Member States, it is very hard to have a decent living standard at the level of the at-risk-of-poverty threshold, and that the at-risk-of-poverty indicator probably underestimates poverty among children.

In Chapter 2, the authors analyze the relation between employment and relative income poverty in the period just before and during the economic crisis in Europe. Their analysis confirms that, for a successful poverty-reduction strategy, employment growth should benefit job-poor households and adequate social welfare systems are required for those who are unable to generate sufficient income from employment.

In Chapter 3, the authors start from a pan-European view to show that strong changes have taken place in the EU-wide distribution of household incomes since the onset of the economic crisis. They find enormous discrepancies between the living standards of Europeans living at the bottom in each country. The authors conclude that reflecting further on the need for mutual insurance and true solidarity across borders is of paramount importance for achieving both social cohesion and social inclusion in the EU, something Cantillon et al. come back to at the end of the book.

The second part of the book evaluates the impact of social and fiscal policies. In Chapter 4, the authors employ a new method to estimate the impact of social transfers on both income poverty and material deprivation, which is usually left out of the picture when evaluating policy impacts. Encouragingly, they find that social transfers not only reduce income poverty but also contribute to a substantial reduction in the extent and depth of material deprivation, although the effects are somewhat smaller. The impact varies in important respects across countries, though. Subsequently, Chapter 5 delves deeper into the impact of social and fiscal policies on poverty in a selection of European countries. The authors use a sophisticated decomposition approach to disentangle the effects on poverty of policy reforms from the effects of economic, social, demographic, and other changes. Remarkably, they find that, although overall poverty trends were disappointing, between 2001 and 2011 in many cases the policy changes taken into consideration did, in themselves, have poverty-reducing effects—implying that welfare states had to work harder to stand still. In Chapter 6, the authors analyze the impact of tax-benefit policies in the European periphery during the crisis. Not entirely surprisingly, they show that, in most of the countries examined, poverty increased, and the policies implemented accounted for a major part of that increase. However, they also identified "fair" austerity measures. Chapter 7 discusses the potential benefit of cash transfers and tax credits to people in paid work but with low earnings. According to the author's analysis, in the Anglo-Saxon world, where employment-conditional tax credits are most prominent, this tool seems to have had a positive impact on employment among low-income families and appears to boost absolute incomes of the poorest households at working age.

The third part of the book focuses on different broad approaches to tackling poverty that have been put forward by some as alternatives—or, more realistically, as supplements—to classic tax-benefit redistributive policies. The past decade has witnessed increasing interest in more decentralized initiatives and policy perspectives. Among these, local forms of "social innovation" as well as "social investment" have become more than buzzwords in policy circles. Chapter 8 assesses the potential of policies promoting social innovation that mobilize an unconventional mix of (local) actors and broad, multifaceted approaches to respond to social needs. Building upon a large number of case studies, the authors argue that local social innovations often are better tied into the life-world of people living in poverty and address multiple forms of exclusion and deprivation in an integrated and customized way; place-based actions are also instrumental in signaling emerging social needs. Rather than conceiving social innovation as a new policy paradigm, the authors claim that social innovation offers instruments that are complementary to the traditional welfare state to improve the situation of the poor.

The authors of Chapter 9 focus on social investment as an important avenue for reducing poverty and meeting the challenges of current and future welfare states. They argue that a distinction should be made between an "enlightened path", the Nordic approach, and the "Third Way" approach to social investment. Policy developments in the Swedish welfare state illustrate that only the former approach to social investment, which includes adequate social protection and redistributive policies, leads to enduring poverty reduction and social inclusion.

Before concluding, the last part of the book focuses on how to circumvent the difficult trade-off between work and poverty reduction and how, in doing so, to improve poverty reduction in the future. In Chapter 10, the authors try to estimate the cost of closing the poverty gap in Belgium, Denmark, and the United Kingdom, while allowing for some "overspill" to keep financial work disincentives in check. The authors find that eradicating poverty does not come cheap: the cost of closing the poverty gap without worsening current incentives at the bottom of the income distribution would be around twice the cost of just lifting all incomes to the level of the poverty threshold. Chapter 11 takes a different perspective and shows how microsimulation techniques can be used to find the most adequate balance between the cost of social policy, jobs, and poverty reduction. By systematically testing alternative policy designs, the authors not only show how important the details of policy reforms are, but also present tools for building smart policies. In Chapter 12, the authors elaborate on the role that the EU could play in realizing a decent income for all in Europe. Their suggestion is that, if poverty reduction is taken seriously, it is time for a decisive advancement of the current European social governance. The chapter argues that decent incomes for the poor are the place to start. Common goals and targets should become more concrete; therefore, there is a need for a move from output to input governance.

In contrast to some of the more disappointing findings related to the recent past, the concluding chapter contends that the implications of the research summarized here can be interpreted more positively. There are many instruments available to governments that offer the prospect of making meaningful progress against poverty. Their effects can be seen in the contrasting experience of different countries at different times that the book describes and analyzes. Particular approaches will be more effective in some countries and settings than in others, and none of the evidence suggests that there is a single "magic bullet" that can achieve substantial change by itself. Rather, policies across a range of approaches will need to be combined, and small changes by themselves will have only small effects. To be successful, welfare states will have to work harder, on many fronts. But if a cohesive Europe is to be achieved for all its citizens, ensuring that fewer of them are left behind the rest is essential.

## NOTES

1  Aaberge, Atkinson, and Sigstad brought together different features of the income distribution in a single framework that allows one to see the relationship between poverty, affluence, and dispersion. The comparison of indicators of poverty (the income gap from the median) and affluence (income minus median) leads to a very important substantive conclusion: "Some countries perform better at the bottom and some at the top of the income distribution, but in general the two move closely together. The different parts of the income distribution story cannot be separated" (Aaberge, Atkinson, & Sigstad, 2017, p. 121).

2  As described by Land and Michalos (2017), the contemporary era of research and reporting on social indicators has its origins in the Social Indicators Movement of some 50 years ago.

3  An extensive collection of papers from the research program, including some more detailed findings related to the chapters in this volume, can be found on the ImPRovE website: http://improve-research.eu/

## REFERENCES

Aaberge, R., Atkinson, A. B., & Sigstad, H. (2017). Income poverty, affluence and polarisation viewed from the median. In A. B. Atkinson, A.-C. Guio, & E. Marlier (eds.), *Monitoring social inclusion in Europe* (pp. 103–122). Luxembourg: Publications Office of the European Union.

Atkinson, A. B. (2015). *Inequality: What can be done?* Cambridge, MA: Harvard University Press.

Atkinson, A. B., Cantillon, B., Marlier, E., & Nolan, B. (2002). *Social indicators: The EU and social inclusion.* Oxford, England: Oxford University Press.

Cantillon, B., & Vandenbroucke, F. (2014). *Reconciling work and poverty reduction. How successful are European welfare states?* Oxford, England: Oxford University Press.

Land, K. C., & Michalos, A. C. (2017). Fifty years after the Social Indicators Movement: Has the promise been fulfilled? *Social Indicators Research, 135*(3), 835–868. doi:10.1007/s11205-017-1571-y

Milanovic, B. (2016). *Global inequality: A new approach for the age of globalization*. Cambridge, MA: Harvard University Press.

Organisation for Economic Co-operation and Development (OECD). (2011). *Divided we stand: Why inequality keeps rising*. Paris, France: OECD Publishing.

Organisation for Economic Co-operation and Development (OECD). (2015). *In it together: Why less inequality benefits all*. Paris, France: OECD Publishing.

Vandenbroucke, F. (2002). Foreword. In A. B. Atkinson, B. Cantillon, E. Marlier, & B. Nolan (Eds.), *Social indicators: The EU and social inclusion* (pp. v–xi). Oxford, England: Oxford University Press.

Zeitlin, J., & Vanhercke, B. (2014). *Socializing the European semester? Economic governance and social policy coordination in Europe 2020* [SIEPS Report 7]. Stockholm: Swedish Institute for European Policy Studies.

# PART 1

# INCOME POVERTY IN EUROPE

SETTING THE SCENE

# 1

# WHAT DOES IT MEAN TO LIVE ON THE POVERTY THRESHOLD? LESSONS FROM REFERENCE BUDGETS

Tim Goedemé, Tess Penne, Tine Hufkens,
Alexandros Karakitsios, Anikó Bernát, Anne Franziskus,
Bori Simonovits, Elena Carillo Álvarez, Eleni Kanavitsa,
Irene Cussó Parcerisas, Jordi Riera Romaní, Lauri Mäkinen,
Manos Matsaganis, Marco Arlotti, Marianna Kopasz,
Péter Szivós, Veli-Matti Ritakallio, Yuri Kazepov,
Karel Van den Bosch, and Bérénice Storms

## INTRODUCTION

Over the past 20 years, the use of the at-risk-of-poverty (AROP) threshold has become increasingly widespread. Furthermore, in this book it takes center stage as a tool for assessing trends in poverty and social exclusion and for evaluating the distributive effects of taxes and social policies. However, as is well known, the indicator builds on a number of assumptions and simplifications that have given rise to several criticisms. In this chapter, we illustrate how reference budgets could help to "contextualize" the AROP threshold by generating more insight into the kind of living standard that can be afforded with an income at the level of the threshold in different countries. Such an approach does not necessarily generate empirical support for the use of the threshold, nor does it offer an alternative to the AROP indicator. Nonetheless, we contend that it provides essential background information for researchers and policymakers who use the AROP indicator.

Especially since the enlargement of the EU in 2004, the AROP indicator has attracted criticism, in spite of its strengths and widespread use, as highlighted in, for instance, Atkinson, Cantillon, Marlier, and Nolan (2002). In this chapter, we argue that reference budgets can help to put into context four weaknesses that are often the subject of criticism.

1. The threshold is defined rather arbitrarily, as 60% of the national median equivalent disposable household income.
2. The AROP line represents very different levels of purchasing power in different countries, and it is not at all obvious that an income at the level of the threshold indicates a similar or comparable situation in terms of poverty or social exclusion.
3. The AROP indicator builds on the assumption that economies of scale at the household level are proportional to the level of household income and are constant across countries, in spite of varying consumption patterns across the income distribution and across countries.
4. The AROP threshold does not take account of cross-national variations in the institutional characteristics of the welfare state and, in particular, variations in the public provision or subsidization of essential goods and services. Obviously, it is a different thing to live on a certain income when essential goods and services (e.g., primary health care, public transport, and education) are freely available or heavily subsidized than when they have to be bought at market prices, ceteris paribus.

For several purposes, these shortcomings are not very problematic. For instance, as many chapters in this volume show, the indicator properly allows for studying the size and characteristics of groups living on a very low income, within and between countries and over time, and it provides useful information on the extent to which social and fiscal policies are targeted at the bottom of the income distribution. In contrast, for other purposes, these aspects may be more problematic. For instance, for the AROP indicator to serve as an indicator of poverty, comparability is undermined if there is no linear relation between the AROP threshold and the necessary resources for having access to a minimum acceptable living standard. Similarly, as a poverty indicator, it may partially fail if economies of scale vary substantially across countries or if the provision and subsidization of essential goods and services vary in important respects within or across countries. Also, when evaluating the adequacy of minimum income support, or when entering into a public debate about an appropriate level of the minimum wage or minimum income support, the arbitrariness of the level of the threshold can be problematic. In these cases, comparable reference budgets can be helpful.

Reference budgets, or budget standards, are illustrative priced baskets of goods and services that represent a certain living standard (cf. Bradshaw, 1993). Reference budgets are mainly used to identify the resources required for a decent living standard. They serve a variety of purposes, including setting income maintenance levels, determining additional income support, debt rescheduling, financial education, and assessing the adequacy of (minimum) wages and benefits (for a review, see Storms et al., 2014). As we have argued elsewhere (Goedemé, Storms, Penne, & Van den Bosch, 2015), if developed in a cross-country comparable way, reference budgets could in addition help to contextualize EU social indicators, to monitor the adequacy of social protection schemes in a comparative perspective, and to facilitate cross-national learning in order to design more effective social policies. However, reference budgets are difficult to construct in a way that is valid, robust, and comparable at the same time. In the ImPRovE project (2012–2016), several country teams have endeavored to construct for the first time cross-nationally comparable reference budgets for six European cities (Antwerp, Athens, Barcelona, Budapest, Helsinki, and Milan). In addition, the same method has been applied to construct reference budgets for Luxembourg, which joined at a later stage (for details, see Franziskus, 2016). The seven cities are located in countries that vary greatly in terms of the size and structure of their welfare state as well as GDP per capita. The main methodological considerations as well as the first results of this endeavor have been described in detail in Goedemé, Storms, Stockman, Penne, and Van den Bosch (2015). In this chapter, we go a step further and explore how comparable reference budgets can be put to use for contextualizing the AROP indicator.

From the ImPRovE project, it has become clear that, due to their complexity, limits to data availability, and the current level of methodological development, reference budgets cannot replace any of the existing indicators of poverty or social exclusion. However, as we show, reference budgets can help to put into context the weaknesses of, for instance, the AROP indicator, so that a better informed interpretation of poverty estimates is possible. In particular, reference budgets help to show what the strong cross-national differences in living standards mean in practice for the adequacy of incomes at the level of the AROP threshold. They also suggest that the poverty risk of some groups (for instance, children and tenants) is underestimated, in absolute terms and relative to that of other groups (such as singles and outright homeowners).

The chapter is structured as follows: first, we elaborate on why it is necessary to contextualize the AROP threshold. Next, we explain the main assumptions underlying the ImPRovE budgets and sketch the method used. Subsequently, we present the ImPRovE reference budgets and explain briefly the most important reasons for the main differences across countries. In the following section, we explore the use of the reference budgets to contextualize the AROP indicator. We conclude with a discussion of what we have learned from the present exercise and how it could be improved in the future.

## WHY CONTEXTUALIZE THE AROP INDICATOR?

The idea that the results of the AROP indicator should be contextualized is not new (cf. Cantillon & Vandenbroucke, 2014). In fact, when Atkinson et al. (2002) made their recommendations for a system of EU social indicators, they wrote that "it is, we believe, possible to 'demystify' the choice of percentage, and thus the level of the poverty line, by explaining what it means in terms of purchasing power in each individual member state" (Atkinson et al., 2002, p. 92). Later, the EU's Indicator Sub-Group emphasized that "for each country, the poverty risk indicator must be assessed by looking at both the share of people whose income is below the threshold and the comparative level (in purchasing power standards [PPS] . . .) of this threshold" (Social Protection Committee—Indicators Sub-Group, 2015, p. 10).

Keeping that recommendation in mind, we can note that, although the percentage of the population at risk of poverty in Hungary, for instance, is on a similar level to that in Belgium and Sweden, the purchasing power of those below the poverty line in Hungary is much lower, because at the level of the threshold, a household in Belgium can afford over 2.5 times more goods and services than a similar household in Hungary (see Figure 1.1). Also—according to these indicators—the poverty situation was worst in Romania, where the AROP rate was clearly the highest, while the threshold was the lowest—nearly seven times lower than the threshold in Luxembourg (that is, accounting for relative price differences). However, interpretation becomes more difficult when thresholds as well as poverty risks are higher, or both are lower (e.g., Luxembourg compared to the Czech Republic). In these cases, it is very difficult to give a consistent interpretation and to provide an answer with regard to where poverty is most likely to be highest. In addition, the vast differences in purchasing power, as indicated by the threshold expressed in PPS, remain abstract.

So, how can one empirically assess in more concrete terms what it means to live on the poverty threshold with a purchasing power that is 2.5 times lower in one country than in another? And, even more challenging, how can one empirically assess whether 60% of the national median equivalent disposable household income is sufficient to have a decent living standard and to avoid poverty? Various options could be explored, including the use of other information regarding

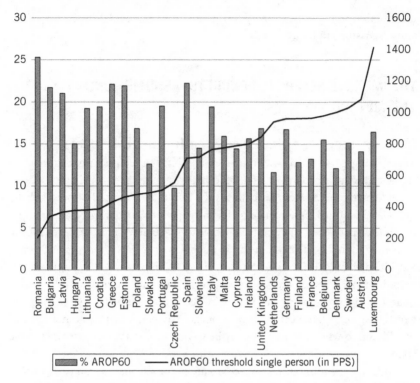

**Figure 1.1.** The at-risk-of-poverty rate (AROP60; 60% threshold, left axis), contextualized by the 60% at-risk-of-poverty threshold in purchasing power standards (PPS; right-hand axis), EU-SILC 2014. *Source*: Eurostat online database (accessed August 2016).

material deprivation or economic stress, subjective poverty lines, or household budget survey data. In fact, many of these options have been considered in the past for defining a reasonable set of poverty lines (for a review, see Atkinson et al., 2002; Deleeck, Van den Bosch, & De Lathouwer, 1992; Van den Bosch, 2001), but none has been very convincing.

In this chapter, we focus on budget standards or reference budgets, an option that has also been suggested by previously cited authors. Various approaches exist for developing reference budgets, differing in particular with regard to the level of detail with which baskets of goods and services are specified and the extent to which one relies on household budget survey data (for a review, see Goedemé, Storms, & Van den Bosch, 2015). In the ImPRovE project, we opted for fully specified reference budgets—that is, reference budgets consisting of a concrete list of goods and services with for each product and service a specification of the type, quality, quantity, lifespan, provider, and price. The budgets were constructed on the basis of a variety of information sources, including public guidelines and regulations, survey data, and discussions in focus groups.

## THE IMPROVE REFERENCE BUDGETS: ASSUMPTIONS AND METHOD

### Main Assumptions Underlying the ImPRovE Budgets

The starting point of developing reference budgets consists in defining the "targeted living standard," that is, the living standard to which the budgets should correspond.[1] In our case, this is the minimum financial resources that a household requires for adequate social participation. Adequate social participation is itself defined as "the ability of people to adequately fulfill the various social roles they should be able to take on as members of society" (Goedemé, Storms, Stockman, et al., 2015, p. 5; cf. Storms, 2012). With regard to the minimum required financial resources, it is important to note that we focus on disposable household income, taking account of subsidized goods and services. In other words, the budgets reflect the out-of-pocket payments by private households, in addition to what they may already be paying through direct taxes and social contributions.

Evidently, the minimum resources required for adequate social participation depend on the characteristics of households as well as their living circumstances. Therefore, fully specified reference budgets can be constructed only for specific hypothetical household types. The hypothetical households are primarily illustrative and should not be considered representative. The compositions of the hypothetical households are defined as:

1. A single person.
2. A single parent with one child, about 10 years old.
3. A couple without children.
4. A couple with two children, a boy about 10 years old and a girl about 14 years old.[2]

The adults are assumed to be about 40 years old. The households live in an urban environment (Antwerp, Athens, Barcelona, Budapest, Helsinki, Luxembourg, and Milan). In addition, we make the following assumptions about:

1. Competences—Family members are well-informed persons, having the necessary competences to make adequate decisions with regard to their health and safety and to be self-reliant. In addition, they are assumed to be able to act economically. For instance, they know their social rights and are willing to exercise them, they know how to access

public goods and services, they are able to compare prices and to buy the products with best value for money, and they can cook economically and healthily with sufficient variation.

2. Health—All household members are in good health. The reason for this assumption is not so much that this is the most common condition, but that costs for health care vary enormously depending on the kind and severity of health problems, each having different implications for the needs of the person affected. Therefore, assuming people are in good health offers a good starting point for comparative analysis, with variations of health to be added in future work.

3. Government-provided or subsidized goods and services—We start from actual provision and actual prices (that is, 'out-of-pocket costs'), insofar as they are accessible for low-income households.

The purpose was to develop long-term reference budgets that should give people access to the targeted living standard for an indeterminate period of time. In other words, the reference budgets include some room for saving in order to gradually replace durables and to cover large one-off or annual costs. This implies that, for instance, if a young person without any assets moves out to start a new family, the reference budgets would not suffice to cover the initial cost of buying all necessary durables at once. If, on the contrary, a household could rely on savings to compensate for an income below the calculated threshold, the reference budget would be overestimated.

These assumptions mean that, in real-life situations, especially for vulnerable families, more resources will be required than those implied by the reference budgets. For example, people are often confronted with physical or mental health problems; in some situations, there is no equal access to information and to public goods and services; and some people's budgeting capacities are limited, so that resources are not always spent in an optimal or most economic way. These assumptions should ensure that the reference budgets are not subject to the critique that they are "too high" when they are used as a benchmark for assessing the adequacy of incomes (cf. Rowntree, 2000). Nonetheless, the concept of adequate social participation will remain somewhat elusive when it is translated into a priced list of goods and services: due to the substantial heterogeneity in living conditions and in personal characteristics and needs, as well as people's diverging experiences and opinions, it is very difficult to define a generally applicable standard in very concrete terms.

## The Procedure for Compiling and Pricing Comparable Reference Budgets

We used a common theoretical and methodological framework to translate the targeted living standard into a concrete set of needs, building to an important extent on Doyal and Gough's theory of human need. In their theory, Doyal and

Gough (1991) identified two universal needs, autonomy and health, and 10 so-called intermediate needs that should be fulfilled in order for anyone to participate adequately in society. For each of these needs, we developed a basket of essential goods and services.[3] The 10 baskets are: adequate housing, food, health care, personal care, clothing, mobility, leisure, rest, maintaining social relations, and safety in childhood.[4]

For drawing up priced lists of goods and services fulfilling the above needs, we used a largely standardized approach, as recommended by Bradshaw and Finch (2000). In order to avoid arbitrary variations across countries in the composition of the baskets, all country teams started from the same assumptions, quality criteria, and one list of goods and services—namely, a list that was developed several years earlier in Belgium (Storms & Van den Bosch, 2009). Each team was asked to adapt the "common base" to the local situation on the basis of a range of information sources, including national regulations and guidelines (e.g., dietary guidelines, regulations for disease prevention, etc.), survey data, national studies on the cost and accessibility of public goods and services, expert opinion, and focus group discussions.[5] A standardized approach benefits comparability and facilitates cross-national learning because it makes it easier to trace and understand cross-national differences in the level of the reference budgets. However, standardization also involves a risk of not reflecting fully the cross-country variation in living conditions, given that differences across countries (cities) were accepted only if they could be well justified on the basis of the evidence collected by the country teams. Hence, the level of the reference budgets could be upwardly biased in some less-well-off countries, insofar as insufficient evidence was available for further deviations from the common list. In the presentation of results below, we come back to this issue. A more in-depth discussion of the ImPRovE method, its strengths and weaknesses, and the issue of comparability can be found in Goedemé, Storms, Stockman, et al. (2015) and Goedemé, Storms, and Van den Bosch (2015).

## COMPARING REFERENCE BUDGETS AND THE EU POVERTY THRESHOLD: WHAT CAN BE LEARNED?

In what follows, we first briefly present the level of the ImPRovE budgets. Subsequently, we illustrate how the reference budgets compare to the AROP threshold. In the third subsection, we turn to the assumptions implied in the AROP indicator with regard to household economies of scale. We first assess economies of scale implicit in the reference budgets and subsequently re-estimate the incidence of child poverty on the basis of the implicit equivalence scale of the budgets.

## The Level of the Reference Budgets in Seven Large EU Cities

Figure 1.2 displays the total reference budgets for four different household types in seven large European cities, differentiated by tenure (rental and ownership) status. The budgets were priced during the first half of 2014 and are expressed in EUR per month.[6] It can be observed that for all family types, the level of the budgets is the highest in Luxembourg and the lowest in Budapest, except for outright home owners, who face the highest costs in Athens. For Budapest, the reference budgets suggest that a single woman who rents a dwelling in the private market needs about 524 EUR per month at the minimum to participate adequately in society, while she needs almost three times that amount (about 1,415 EUR per month) in Luxembourg in order to reach the same living standard. Yet, the variation of reference budgets across cities is smaller than the variation of national median equivalent net incomes, even when expressed in PPS. The highest reference budget for a single person renting a dwelling in the private market is

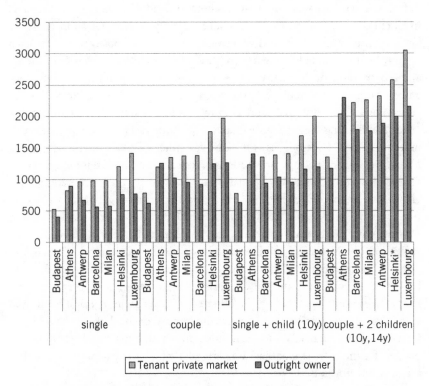

**Figure 1.2.** Total ImPRovE reference budgets (EUR per month) for four household types, in six large EU cities, 2014. *Notes*: The single category and single-parent category are both assumed to be female. *In Helsinki the children of the couple are assumed to be 4 and 10 years old instead of 10 and 14 years old. Cities are ordered by the level of the budget for tenants on the private market.

equal to 2.7 times the lowest budget, while the highest median equivalent net income in PPS (for the seven countries) is equal to 3.7 times the lowest median income. Overall, the level of the budgets is positively correlated with national median equivalent disposable household incomes in PPS, but there are important exceptions, such as Athens in the case of outright homeowners (relatively expensive), and Antwerp for families without children (relatively inexpensive).

The figure also illustrates how reference budgets increase with family size, but not proportionally, due to economies of scale. Housing costs in particular do not change in proportion to household size. Furthermore, the cost of children generally increases with the age,[7] which is mainly due to increasing costs for food, education, personal care, and mobility. Note that we did not include child-care costs. Hence, the real costs of younger children will be underestimated when families have to make use of child-care services, which probably would also increase differences across countries (Hufkens & Verbist, 2016).

The observed cross-national variation in the absolute level of the reference budgets can be explained by several factors. Most of the variation is due to differences in price levels, although the choice of products is not exactly the same in all cities. For instance, we observe a remarkably large variation in reference housing costs as a result of the distinctive structure of the housing market in each region. Another example is the relatively high cost of clothing in Helsinki, Milan, and Luxembourg, or the relatively low cost of membership in youth associations and sporting clubs in Budapest. The reference budgets are also affected by the climatological, institutional, and cultural context. Climatological differences affect the clothing basket, and we allow for more variation in countries with more pronounced seasons, as is the case for Athens, Barcelona, Budapest, and Milan. Not surprisingly, the institutional context has an important effect on the accessibility and affordability of health care (e.g., co-payments are required for visits to a general practitioner in Antwerp and Luxembourg, but such visits are free of charge in the other cities), education (high cost in Barcelona, low cost in Helsinki), and public transport (high cost in Helsinki, Barcelona, and Milan, relatively low cost in Antwerp and Luxembourg). Institutional variation in terms of public guidelines and regulations appears to be particularly relevant for the food basket. In Greece, Spain, and Italy, remarkably larger quantities of meat, fish, and fruit are recommended than in the other countries. Finally, cultural habits and social expectations explain some of the differences, particularly for baskets fulfilling sociocultural needs, such as leisure and maintaining social relations. The budgets for the latter two baskets are particularly high in Luxembourg, and they are relatively low in Budapest.

## The AROP Threshold in Perspective

Figure 1.3 shows how the reference budgets can help in understanding what kind of living standard can be achieved with an income at the level of the poverty threshold. For this purpose, we express the reference budgets for a single woman

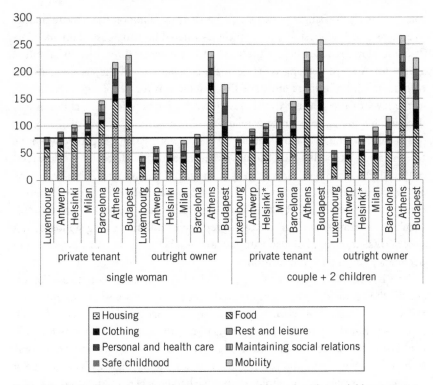

**Figure 1.3.** Total reference budgets of a single woman and a couple with two children (private tenant or outright owner) expressed as percentage of the at-risk-of-poverty threshold in seven cities, 2014. *Note:* *In Helsinki, the children of the couple are assumed to be 4 and 10 years old instead of 10 and 14 years old. At-risk-of-poverty threshold retrieved from Eurostat on August 25, 2016. Values refer to 2014 (EU-SILC 2015).

and a couple with two children as a percentage of the AROP threshold.[8] In Athens and Budapest, the AROP threshold is clearly far below the level of the reference budgets, suggesting that it is not possible to participate adequately in society at the level of the threshold. In contrast, the AROP threshold is higher than the reference budgets for Luxembourg and approaches the level of the reference budgets in Antwerp and Helsinki, in particular in the case of tenants, suggesting that, for these cities, the AROP threshold captures better the minimum cost of participating adequately in society. For outright owners, the AROP threshold is even substantially higher than the reference budgets for a good number of cities. In the case of Barcelona and Milan, outright homeownership seems to determine whether or not an income at the level of the AROP threshold allows for participating adequately in society. Please note that the prevalence of particular occupancy statuses varies strongly across countries.

For families with children, except for Luxembourg, an income at the level of the poverty threshold is generally more inadequate, especially in Athens and Budapest. Furthermore, the figure illustrates how housing costs play a major role. Strikingly, for single persons renting their dwelling on the private market in Athens and Budapest, the level of the estimated housing cost of an adequate dwelling alone reaches nearly the level of the poverty threshold. In all cities, except for Athens, housing costs decrease substantially in the case of outright owners, resulting in more adequate living standards for people with an income at the level of the poverty threshold. However, for families with children, the decreasing housing costs become relatively less important because of economies of scale in housing (cf. below). Finally, it is noteworthy that the gap between the reference budgets and the threshold is larger in countries where the absolute level of the AROP threshold is low or very high (as in Luxembourg). Clearly, having an income at the level of the AROP threshold means different things in different countries in terms of the ability to participate adequately in society. In sum, this graph shows how the AROP threshold represents different living standards not only across countries, but also within countries, between households varying in occupancy status and composition.

The ImPRovE budgets may appear to be high for some countries. For instance, the Hungarian team emphasized that the various baskets for Budapest reflected the minimum necessary for adequate participation in each domain separately, but that, still, for many Hungarians, the sum of all baskets together could be perceived as being relatively high. Yet, the results above imply that some trade-offs between essential goods and services are to be made with an income at the level of the poverty threshold. Even if we had largely overestimated the minimum cost of adequate social participation for Athens and Budapest (although we have no indication that this is indeed the case), it is clear that households with an income at the level of the AROP threshold have a (much) harder time making ends meet in the latter two cities than in the other cities. In the case of Athens, the relatively high housing costs stand out, partially due to relatively high property taxes for homeowners in Athens in 2013. It is also worth saying that, in Greece between 2009 and 2014, the AROP threshold declined by nearly 40% in real terms (cf. Chapter 6). If the threshold of 2009 still applied, the ratio of the reference budgets to the threshold would be only 60% of its current level, considerably altering the picture. In contrast, the budgets for Luxembourg may be perceived to be low from a national perspective.

Within the ImPRovE project, full budgets were developed for only seven cities. In another project, in most of the remaining EU capital cities, the minimum cost of a healthy diet was established in accordance with national dietary guidelines. To give a sense of the meaning of the AROP threshold in these EU countries, Figure 1.4 shows the resulting food budgets, as a percentage of the threshold (Storms et al., 2015).[9] As can be observed from the graph, the degree to which households with an income at the level of the AROP threshold have sufficient income for affording a diet in accordance with the national food-based dietary guidelines varies substantially across EU Member States. The level of the threshold appears to be very low, especially in Bulgaria and Romania. If

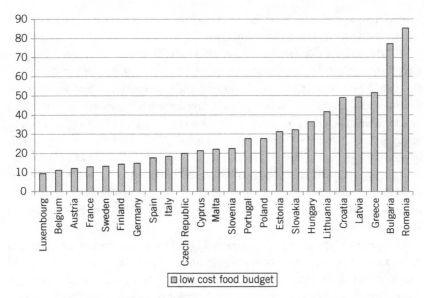

**Figure 1.4.** The low-cost food basket expressed as a percentage of the at-risk-of-poverty threshold for a single person (woman) in 24 countries (data are not available for Denmark, Ireland, the Netherlands, Slovakia, and the United Kingdom), 2013. *Note: Price levels refer to the capital city. Food baskets are converted to price levels of 2013, making use of the official food-specific HICP, published by Eurostat. At-risk-of-poverty thresholds taken from Eurostat on August 25, 2016 (EU-SILC 2014).*

households in Romania and Bulgaria in the capital city living at the level of the AROP threshold prefer to eat a healthy diet (or governments would want them to do so), they would have to spend their income nearly completely on food, neglecting all other essential expenses, including housing. Maybe this is why anti-poverty NGOs in these countries are hesitant to back the AROP threshold as a benchmark for minimum income protection (cf. Van Lancker, 2015) and encounter difficulties in explaining the threshold to their members: an income at the level of the threshold can barely be considered adequate. Even if we had overestimated the cost of food in a number of countries, our results indicate that the AROP threshold in Bulgaria and Romania not only is much lower than the one in the richer Member States in terms of purchasing power, but also allows only a very restricted consumption level, at best.

## Economies of Scale and the Poverty Risk of Children

One of the criticisms of the AROP indicator is that economies of scale at the household level are overly simplified and do not sufficiently take into account the needs and effective costs that people face. Obviously, reference budgets are not required for knowing that the relative poverty risk of persons facing special needs is underestimated (as in the case of a disability or very high health care costs). In contrast, it is not obvious that this is also the case for differences in needs across age groups and different household sizes, given that an equivalence scale is used for capturing these differences.

In Table 1.1, we express the costs of additional household members as a proportion of the ImPRovE reference budget for a single person. Given that housing costs are the primary driver of economies of scale, we make a distinction between tenants and outright homeowners. When housing costs increase, the relative cost of additional household members decreases, resulting in a flatter implicit equivalence scale. The table shows that the modified OECD equivalence scale, which is used for calculating the AROP threshold, neglects differences in economies of scale by tenure status and across countries. Furthermore, it seems to underestimate the additional cost of children, especially for families with older children and with low housing costs (outright owners or those who benefit from subsidized rent).[10]

In order to illustrate how the modified OECD scale results most probably in an underestimation of poverty among children, we have re-estimated the AROP rate using an alternative equivalence scale, derived from the reference budgets. Given that we do not have reference budgets for owner-occupiers with a mortgage, which is a common situation in the population, we do not make a distinction by tenure status. Instead, we take the equivalence scale of households renting on the private market from the table above, so as to estimate a lower bound on the potential underestimation of child poverty (as is indicated by Table 1.1, the relative cost of children can be expected to be higher for other tenure statuses). For Finland, we assume that economies of scale for a child in secondary education are similar to those for a second adult (similar to previous results of reference budget research in Finland). We leave the weight of a child below the age of 6 unchanged (i.e., 0.3, as is the case for the modified OECD equivalence scale). Furthermore, we give students up to the age of 25 the same weight as teenagers, although there are indications that the cost of students is higher (Van Thielen et al., 2010). In other words, we recalculate the AROP indicator (including the threshold) by changing the equivalence scale used.[11] Admittedly, this remains a very rough approximation: we start from a very limited set of hypothetical household types and, for instance, do not correct for changes in economies of scale as the household size increases further, or for additional needs not covered by the budgets (e.g., child care or special health care).

The results are summarized in Figure 1.5. In all countries, the poverty risk of children less than 18 years old increases substantially (and significantly at the 95% confidence level) when the alternative equivalence scale is used. The increase is largest in Belgium and Hungary and smallest in Finland and Spain. Furthermore, in all countries, the ratio of the poverty risk of children and the poverty risk of adults is significantly larger with the new equivalence scale than with the modified OECD equivalence scale.

**Table 1.1.** Implicit Equivalence Scales of the ImPRovE Reference Budgets, Compared with the Modified OECD Scale (2014)

| | Modified OECD scale | Reference budgets—private tenant | | | | | | | Reference budgets—outright owner | | | | | | |
|---|---|---|---|---|---|---|---|---|---|---|---|---|---|---|---|
| | | BE | EL | ES | HU | FI | IT | LU | BE | EL | ES | HU | FI | IT | LU |
| 1st Adult | 1 | 1 | 1 | 1 | 1 | 1 | 1 | 1 | 1 | 1 | 1 | 1 | 1 | 1 | 1 |
| 2nd Adult | 0.5 | 0.39 | 0.47 | 0.39 | 0.52 | 0.46 | 0.42 | 0.38 | 0.52 | 0.41 | 0.60 | 0.59 | 0.66 | 0.70 | 0.63 |
| Child 6–11 y | 0.3 | 0.43 | 0.51 | 0.36 | 0.50 | 0.41 | 0.45 | 0.41 | 0.53 | 0.57 | 0.63 | 0.62 | 0.54 | 0.70 | 0.54 |
| Child 12–17 y | 0.5 | 0.57 | 0.56 | 0.47 | 0.64 | | 0.57 | 0.48 | 0.74 | 0.62 | 0.82 | 0.80 | | 0.91 | 0.68 |

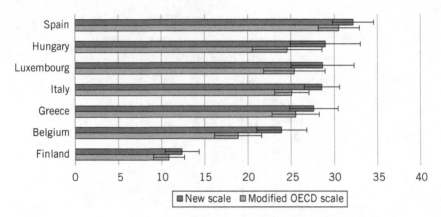

**Figure 1.5.** The at-risk-of-poverty rate (AROP60) for persons less than 18 years old, with the modified OECD equivalence scale, and the alternative scale based on the reference budgets, EU-SILC 2014. *Note*: 95% confidence intervals, sample design taken into account (cf. Goedemé, 2013). Overlapping confidence intervals do not necessarily imply a nonsignificant difference (e.g. Afshartous & Preston, 2010). *Source*: EU-SILC 2014 version 1, authors' calculations.

## CONCLUSION

This chapter uses reference budgets to contextualize the AROP indicator. The budgets were developed by making use of an empirical needs-based approach, without making any ex ante assumption about the appropriate level of the budgets in relation to the average income in a country. The budgets are fully specified, in the sense that they cover concrete lists of goods and services representing the minimum resources required for adequate social participation. They are priced at actual prices faced by households, taking publicly provided or subsidized goods and services into account. In addition, they are developed so as to maximize cross-national comparability. For this reason, they are somewhat different from the budgets developed for national purposes (for instance, Storms, Van Thielen, Penne, & Goedemé, forthcoming).

The ImPRovE budgets make clear that the AROP threshold not only varies across countries in terms of purchasing power, but also has real impacts on the extent to which a decent living standard can be reached with an income at the level of the threshold. In the capital cities of Bulgaria and Romania, the AROP threshold is barely sufficient for having access to a healthy diet in accordance with national guidelines, whereas in Budapest and Athens, an income at the level of the threshold allows for adequate food and clothing, but remains insufficient to fulfill other essential needs, such as housing. In contrast, in Antwerp, Helsinki, and especially Luxembourg, it seems more realistic that it is possible to participate adequately in society with an income at the level of the threshold. To some extent, this is the result of differences in the degree to which households can rely on publicly provided or subsidized goods and services, although differences in the level of the median income across countries seem to be the main driving factor. In addition, the budgets show that the AROP indicator is a relatively rough measure, neglecting differences in household economies of scale between groups in society (notably by tenure status and age) and across countries. As a result, the poverty risk of children is probably underestimated.

By making more concrete the income that is necessary for obtaining a certain living standard, reference budgets help to clarify the actual meaning of being at risk of poverty in countries that vary strongly in their average standard of living (cf. Chapter 3). In our view, due to their clarity and empirical character, the reference budgets also provide policymakers and NGOs with a stronger foothold for assessing the adequacy of minimum income support and for having an evidence-based debate about an appropriate level of minimum incomes. Furthermore, it is clear that, in some countries, there is a problem not only of limited redistribution toward the bottom but also of a generally low standard of living in the population. In these cases, reference budgets could help to define intermediate goals and to select priorities, both for improving the adequacy of wages and for tax-benefit policies. Furthermore, this also raises the question about the desirability of increased cross-national solidarity in the EU.

As we emphasized from the outset, we do not think that reference budgets should or could replace any of the existing indicators of poverty or social exclusion. Reference budgets are still in development, and more and better data (e.g., on prices and living patterns) as well as methodologies (e.g., for the consultation of citizens) are required to come up with robust and comparable reference budgets that are more generalizable than those developed for four household types in the ImPRovE project. In that sense, much more research is still necessary for developing reference budgets that are valid, robust, and comparable at the same time. ImPRovE has taken a very valuable first step and was successful in developing and applying for the first time a method that resulted in largely comparable reference budgets. It has led to useful results and has shown that considerable cross-national coordination is required to come up with comparable budgets. The field is open for further exploration, expansion, and improvement. As we have tried to show, reference budgets bring in a new type of information that is very helpful for better understanding the limits of the AROP indicator when the latter is used for measuring poverty within and across countries, or as a benchmark for the adequacy of social policies. Combining the results of reference budgets research with those of other approaches (e.g., the study of actual spending patterns as documented in household budget survey data) could further improve our understanding of poverty in Europe and could help to foster an evidence-based debate on the policies that are required to improve the adequacy of incomes throughout Europe.

## NOTES

We are grateful to Jonathan Bradshaw, Peter Saunders, and all members of the ImPRovE Consortium for valuable comments and suggestions throughout the ImPRovE project. In particular we would like to thank Bea Cantillon, Anne Van Lancker, and Fintan Farrell for the exchanges we had when developing this chapter. Our research was financially supported by the European Union 7th Framework Programme (FP7/2012–2016) under Grant Agreement N. 290613 (ImPRovE project). We made use of anonymized microdata from the EU Statistics on Income and Living Conditions (EU-SILC), provided by Eurostat (175/2015-EU-SILC-ECHP-LFS). The usual disclaimers apply.

1  This subsection relies strongly on Goedemé, Storms, Stockman, et al. (2015).
2  In Finland, researchers made use of the results from some previous work (Lehtinen, Varjonen, Raijas, & Aalto, 2011) and assumed, for this reason, that the children of the couple are a boy 4 years old and a girl 10 years old.
3  We also built upon other sources, such as international declarations (e.g., Council of Europe, 1996; United Nations General Assembly, 1989). The theoretical framework is discussed in more depth in Storms, Goedemé, Van den Bosch, and Devuyst (2013).
4  This is a somewhat adapted version of the initial list of Doyal and Gough (1991), to make it fit better for the purpose of developing coherent baskets of goods and services. The list of intermediate needs is not exhaustive. For instance, the needs *security* and *lifelong learning* are not covered in the ImPRovE budgets.
5  For the estimation of housing costs, we followed the same rationale, but applied a different procedure given the heterogeneity of housing markets as well as the availability of representative survey data. More precisely, on the basis of EU-SILC, the cost of an adequate dwelling was estimated at the 30th percentile for the Nomenclature of Territorial Units for Statistics 2 (NUTS2) region in which the city is located, differentiating across tenure status. In order to define an adequate dwelling, a set of minimum quality criteria was applied to all seven countries, mainly building upon EU housing indicators (Van den Bosch, Goedemé, Schuerman, & Storms, 2016).
6  Note that, for our purposes, reference budgets are best expressed in EUR rather than PPS, given that they already incorporate price differences across countries. The exchange rate that we have applied for Hungary is 300 HUF (Hungarian forints) to the EUR.
7  In Helsinki, the age of the second child is 4 years instead of 14 years, which explains partly why the gap between Helsinki and the other cities is relatively small for couples with children.
8  The level of the AROP threshold is subject to sampling error. Estimations for EU-SILC 2014 show that the sampling variance of the ratio of the reference budgets and the AROP threshold is relatively small. For tenants renting at market prices in Athens, the 95% confidence interval spans 6 percentage

points below and above the value shown in Figure 1.3. For the other cases, the confidence interval is smaller.

9  The methodology for this basket is largely similar to the ImPRovE methodology. For a complete discussion, see Goedemé, Storms, Penne, et al. (2015).

10  We would like to mention here that the importance of housing costs, or of its complement, the returns to home ownership, has been recognized by those responsible for EU-SILC. The proposal was made that imputed rent for home owners and those renting below market rent should be included in disposable income. Problems with the data quality and the estimation methods of imputed rent made this impossible, unfortunately. See Törmälehto and Sauli (2013).

11  In Penne, Cussó Parcerisas, Mäkinen, Storms, and Goedemé (2016), we go a step further and illustrate how reference budgets themselves could be used as a poverty line.

## REFERENCES

Afshartous, D., & Preston, R. A. (2010). Confidence intervals for dependent data: Equating non-overlap with statistical significance. *Computational Statistics and Data Analysis, 54*(10), 2296–2305.

Atkinson, A. B., Cantillon, B., Marlier, E., & Nolan, B. (2002). *Social indicators: The EU and social inclusion.* Oxford, England: Oxford University Press.

Bradshaw, J. (1993). *Budget standards for the United Kingdom.* Aldershot, England: Avebury.

Bradshaw, J., & Finch, N. (2000). Conclusions and recommendations. In J. Bradshaw, B. Nolan, B. Maître, & N. Finch (Eds.), *The measurement of absolute poverty—Final report for Eurostat* (pp. 63–79). York, England: Social Policy Research Unit, University of York.

Cantillon, B., & Vandenbroucke, F. (2014). Conclusion. In B. Cantillon & F. Vandenbroucke (Eds.), *Reconciling work and poverty reduction: How successful are European welfare states?* (pp. 319–324). Oxford, England: Oxford University Press.

Council of Europe. (1996). *European Social Charter (Revised).* Strasbourg, France: Council of Europe.

Deleeck, H., Van den Bosch, K., & De Lathouwer, L. (1992). *Poverty and the adequacy of social security in the EC: A comparative analysis.* Aldershot, England: Avebury.

Doyal, L., & Gough, I. (1991). *A theory of human need.* Houndmills, England: Macmillan.

Franziskus, A. (2016). Quels besoins pour une vie décente? Vers un budget de référence pour le Luxembourg. Cahier Économique 122. Luxembourg: STATEC.

Goedemé, T. (2013). How much confidence can we have in EU-SILC? Complex sample designs and the standard error of the Europe 2020 poverty indicators. *Social Indicators Research, 110*(1), 89–110.

Goedemé, T., Storms, B., Penne, T., & Van den Bosch, K. (Eds.). (2015). *The development of a methodology for comparable reference budgets in Europe— Final report of the pilot project.* Brussels, Belgium: European Commission.

Goedemé, T., Storms, B., Stockman, S., Penne, T., & Van den Bosch, K. (2015). Towards cross-country comparable reference budgets in Europe: First results of a concerted effort. *European Journal of Social Security (EJSS), 17*(1), 3–31.

Goedemé, T., Storms, B., & Van den Bosch, K. (2015). *Proposal for a method for comparable reference budgets in Europe.* Brussels, Belgium: European Commission.

Hufkens, T., & Verbist, G. (2016). *The distributive effects of work-family life policies in European welfare states.* Antwerp, Belgium: Herman Deleeck Centre for Social Policy, University of Antwerp.

Lehtinen, A.-R., Varjonen, J., Raijas, A., & Aalto, K. (2011). *What is the cost of living? Reference budgets for a decent minimum standard of living in Finland.* Helsinki, Finland: National Consumer Research Centre.

Organisation for Economic Co-operation and Development (OECD). (2016). *Average annual wages.* Paris, France: OECD.

Penne, T., Cussó Parcerisas, I., Mäkinen, L., Storms, B., & Goedemé, T. (2016). *Can reference budgets be used as a poverty line?* Antwerp, Belgium: Herman Deleeck Centre for Social Policy, University of Antwerp.

Rowntree, B. S. (2000 [1901]). *Poverty: A study of town life.* Bristol, England: The Policy Press.

Social Protection Committee—Indicators Sub-Group. (2015). *Portfolio of EU social indicators for the monitoring of progress towards the EU objectives for social protection and social inclusion: 2015 update.* Luxembourg: Publications Office of the European Union.

Storms, B. (2012). *Referentiebudgetten voor maatschappelijke participatie [Reference budgets for social participation]* (Doctoral thesis, University of Antwerp, Antwerp, Belgium).

Storms, B., Goedemé, T., Van den Bosch, K., & Devuyst, K. (2013). *Towards a common framework for developing cross-nationally comparable reference budgets in Europe.* Antwerp, Belgium: Herman Deleeck Centre for Social Policy, University of Antwerp.

Storms, B., Goedemé, T., Van den Bosch, K., Penne, T., Schuerman, N., & Stockman, S. (2014). *Review of current state of play on reference budget practices at national, regional, and local level.* Brussels, Belgium: European Commission.

Storms, B., Penne, T., Carrillo Alvarez, E., Boeckx, H., Stockman, S., Pintó, G., & Goedemé, T. (2015). The food basket. In T. Goedemé, B. Storms, T. Penne, & K. Van den Bosch (Eds.), *The development of a methodology for comparable reference budgets in Europe—Final report of the pilot project* (pp. 64–104). Brussels, Belgium: European Commission.

Storms, B., & Van den Bosch, K. (2009). *What income do families need for social participation at the minimum? A budget standard for Flanders.* Antwerp, Belgium: Herman Deleeck Centre for Social Policy, University of Antwerp.

Storms, B., Van Thielen, L., Penne, T., & Goedemé, T. (Eds.). (forthcoming). *Hoeveel inkomen is minimaal nodig? Referentiebudgetten voor maatschappelijke participatie.* Brugge, Belgium: Die Keure.

Törmälehto, V.-M., & Sauli, H. (2013). *The distributional impact of imputed rent in EU-SILC 2007–2010.* Luxembourg: Publications Office of the European Union.

United Nations General Assembly. (1989). *Convention on the rights of the child.* https://www.ohchr.org/en/professionalinterest/pages/crc.aspx (last accessed July 2018).

Van den Bosch, K. (2001). *Identifying the poor: Using subjective and consensual measures.* Aldershot, England: Ashgate.

Van den Bosch, K., Goedemé, T., Schuerman, N., & Storms, B. (2016). *Reference housing costs for adequate dwellings in ten European capitals. Critical Housing Analysis, 3*(1), 1–9.

Van Lancker, A. (2015). *Toward adequate and accessible minimum income schemes in Europe—Synthesis report.* Brussels, Belgium: European Commission.

Van Thielen, L., Deflandre, D., Baldewijns, K., Boeckx, H., Leysens, G., Storms, B., Casman, M.-T., & Van den Bosch, K. (2010). *Minibudget. Wat hebben gezinnen nodig om menswaardig te leven in België?* Geel, Belgium: Katholieke Hogeschool Kempen.

# 2

# EMPLOYMENT AND POVERTY DYNAMICS BEFORE, DURING, AND AFTER THE CRISIS

**András Gábos, Réka Branyiczki, Barbara Binder, and István György Tóth**

## INTRODUCTION AND RESEARCH QUESTIONS

This chapter investigates the existence and strength of the relationship between employment and poverty. We also contribute to the understanding of the missing links between individual employment rates, household employment patterns, and poverty outcomes—relevant only at the household level. We differentiate between the 2005–2008 period and the 2008–2012 period to emphasize that, for many countries (although not all), the advent of the Great Recession constituted a relevant turning point.

Lessons learned from past economic downturns reveal the relationship between macroeconomic change and household income distribution (and its lower tail, relative poverty) is not straightforward. A recession that reduces real income levels in general is only going to raise poverty rates if they are measured in real income terms by an anchored poverty line. With regard to the relative at-risk-of-poverty (AROP) rate, this is not necessarily the case; developments for the poverty rate also depend on what impact the economic downturn has on income distribution, that is, which population groups are affected and where exactly they are located in the distribution. Further, not only the recession itself but also policy responses to it shape the income distribution, resulting in inequalities and developments in poverty figures. The variance of consequences across countries therefore depends not only on how far, and in what ways, the economic downturn hits a country but also on the country's system of social protection, its labor market institutions, and the role of automatic stabilizers (Jenkins, Brandolini, Micklewright, & Nolan, 2012).

Marx, Horemans, Marchal, Van Rie, and Corluy (2013, p. 9) noticed that the overall relationship between employment and poverty in a cross-country perspective became stronger between 2008 and 2011 than it had been before. This is the starting point of our analysis. After presenting the data and methods in the next section, we present country-by-country trajectories of employment and poverty. After this, we analyze the correlations between these variables: we set up various regression models to estimate the strength of the relationship. The discussion then turns to the decomposition exercise proposed by Corluy and Vandenbroucke (2014), followed by an analysis of the role of social expenditures in poverty alleviation. Then we summarize our results on a country-by-country basis. The concluding discussion summarizes and interprets our results.

## DATA AND METHODS

To better understand the relationship between employment and poverty, we first develop country groupings based on their employment trajectories before the crisis hit and thereafter. Then we examine how employment trends translate into developments in poverty in these country groupings. The analyses are restricted to the active-age population (i.e., those between the age of 20 and 59 years[1]). A simple presentation of trends and correlations of employment and poverty is then followed by a panel regression analysis to quantify the relationship (i.e., the elasticity of the variables). A decomposition analysis further elaborates on the missing link between individual employment rates and poverty outcomes measured on the household level.

Eight waves of the European Union (EU) Statistics on Income and Living Conditions (EU-SILC) cross-sectional dataset covering the EU27 Member States[2] are used for the analysis. Income data are available for the time periods 2005–2008 and 2009–2012 (survey years). The first period reflects steady global economic growth before the international financial crisis began and, therefore, also before it spilled over to the "real" economy. The downturn began in 2008, but across the Organisation for Economic Co-operation and Development (OECD) countries, 2009 was the peak of the recession, when nominal GDP shrank, unemployment rates rose sharply, and public deficits increased due to falling revenue and increased expenditure. In late 2009 and early 2010, several EU countries came under pressure from sovereign debt markets, putting the other Member States under considerable strain as well (Starke, Kaasch, & Van Hooren, 2013, p. 125). Accordingly, the income reference periods of 2008 (EU-SILC 2009) onward should display data that are affected by the economic downturn.

The core indicator investigated is the AROP rate after social transfers.[3] The basic idea of this indicator as it is defined by the European Commission is that each household should have at its disposal a minimum income required for participation in society. For this reason, the threshold that separates those at risk from those who are not is nation specific. The AROP indicator is relative, as the threshold is set at 60% of the median equivalent income of the population and therefore depends on the respective income distribution of the current year (Atkinson et al., 2002; Decancq et al., 2014; for a critical review of the conceptual and methodological shortcomings, see Decancq et al., 2014).

Although the AROP indicator is a headcount measure and refers to individuals living below a certain standard of living, the basis of the indicator lies on the household level, because it is household income that it is drawn upon. Therefore, we consider the household a relevant level of analysis, the main indicator being the household's work intensity (WI), which distinguishes between jobless and non-jobless households. The underlying assumption is that households' WI provides an indication of their need for social protection, under given labor market conditions and policies (see also Cantillon, Van Mechelen, Pintelon, & Van den Heede, 2014, p. 17). Insufficient work participation resulting from very short part-time work or short employment spells over the year is often related to in-work poverty. Therefore, instead of distinguishing between a number of various employment risk groups, WI is used as a suitable proxy variable. Jobless households are those that have a WI = 0, and non-jobless households are defined as those having a WI > 0.

## TRENDS IN EMPLOYMENT AND POVERTY, 2005–2012/13

Time trends in employment as well as in poverty can be seen as a series of episodes of boom and bust, rise and decline.[4] Creating country groupings by means of employment trends before and after the onset of the crisis yields five clusters differing in their employment trajectories.[5] Based on this, we examine whether the observed employment trends translate into the expected developments in poverty, and if there is a stronger employment/poverty relationship in the crisis period than in the pre-crisis period, as indicated by Marx and colleagues (2013, p. 9).

Data on individual employment trends (annual average of employment rate for age 20 to 64, %, men and women together) and on poverty trends for age group 20–59[6] are shown in Tables 2.1 and 2.2, respectively.

**Table 2.1.** Employment Rate of Individuals Age 20 to 64, Annual Average (%)

|  |  | 2005 | 2006 | 2007 | 2008 | 2009 | 2010 | 2011 | 2012 | 2013 |
|---|---|---|---|---|---|---|---|---|---|---|
| **Group A** | Bulgaria | 61.9 | 65.1 | 68.4 | 70.7 | 68.8 | 65.4 | 62.9 | 63.0 | 63.5 |
| | Cyprus | 74.4 | 75.8 | 76.8 | 76.5 | 75.3 | 75.0 | 73.4 | 70.2 | 67.2 |
| | Spain | 67.2 | 69.0 | 69.7 | 68.5 | 64.0 | 62.8 | 62.0 | 59.6 | 58.6 |
| | Greece | 64.6 | 65.7 | 66.0 | 66.5 | 65.8 | 64.0 | 59.9 | 55.3 | 53.2 |
| | Ireland | 72.6 | 73.4 | 73.8 | 72.3 | 66.9 | 64.6 | 63.8 | 63.7 | 65.5 |
| | Portugal | 72.3 | 72.7 | 72.6 | 73.1 | 71.2 | 70.5 | 69.1 | 66.5 | 65.6 |
| | Slovenia | 71.1 | 71.5 | 72.4 | 73.0 | 71.9 | 70.3 | 68.4 | 68.3 | 67.2 |
| **Group B** | Denmark | 78.0 | 79.4 | 79.0 | 79.7 | 77.5 | 75.8 | 75.7 | 75.4 | 75.6 |
| | Finland | 73.0 | 73.9 | 74.8 | 75.8 | 73.5 | 73.0 | 73.8 | 74.0 | 73.3 |
| | Hungary | 62.2 | 62.6 | 62.6 | 61.9 | 60.5 | 60.4 | 60.7 | 62.1 | 63.2 |
| | Italy | 61.6 | 62.5 | 62.8 | 63.0 | 61.7 | 61.1 | 61.2 | 61.0 | 59.8 |
| | Netherlands | 75.1 | 76.3 | 77.8 | 78.9 | 78.8 | 76.8 | 77.0 | 77.2 | 76.5 |
| | Sweden | 78.1 | 78.8 | 80.1 | 80.4 | 78.3 | 78.1 | 79.4 | 79.4 | 79.8 |
| | Slovakis | 64.5 | 66.0 | 67.2 | 68.8 | 66.4 | 64.6 | 65.0 | 65.1 | 65.0 |
| **Group C** | Estonia | 72.0 | 75.9 | 76.9 | 77.1 | 70.0 | 66.8 | 70.6 | 72.2 | 73.3 |
| | Lithuania | 70.7 | 71.3 | 72.7 | 72.0 | 67.0 | 64.3 | 66.9 | 68.5 | 69.9 |
| | Latvia | 70.3 | 73.5 | 75.2 | 75.4 | 66.6 | 64.3 | 66.3 | 68.1 | 69.7 |
| **Group D** | Austria | 71.7 | 73.2 | 74.4 | 75.1 | 74.7 | 74.9 | 75.2 | 75.6 | 75.5 |
| | Germany | 69.4 | 71.1 | 72.9 | 74.0 | 74.2 | 74.9 | 76.3 | 76.7 | 77.1 |
| | Malta | 57.4 | 57.9 | 58.6 | 59.2 | 59.0 | 60.1 | 61.6 | 63.1 | 64.8 |
| | Poland | 58.3 | 60.1 | 62.7 | 65.0 | 64.9 | 64.3 | 64.5 | 64.7 | 64.9 |
| **Group E** | Belgium | 66.5 | 66.5 | 67.7 | 68.0 | 67.1 | 67.6 | 67.3 | 67.2 | 67.2 |
| | Czech Republic | 70.7 | 71.2 | 72.0 | 72.4 | 70.9 | 70.4 | 70.9 | 71.5 | 72.5 |
| | France | 69.4 | 69.3 | 69.8 | 70.4 | 69.5 | 69.2 | 69.2 | 69.4 | 69.5 |
| | Luxembourg | 69.0 | 69.1 | 69.6 | 68.8 | 70.4 | 70.7 | 70.1 | 71.4 | 71.1 |
| | Romania | 63.6 | 64.8 | 64.4 | 64.4 | 63.5 | 63.3 | 62.8 | 63.8 | 63.9 |
| | United Kingdom | 75.2 | 75.2 | 75.2 | 75.2 | 73.9 | 73.6 | 73.6 | 74.2 | 74.9 |

*Source*: Eurostat Statistical Database.

**Table 2.2.** At-risk-of-poverty Rates (%) Among Individuals Age 20 to 59 (AROP(a) Rates), EU27, 2005–2012

|         |             | 2005 | 2006 | 2007 | 2008 | 2009 | 2010 | 2011 | 2012 |
|---------|-------------|------|------|------|------|------|------|------|------|
| Group A | Bulgaria    | —    | —    | 18.4 | 16.3 | 15.3 | 15.1 | 17.6 | 16.7 |
|         |             | —    | —    | 1.15 | 1.11 | 0.91 | 0.86 | 0.79 | 0.79 |
|         | Cyprus      | 10.2 | 9.7  | 9.3  | 10.2 | 9.8  | 11.2 | 10.9 | 11.9 |
|         |             | 0.58 | 0.58 | 0.59 | 0.69 | 0.74 | 0.74 | 0.72 | 0.64 |
|         | Spain       | 15.5 | 15.3 | 15.9 | 15.9 | 16.5 | 19.5 | 20.6 | 22.0 |
|         |             | 0.46 | 0.48 | 0.49 | 0.54 | 0.55 | 0.59 | 0.66 | 0.63 |
|         | Greece      | 16.4 | 17.8 | 18.2 | 18.1 | 17.5 | 18.7 | 19.7 | 23.6 |
|         |             | 0.77 | 0.80 | 0.73 | 0.72 | 0.83 | 0.99 | 0.85 | 1.11 |
|         | Ireland     | 14.8 | 14.6 | 12.8 | 12.3 | 12.2 | 13.7 | 14.0 | 14.9 |
|         |             | 0.80 | 0.85 | 0.89 | 0.85 | 0.92 | 0.99 | 0.91 | 0.90 |
|         | Portugal    | 15.4 | 14.9 | 14.2 | 15.5 | 15.2 | 15.4 | 15.7 | 16.5 |
|         |             | 0.87 | 0.86 | 0.90 | 0.94 | 0.93 | 0.99 | 0.90 | 0.70 |
|         | Slovenia    | 10.1 | 9.5  | 9.6  | 10.3 | 9.0  | 10.6 | 11.4 | 12.3 |
|         |             | 0.45 | 0.35 | 0.41 | 0.42 | 0.39 | 0.45 | 0.46 | 0.47 |
| Group B | Denmark     | 11.5 | 11.3 | 11.2 | 11.7 | 12.2 | 13.3 | 13.6 | 13.8 |
|         |             | 0.68 | 0.69 | 0.72 | 0.76 | 0.77 | 0.81 | 0.88 | 1.03 |
|         | Finland     | 10.4 | 11.0 | 11.3 | 11.7 | 11.9 | 12.3 | 12.8 | 12.3 |
|         |             | 0.39 | 0.42 | 0.45 | 0.47 | 0.47 | 0.48 | 0.52 | 0.49 |
|         | Hungary     | 13.7 | 14.8 | 11.8 | 12.3 | 12.2 | 12.1 | 13.7 | 13.6 |
|         |             | 0.67 | 0.65 | 0.52 | 0.61 | 0.53 | 0.61 | 0.59 | 0.47 |
|         | Italy       | 16.1 | 17.5 | 17.5 | 16.2 | 16.3 | 17.0 | 18.8 | 18.8 |
|         |             | 0.52 | 0.55 | 0.52 | 0.55 | 0.52 | 0.56 | 0.58 | 0.50 |
|         | Netherlands | 10.1 | 9.5  | 9.1  | 10.0 | 10.4 | 9.9  | 10.6 | 10.0 |
|         |             | 0.61 | 0.63 | 0.61 | 1.03 | 0.87 | 0.84 | 0.93 | 0.64 |
|         | Sweden      | 8.9  | 11.2 | 9.9  | 11.1 | 11.7 | 11.8 | 12.6 | 13.1 |
|         |             | 0.43 | 0.52 | 0.44 | 0.46 | 0.51 | 0.48 | 0.52 | 0.53 |
|         | Slovakia    | 12.9 | 10.7 | 9.2  | 9.4  | 9.6  | 11.3 | 12.6 | 12.5 |
|         |             | 0.56 | 0.52 | 0.48 | 0.47 | 0.49 | 0.57 | 0.63 | 0.63 |
| Group C | Estonia     | 16.2 | 15.2 | 15.4 | 13.9 | 14.9 | 15.3 | 18.3 | 17.4 |
|         |             | 0.74 | 0.65 | 0.67 | 0.64 | 0.70 | 0.72 | 0.79 | 0.72 |
|         | Lithuania   | 18.6 | 17.6 | 14.8 | 16.0 | 17.8 | 21.8 | 19.9 | 16.8 |
|         |             | 0.79 | 0.93 | 0.77 | 0.99 | 0.98 | 1.15 | 1.05 | 0.95 |
|         | Latvia      | 17.7 | 19.3 | 17.3 | 18.5 | 19.3 | 19.8 | 20.4 | 19.2 |
|         |             | 0.95 | 0.89 | 1.12 | 1.10 | 0.89 | 0.82 | 0.76 | 0.69 |

**Table 2.2.** Continued

|  |  | 2005 | 2006 | 2007 | 2008 | 2009 | 2010 | 2011 | 2012 |
|---|---|---|---|---|---|---|---|---|---|
| Group D | Austria | 11.1 | 11.2 | 10.8 | 10.9 | 10.6 | 10.6 | 10.9 | 13.4 |
|  |  | 0.55 | 0.59 | 0.55 | 0.65 | 0.58 | 0.58 | 0.61 | 0.67 |
|  | Germany | 11.8 | 12.6 | 14.7 | 15.1 | 15.6 | 15.3 | 16.0 | 16.0 |
|  |  | 0.40 | 0.41 | 0.41 | 0.42 | 0.43 | 0.42 | 0.43 | 0.46 |
|  | Malta | — | — | — | — | 11.7 | 12.2 | 13.0 | 12.0 |
|  |  | — | — | — | — | 0.64 | 0.73 | 0.69 | 0.69 |
|  | Poland | 20.7 | 19.1 | 17.2 | 16.2 | 15.8 | 16.9 | 17.0 | 16.4 |
|  |  | 0.48 | 0.49 | 0.46 | 0.50 | 0.47 | 0.52 | 0.51 | 0.50 |
| Group E | Belgium | 11.3 | 11.6 | 12.0 | 11.3 | 11.5 | 11.8 | 12.7 | 13.2 |
|  |  | 0.89 | 0.76 | 0.80 | 0.67 | 0.73 | 0.73 | 0.87 | 0.67 |
|  | Czech Republic | 9.8 | 8.8 | 8.7 | 8.3 | 7.3 | 8.0 | 9.1 | 9.3 |
|  |  | 0.77 | 0.53 | 0.51 | 0.49 | 0.45 | 0.44 | 0.49 | 0.52 |
|  | France | 11.4 | 12.1 | 12.0 | 11.8 | 11.8 | 12.9 | 13.7 | 13.7 |
|  |  | 0.42 | 0.48 | 0.47 | 0.52 | 0.56 | 0.49 | 0.53 | 0.45 |
|  | Luxembourg | 12.8 | 13.7 | 13.0 | 13.4 | 14.2 | 14.2 | 13.3 | 14.6 |
|  |  | 1.01 | 0.95 | 1.03 | 1.10 | 0.97 | 0.88 | 0.85 | 0.86 |
|  | Romania | — | — | 20.6 | 20.0 | 20.1 | 19.2 | 21.6 | 22.3 |
|  |  | — | — | 1.06 | 1.10 | 1.19 | 1.13 | 1.19 | 0.84 |
|  | United Kingdom | 15.5 | 15.3 | 14.5 | 14.2 | 14.2 | 14.5 | 13.6 | 15.1 |
|  |  | 0.60 | 0.54 | 0.56 | 0.60 | 0.69 | 0.70 | 0.67 | 0.58 |

*Source*: Authors' calculations based on EU-SILC 2005–2012 (releases and coverage specified in Endnote 4).

- Group A includes Greece, Spain, Portugal, Cyprus, Bulgaria, Slovenia, and Ireland. These member states were characterized by increasing employment among the active-age population in the first half of the period of analysis. After employment reached its peak in 2008 (2007 in Spain), a large and persistent drop in employment is observable, with no signs of recovery until 2013 (2012 in Ireland). Poverty rates in this group showed a distinctive pattern, especially from the onset of the crisis onward. The strong drop in employment was clearly mirrored in increasing poverty rates, which showed no change until the onset of the crisis and then rose right after.[7] Employment and poverty trends seemed to correlate very strongly in this group.
- In Group B, Denmark, Sweden, Finland, Slovakia, Hungary, Italy, and the Netherlands, the employment drop around 2008 was also measurable; however, it did not seem to be followed by a long-term declining trend. The paths these countries followed after 2008 are not uniform,

though. Some (like Sweden and Hungary, for example) showed recovery by 2012, others seemed to stagnate (Slovakia and Finland after 2010), and some (like Italy) were on a slight decline afterward. Although Group B had more variation in poverty trends than Group A, a generally increasing trend was clearly observable in the crisis period (except in the Netherlands). While the poverty rates in Finland, Sweden, and Denmark were overall on the rise from 2005 on, we observe a U-shape curve for the trend in Slovakia, Hungary, and partly in Italy, while rates were relatively stable in the Netherlands. The mirrored trends of employment and poverty after the crisis hit seem to be prevalent here as well, although the poverty trend does not seem to even out as much as the employment trends do after the crisis. In the previous period, a generally increasing employment rate was not accompanied by decreasing poverty rates; this was especially the case in Finland.

- Group C contains the three Baltic countries, Estonia, Latvia, and Lithuania, showing the most volatile trends. This group had continued employment growth between 2006 and 2008, accompanied by decreasing poverty rates (on generally high levels) in Estonia and Lithuania. This was followed by a large employment drop in the two years afterward and rising poverty rates. Between 2011 and 2013, a quick recovery of labor markets was seen, reaching the start levels (2005) by 2013. The rise in poverty converted and stabilized (or even decreases) after a short lag.

- In Group D, Malta, Poland, Germany, and Austria stand out as the countries where employment never really declined throughout the period (except the slight drop in Poland between 2009 and 2010). While the rise in employment came to a standstill in Austria and in Poland, Germany and (even more) Malta witnessed further employment growth after 2010. Poverty trends clearly mirrored employment trends in Poland and mostly stagnated in Austria. Germany stands out with a strong increase in poverty rates although it witnessed steady employment growth. The poverty series in Malta was too short for a clear pattern to emerge.

- Finally, Group E, comprised of Belgium, Luxembourg, France, the Czech Republic, Romania, and the United Kingdom, evidenced only slight changes (as compared to the first four country groupings) in employment trends. For poverty, there are diverse trends in this group. In Romania and in the Czech Republic, longer decline periods (2007–2010 and 2005–2009, respectively) of poverty were followed by a sharp increase afterward (in 2011–2012 and in 2010–2012, respectively). In Belgium and France, increasing poverty rates were observed despite only marginal changes in employment. Luxembourg and the United Kingdom showed relatively small changes of poverty accompanying similarly small changes in employment.

On the basis of these trends in the country groupings, two periods and two respective developments can be distinguished. In the first one, rising employment rates until the onset of the crisis did not result in the expected decreasing poverty rates. The second period was characterized by decreasing employment rates in the recession, which settled in increasing poverty rates to a different degree. In general, relatively larger changes in employment seemed to be accompanied by reverse trends in poverty. However, trends in poverty under no change in employment patterns turn out to be very heterogeneous—perhaps due to different policies in labor markets and in social transfers. Also, the elasticity of poverty change to employment seems to vary in different countries. The next section is devoted to the estimation of the magnitude of the correlation between employment and poverty.

## THE RELATIONSHIP BETWEEN EMPLOYMENT TRENDS AND OVERALL POVERTY CHANGE

To provide evidence on the correlation between employment and poverty, employment rate was regressed on AROP(a) rates for the EU27 Member States, for the time period from 2004 until 2013.

There are a number of caveats of the dataset to consider. First of all, AROP(a) is a household level indicator, estimated for the age cohort 20–59. By contrast, employment rate is measured at the individual level for the age cohort 20–64. While we think that the inconsistencies between the age cohort do not cause extremely large distortions, they cannot be ignored. Furthermore, the EU-SILC indicator of poverty for survey years 2005 to 2012 refers to income years 2004 to 2011. The regressions were run on an adjusted dataset, where the poverty indicators and the employment rate referred to the same years. The underlying assumption was that employment loss immediately causes a drop in the incomes of the household, leading to an immediate increase in poverty risk.[8] Finally, the panel dataset was unbalanced because there were missing cases of AROP(a) rates in the EU-SILC datasets: observations were missing for Malta in 2005–2008 and for Romania and Bulgaria in 2005 and 2006.

Several models were run to assess the relationship between individual employment and poverty risk after social transfers in the EU in the time period of 2004 until 2012.[9] Models 1, 2, and 3 are first differences (FD) regressions to assess how changes in employment rates from one year to another are associated with changes in poverty rates. Recalling the opposite employment trends in the two (pre-crisis and crisis) periods defined in the introduction, we introduced a crisis dummy in Model 2 (during the years 2008–2012, the dummy equals 1, while for the pre-crisis period 2004–2007, the dummy equals 0), ceteris paribus.[10] In Model 3, year dummies are introduced. Finally, country fixed effects (FE) are introduced in Models 4, 5, and 6 (together with a crisis dummy in Model 5 and with year dummies in Model 6), to control for country specificities of the time trends and to observe possible longer-term stable relationships between employment and poverty.

Our results are summarized in Table 2.3. Model 1 shows that a 10 percentage point increase in employment rate between two years, on average, is associated with a 2.9 percentage point decrease in AROP(a). The introduction of the crisis dummy (which was significant only at a 10% level) slightly decreased the coefficient of the employment rate from 0.29 to 0.26 (Model 2). Similarly, when the time dummies were included to control for an arbitrary time trend of poverty that is common across all countries (Model 3), the estimated coefficient became smaller: in a country where employment rate increases by 10 percentage points between two years, the AROP rate decreased by 2.5 percentage points on average. The estimated coefficients of the employment rate were significant at a 1% level. The underlying assumption that a change in employment has immediate, short-term effects was supported by the finding that the estimated coefficient of a one-year lag of the employment rate, which could have captured the delayed effects, was not significant.

Compared to the FD models, the FE models looked at long-term differences. Model 4 reveals that, in countries where employment was 10 percentage

**Table 2.3.** Coefficient Estimates of Regression Analyses Predicting Poverty, AROP(a) Rates by Employment, EU27, 2005–2012

| Dependent variable: AROP(a) rate | Model 1 | Model 2 | Model 3 | Model 4 | Model 5 | Model 6 |
|---|---|---|---|---|---|---|
| | FD | FD | FD | FE | FE | FE |
| Employment rate (%) | −0.29*** | −0.26*** | −0.25*** | −0.27*** | −0.25*** | −0.19** |
| (SE) | (0.06) | (0.06) | (0.07) | (0.08) | (0.08) | (0.09) |
| Crisis dummy | — | 0.21* | — | — | 0.83*** | — |
| (SE) | | (0.12) | | | (0.22) | |
| Constant | 0.20*** | 0.08 | 0.28 | 34.0*** | 31.1*** | 28.0*** |
| (SE) | (0.07) | (0.12) | (0.21) | (5.5) | (5.3) | (6.1) |
| Time dummies | — | — | Yes | — | — | Yes |
| $r^2$ | 0.19 | 0.20 | 0.23 | 0.20 | 0.32 | 0.39 |
| Observations | 181 | 181 | 181 | 208 | 208 | 208 |

Notes: Standard errors are shown in parentheses. Coefficients are significant at *** $p < 0.01$, ** $p < 0.05$, * $p < 0.10$ levels. Please note that standard errors are cluster standard errors in the case of FD and FE models. $r^2$ is within $r^2$ in the FE models.

Source: AROP(a) rate: Authors' calculations based on EU-SILC 2005–2012 (releases and coverage specified in Endnote 4). Employment rate: Eurostat, Eurostat Statistical Database, based on EU-LFS (last update July 10, 2014).

points higher than the country's long-term country-specific mean, AROP(a) rate was 2.7 percentage points lower than the long-run country-specific mean, on average. The introduction of the crisis dummy in Model 5 and the year dummies in Model 6 to control for an arbitrary time trend of poverty that was common across all countries resulted in a smaller coefficient in absolute terms: in a country where employment was 10 percentage points higher than the country's long-term country-specific average, the AROP rate was expected to be 2.5 and 1.9 percentage points lower than its long-run country-specific mean, respectively. The estimated coefficients were significant at a 1% or 5% level. The crisis dummy was significant, indicating that, in times of crisis, the country's poverty rate was expected to be 0.83 percentage points higher than the country's long-term average poverty rate, holding other explanatory variables constant.

Altogether, the regression results show that there is a significant negative association between employment and poverty risk. The higher the employment, the lower the AROP rate. We suggest taking Model 3 (first differences with year dummies) and Model 6 (country fixed effects with year dummies) as benchmarks.

(Model 3)    $\Delta Pov_{it} = \alpha + \beta \Delta Emp_{it} + \delta_t + \upsilon_{it}$
(Model 6)    $\Delta Pov_{it} = \alpha + \beta \Delta Emp_{it} + \gamma \Delta Emp_{it-1} + \upsilon_{it}$

where subscript i indicates country, t is year, Pov is poverty rate, Emp is employment rate, and $\delta_t$ stands for time (year) dummies.

The other panel regression models may serve as robustness checks: the sign of the estimated coefficients for employment was always negative (as expected) and significant at 1% or 5% level. The magnitudes of the coefficients were also similar, with values ranging from −0.19 to −0.29. It might be a matter of discussion whether this is a large or a small effect. If we consider that employment rates are measured for individuals, while poverty is a household characteristic, the relationship between individual employment rates and household poverty rates can be considered surprisingly high.[11]

Corluy and Vandenbroucke (2014) also found evidence for a negative correlation between the levels of individual employment rates and AROP(a) rates in 2005–2008. However, they reported that household joblessness rates showed no correlation with poverty rates for the same years. According to a simulation model by Marx, Vandenbroucke, and Verbist (2011), employment growth does not necessarily result in lower relative poverty shares.

The elasticity of the employment:poverty ratio—while it looks sizable for the whole sample on average—seems to vary across countries and periods. As shown in Table 2.1, for example, the Belgian poverty rate increased despite no change in employment trends in the last phase of the period. Also, AROP rates in the United Kingdom seemed to deviate from employment trends. Reasons for these alterations may lie in policies, labor markets, or fiscal and welfare regimes alike.

In what follows, we account for the link between individual employment and income poverty by investigating how changes in individual employment are translated into household WI, how changes in household WI contribute to changes in poverty rates, and how the latter is mitigated by social transfers.

## DECOMPOSITION OF LABOR MARKET TRENDS AND POVERTY CHANGES

When analyzing poverty and social exclusion trends, it is of primary importance to understand the way in which changes in individual-level employment transform into household-level outcomes. Depending on how the newly evolving jobs distribute across households according to their WI and to the underlying dynamics of the process, changes in the overall risk of income poverty may strongly differ, also depending on the design of and the changes in the welfare benefit system that contribute to variances among Member States (Marx et al., 2013). Corluy and Vandenbroucke (2014) provided an insight into the effects of unequal distribution of employment over households in the EU Member States between 1995 and 2008. They find that, in most of the countries, the actual household joblessness rate was higher in both 1995 and 2008 than what one would have expected on the basis of a random distribution. This was the case mainly in the southern countries, and, less so, in the new Member States, where a more even distribution of employment gain across households was observed. Hereafter, we also consider both levels of analysis by first looking at developments in individual employment and then switching to the household level by distinguishing between jobless and non-jobless households. We follow the methodology proposed by Corluy and Vandenbroucke (2014) to decompose the contribution of various labor-market developments to trends in poverty. They suggest the following equation:

$$\Delta pov = \overline{wr_i}\Delta pwr_i + \overline{wr_i}\Delta pwp_i + \left(\overline{pwp_i} - \overline{pwr_i}\right)\Delta wp_i \tag{1}$$

where $\Delta pov$ is the change in the AROP(a) rate in the period; $wp$ is the share of individuals in jobless households, where WI = 0; $wr$ is the share of individuals in non-jobless households, where WI > 0 ($wr = 1 - wp$); $pwp_i$ is the AROP(a) rate for individuals in jobless households—AROP(a) rate where WI = 0; and $pwr_i$ is the AROP(a) rate for individuals in non-jobless households—AROP(a) rate where WI > 0.

We differentiate between two periods for the decomposition analysis: 2005–2008 and 2008–2012.[12]

Poverty change can therefore be decomposed into a sum of three factors:

- A contribution by the (average) change in the AROP rate of individuals in non-jobless households ($\overline{wr_i}\Delta pwr_i$)
- A contribution by the (average) change in the AROP rate of individuals in jobless households ($\overline{wr_i}\Delta pwr_i$)
- A contribution by the (structural) change in the share of the population living in jobless households $\left(\overline{pwp_i} - \overline{pwr_i}\right)\Delta wp_i$.

Results for this decomposition are shown in Table 2.4 (period 2005–2008) and in Table 2.5 (period 2008–2012). Countries (rows) are ranked according to the magnitude of the poverty change within the period. Shades correspond to the magnitudes of the indicators: dark grey (with pattern) is for deterioration (poverty increase), while light grey is for improvements (poverty decrease). A combined analysis of the two tables reveals the following findings.

- In the first period, the overall trend in poverty change was a decline or no change in most of the countries (exceptions being Finland, Greece, Sweden, and Germany, where poverty increase exceeded 1%), while the trend was an increase or no change in all countries in the second period.[13]
- Countries differ in the portion of overall poverty changes attributable to alteration in the poverty risk of jobless and non-jobless households, as well as in the share attributable to changes in the population share of those in jobless households.
- The decline in the share of persons living in jobless households had a sizable contribution to the decline in poverty rates in the first period. For example, this is the case in Estonia, where the contribution of increasing poverty rates of those in jobless households was offset by the effect of the declining share of this group. Similarly, the declining poverty rate in the United Kingdom can be attributable to a large extent to the decline in the share of those living in jobless households. Similar tendencies (albeit to a smaller extent) could be traced in Poland and Lithuania. The case of Belgium is of special interest: the overall no-change in AROP(a) was a result of the fact that the beneficial effects of the declining share of jobless households were completely offset by the increasing poverty rates in both jobless and non-jobless households.
- In the second period, the share of people living in jobless households increased in many countries, contributing to an overall increase in poverty. This was especially the case in Ireland, Spain, and Estonia, whereas in Latvia and Lithuania the increasing share of jobless households did not result in a significant rise in poverty. Germany is the only case where the

**Table 2.4.** Decomposition of Changes in Poverty Rates in the EU Member States Between 2005 and 2008—Analysis of Jobless (WI = 0) and Non-jobless (WI > 0) Households (Percentage Points)

| Country | Change in the AROP rate of active-age individuals $\Delta pov = pov_{i1} - pov_{i0}$ | | Change in the AROP rate of individuals in non-jobless households $awr * \Delta pwr$ | | Change in the AROP rate of individuals in jobless households $awp * \Delta pwp$ | | Change in the share of individuals in jobless households $(apwp - apwr) * \Delta wp$ | |
|---|---|---|---|---|---|---|---|---|
| Germany | 3.30 | *** | 1.40 | *** | 1.88 | *** | −0.14 | |
| Sweden | 2.17 | *** | 1.80 | *** | 0.67 | *** | −0.36 | ** |
| Greece | 1.73 | * | 1.79 | * | −0.17 | | 0.01 | |
| Finland | 1.29 | ** | 1.27 | *** | 0.75 | *** | −0.63 | *** |
| Latvia | 0.85 | | 2.21 | * | 0.64 | *** | −2.02 | *** |
| Luxembourg | 0.62 | | 0.54 | | 0.58 | | −0.43 | ** |
| France | 0.49 | | 0.39 | | 0.12 | | 0.03 | |
| Spain | 0.38 | | 0.47 | | 0.02 | | −0.10 | |
| Slovenia | 0.23 | | 0.49 | | 0.43 | | −0.68 | *** |
| Denmark | 0.22 | | 0.88 | | −0.53 | | −0.25 | |
| Portugal | 0.12 | | 0.24 | | −0.05 | | −0.02 | |
| Cyprus | 0.07 | | 0.25 | | 0.05 | | −0.18 | |
| Italy | 0.05 | | 0.16 | | −0.03 | | −0.11 | |
| Belgium | 0.03 | | 0.56 | | 0.82 | * | −1.28 | *** |
| Netherlands | −0.05 | | −0.61 | | 0.23 | | −0.48 | ** |
| Austria | −0.18 | | −0.95 | | 0.49 | | 0.36 | |
| United Kingdom | −1.23 | | −0.03 | | −0.12 | | −1.11 | *** |
| Hungary | −1.45 | | −1.51 | ** | −0.49 | | 0.31 | * |
| Czech Republic | −1.50 | | −0.46 | | −0.22 | | −0.76 | ** |
| Estonia | −2.30 | ** | −0.42 | | 0.41 | * | −2.49 | *** |
| Ireland | −2.52 | ** | −0.03 | | −2.39 | *** | 0.10 | |
| Lithuania | −2.58 | ** | −0.87 | | −0.12 | | −1.60 | *** |
| Slovakia | −3.53 | *** | −3.09 | *** | 0.12 | | −0.49 | *** |
| Poland | −4.45 | *** | −2.67 | *** | −0.38 | * | −1.40 | *** |

*Note*: Countries are ranked by percentage point changes in the poverty rate. Shades correspond to the magnitudes of the indicators: dark grey (with pattern) is for deterioration (poverty increase), while light grey is for improvements (poverty decrease). Changes are significant at *** p< 0.01, ** p<0.05, * p<0.1 levels.

*Source*: Authors' calculations based on EU-SILC 2005–2012 (releases and coverage specified in Endnote 4).

**Table 2.5.** Decomposition of Changes in Poverty Risk in the EU Member States Between 2008 and 2012—Analysis of WI = 0 and WI > 0 Households

| Country | Change in the AROP rate of active-age individuals $\Delta pov = pov_{i1} - pov_{i0}$ | | Change in the AROP rate of individuals in non-jobless households $awr * \Delta pwr$ | | Change in the AROP rate of individuals in jobless households $awp * \Delta pwp$ | | Change in the share of individuals in jobless households $(apwp - apwr) * \Delta wp$ | |
|---|---|---|---|---|---|---|---|---|
| Spain | 6.11 | *** | 3.24 | *** | 0.53 | | 2.33 | *** |
| Greece | 5.48 | *** | 2.35 | ** | 2.01 | *** | 1.61 | *** |
| Estonia | 3.54 | *** | 1.86 | ** | −0.81 | ** | 2.16 | *** |
| Slovakia | 3.07 | *** | 1.06 | | 2.42 | *** | 0.65 | *** |
| Ireland | 2.57 | ** | −0,79 | | 0.37 | | 2.82 | *** |
| Italy | 2.56 | *** | 2.24 | *** | 0.17 | | 0.06 | |
| Austria | 2.53 | *** | 2.82 | *** | −0.17 | | −0.42 | * |
| Romania | 2.33 | * | 2.22 | * | 0.27 | | −0.22 | |
| Denmark | 2.13 | * | 0.97 | | 0.03 | | 0.83 | ** |
| Sweden | 2.04 | *** | 0.83 | | 2.05 | *** | −0.14 | |
| Belgium | 1.98 | ** | 0.73 | | 0.61 | | 0.67 | * |
| Slovenia | 1.97 | *** | 1.23 | ** | 0.15 | | 0.58 | *** |
| France | 1.85 | *** | 1.40 | ** | 0.73 | ** | −0.20 | |
| Cyprus | 1.71 | * | 1.47 | * | −0.68 | | 0.65 | *** |
| Hungary | 1.37 | * | 1.13 | * | 1.30 | *** | −0.47 | *** |
| Luxembourg | 1.26 | | 0.94 | | −0.36 | | 0.52 | *** |
| Czech Republic | 1.04 | | 1.15 | * | −0.03 | | −0.18 | |
| Germany | 0.93 | | 1.28 | *** | 0.87 | *** | −1.10 | *** |
| Portugal | 0.93 | | −0.62 | | 0.61 | | 1.12 | *** |
| United Kingdom | 0.88 | | 0.79 | | −0.97 | *** | 0.90 | *** |
| Lithuania | 0.83 | | −1.02 | | −0.64 | | 2.37 | *** |
| Latvia | 0.69 | | −1.19 | | −2.02 | *** | 3.32 | *** |
| Finland | 0.57 | | −1.15 | ** | 0.72 | ** | 0.83 | *** |
| Bulgaria | 0.46 | | −0.47 | | −0.73 | * | 1.49 | *** |
| Poland | 0.13 | | −0.13 | | 1.08 | *** | −0.36 | *** |
| Netherlands | 0.00 | | −0.56 | | 0.66 | | 0.32 | |

*Note*: Countries are ranked by the percentage point changes in the poverty rate. Shades correspond to the magnitudes of the indicators: dark grey (with pattern) is for deterioration (poverty increase), while light grey is for improvements (poverty decrease). Changes are significant at *** $p < 0.01$, ** $p < 0.05$, * $p < 0.1$ levels.

*Source*: Authors' calculations based on EU-SILC 2005–2012 (releases and coverage specified in Endnote 4).

increase of poverty rates most probably would have been much higher if the share of people living in jobless households had not declined.

- However, it is not just the structural effect that played a role in overall poverty change in the two periods. The increased poverty rate of the jobless was a significant contributor to poverty change in Germany between 2005 and 2008 and in Slovakia between 2008 and 2012. However, an interesting finding is that changing relative poverty of the non-jobless households also matters a lot. In Poland and in Slovakia, for example, a sizable part of the decline in poverty is accounted for by decreasing poverty rates of the non-jobless households, while in Finland, Greece, Sweden, and Germany, a sizable part of the increase in poverty is accounted for by increasing poverty rates of the non-jobless households between 2005 and 2008.
- In Spain, Greece, Estonia, Slovakia, Ireland, Italy, Austria, Romania, Denmark, and Sweden, the rise of poverty exceeded 2 percentage points in the second period. The increased poverty rate of non-jobless households played a role in this increase in six of the ten countries (exceptions are Ireland, Slovakia, Denmark, and Sweden).

It would be very difficult to find any pattern or relationship between our country groupings (organized preliminarily by the observed employment paths) and the relative contributions of the various factors to poverty change, which points to the role of institutional and contextual factors in shaping individual country stories. The really interesting phase is the crisis period. One sees large poverty increases in Greece and in Spain, in both countries mainly driven by increased poverty of non-jobless households. At the same time, poverty did not increase significantly in Finland in this period, mostly because of the decline in poverty rates of non-jobless households. The analysis could go further for the various groups without finding systematic patterns at this level of data detail.[14]

## THE ROLE OF SOCIAL EXPENDITURES

Poverty rates are jointly determined by employment patterns and by social expenditures.[15] The main tool welfare states have at their disposal for redistributing income is social protection, including cash transfers through social insurance and social assistance. The variable we use here captures all active-age cash benefits accruing to individuals aged 20 to 59 (i.e., unemployment benefits, sick pay/disability pay, social assistance, and family-related allowances or housing allowances; pensions are excluded).[16] To measure the difference in the AROP rate before and after social transfers (excluding pensions), we apply the standard measure of withdrawal rates,[17] defined as:

$$PRI = \left( preAROP(a) - AROP(a) \right) / preAROP(a) * 100,$$

where preAROP(a) is the AROP rate before social transfers (excluding pensions) of the active-age population and PRI is the poverty reduction index.

At the beginning of the crisis (2008), PRI was the highest (above 50%) in the Nordic countries, Belgium, Ireland, Austria, the Czech Republic, Hungary, and Slovenia. The lowest PRIs (below 25%) in 2008 were observed in the Mediterranean countries (Greece, Spain, Italy) and in Latvia, as well is in some other new Member States (Bulgaria, Poland, and Romania).

In countries with a high poverty-reduction effect of social transfers by 2008, the poverty-alleviation capacity of cash benefits either diminished or leveled between 2008 and 2012 (see Table 2.6). Contrarily, half of the countries with medium PRI seemingly made efforts to compensate for the negative effects of the crisis via income redistribution. In these countries, poverty trends were mixed: in the Netherlands, the poverty rate stagnated, in Cyprus and the United Kingdom it increased significantly, but not largely. In Estonia and Lithuania, the volatility of poverty rates was very high in this period, similar to individual employment rates. In some other countries with medium PRI, no sizable change in the poverty-reduction effect of transfers could be observed. Countries with low PRI showed different patterns in the latter period: the effectiveness of poverty reduction increased in Latvia and Spain, while in Romania and Poland, PRI diminished by one quarter compared to the 2008 levels.

Overall, public social expenditures remained an important factor in the fight against poverty. However, the effectiveness of social systems declined in the crisis years in many countries, mostly in those where the PRI was high before: Austria, the Czech Republic, Hungary, and Sweden. Contrarily, low

**Table 2.6.** EU Member States' Classification According to the Poverty-Reduction Effects of Social Transfers

| PRI in 2008 | Increase between 2008 and 2012 | No sizable change between 2008 and 2012 | Decrease between 2008 and 2012 |
|---|---|---|---|
| High PRI | — | Ireland, Denmark, Finland, Slovenia, Belgium | Hungary, Sweden, Austria, the Czech Republic |
| Medium PRI | Cyprus, Estonia, Lithuania, the Netherlands, the United Kingdom | Portugal, (Malta), France, Luxembourg | Slovakia, Germany |
| Low PRI | Latvia, Spain | Greece, Bulgaria, Italy | Romania, Poland |

*Note:* High PRI: PRI in 2008: > 50%, Low PRI in 2008: < 25%. Increase between years 2008 and 2012: increase in PRI value by at least 10%. Decrease between years 2008 and 2012: decrease by at least 10%.

*Source:* Authors' classification based on PRI figures in Gábos et al. (2015, pp. 44–47).

pre-crisis poverty-reduction effect of benefits does not seem to correlate with post-crisis performance.

## SUMMARY AND CONCLUSIONS

Taking into account recent publications on the mechanics of the employment–poverty relationship (Cantillon, Van Mechelen, Pintelon, & Van den Heede, 2014; Corluy & Vandenbroucke, 2014; Marx et al., 2013), this chapter examines both micro- and macro-level correlations, with the aim of contributing to a better understanding of how employment change relates to changes in poverty in EU Member States. In addition, we point to the cross-country variance of this relationship and present the factors affecting the transmission mechanisms between individual employment and household-level income poverty. Our focus is on the period between 2005 and 2012, within which we differentiated between pre-crisis (2005–2008) and crisis (2008–2012) periods—with the advantage of examining both periods of employment growth and periods of losses or recoveries. We also kept in mind recent research results indicating that the overall relationship between employment and poverty in an across-country perspective became stronger between 2008 and 2011 than it had been before (Marx et al., 2013, p. 9).

Overall, the results of our EU-wide analysis support the evidence on the negative relationship between individual employment and poverty (Corluy & Vandenbroucke, 2014, p. 27).

- Our estimates indicate that post-transfer poverty to employment elasticity has been around 25% on average in the EU in the period between 2004 and 2011. The elasticity of the employment:poverty ratio—while it looks sizable for the whole sample on average—seems to have some variations across countries and periods.
- The crisis has resulted in very different employment trajectories. We have seen that relatively larger changes in employment seem to have been accompanied with reverse trends in poverty rates: when employment increases, poverty declines in most cases (and vice versa, when employment declines, poverty rises). However, in contrast to Marx et al. (2013), we found no clear evidence that the relationship between employment and poverty rates differ between the pre-crisis and the crisis periods.

Countries differ greatly in how far a change in the overall poverty rate can be attributed to changes in the share of jobless households in the population on the one hand, and to the changes in the poverty rates of individuals living in jobless and non-jobless households on the other hand.

- The declining share of persons in jobless households between 2005 and 2008 played a very important (relative) role in the large poverty drops observed in Poland, Slovakia, Lithuania, Ireland, and Estonia. In the second period, the share of jobless households increased in most of the countries, contributing to an overall increase in poverty. Largest contributions of this factor to poverty change were measured in Estonia and Spain. In both countries, the massive rise of poverty was accompanied by a large increase in the share of jobless households.

- However, it is not just the structural effect that played a role in overall poverty change in the two periods. The increased poverty rate of the jobless was a significant contributor to poverty change in Germany between 2005 and 2008 and in Slovakia between 2008 and 2012. Moreover, changing relative poverty of the non-jobless households also matters a lot. In Poland and Slovakia, for example, a considerable part of the decline in poverty is accounted for by decreasing poverty rates of non-jobless households, while in Latvia, Finland, Greece, Sweden, and Germany, a sizable part of the increase in poverty is attributable to increasing poverty rates of non-jobless households. In the second period, countries like Spain, Greece, Estonia, Austria, Italy, and Romania observed poverty increases by more than 2 percentage points, the increased poverty rate of households having at least one employed household member has played a role in this overall increase.

We conclude that the success of poverty reduction depends to a large extent on three factors: the dynamics of overall employment growth, the fair distribution of the employment growth across households with different WI (as found by Corluy & Vandenbroucke, 2014, and supported indirectly by our WI group-specific results), and properly designed social welfare systems to smooth out the income losses of those families who are, for some reason, unable to generate sufficient income from employment to participate in society.

## NOTES

This chapter is based on Gábos et al. (2015), ImPRovE Working Paper No. 15/06, at http://improve-research.eu/?page_id=37. That document presents a more complete analysis of how changes in individual employment translate to household level poverty outcomes. This chapter is more restrictive, but we refer to our related findings when necessary. The research on which this chapter is based is financially supported by the European Union's 7th Framework Programme (FP7/2012–2016) under Grant Agreement N. 290613 (project title: ImPRovE). We thank John Hills, Frank Vandenbroucke, Bea Cantillon, Tim Goedemé, Diego Collado, and the participants of the ImPRovE project meeting in Budapest (November 26–27, 2014) for valuable comments and support.

1  To denote this restriction, we refer to at-risk-of-poverty rates of the active-age population only as AROP(a) rates, instead of AROP rates (at-risk-of-poverty rates referring to the whole population).

2  Versions of these eight waves are as follows: 2005-5, 2006-4, 2007-6, 2008-5, 2009-5, 2010-4, 2011-4, and 2012-2. The most recent waves are 2011-4 and 2012-2, released on August 1, 2014. Data for 2011 and for 2012 are still subject to revisions in subsequent releases. In all countries except Ireland and the United Kingdom, the income reference period is equal to the calendar year preceding the survey year. In Ireland, the income reference period is the 12 months preceding the interview; in the United Kingdom, the current income is extrapolated in order to get a figure for the whole year. Notations for dates refer to survey years throughout the paper. Data for Bulgaria and Romania are available from 2007 onward; data for Malta is available from 2009 onward. The validity of data for Germany until 2008 has been questioned because quota sampling was practiced in a transition period until full random sampling was finally established.

3  Definitions of the core indicators are summarized in Gábos et al. (2015, p. 10).

4  Various country stories of poverty and inequality are given in detail by Nolan et al. (2014) for the periods 1980–2010. A summary of the country stories in a comparative manner is provided by Tóth (2014). Concluding remarks about the changing inequalities and related policies in rich countries are summarized by Salverda et al. (2014).

5  For further information on the methods, see Gábos et al. (2015, pp. 16–24).

6  We use age bracket 20–64 for employment statistics, which is the age bracket least deviating from our preferred age bracket for poverty measurement available in the Eurostat public database.

7  Lags in the poverty rate (in this case, especially in Greece, Slovenia, and Bulgaria) might be rooted both in the fact that the poverty measure refers to the survey year and not the income reference year (the previous year in most of the countries) and in a lag of the effect of the crisis until it reached certain countries.

8  For example, Ayllón and Gábos (2015) found in their individual-level dynamic analysis that income poverty and low WI are related via current effects instead of feedback effects, which also indicates that effects are immediate within the reference period of the previous year.

9  For an extended set of regression models, which includes pooled ordinary least squares (OLS) models of AROP(a) and AROP(a) before social transfers, see Gábos et al. (2015, pp. 27–29).

10 It can be argued that the crisis dummy we applied may not be the best proxy to approximate the direction of employment changes, given that it reflects two time periods, irrespective of the economic developments within the periods. In a subsequent version of this chapter we plan to tag upward and downward

spells to get further insights into the nature of the employment–poverty relationship.

11 An extended version of the paper (Gábos et al., 2015) includes regression models of AROP rates before social transfers. Employment had a higher impact on AROP rates prior to transfers (the estimates ranged from −0.54 to −0.73, compared to the range from −0.19 to −0.29 in the AROP(a) models), which may be explained by the moderating role of the welfare state that counteracts market (and private transfer) income inequalities. These mechanisms may come into effect via automatic stabilizers or direct government interventions.

12 When the working-age population is split up according to the households' WI, the sample size is somewhat reduced, because we lose the households having only people with self-declared student status in the age group 20–24 and therefore have missing values on the household WI variable. However, this concerns only < 1% of households and is not systemic across countries.

13 We shall, however, recall that, in some countries, some within-period non-linear trends were also observable: see the examples of Latvia and Poland.

14 Please note that our analysis is not yet extended to decompositions of pretransfer poverty rates. This is a direction into which we could move in the next version of the chapter.

15 A more detailed analysis of the role of social expenditures can be found in Gábos et al. (2015, pp. 39–49). The chapter includes an analysis of the trends in benefit size and PRI in the Member States (in the periods 2005–2008 and 2008–2012 in both jobless and non-jobless households).

16 While pensions are excluded from cash welfare benefits in this exercise, we should mention here that, in some Member States (e.g., Southern and Central-Eastern European countries), pensions might be an important source of income in multigenerational households.

17 The counterfactual nature of the withdrawal rate and the problems related to it, as well as the validity of the conclusions, are discussed elsewhere in the literature (Blundell et al., 2011; Diris et al., 2014; Doerrenberg & Peichl, 2012; Förster & Tóth, 2015,). A brief overview is provided by Gábos et al. (2015, pp. 8–9).

# REFERENCES

Ayllón, S., & Gábos, A. (2015). *The interrelationships between the Europe 2020 social inclusion indicators* [ImPRovE Discussion Paper No. 15/01]. Herman Deleck Centre for Social Policy: Antwerp, Belgium.

Atkinson, A. B., Cantillon, B., Marlier, E., & Nolan, B. (2002). *Social indicators: The EU and social exclusion.* Oxford, England: Oxford University Press.

Becker, G. S. (1981). *A treatise on family*. Cambridge, MA: Harvard University Press.

Blundell, R., Bozio, A., & Laroque, G. (2011). Labour supply and the extensive margin. *American Economic Review, 101*(3), 482–486.

Cantillon, B., & Vandenbroucke, F. (2014). *Reconciling work and poverty reduction: How successful are European welfare states?* Oxford, England: Oxford University Press.

Cantillon, B., Van Mechelen, N., Pintelon, O., & Van den Heede, A. (2014). Social redistribution, poverty and the adequacy of social protection. In B. Cantillon & F. Vandenbroucke (Eds.), *Reconciling work and poverty reduction: How successful are European welfare states?* (pp. 157–184). Oxford, England: Oxford University Press.

Corluy, V., & Vandenbroucke, F. (2014). Individual employment, household employment, and risk of poverty in the European Union: A decomposition analysis. In B. Cantillon & F. Vandenbroucke (Eds.), *Reconciling work and poverty reduction: How successful are European welfare states?* (pp. 94–130). Oxford, England: Oxford University Press.

Decancq, K., Goedemé, T., Van den Bosch, K., & Vanhille J. (2014). The evolution of poverty in the European Union: Concepts, measurement, and data. In B. Cantillon & F. Vandenbroucke (Eds.), *Reconciling work and poverty reduction: How successful are European welfare states?* (pp. 60–93). Oxford, England: Oxford University Press.

Doerrenberg, P., & Peichl, A. (2012). *The impact of redistributive policies on inequality in OECD countries* [IZA DP No. 6505]. IZA—Institute of Labour Economics: Bonn, Germany.

Diris, R., Vandenbroucke, F., & Verbist, G. (2014). Child poverty: What can social spending explain in Europe? [Discussion Paper Series, DPS14.20]. Leuven, Belgium: KU Leuven, Center for Economic Studies.

Förster, M., & Tóth, I. G. (2015). Cross-country evidence of the multiple drivers of inequality changes in the OECD area. In A. B. Atkinson & F. Bourguignon (Eds.), *Handbook of income distribution* (pp. 1729–1843). Amsterdam, The Netherlands: Elsevier.

Gábos, A., Branyiczki, R., Lange, B., & Tóth, I. G. (2015). *Employment and poverty dynamics in the EU countries before, during and after the crisis* [ImPRovE Working Paper No. 15/06]. Antwerp, Belgium: Herman Deleeck Centre for Social Policy, University of Antwerp.

Jenkins, S. P., Brandolini, A., Micklewright, J., & Nolan, B. (2012). *The Great Recession and the distribution of household income*. Oxford, England: Oxford University Press.

Marx, I., Vandenbroucke, P., & Verbist, G. (2011). Can higher employment levels bring lower poverty in the EU? Regression based simulations of the Europe 2020 target. [Discussion Paper series No. 6068]. IZA—Institute of Labour Economics: Bonn, Germany.

Marx, I., Horemans, J., Marchal, S., Van Rie, T., & Corluy, V. (2013). *Towards a better marriage between job growth and poverty reduction* [GINI Policy Paper No. 5]. Amsterdam, The Netherlands: Amsterdam Institute for Advanced Labor Studies.

Nolan, B., Salverda, W., Checchi, D., Marx, I., McKnight, A., Tóth, I. G., & van de Werfhorst, H. G. (Eds.). (2014). *Changing inequalities and societal impacts in rich countries: Thirty countries' experiences.* Oxford, England: Oxford University Press.

Salverda, W., Nolan, B., Checchi, D., Marx, I., McKnight, A., Tóth, I. G., & van de Werfhorst, H. G. (2014). Conclusions: Inequality, impacts, and policies. In W. Salverda, B. Nolan, D. Checchi, I. Marx, A. McKnight & I. G. Tóth (Eds.), *Changing inequalities in rich countries: Analytical and comparative perspectives* (pp. 328–349). Oxford, England: Oxford University Press.

Tóth, I. G. (2014). Revisiting grand narratives of growing income inequalities: Lessons from 30 country studies. In B. Nolan, W. Salverda, D. Checchi, I. Marx, A. McKnight, I. G. Tóth, & H. G. van de Werfhorst (Eds.), *Changing inequalities and societal impacts in rich countries: Thirty countries' experiences* (pp. 11–47). Oxford, England: Oxford University Press.

Starke, P., Kaasch, A., & Van Hooren, F. (2013). *The welfare state as crisis manager: Explaining the diversity of policy responses to economic crisis.* New York, NY: Palgrave-MacMillan.

# 3

# A PAN-EUROPEAN PERSPECTIVE ON LOW-INCOME DYNAMICS IN THE EUROPEAN UNION

Tim Goedemé, Lorena Zardo Trindade, and Frank Vandenbroucke

## INTRODUCTION

Income poverty and income inequality are complex phenomena. In Europe, they are most often studied from a national perspective. Indicators of relative inequality, such as the Gini coefficient, are predominantly used to study inequality within European Union (EU) countries, while the at-risk-of-poverty (AROP) indicator compares incomes with 60% of the national median income. As a result, important pan-European dynamics in household incomes remain largely invisible. However, both a national and a pan-European perspective are required for understanding poverty and inequality and the complex challenge of solidarity in the EU. By assessing household incomes with a common European standard, it is possible to gain more insight into the improvement or deterioration of the standard of living of the poorest people in the EU compared to the rest of the EU's population. This helps to shed an alternative light on progress toward the goal of greater social cohesion in the EU (e.g., Brandolini, 2007; Fahey, 2007), complementing the predominant analyses. In addition, it facilitates a better understanding of trends in the disparities of living standards between EU Member States, which pose an important challenge for European solidarity and social policy initiatives (cf. Goedemé & Van Lancker, 2009; Levy, Matsaganis, & Sutherland, 2013; Vandenbroucke, Cantillon, Van Mechelen, Goedemé, & Van Lancker, 2013). Therefore, this chapter studies recent trends in low-income dynamics from a pan-European perspective, complementing the analyses in other chapters that are mostly based on the AROP indicator.

Several authors have shed light on poverty and inequality from a pan-European perspective by directly comparing the living standard of EU citizens. Some have looked at pan-European poverty and inequality excluding the post-2004 EU Member States (Atkinson, 1996; Beblo & Knaus, 2001; Berthoud, 2004; de Vos & Zaidi, 1998; Eurostat, 1990; Kangas & Ritakallio, 2007), or including at least some post-2004 EU Member States (Boix, 2004; Bönke & Schröder, 2015; Brandolini, 2007; Fahey, 2007; Förster, 2005; Lelkes, Medgyesi, Tóth, & Ward, 2009; Whelan & Maître, 2010). However, few authors have looked into changes over time, and, if they have done so, they have mainly focused on the EU as a whole or on trends characterizing clusters of countries (Goedemé & Collado, 2016). Previous studies have highlighted the following trends. First, developments and policies at the EU level impact upon the distribution of income, both within and between Member States (Heidenreich, 2016). Second, the distribution of those with a relatively low income is very different from a pan-European perspective compared to a national perspective. With the (national) AROP indicator, those at risk of poverty tend to live predominantly in the "old" EU Member States. In contrast, when a pan-European benchmark is used, about 40% of those with a low income tend to live in the Member States that have joined the EU since 2004, in spite of their relatively low population share. Third, dynamics in national AROP rates can be very different from pan-European dynamics in living standards: the low-income proportion (LIP) with a pan-European threshold has tended to decrease and then stabilize between 2005 and 2014, while it increased in several periods if national thresholds are used. Fourth, in the same period, substantial changes in the pan-European income distribution have taken place, mainly as a result of strong reductions in the number of households with an income below 40% of the EU-wide median in the Member States that joined the EU in 2004 (Goedemé & Collado, 2016; Goedemé, Collado, & Meeusen, 2014).

In contrast to previous contributions, this chapter disaggregates trends in pan-European low-income dynamics and tracks country-specific patterns in the EU. The focus is on trends since the onset of the financial and economic crisis. To do so, we make use of two indicators: the EU-wide LIP and the EU-wide low-income gap ratio (LIG). Both indicators compare household incomes to a threshold that is defined as a percentage of the EU-wide median income, controlling for average price differences across countries. With the LIP, we look at the percentage of the population with an income below the threshold, while with the LIG, we look at the size of the gap between household incomes and the common threshold. We focus on four questions: How have the EU-wide LIP and LIG evolved in individual EU Member States? How has the composition of the bottom of the pan-European distribution of incomes changed since the onset of the crisis? Which countries have contributed most to (changes in) the EU-wide LIP and LIG? How do these changes compare with trends in the AROP rate? For the analysis, we use European Union Statistics on Income and Living Conditions (EU-SILC) 2008–2014 data. We consider all EU Member States except for Croatia, because it joined the EU during the period under consideration.

The chapter begins by setting the scene and describes our choice of indicators with reference to the original inspiration of the European project, that is, the simultaneous pursuit of upward convergence across the Member States and social cohesion within the Member States. The second section briefly explains our most important methodological choices and presents the data used. The third section presents the empirical findings and discusses consecutively the four questions highlighted before. The last section presents the conclusions.

## TWO PERSPECTIVES ON COHESION

The empirical findings presented in this chapter illustrate two different perspectives on "cohesion" in the EU. On the one hand, there is a well-known national perspective on cohesion, in which the term *cohesion* is associated with social inclusion as we traditionally understand it. On the other hand, there is a pan-European perspective, in which cohesion is associated with the aspiration of upward convergence in prosperity across the Member States of the EU. Indeed, cohesion policy is a well-known dimension of EU policies. Economic and social cohesion—as defined in the 1986 Single European Act—is about "reducing disparities between the various regions and the backwardness of the least-favored regions." The EU's most recent treaty, the Lisbon Treaty, adds another facet to cohesion, referring to "economic, social, and territorial cohesion."

The overarching indicator used to assess social inclusion at the national level is the AROP rate, with a threshold set at 60% of national median income (i.e., the percentage of individuals living with an income below 60% of the national median). Admittedly, the AROP rate is but one indicator among many. Nevertheless, we believe there are strong arguments to use this relative AROP measure as a central and overarching measure in order to gauge, at the national level, social inclusion, and thus social cohesion as we wish to understand it here (for the original argument, see Atkinson, Cantillon, Marlier, & Nolan, 2002; for a more recent affirmation of the same view, see Cantillon, 2014). In this chapter we apply a (technically) similar indicator at the pan-European level (the percentage of individuals living with an income below 60% or 40% of the European median), but we do not argue that applying it with a 60% threshold yields an indicator of "relative poverty" at the pan-European level. We do not elaborate upon the complex and multifaceted discussion on the meaning and measurement of "poverty" in today's integrated Europe (see, for instance, Berthoud, 2012; Fahey, 2007; Goedemé & Rottiers, 2011; Whelan & Maître, 2009a, 2009b); for this reason, we use the more neutral expressions LIP and LIG for the pan-European measure. However, LIP and LIG are useful indicators for assessing the historical point and purpose of the European project in the socioeconomic domain: upward convergence in prosperity across the Union. This is not to say that LIP and LIG are the only indicators one should study to gauge upward convergence across the EU Member States; yet, the proportion of residents in a Member State who live with an income that is considerably below the European median provides a measure of the extent to which upward convergence in economic prosperity is a reality for a sufficiently large share of the population in that Member State. This provides a useful complement to the predominant analyses that focus on trends in GDP per capita. In addition, the technical similarity of the national and the pan-European measures, both using 60% (or 40%) of the respective median income as a cut-off, sheds an interesting light on what we consider to be the fundamental aspiration of the founders of the European project.

The European integration project has been described as a "convergence machine" (Gill & Raiser, 2012). Convergence was not just a result, it was also a precondition for continuing European integration: the "output legitimacy" of integration was based on the simultaneous pursuit of economic progress on the one hand, and of social progress and cohesion on the other hand, both within countries (through the gradual development of welfare states) and between countries (through upward convergence across the EU). The founders of the European project who prepared the Treaty of Rome optimistically assumed that growing cohesion both between and within countries could be reached by supranational economic cooperation, together with some specific instruments for raising the standard of living across the Member States (which were later brought together in the EU's cohesion policy). Economic integration was to be organized at the EU level and would boost economic growth and create upward convergence; domestic social policies were to redistribute the fruits of economic progress, while remaining a national prerogative. With hindsight (and in a slightly benign interpretation), one may say that the founders of the European project created two perspectives on social cohesion: a pan-European perspective and a national perspective. Certainly, apart from redistributive aspects of the common agricultural policy and a limited degree of cross-country redistribution in favor of less-developed regions through structural funds, in the context of the specific cohesion policy, their approach was not redistributive across borders. Nor was it about the mutual insurance of risks across borders. In other words, they did not envisage the organization of solidarity as we normally understand it within welfare states, which implies mixtures of redistribution and insurance. Historically, the founders' approach predominantly implied fair access to opportunities: trade and investment opportunities for countries joining the EU and personal opportunities for all their citizens wanting or needing to be mobile.

Stretching the notion of inclusion, one might also say that, in pursuing cohesion, from the start the EU was motivated by a (relatively vague) notion of inclusion on a pan-European scale. It is this notion of inclusion on a pan-European scale that is explored in this chapter, from an empirical perspective.

Until the mid-2000s, the EU's approach to social progress and cohesion was considered to be, by and large, successful, and the founders seemed vindicated in their optimistic belief. Since then, the model clearly broke down, and the EU stopped being a convergence machine. Overall, new Member States recorded impressive economic growth after their accession to the EU, but the eurozone crisis triggered divergence among the eurozone members (European Commission, 2014). Within the Member States, the overall position of pensioners has improved, but, among the non-elderly population, two mutually reinforcing processes of polarization are leading to more inequality at the bottom end of the income distribution in a significant number of Member States. First, more people are living in work-poor households (i.e., households with a weak attachment to the labor market), and, second, these households are experiencing higher poverty risks. The latter trend already started before the crisis (Cantillon & Vandenbroucke, 2014; Vandenbroucke & Rinaldi, 2015). This chapter focuses on the dynamics of pan-European social cohesion since the crisis.

## DATA AND MEASUREMENT

In order to assess pan-European dynamics in living standards, we make use of the EU-SILC data, which provide harmonized individual- and household-level information for income as well as additional social indicators. EU-SILC is meant to be a representative sample of persons living in private households. We consider all countries that were an EU Member State between 2008 and 2014.[1] With the exception of Ireland and the United Kingdom, income data refer to the year before the survey year, while other information (e.g., on household composition) refers to the survey year.[2] Nevertheless, the years reported in the figures below refer to the year of the survey, rather than to the income reference year. Although EU-SILC data are available annually from 2005, the analysis focuses on the period between 2008 and 2014[3] in order to limit the number of countries with a break in the time series for income.[4] Although EU-SILC data are to an important extent harmonized, large differences remain with regard to the source of income data (e.g., survey vs. register data), data collection modes, weighting schemes and imputation procedures. At the same time, EU-SILC constitutes the best available source for comparative studies on income and living conditions in the EU.

Given that EU-SILC data are based on complex sample designs, standard errors calculated under the assumption of simple random sampling are strongly downwardly biased. For this reason, as recommended by Goedemé (2013), the analysis considers reconstructed sample design variables[5] that make optimal use of the sample design information in the data (see also Zardo Trindade & Goedemé, 2016). However, because it is not possible to calculate the covariance over different EU-SILC waves, standard errors of changes over time can be expected to be overestimated. As has been noted by several authors, the fact that the low-income threshold is estimated as a share of median income, which itself is an estimate on the basis of the data, may have a non-negligible effect on the sampling variance (Berger & Skinner, 2003; Preston, 1995). We take this into account by making use of the DASP (Distributive Analysis Stata Package) module developed for Stata (Araar & Duclos, 2007). For technical reasons, this effect is not taken into account when decomposing the LIP and LIG. Changes over time are considered statistically significant at the 95% confidence level.

In order to calculate the LIP and LIG, we start from equivalent disposable household income.[6] Equivalent disposable household income equals the sum of all after-transfer incomes of all household members, net of taxes and social contributions, adjusted for differences in needs between households by making use of the modified Organisation for Economic Co-operation and Development (OECD) equivalence scale.[7] Given that we are interested in comparing cross-national differences in real income, differences in currencies and price levels across the selected countries are taken into account. Therefore, we first convert incomes expressed in national currencies into purchasing power standards (PPS) by using purchasing power parities (PPPs) for final household consumption, calculated by Eurostat (cf. European Commission and Eurostat, 2012). Although PPPs are the best tool available for making incomes cross-nationally comparable, they have some limitations. First, income in PPS is not comparable across time. Therefore, we express incomes in PPS as a percentage of the year-specific EU-wide median income in PPS. This allows us to focus on how income levels in individual countries change in comparison with the EU-wide median. Second, the reference consumption bundle that is used for calculating the PPPs may be more representative for some countries than for others, which may lead to biased estimates of real income levels and trends in the EU-wide LIP. Furthermore, PPPs are not necessarily constructed on the basis of a basket of goods and services that reflects consumption patterns of low-income groups and neglect within-country differences in price levels (Deaton, 2002; Milanovic, 2005). From this point forward, we simply refer to "income" to denote equivalent disposable household income in PPS.

In this chapter, pan-European low-income dynamics are studied by calculating two related measures. The EU-wide LIP is equal to the percentage of the population with an income below a percentage of the pan-European median income. The EU-wide LIG equals the gap between the low-income threshold and the income of the poor expressed as a percentage of the low-income threshold, averaged over the total population. Both measures are part of the Foster–Greer–Thorbecke (FGT) index (Foster, Greer, & Thorbecke, 1984, 2010). A more elaborate discussion of the various aspects of the FGT index and the measurement of income poverty in the EU can be found in Decancq et al. (2014).

## RESULTS[8]

So far, low-income dynamics from a pan-European perspective have mainly been studied at the aggregate level, for groups of countries. In order to shed more light on low-income dynamics in the EU, we highlight consecutively (1) trends in levels at the aggregate level and in individual Member States, (2) changes in the composition of the EU-wide LIP and LIG, (3) the contribution of individual countries to (changes in) the EU-wide LIP and LIG, and (4) the correlation between changes in the EU-wide LIP and LIG and the AROP indicator.

### Pan-European Low-Income Dynamics at a Glance

In order to better grasp the changes in the pan-European income distribution, it is useful to first consider the changes in the wider distribution of incomes in each EU Member State. In Figures 3.1, 3.2 and 3.3, we depict kernel density curves of each national income distribution, expressing incomes as a percentage of the year-specific EU-wide median income (while taking price differences into account). We do so for EU-SILC 2008 and 2014. From the graphs, it is clear that re-ranking has taken place throughout the pan-European income distribution. In comparison with the EU-wide median income, the richer EU Member States Austria, Belgium, Denmark, Finland, and Sweden, as well as Malta, have experienced growing incomes across most of the distribution and throughout the period under consideration. However, given their relatively high income levels, except for Malta, these changes have happened mainly above 60% of the EU-wide median income. In contrast, the Netherlands, Ireland, the United Kingdom, and especially Greece, Italy, Spain, and Cyprus, have clearly seen their income distributions fall in comparison with the pan-European median income. Changes in the income distribution in the Central and Eastern European Member States have immediate effects for the EU-wide LIP, given their relatively low level of incomes. Over the period under consideration, Poland, the Czech Republic, and Romania have seen their income levels grow across the distribution, as have Bulgaria, Hungary, Lithuania, and Slovakia (although with a decrease in some years). In Slovenia, decreases have been somewhat more predominant, depending also on the part of the income distribution under consideration.

Although kernel density curves are helpful for giving a quick picture of the changes that have taken place, they do not allow for a very precise interpretation of what has happened at the bottom of the income distribution. A more direct estimation of the LIP and LIG is more helpful in that regard. Given the considerable changes in the pan-European distribution of incomes, we can expect relatively strong movements in the EU-wide LIP at the Member State level, but it is

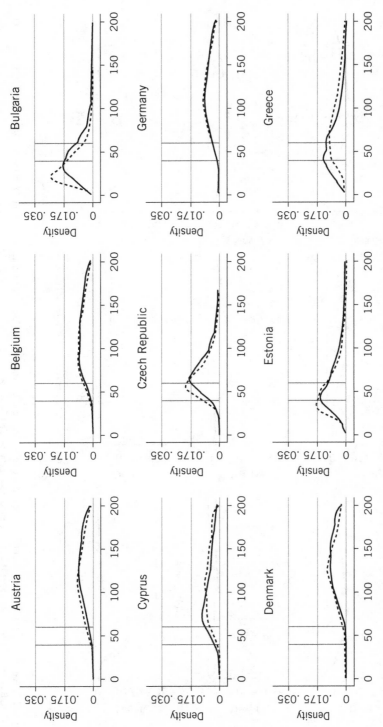

**Figure 3.1.** Kernel density curves of national income distributions relative to the year-specific EU-wide median income (EU27), EU-SILC 2008–2014. (1/3) *Notes:* Breaks in series in Denmark (2011), and Estonia (2014). *Source:* EU-SILC UDB 2008–2014, authors' calculations (see methodological section for details).

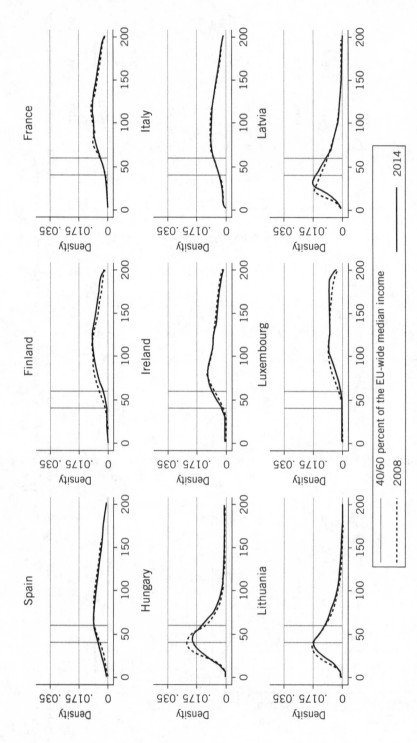

**Figure 3.2.** Kernel density curves of national income distributions relative to the year-specific EU-wide median income (EU27), EU-SILC 2008–2014. (2/3) *Source:* EU-SILC UDB 2008–2014, authors' calculations (see methodological section for details).

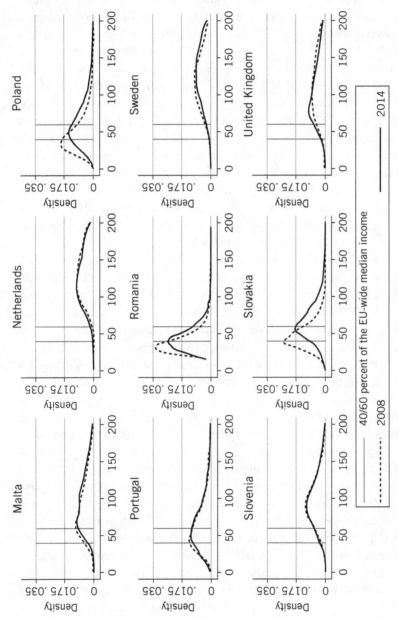

**Figure 3.3.** Kernel density curves of national income distributions relative to the year-specific EU-wide median income (EU27), EU-SILC 2008–2014. (3/3) *Notes:* Break in series in the United Kingdom (2012). *Source:* EU-SILC UDB 2008–2014, authors' calculations (see methodological section for details).

unclear how trends have been at the aggregate level. In previous work, we found that the total EU-wide LIP fell between EU-SILC 2005 and EU-SILC 2009, but changed much less in the following two years (Goedemé et al., 2014, Goedemé & Collado, 2016). Also, between EU-SILC 2010 and 2014, year-to-year changes were very modest and mostly not statistically significant (at the 95% confidence level). Overall, between EU-SILC 2008 and EU-SILC 2014, at 40% of the EU-wide median income, the LIP dropped from 13.1% to 11.3%, while at 60% of the EU-wide median, it dropped from 24.6% to 22.9%. Over three quarters of this drop was realized before EU-SILC 2011. At the same time, with the threshold set at 40% of the EU-wide median income, the LIG dropped from 5.1% in EU-SILC 2008 to 4.4% in EU-SILC 2010, after which it remained at about the same level. A similar pattern can be observed when the threshold is set at 60% of the EU-wide median income. The stagnation (LIG) and modest changes (LIP) since EU-SILC 2010 are rather surprising, given that the crisis and the policy responses that followed continued to affect national income distributions and absolute changes in living standards after 2010 (Matsaganis & Leventi, 2014). This apparent stagnation at the EU level contrasts sharply with the strong changes that can be observed in a number of EU Member States.

Figure 3.4 shows recent changes in the EU-wide LIP and LIG in more detail. First, it is clear that the variation between EU Member States in the level of the LIP and LIG is enormous. With the threshold set at 60% of the EU-wide median income, the LIP in Luxembourg, Finland, and Austria was below 5% in EU-SILC 2014. In contrast, in Greece, Lithuania, Latvia, Hungary, and Bulgaria, it was over 50%, and even over 90% in Romania, by far the poorest country in the EU. A similar variation can be found when looking at the LIG, although there is some re-ranking of countries, and relative differences between Luxembourg and Romania are much larger.

Second, changes in the LIP and LIG also vary strongly across countries. Over the entire period, Slovakia (−33 percentage points) and Poland (−22 percentage points) display the strongest decreases in the LIP with a 60% threshold, while the LIP increased most strongly in Greece (+25 percentage points). Substantial decreases have also taken place in other new Member States, notably Bulgaria, Estonia,[9] Hungary, and the Czech Republic (all −10 percentage points or more), whereas more modest increases (between 4 and 7 percentage points) have taken place in Cyprus, Spain, and Ireland. Remarkably, Romania does not figure in the list of countries with strong decreases. This is somewhat different if we consider the LIG, indicating that changes may have had a stronger impact on the LIP if the threshold had been set lower. This is not surprising, if we consider the overall level of the income distribution in Romania, as depicted in Figure 3.3. Third, it is worth pointing out that the timing of changes in the LIG and LIP varies substantially across countries. In some, the biggest changes were concentrated between EU-SILC 2008 and 2010, notably in Slovakia; in others, the next two years witnessed the biggest change, notably in Greece and Hungary; whereas

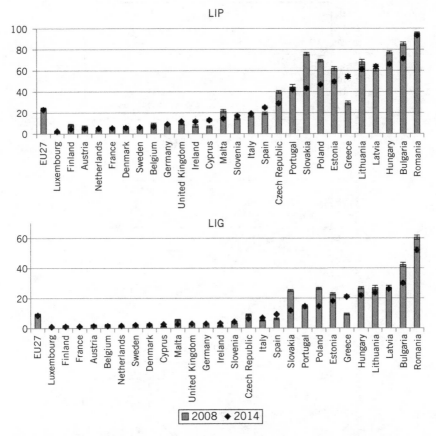

**Figure 3.4.** The EU-wide low-income proportion (LIP) and low-income gap ratio (LIG; EU27), with the threshold set at 60% of the year-specific EU-wide median income, EU-SILC 2008–2014. *Notes:* 95% confidence intervals. Countries ranked by EU-SILC 2014 values. Breaks in series in Denmark (2011), United Kingdom (2012), and Estonia (2014). *Source:* EU-SILC UDB 2008–2014, authors' calculations (see methodological section for details).

the strongest increase in the EU-wide LIP was observed between EU-SILC 2012 and 2014 in Cyprus. Other countries display more varied patterns, including Bulgaria, Latvia, and Lithuania.

Given the relatively strong decreases in most new EU Member States, one may wonder whether stronger changes have taken place lower down the pan-European income distribution, so that we can observe convergence in the level of LIP and LIG across countries over the period of observation. Figure 3.5 compares the level of the LIP and LIG in EU-SILC 2008 with the percentage point change between EU-SILC 2008 and 2014. This graph shows some convergence in the LIP and LIG at both the 40% and the 60% threshold,[10] while convergence is stronger the more we focus on the bottom of the distribution (i.e., by looking at the gap rather than the LIP or by taking a lower threshold). The graph also highlights

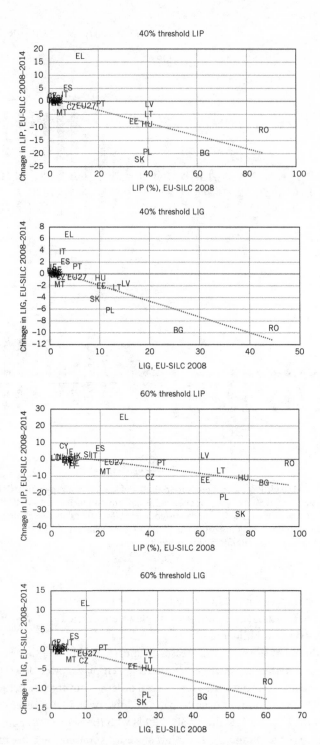

**Figure 3.5.** Percentage point change in the EU-wide low-income proportion (LIP) and the EU-wide low-income gap ratio (LIG). *Notes*: The dotted line is a linear regression line. Please note that the x-axis and y-axis are not on a similar scale for each graph. Breaks in series in Denmark (2011), United Kingdom (2012), and Estonia (2014). *Source*: EU-SILC UDB 2008–2014, authors' calculations (see methodological section for details).

the diverging pattern of the Baltic countries, Hungary, Poland, and Slovakia with regard to the LIP with a 40% of median income threshold and the LIG with a 60% of median income threshold. In EU-SILC 2008, all six countries had a LIP of about 40% and a LIG of about 26% (with somewhat lower figures for Estonia). Six years later, Slovakia and Poland had seen far stronger reductions in the LIP than the other four countries. Finally, countries like the Czech Republic, Estonia, Malta, Poland, and Slovakia succeeded in reducing the number of people with an income between 40% and 60% of the EU-wide median income, while at the same time lifting incomes above the 40% threshold, whereas this was not the case for Romania and Bulgaria. In these countries, the number of households lifted above the 60% threshold was far more limited than those lifted above the 40% threshold.

## The Changing Composition of the EU-wide Low-Income Population

As observed in the previous section, the EU-wide LIP has changed considerably in Eastern Europe and Greece. This suggests that the composition of the population with an income below the pan-European threshold has changed in important respects. Figure 3.6 captures the considerable changes in the composition of the pan-European low-income population between EU-SILC 2008 and 2014 in more detail. In EU-SILC 2008, the composition of those with an income below the low-income threshold and the composition of the LIG was heavily dominated by only two countries: Romania and Poland. Furthermore, the more we focus on the bottom of the distribution, the stronger this concentration was. With the threshold set at 60% of the EU-wide median income, in EU-SILC 2008, nearly 40% of those with an income below the threshold lived either in Romania or Poland. With the threshold set at 40% of the EU-wide median income, the two countries accounted for about 56% of the LIG.[11] In EU-SILC 2014, the composition of the LIP and the LIG has changed substantially, while also becoming less concentrated. These changes have been strongest if the focus is on the LIG with the threshold set at 40% of the EU-wide income. Whereas Poland initially accounted for about 18% of the total LIG, by EU-SILC 2014, its share was halved. In contrast, Italy, Spain, Greece, and also Germany accounted for a substantially increased share of the LIG. As a result, the share of the EU15 in the LIG with the threshold set at 40% of the EU-wide median income had increased from 26% in 2008 to 43% in EU-SILC 2014. Still, a third of the LIG was on the account of Romania. In many countries, as a consequence of these changes, the country share in the LIG has tended to become somewhat closer in line with each country's population share. Nonetheless, strong deviations still exist: Romania, Bulgaria, Hungary, the Baltic countries, and now also Greece are strongly overrepresented in the EU-wide low-income population and LIG.

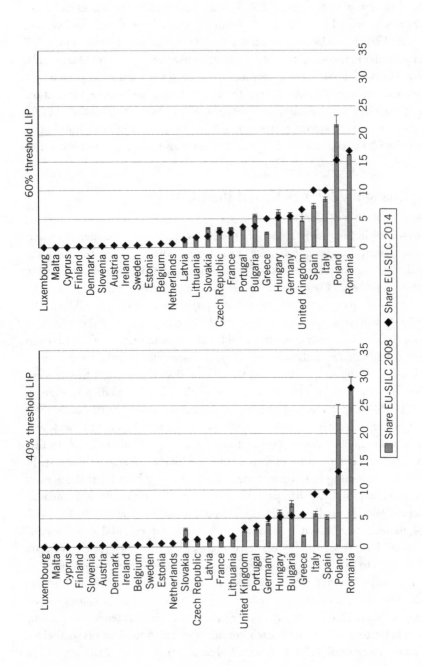

60% threshold LIP

Luxembourg
Malta
Cyprus
Finland
Denmark
Slovenia
Austria
Ireland
Sweden
Estonia
Belgium
Netherlands
Latvia
Lithuania
Slovakia
Czech Republic
France
Portugal
Bulgaria
Greece
Hungary
Germany
United Kingdom
Spain
Italy
Poland
Romania

40% threshold LIP

Luxembourg
Malta
Cyprus
Finland
Slovenia
Austria
Denmark
Ireland
Belgium
Sweden
Estonia
Netherlands
Slovakia
Czech Republic
Latvia
France
Lithuania
United Kingdom
Portugal
Germany
Hungary
Bulgaria
Greece
Italy
Spain
Poland
Romania

■ Share EU-SILC 2008     ◆ Share EU-SILC 2014

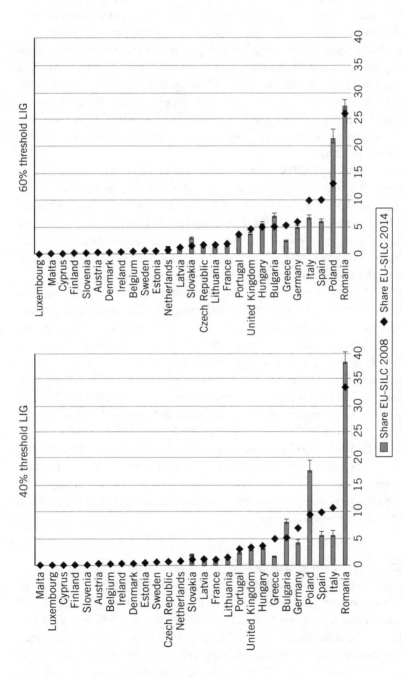

**Figure 3.6.** The share of EU Member States in the EU-wide low-income proportion (LIP) and their share in the EU-wide low-income gap ratio (LIG), EU-SILC 2008–2014. *Notes:* The 95% confidence intervals take account of the sample design (Goedemé, 2013) but assume an exogenous low-income threshold. Countries ranked by EU-SILC 2014 values. Breaks in series in Denmark (2011), United Kingdom (2011), United Kingdom (2012), and Estonia (2014). *Source:* EU-SILC UDB 2008–2014, authors' calculations (see methodological section for details).

## The Contribution of Individual Countries to the Overall Trend

Although the EU-wide LIP has changed most in countries, such as Slovakia, Poland, Bulgaria, and Greece, this does not necessarily imply that trends in these countries can explain overall trends in the total LIP, given—except for Poland—their relatively small populations. The composition of the pan-European low-income population also shows that bigger countries, such as Italy, Spain, and Germany, contribute substantially to the EU-wide LIG. It is possible to quantify with more precision the contribution of each country to the overall change in the EU-wide LIP, at least in a mechanical way (that is, not in a causal framework). To do so, we follow an accounting approach spelled out by Corluy and Vandenbroucke (2012).[12,13]

Overall, between EU-SILC 2008 and 2014, the EU-wide LIP decreased from 24.6% to 22.9% with threshold set at 60% of the EU-wide median income. In the same period, the LIG declined from 5.1% to 4.5% with the threshold set at 40% of the EU-wide median income. As mentioned earlier, most of the decline was realized in the first years of observation. The subsequent stability was not so much the result of inertia in the relative income levels of individual countries, but the result of compensatory trends across EU Member States.

Figure 3.7 and Figure 3.8 depict the contribution of each Member State to the overall trend in more detail, while neglecting the small contribution of the change in population shares. Remarkably, but not entirely unexpectedly, almost half of the Member States have had nearly no impact on the overall change (or lack thereof) in the total EU-wide LIP or LIG. Furthermore, changes in Poland have been most important as a factor for reducing the total EU-wide LIP and LIG. Nonetheless, other Member States also contributed a substantial share to keeping the LIP low or reducing it, most notably Romania and Bulgaria (especially if one focuses on the LIG or a threshold at 40% of the EU-wide median income). On the other side, upward pushes contributing to an increase in the LIP came primarily, and more evenly, from three crisis-hit countries: Spain, Greece, and Italy. Remarkably, at times Germany and the United Kingdom also had an important impact on the total change, although—especially in Germany—changes in the EU-wide LIP have been rather modest.

## Contrasting a Pan-European with a National Perspective

In the introduction, we argue that for understanding poverty and inequality in the EU, both a national and a pan-European perspective are indispensable. In the specific context of EU enlargement, it is interesting to verify whether or not countries that see a growing proportion of their population obtaining incomes above 40% or 60% of the EU-wide median are typically countries in which the AROP indicator (which uses a national threshold) improves or not. In other words, the question is whether or not we see the simultaneous achievement of catching-up processes in terms of economic prosperity for a middle group of people, whose

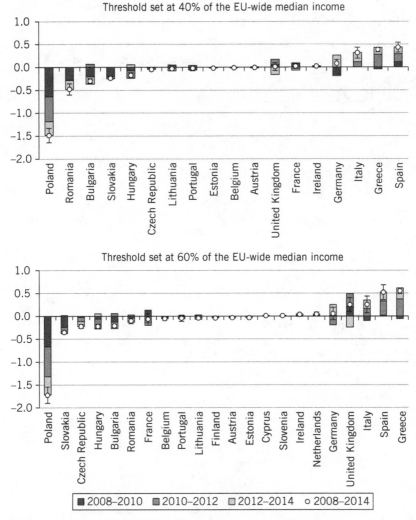

**Figure 3.7.** The contribution of the change in the EU-wide low-income proportion (LIP) in each Member State to the total change in the EU-wide LIP (EU27), EU-SILC 2008–2014. *Notes:* Countries are sorted by total contribution to the change in the LIP. Countries are included in the graphs only if they have a contribution rate of ≥ 0.01 for changes in the period 2008–2014. The 95% confidence intervals take account of the sample design (Goedemé, 2013), but assume an exogenous low-income threshold. Breaks in series in Denmark (2011), United Kingdom (2012), and Estonia (2014). *Source:* EU-SILC UDB 2008–2014, authors' calculations (see methodological section for details).

position shifts over the EU-wide 60% threshold, and improvements in the internal income distribution (from the perspective of the bottom end of the national distribution of incomes). From Figure 3.9 it can be observed that there are hardly any countries that achieve such a combination. Latvia, Lithuania, and Malta have combined a decrease in the LIP and LIG with a national and EU-wide

Threshold set at 40% of the EU-wide median income

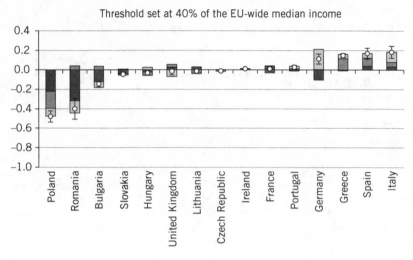

Threshold set at 60% of the EU-wide median income

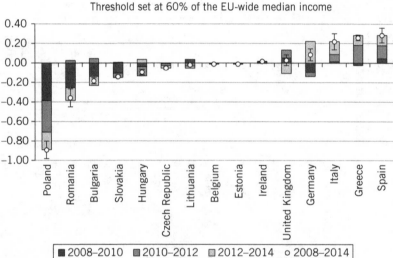

■ 2008–2010   ■ 2010–2012   ▢ 2012–2014   ○ 2008–2014

**Figure 3.8.** The contribution of the change in the EU-wide low-income gap ratio (LIG) in each Member State to the total change in the EU-wide low-income gap ratio (EU27), EU-SILC 2008–2014. *Notes*: Countries are sorted by total contribution to the change in the LIG. Countries are included in the graphs only if they have a contribution rate of ≥ 0.01 for changes in the period 2008–2014. The 95% confidence intervals take account of the sample design (Goedemé, 2013) but assume an exogenous low-income threshold. Breaks in series in Denmark (2011), United Kingdom (2012), and Estonia (2014). *Source*: EU-SILC UDB 2008–2014, authors' calculations (see methodological section for details).

threshold in some instances, but not at all levels of the low-income threshold and with rather modest decreases in the EU-wide LIP. Notably, none of the new Member States that have witnessed the strongest decreases in the EU-wide LIP and LIG has combined this with a substantial drop in the LIP and LIG with a national threshold. Potentially, this signals a kind of "trade-off." However, when

Percentage point change in LIP

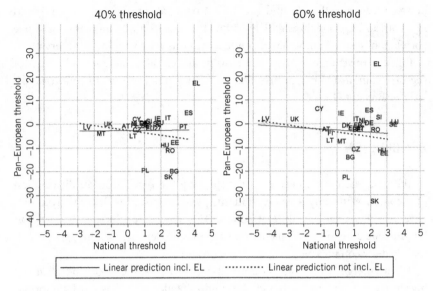

40% threshold            60% threshold

——— Linear prediction incl. EL     ·········· Linear prediction not incl. EL

Percentage point change in LIG

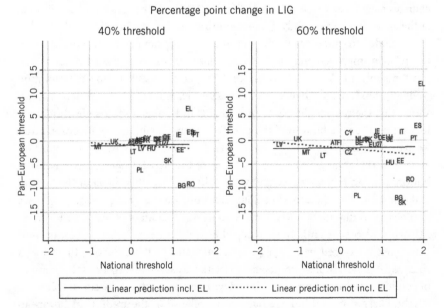

40% threshold            60% threshold

——— Linear prediction incl. EL     ·········· Linear prediction not incl. EL

**Figure 3.9.** The change in the low-income proportion between EU-SILC 2008 and 2014. A comparison of the trend with a pan-European and a national threshold. *Notes*: The *x*-axis and *y*-axis are not on a similar scale for each graph. Breaks in series in Denmark (2011), United Kingdom (2012), and Estonia (2014). *Source*: EU-SILC UDB 2008–2014, authors' calculations (see methodological section for details).

looking at all EU Member States, we do not observe a strong negative correlation between trends in the LIP and LIG with a national threshold and the LIP and LIG with an EU-wide threshold. Presumably, the reason why there is no negative correlation over the whole set of countries (in this brief window of observation) is linked to the eurozone crisis: the crisis produced the simultaneous increase of the LIP from an EU perspective and more "national poverty" in countries like Italy, Spain, and Greece.

## CONCLUSION

In the past, there have been calls for studying the pan-European distribution of incomes. With only a few exceptions, pan-European low-income dynamics have received relatively little attention. This chapter explores pan-European low-income dynamics, complementing the picture depicted in Chapter 2, which mainly draws on the (national) AROP indicator.

What emerges from trends observed between EU-SILC 2008 and 2014 is a highly dynamic picture. Although the window of observation is short, important changes have taken place. Since EU-SILC 2010, these changes have been limited at the aggregate level, mainly because continuing changes in individual Member States tended to cancel each other out. A pan-European perspective underscores the relative improvements in living standards in the new EU Member States, most notably in Poland, Slovakia, and Bulgaria, as well as the deterioration of living standards in Greece, and to a lesser extent in Spain and Italy. Also, it shows that the non-negligible improvements in Romania are visible only if one focuses on the very bottom of the pan-European distribution of incomes, given Romania's overall very low living standards. These trends mark an important change in the composition of the bottom of the pan-European income distribution, with an increasing weight of the "old" EU Member States at the bottom end, most notably the crisis-hit Southern European countries. Worryingly, we also observed that no country succeeded in substantially reducing the EU-wide LIP while also substantially reducing the AROP rate. In other words, upward convergence stopped being the general rule, and in the eurozone there was a sharp divergence. Moreover, insofar as there was still convergence for a number of countries, it was often not combined with increased domestic social cohesion.

The likely story behind the data—the collapse of the traditional European convergence machine—is a mixture of design failures in the architecture of the eurozone, the impact of the increasing heterogeneity of the enlarged EU, and longer-term domestic trends that generate more poverty within a significant number of Member States, notably within the working-age population. Whatever the solutions that are proposed to a variety of problems besetting the monetary union (e.g., a banking union, a fiscal capacity at the eurozone level, possibly associated with a re-insurance of national unemployment insurance schemes or a genuine EU unemployment insurance scheme), these solutions always entail the ex ante organization of solidarity mechanisms. In short, a polity that initially emerged as an "opportunity structure," motivated by the aspiration of growing cohesion, is in need of mutual insurance and true solidarity across borders. Simultaneously, supporting convergence across the enlarged EU presupposes a much more active social and "human capital" dimension in the EU's policies than the founders deemed necessary (Vandenbroucke & Rinaldi, 2015).

Thus, a dual perspective on solidarity, national and pan-European, is the logical consequence of developments that started more than 60 years ago. In fact, one might consider such a dual perspective on solidarity to be the defining normative feature of "the European Social Model." The European Social Model is not simply a summary description of a set of coexisting national social models; it also describes the way the national welfare states interact with each other—or are supposed to interact with each other—in Europe. Hence, we need a conceptual and empirical apparatus to describe the income dimension of this interaction in an integrated way; the methodology and data presented in this chapter provide a promising means to that end.

## NOTES

We are grateful to John Hills, Bea Cantillon, and Zach Parolin for comments and suggestions and to Mary van Beuren for language editing. The research for this article has benefited from financial support by the Flemish Methusalem Programme. The data were made available by Eurostat (Contract RPP 175/2015-EU-SILC-ECHP-LFS). The usual disclaimers apply.

1   At the time of writing, the Brexit referendum took place. Given that our period of analysis covers the pre-Brexit period, we include the United Kingdom in the analysis.

2   In Ireland, the income reference period equals the 12 months preceding the interview, whereas in the United Kingdom current income is multiplied by 52 or 12 (depending on whether it has been recorded as a weekly or a monthly amount). For more information on EU-SILC, we refer to Marlier, Atkinson, Cantillon, and Nolan (2007), Iacovou, Kaminska, and Levy (2012), and Decancq, Goedemé, Van den Bosch, and Vanhille (2014).

3   Data for 2008 is based on EU-SILC 2008 User Database (UDB) version 7 and EU-SILC 2007 UDB version 6 for the United Kingdom. For 2009, references are EU-SILC 2009 UDB version 7 and EU-SILC 2008 UDB version 7 for the United Kingdom. For 2010, we make use of EU-SILC 2010 UDB version 6, and EU-SILC 2009 UDB version 7 for the United Kingdom. For 2011, we make use of EU-SILC 2011 UDB version 5 and EU-SILC 2010 UDB version 6 for the United Kingdom. For 2012, we make use of EU-SILC 2012 UDB version 3 and

EU-SILC 2011 UDB version 5 for the United Kingdom. For 2013, references are EU-SILC 2013 UDB version 2 and EU-SILC 2012 UDB version 3 for the United Kingdom. Finally, data for 2014 is based on EU-SILC 2014 UDB version 1 and EU-SILC 2013 UDB version 2 for the United Kingdom.

4  Four countries have a break in time series in 2008: Spain, France, Austria, and Cyprus. Other breaks in series have appeared after this date: for the 2011 wave in Denmark, the 2012 wave in the United Kingdom, and the 2014 wave in Estonia. We have not attempted to apply any correction for these breaks in series. The equivalent disposable household income in the UDB has been multiplied by correction factors in order to ensure perfect alignment of estimated national median incomes with Eurostat estimates.

5  The sample design variables that we use can be downloaded from https://timgoedeme.com/eu-silc-standard-errors/.

6  Incomes are bottom-coded at 1% of the country-year specific average equivalent disposable household income and top-coded at 10 times non-equivalized disposable household income (the so-called "LIS procedure"). See Van Kerm (2007) for a discussion of the treatment of extreme income values in EU-SILC.

7  The modified OECD equivalence scale attaches a weight of 1 to the first adult, 0.5 to all other household members age 14 and older, and 0.3 to all household members less than 14 years old.

8  Some of the graphs make use of the following country labels: AT= Austria, BE = Belgium, BG = Bulgaria, CY = Cyprus, CZ = Czech Republic, DE = Germany, DK = Denmark, EE = Estonia, EL = Greece, ES = Spain, FI = Finland, FR = France, HU = Hungary, IE = Ireland, IT = Italy, LT = Lithuania, LU = Luxembourg, LV = Latvia, MT = Malta, NL = Netherlands, PL = Poland, PT = Portugal, RO = Romania, SE = Sweden, SI = Slovenia, SK = Slovakia, UK = United Kingdom.

9  Some caution is required for the Estonian estimate, given a break in series in EU-SILC 2014.

10 In line with Sala-i-Martin (1996), we linearly regress the annual growth rate of the LIP between 2008 and 2014 on the level of the LIP at the beginning of the period. The coefficient for absolute beta-convergence is estimated using an ordinary least square regression model across the EU27 countries. For the LIP, it ranges from −0.16 for a 40% threshold to −0.065 for a 60% threshold. For LIG, it ranges from −0.27 for a 40% threshold to −0.23 for a 60% threshold. Since the coefficients are negative, we can say that there is absolute convergence in the EU-wide LIP and LIG across countries.

11 Please note that given price differences across countries, as well as differences in population composition, the numbers in Figure 3.4 do not exactly tell how financial resources in EUR should be redistributed across Europe in order to reduce the LIG to zero. For a given LIG measured by equivalent income in purchasing power standards, ceteris paribus, more resources in

EUR are required if households are smaller, or if price levels are higher. In other words, the graphs underestimate the resources that would need to flow to the richer EU Member States in order to reduce the LIG to zero.

12   The total change in the LIP ($\Delta LIP$) is decomposed as follows:

$$\Delta LIP = \overline{Share_{country\,x}} * \Delta LIP_{country\,x} + \overline{Share_{EU27-country\,x}} * \Delta LIP_{EU27-country\,x}$$
$$+ (\overline{LIP_{EU27-country\,x}} - \overline{LIP_{country\,x}}) * \Delta Share_{country\,x}$$

The first component consists of the average share of the country under consideration in the total population, multiplied by $\Delta LIP$ in that country. The component reflects the direct effect of a change in the LIP in the country under consideration. The second component does exactly the same for the $\Delta LIP$ in the remaining countries. Finally, the third factor estimates the impact of the change in the share ($\Delta Share$) of the country under consideration in the total population. Given that the effect of changes in population shares is rather small and mostly not statistically significant (at the 95% confidence level), we only consider the effect of the change in the LIP and LIG in each individual Member State.

13   Although the decomposition is useful for our purposes, at least two caveats should be kept in mind. First, the decomposition assumes that the income threshold is given and ignores the effect that each country may have on the total LIP via its effect on the EU-wide median income, either by differential income growth or by changing its share in the total population. Second, the decomposition is a mere accounting approach and is not an attempt to construct a realistic counterfactual. A more detailed discussion of the limits of the decomposition can be found in Corluy and Vandenbroucke (2012).

## REFERENCES

Araar, A., & Duclos, J.-Y. (2007). *DASP: Distributive Analysis Stata Package.* Québec, Canada: PEP, CIRPÉE and World Bank, Université Laval.

Atkinson, A. B. (1996). Income distribution in Europe and the United States. *Oxford Review of Economic Policy, 12*(1), 15–28.

Atkinson, A. B., Cantillon, B., Marlier, E., & Nolan, B. (2002). *Social indicators: The EU and social inclusion.* Oxford, England: Oxford University Press.

Beblo, M., & Knaus, T. (2001). Measuring income inequality in Euroland. *Review of Income and Wealth, 47*(3), 301–320.

Berger, Y. G., & Skinner, C. J. (2003). Variance estimation for a low income proportion. *Journal of the Royal Statistical Society, Series C (Applied Statistics), 52*(4), 457–468.

Berthoud, R. (2004). *Patterns of poverty across Europe.* Bristol, England: The Policy Press.

Berthoud, R. (2012). *Calibrating a cross-European poverty line.* Colchester, England: ISER.

Boix, C. (2004). *The institutional accommodation of an enlarged Europe.* Bonn, Germany: Friedrich Ebert Stiftung.

Bönke, T., & Schröder, C. (2015). *European-wide inequality in times of the financial crisis.* Berlin, Germany: DIW.

Brandolini, A. (2007). Measurement of income distribution in supranational entities: The case of the European Union. In S. P. Jenkins & J. Micklewright (Eds.), *Inequality and poverty re-examined* (pp. 62–83). Oxford, England: Oxford University Press.

Cantillon, B. (2014). Beyond social investment: Which concepts and values for social policy-making in Europe. In B. Cantillon & F. Vandenbroucke (Eds.), *Reconciling work and poverty reduction: How successful are European welfare states?* (pp. 286–318). Oxford, England: Oxford University Press.

Cantillon, B., & Vandenbroucke, F. (Eds.). (2014). *Reconciling work and poverty reduction: How successful are European welfare states?* Oxford, England: Oxford University Press.

Corluy, V., & Vandenbroucke, F. (2012). *Individual employment, household employment and risk of poverty in the EU: A decomposition analysis* [CSB Working Paper]. Antwerp, Belgium: Herman Deleeck Centre for Social Policy, University of Antwerp.

de Vos, K., & Zaidi, A. M. (1998). Poverty measurement in the European Union: Country-specific or Union-wide poverty lines? *Journal of Income Distribution, 8*(1), 77–92.

Deaton, A. (2002). *Data for monitoring the poverty MDG.* New York, NY: United Nations Development Programme.

Decancq, K., Goedemé, T., Van den Bosch, K., & Vanhille, J. (2014). The evolution of poverty in the European Union: Concepts, measurement and data. In B. Cantillon & F. Vandenbroucke (Eds.), *Reconciling work and poverty reduction in Europe: How successful are European welfare states?* (pp. 60–93). Oxford, England: Oxford University Press.

European Commission. (2014). *Investment for jobs and growth—Promoting development and good governance in EU regions and cities* [Sixth report on economic, cohesion and territorial cohesion]. Luxembourg: Publications Office of the European Union.

European Commission & Eurostat. (2012). *Eurostat-OECD methodological manual on purchasing power parities.* Luxembourg: Publications Office of the European Union.

Eurostat (1990). *Poverty in Figures: Europe in the Early 1980s.* Luxembourg: Office for Official Publications of the European Communities.

Fahey, T. (2007). The case for an EU-wide measure of poverty. *European Sociological Review, 23*(1), 35–47.

Förster, M. F. (2005). The European social space revisited: Comparing poverty in the enlarged European Union. *Journal of Comparative Policy Analysis, 7*(1), 29–48.

Foster, J., Greer, J., & Thorbecke, E. (1984). A class of decomposable poverty measures. *Econometrica, 52*(3), 761–766.

Foster, J., Greer, J., & Thorbecke, E. (2010). The Foster-Greer-Thorbecke (FGT) poverty measures: 25 years later. *Journal of Economic Inequality, 8*(4), 491–524.

Gill, I. S., & Raiser, M. (2012). *Golden growth: Restoring the lustre of the European economic model.* Washington, DC: The World Bank.

Goedemé, T. (2013). How much confidence can we have in EU-SILC? Complex sample designs and the standard error of the Europe 2020 poverty indicators. *Social Indicators Research, 110*(1), 89–110.

Goedemé, T., & Collado, D. (2016). The EU convergence machine at work: To the benefit of the EU's poorest citizens? *Journal of Common Market Studies, 54*(5), 1142–1158.

Goedemé, T., Collado, D., & Meeusen, L. (2014). *Mountains on the move: Recent trends in national and EU-wide income dynamics in old and new EU Member States.* Antwerp, Belgium: Herman Deleeck Centre for Social Policy, University of Antwerp.

Goedemé, T., & Rottiers, S. (2011). Poverty in the enlarged European Union: A discussion about definitions and reference groups. *Sociology Compass, 5*(1), 77–91.

Goedemé, T., & Van Lancker, W. (2009). A universal basic pension for Europe's elderly: Options and pitfalls. *Basic Income Studies, 4*(1), Article 5.

Heidenreich, M. (2016). The Europeanization of income inequality before and during the Eurozone crisis: Inter-, supra-and transnational perspectives. In M. Heidenreich (Ed.), *Exploring inequality in Europe: Diverging income and employment opportunities in the crisis* (pp. 22–47). Cheltenham, England: Edward Elgar.

Iacovou, M., Kaminska, O., & Levy, H. (2012). *Using EU-SILC data for cross-national analysis: Strengths, problems and recommendations.* Essex, England: ISER.

Kangas, O., & Ritakallio, V.-M. (2007). Relative to what? Cross national pictures of European poverty measured by regional, national and European standards. *European Societies, 9*(2), 119–145.

Lelkes, O., Medgyesi, M., Tóth, I. G., & Ward, T. (2009). Income distribution and the risk of poverty. In T. Ward, O. Lelkes, H. Sutherland, & I. G. Tóth (Eds.), *European inequalities: Social inclusion and income distribution in the European Union* (pp. 17–44). Budapest, Hungary: Tárki.

Levy, H., Matsaganis, M., & Sutherland, H. (2013). Towards a European Union child basic income? Within and between country effects. *International Journal of Microsimulation, 6*(1), 63–85.

Marlier, E., Atkinson, A. B., Cantillon, B., & Nolan, B. (2007). *The EU and social inclusion: Facing the challenges*. Bristol, England: The Policy Press.

Matsaganis, M., & Leventi, C. (2014). The distributional impact of austerity and the recession in Southern Europe. *South European Society and Politics, 19*(3), 393–412.

Milanovic, B. (2005). *Worlds apart: Measuring international and global inequality*. Princeton, NJ: Princeton University Press.

Preston, I. (1995). Sampling distributions of relative poverty statistics. *Journal of the Royal Statistical Society, Series C (Applied Statistics), 44*(1), 91–99.

Sala-i-Martin, X. (1996). The classical approach to convergence analysis. *The Economic Journal, 106*(437), 1019–1036.

Van Kerm, P. (2007). Extreme incomes and the estimation of poverty and inequality indicators from EU-SILC (No. 2007-01). Luxembourg: CEPS-Instead.

Vandenbroucke, F., Cantillon, B., Van Mechelen, N., Goedemé, T., & Van Lancker, A. (2013). The EU and minimum income protection: Clarifying the policy conundrum. In I. Marx & K. Nelson (Eds.), *Minimum income protection in flux* (pp. 271–317). Hampshire, England: Palgrave-Macmillan.

Vandenbroucke, F., & Rinaldi, D. (2015). Social inequalities in Europe—The challenge of convergence and cohesion. In Vision Europe Summit Consortium (Ed.), *Redesigning European welfare states—Ways forward* (pp. 38–77). Gütersloh, Germany: Bertelsmann Stiftung.

Whelan, C. T., & Maître, B. (2009a). The "Europeanisation" of reference groups: A reconsideration using EU-SILC. *European Societies, 11*(2), 283–309.

Whelan, C. T., & Maître, B. (2009b). Europeanization of inequality and European reference groups. *Journal of European Social Policy, 19*(2), 117–130.

Whelan, C. T., & Maître, B. (2010). Comparing poverty indicators in an enlarged European Union. *European Sociological Review, 26*(6), 713–730.

Zardo Trindade, L., & Goedemé, T. (2016). *Notes on updating the EU-SILC UDB sample design variables 2012–2014*. Antwerp, Belgium: Herman Deleeck Centre for Social Policy, University of Antwerp.

# PART 2

# THE ROLE OF SOCIAL PROTECTION

# 4

# THE IMPACT OF SOCIAL TRANSFERS ON INCOME POVERTY AND MATERIAL DEPRIVATION

## Geranda Notten and Anne-Catherine Guio

## INTRODUCTION

In 2010, European Union (EU) heads of state and government launched the Europe 2020 strategy and committed to lifting at least 20 million people out of poverty and social exclusion—that is, from around 116.5 million, based on 2008 EU Statistics on Income and Living Conditions (EU-SILC)[1] figures, down to 96.5 million. The EU social inclusion target is based on a combination of three indicators: income poverty (also referred to as "poverty risk" or "relative poverty"), severe material deprivation (SMD), and (quasi-)joblessness. According to the 2013 EU-SILC data (the most recent data available during the writing of this chapter), the number of people at risk of poverty or social exclusion was 121.6 million, a jump of more than 5 million people since the adoption of the EU target. The jump mainly resulted from the Great Recession and subsequent austerity policies implemented by EU Member States.

The three indicators combined in the EU social inclusion target are part of a larger set of commonly agreed EU social indicators, which are used by the European Commission and Member States to monitor progress on poverty and social exclusion. Among the EU social indicators, there are two indicators of income poverty before social transfers (one considering pensions and old-age benefits as social transfers, the other including them as non-transfers income). When compared with the income poverty rate after social transfers, the poverty rates before social transfers allow assessment (crudely) of the impact of social transfers. This chapter develops a similar approach by estimating the effects of social transfers on material deprivation (i.e., by predicting a material deprivation rate before social transfers), showing thereby the effects of social transfers that we miss by considering only their impact on income poverty. This is important because neglecting the impact of social transfers on material deprivation and focusing only on their impact on income poverty understates both their effectiveness (i.e., the impact of social transfers on expected outcomes, such as reducing the number of targeted people in poverty and social exclusion) and their efficiency (i.e., the relative cost of this reduction). Furthermore, evidence shows that a family can be materially deprived even when their income is above the poverty threshold, and vice versa (see, among others, Guio, Gordon, & Marlier, 2012; Nolan & Whelan, 2010). Using both indicators allows better accounting for a larger diversity of situations of poverty and social exclusion, as recognized by the EU social inclusion target. Using the 2008 and 2013 EU-SILC data, this chapter focuses on four Member States— Germany (DE), Greece (EL), Poland (PL), and the United Kingdom (UK)—which have been chosen because they have different levels of living standards and redistributive capacity and because the crisis affected their economies differently.

The method used in this chapter is still under development. In future work, it will need to be refined and expanded to all EU countries. However, the results presented already highlight the importance of assessing the impact of social transfers on material deprivation, and they show how this approach can usefully complement the current EU approach, which looks only at the impact of social transfers on income poverty.

The next section of this chapter sets the scene; it briefly discusses the concepts of income poverty and material deprivation and provides a description of trends in economic growth, poverty, and social protection expenditures in the four selected Member States between 2008 and 2013. After that, the methods are presented, followed by the results. The conclusion summarizes the main findings.

## SETTING THE SCENE

### The Concepts of Income Poverty and Material Deprivation

The EU indicator of income poverty, also called at-risk-of poverty (AROP) rate, is defined as the percentage of the population living in a household whose equivalized income is below 60% of the national median equivalized disposable income. Disposable income is the total income of a household that is available for spending or saving, after tax and other deductions. All monetary income received from any source by each member of the household is added up; this includes income from work, income from capital and social benefits, and any other household income; taxes, social contributions, and regular interhousehold cash transfers that have been paid are deducted. To account for differences in the size and composition of households, disposable income is divided by the number of "equivalent adults," using the modified Organisation for Economic Co-operation and Development (OECD) scale, which gives a weight of 1.0 to the first adult, 0.5 to the second adult and each subsequent person age 14 and over, and 0.3 to each child less than 14 years old. The income reference period is the previous calendar year for all countries except the United Kingdom, where the income reference period is the current year. Two other EU social indicators are the income poverty rates before social transfers where one considers pensions and old-age benefits as social transfers, and the other includes them as non-transfers income. These indicators measure the percentage of persons living in households whose equivalized disposable income before social transfers is below the AROP threshold (calculated using income after social transfers).

Since 2009, the EU portfolio of social indicators also includes a material deprivation measure that complements the income poverty indicators (see Guio, 2009). The household deprivation information is collected at the household level and is assigned to all household members (including children). This indicator considers nine deprivations: the household cannot (1) afford one week of annual holiday away from home; (2) face unexpected expenses; (3) avoid arrears (mortgage or rent, utility bills, or loans); (4) afford a meal with meat, chicken, fish, or vegetarian equivalent every second day; (5) afford to keep their home adequately warm; (6) afford to have a car or van for private use (if wanted[2]); (7) afford to have a washing machine (if wanted); (8) afford to have telephone (if wanted); and (9) afford to have a television (if wanted).

A person is deprived if his or her household lacks three or more items (standard definition). The policy importance of the concept of material deprivation has increased in 2010, because an indicator of SMD (with a threshold set at four) is one of the three indicators the Europe 2020 social inclusion target is based on. Therefore, this chapter focuses on SMD. The EU indicators for material deprivation are under revision (see Guio et al., 2012).

Material deprivation indicators have also gained importance outside Europe, in Australia, Canada, and New Zealand, for example (Notten, 2015; Perry, 2015; Saunders & Wong, 2011). In the United States, research communities use similar, although not identical, "material hardship" indicators (Cancian & Meyer, 2004; Huston & Bentley, 2010; Wu & Eamon, 2010).

Income and material deprivation are complementary because they reflect related but different concepts of material well-being and each has its own specific measurement challenges (see Battiston et al., 2013; Bossert & D'Ambrosio, 2014; Cancian & Meyer, 2004; Guio et al., 2012, Marlier et al., 2007; Nolan &

Whelan, 2010). Consequently, while income and material deprivation indicators often "agree" about a person's material well-being, they also regularly "disagree." It is important to understand the reasons for this (Fusco, Guio, & Marlier, 2011). In Western Europe, for instance, the negative but relatively modest correlations between equivalized income and the number of deprivations range from −0.17 in Denmark to −0.36 in Belgium, resulting in mixed status (deprived but not income-poor or income-poor but not deprived) of 12% to 20% of the population (Fusco, Guio, & Marlier, 2010, Tables 6.1 and A4). The results are similar when using somewhat different definitions (Cancian & Meyer, 2004; Nolan & Whelan, 2010).

The empirically observed disagreement between income and material deprivation indicators arises not only because the indicators measure related but distinct concepts of well-being but also because each indicator has its own specific measurement issues. Ringen (1988) conceptualizes material well-being in terms of either consumption (direct concept) or resources (indirect concept). A direct concept should be operationalized using a direct indicator (i.e., material deprivation, expenditures) and an indirect concept with an indirect indicator (i.e., income, wealth). Moreover, measurement imperfections, including errors, also play a role: an indirect indicator may not reflect a person's potential living standard and a direct indicator may not reflect a person's actual living standard.

There are several conceptual and measurement issues that explain discrepancies between a household's income and its potential living standard. Conceptually, the rationale for using income is that, for most households, it is the largest source for funding consumption. However, households can also fund their living standard by depleting assets or taking up loans (Brandolini, Magri, & Smeeding, 2010). Income indicators are often not adjusted for receipt of in-kind transfers and payments of indirect taxes (Aaberge, Langørgen, & Lindgren, 2017; Garfinkel, Rainwater, & Smeeding, 2006; Paulus, Sutherland, & Tsakloglou, 2010). While commonly adjusted for differences in household size, income indicators are usually not adapted for differences in needs, such as chronic illness or disability of household members (Sen, 1999). An implicit assumption underlying a resource-based indicator is also that needed goods and services can be purchased in well-functioning markets (Bourguignon & Chakravarty, 2003). Furthermore, in some surveys, income from the previous year is seen as the best proxy for current income, even if this implies inconsistencies between income and the current household composition and activity status information. Finally, measurement errors due to intentional (informal earnings, tax evasion) or unintentional (memory failure) misreporting tend to under- or overestimate actual income levels.

Material deprivation indicators measure a household's actual living standard more directly by focusing on the affordability of items considered essential to having a decent standard of living in the society where people live (Guio, 2009; Guio et al., 2012; Townsend, 1979). The items typically reflect common perceptions of what are social necessities. Material deprivation indicators thereby circumvent the challenges of accounting for alternative resources, needs, and noncash or durable consumption when constructing monetary indicators, such as income or consumption. There are, however, various reasons for having discrepancies between a household's responses to the material deprivation questions in the survey and its actual living standard. First, the selection of deprivation items assumes a common prioritization of needs in society. Differences in needs and priorities by minority groups may thus be overlooked or mistakenly interpreted as deprivation. Second, adverse circumstances may lower a person's aspirations to the degree that she responds by not having an item because she does not want it (Guio, 2009; Guio et al., 2012). Third, feelings of shame may also result in underreporting of deprivation (Breunig & McKibbin, 2011). Finally, information regarding the quality of the different goods and their longevity (e.g., durables) is usually not taken into account.

## Trends in Income Poverty, Material Deprivation, Economic Growth, and Social Protection Expenditures

The 2008 economic and financial crisis and its aftermath had very different effects on poverty in EU Member States. The four countries we study in this chapter were selected to illustrate that variation in experiences (summarized in Table 4.1). Between 2008 and 2013, income poverty increased in Greece, remained stable in Germany and Poland, and declined in the United Kingdom. During the same period, material deprivation increased in Greece, remained stable in Germany, and decreased in Poland. Material deprivation also increased in the United Kingdom since 2009. However, the large increase between 2011 and 2012 (2.7 percentage points, to 7.8%) coincides with a switch to another survey instrument and could also reflect differences in data collection.

The pattern of economic growth is a key factor explaining these trends. The United Kingdom and Greece were hard hit by the recession. The United Kingdom's economy was in recession for two years (2008 and 2009), while Greece's economy shrank for six consecutive years (2008 to 2013). Severe austerity measures and

**Table 4.1.** Income Poverty and Material Deprivation Trends (2008–2013)

|                | At-risk-of-poverty rate | Severe material deprivation rate |
|----------------|-------------------------|----------------------------------|
| Germany        | Stable                  | Stable                           |
| Greece         | Increase                | Increase                         |
| Poland         | Stable                  | Decrease                         |
| United Kingdom | Decrease                | Increase                         |

*Note:* Table A1 in Notten & Guio (2016) presents the time-series data.
*Source:* Eurostat (2017).

reforms followed. In the United Kingdom, the recession reduced median income proportionally more than the lower incomes, shifting both the income poverty threshold and the income poverty rate downward. At the same time, the inability to afford four or more deprivation items increased somewhat until 2011. In Greece, lower incomes were harder hit by the recession and cutbacks, resulting in increased income poverty and in a decline in the standard of living. Poland's economic growth slightly slowed down but the economy did not enter a recession. Germany's economy shrank only in 2009, after which it rebounded strongly. In both countries, the income poverty threshold rose gradually and at roughly the same pace in the middle and bottom of the income distribution. Yet, in Poland, the living standard of those with many deprivations also improved gradually, while it did not in Germany.

Social protection expenditures are known to be an influential factor, too. In a recession, the expenditures accruing to working-age individuals and their families work as automatic stabilizers (partially) compensating for market income lost due to the contraction of the economy. The size of the effect on income poverty and material deprivation depends on the design of the country's social safety net. Changes in income poverty and material deprivation over time depend on if, and how, the safety net has been reformed as part of austerity measures. Table 4.2 provides some first clues by summarizing the social protection expenditure trends. Comparing 2008 and 2012, expenditures per capita (at constant prices) rose in all categories in Germany and the United Kingdom. In Greece, except for old-age pension and survivor benefits, all other categories declined. Total expenditures in Poland remained stable, although old-age pension and survivor benefits gained importance relative to family, housing and social exclusion benefits. The remainder of this chapter quantifies the impact of these spending categories on income poverty and material deprivation.

**Table 4.2.** Trends in Social Protection Expenditures (2008–2012, per Inhabitant at Constant Prices)

| | Social protection | Old-age pensions and survivors benefits | Work-age social insurance | Family, housing, & social exclusion |
|---|---|---|---|---|
| Germany | Increase | Increase | Increase | Increase |
| Greece | Decrease | (Net) increase | Decrease | Decrease |
| Poland | Stable | (Net) increase | Stable | (Net) decrease |
| United Kingdom | Increase | Increase | Increase | Increase |

Note: The data for Greece are provisional. Table A1 in Notten and Guio (2016) presents the time-series data.
Source: Eurostat.

# METHOD

This study estimates the effect of transfers on material deprivation and compares it to the effect of transfers on income poverty. It assesses the effect of transfers (total transfers and by type) on the number of deprivations, the SMD rate, and the AROP rate. The latter two indicators have significant political importance because they are used to monitor progress on the EU's social inclusion target, which is to be met by 2020. We are the first to develop and test a regression approach to predict the effect of social transfers on material deprivation. For income poverty, we use the method that is already routinely used at the EU level to calculate such effects. As the Great Recession in 2008/9 and the following austerity measures have made meeting the EU's social inclusion target more challenging, we also compare 2008 (our pre-crisis yardstick[3]) and 2013 EU-SILC data (the most recent available data at the time of writing) to see whether the poverty-reduction effects of transfers have changed.

At the EU level, the impact of social transfers on income poverty is assessed by comparing income poverty rates on the basis of total household disposable income with and without social transfers (there are two indicators: one indicator counting pensions as non-transfers and one counting pensions as transfers). For both poverty rates (before and after transfers), the threshold used is the post-transfers income poverty threshold (see the section "The Concepts of Income Poverty and Material Deprivation"). This method overestimates the effects of transfers on income poverty, first because it assumes that the receipt of transfers does not change the behavior of persons and households, but when transfers are large, this assumption is likely to be violated; and second because it fails to take into account that receiving one transfer may affect a person or household's eligibility for other transfers. Advanced microsimulation models would lead to better estimates because they take tax–benefit rules and/or behavioral effects into account (Figari et al., 2015). Our focus here is on developing and testing a method that yields estimates of the effects of transfers on material deprivation. Incorporating the technique into more sophisticated models is left for future research.

The post-transfers income indicator is the EU-SILC's total disposable household income variable (Di Meglio, Dupré, Montaigne, & Wolff, 2017). We also use five pre-transfer income indicators. The first is total disposable household income before all social transfers. This variable is constructed by subtracting all gross social transfer amounts from a household's total disposable income (old-age and survivor pensions, social insurance, family, housing, social assistance, and other benefits/allowances). The second is total disposable household income before all social transfers except old-age and survivor pensions. The other three pre-transfers income variables measure income before old-age and survivor pensions, income before gross social insurance benefits (unemployment, sickness, disability), and income before gross household transfers (family allowances, social assistance, housing allowances). All income variables are adjusted using the modified OECD equivalence scale (Table 4.3). All results are weighted using the EU-SILC's household cross-sectional weights (households) or individual cross-sectional weights (individuals).

The post-transfers material deprivation indicator is based on the number of deprivations a household cannot afford (see the section "The Concepts of Income Poverty and Material Deprivation"). To estimate what the number of deprivations would be before transfers, we first estimate a multivariate regression model for each country separately, using the household as the unit of analysis. The dependent variable, the number of (post-transfers) deprivations, is regressed on disposable income (in natural logarithm) and various controls. We use the resulting income elasticity of material deprivation to predict a household's number of deprivations using pre-transfers and post-transfers income. The difference between these predictions reflects the change in the number of deprivations due to social transfers. To calculate the EU's SMD rate before transfers we add the difference in count to the observed deprivation count. This method assumes that different sources of income contribute similarly to avoiding material deprivation.

Estimating income elasticity is the crucial step in our method and thus requires the selection of an appropriate multivariate estimator and model specification. Our preferred estimator is a maximum likelihood estimator based on a negative binomial regression model (Hilbe, 2011) because the dependent variable reflects count data (the number of deprivations) for which the variance is larger than the mean (overdispersion). Various alternative estimators have been used to investigate the relation between income and material deprivation. Focusing on explaining cross-national differences in material deprivation, Nelson (2012) chose a Probit model but discarded a lot of information by creating a binomial dependent variable. Muffels and Fouarge (2004) used a Tobit regression model. However, Angrist and Pischke (2009) argued that a Tobit model is only needed when data are truly censored (p. 102). Relying on this argument, Figari (2012) used a linear fixed-effects model and longitudinal data to explain cross-national differences in material deprivation. However, a linear estimator relies on the assumption of a normal distribution, while count data typically have a Poisson-like distribution. Our tests show that this also holds for our dependent variable.

We determine the preferred model specification with the principal aim of obtaining an income elasticity of material deprivation that is representative for the population of interest—namely, households receiving transfers who are at considerable risk of material deprivation. The choice of control variables has further been driven by the theoretical and empirical evidence regarding the nature of the relationship between income and material deprivation. As discussed earlier, for similar income levels, material deprivation may differ, depending on the debt/wealth level, specific needs and costs (housing, child care, health), or other measurement issues (diversity of preferences, or difficulties in measuring incomes, such as self-employment or capital incomes). Other considerations

**Table 4.3.** Summary Statistics

| | Germany | | Greece | | Poland | | United Kingdom | |
|---|---|---|---|---|---|---|---|---|
| | **2008** | **2013** | **2008** | **2013** | **2008** | **2013** | **2008** | **2013** |
| **Greece** | | | | | | | | |
| • Individuals | 28,785 | 26,633 | 16,748 | 17,909 | 41,120 | 36,413 | 20,962 | 23,168 |
| • Households | 13,247 | 12,656 | 6,455 | 7,385 | 13,951 | 12,884 | 8,886 | 10,114 |
| **Equivalized income (nominal annual mean, in EUR)** | | | | | | | | |
| • Before all transfers | 14,724 | 15,702 | 9,611 | 5,834 | 3,636 | 4,402 | 17,166 | 15,330 |
| • Before old-age and survivor pensions | 16,816 | 17,873 | 9,999 | 6,266 | 3,954 | 4,693 | 19,061 | 17,790 |
| • Before transfers other than pensions | 18,974 | 20,407 | 12,391 | 8,932 | 4,630 | 5,689 | 20,694 | 19,284 |
| • Before social insurance benefits | 20,107 | 21,789 | 12,554 | 9,091 | 4,752 | 5,802 | 22,129 | 21,101 |
| • Before household social transfers | 20,001 | 21,284 | 12,626 | 9,210 | 4,833 | 5,877 | 21,265 | 20,011 |
| • Disposable | 21,066 | 22,577 | 12,779 | 9,365 | 4,948 | 5,981 | 22,589 | 21,744 |
| **Distribution of the population by number of deprivations:** | | | | | | | | |
| • 0 | 57.3 | 60.1 | 40.2 | 28.2 | 27.2 | 30.2 | 64.2 | 49.4 |
| • 1 | 16.9 | 16.8 | 23.1 | 19.0 | 18.6 | 19.7 | 13.1 | 19.0 |
| • 2 | 12.8 | 11.5 | 15.1 | 15.7 | 21.8 | 24.5 | 11.4 | 14.2 |
| • 3 | 7.5 | 6.2 | 10.6 | 17.0 | 14.6 | 13.6 | 6.8 | 9.1 |
| • 4+ | 5.5 | 5.4 | 11.0 | 20.0 | 17.8 | 11.9 | 4.5 | 8.3 |
| **Correlation** | | | | | | | | |
| • Log disposable income & number of deprivations | −0.472 | −0.506 | −0.537 | −0.545 | −0.482 | −0.509 | −0.347 | −0.432 |
| **Number of households excluded from analysis** | | | | | | | | |
| • Disposable income ≤ 0 | 66 | 20–49 | 20–49 | 54 | 20–49 | < 20 | 20–49 | 58 |

*Notes:* Income is expressed in EUR in the EU-SILC data and the exchange rate used is provided by the HX010 variable. Discrepancies between the SMD rate and that reported by Eurostat are due to the exclusion of observations with negative disposable income.

*Source:* Authors' computation, UDB August 2010 and March 2015.

involve the cross-national comparability of control variables: to enhance comparability, we use the same model specification for each country. Our preferred model specification includes variables controlling for:

- Survey year (a dummy for the 2013 wave)
- High-income household (a dummy indicating whether the household's income is ranked in the top deciles of the income distribution)[4]
- Very-low-income household (a dummy indicating whether the household's income is below that of the first percentile of the income distribution)
- High-transfers household (a dummy indicating whether the household's nonpension-transfers income is above 25% of disposable income)
- Debt burden (two dummies indicating whether debt repayment is a heavy or modest burden for the household)
- Housing costs (two dummies indicating whether housing costs are a heavy or modest burden for the household)
- Home ownership (a dummy indicating whether the household's residence is rented)
- Proxy health costs (one dummy indicating whether at least one adult member has a chronic illness, derived from variable "Suffer from any chronic (long-standing) illness or condition" (PH020)
- Household demographics (six household-type dummies derived from variable "Household type" (HX060) and three variables indicating the number of children, adults, and elderly)
- Education level (four dummies constructed from variable "Highest ISCED level attained" (PE040) indicating the highest level of education attained for the adult household member with the highest education)
- Self-defined economic status (eight dummies constructed from variable "Self-defined current economic status" (PL030) indicating whether at least one adult member is in full-time employment, part-time employment, self-employed, unemployed, retired, inactive due to disability, fulfilling domestic work, or otherwise inactive)
- Citizenship (two dummies indicating that at least one adult member has EU or non-EU citizenship).

## RESULTS

### The Income Elasticity of Material Deprivation

Table 4.4 summarizes the key results of our preferred model estimated using a negative binomial (NB) regression, our preferred estimator, and those using ordinary least squares (OLS).[5] The income elasticity of material deprivation ranges from −0.33 for the United Kingdom to −0.51 in Germany, indicating that a 1%

increase in household income reduces the household's number of deprivations by 0.33 to 0.51. Using an OLS estimator, the estimated income elasticity is close to the NB elasticity for Germany (−0.57) and higher for Greece (−0.87) and Poland (−0.74) but lower for the United Kingdom (−0.17). The high percentage of zero deprivations (Table 4.3) suggests that the values violate the normal distribution assumption required for a linear estimator. The zero $p$-values of the likelihood-ratio test of alpha (Table 4.4) indicates that the variance is larger than the mean for most countries, confirming that a NB regression model is a better fit than a Poisson model. For Poland, a model without an alpha (Poisson) would be somewhat more efficient.

With the exception of Germany, the 2013 dummy is significant, indicating that material deprivation levels differ across survey waves, being positive in 2013 in Greece and the United Kingdom and negative in Poland. The inclusion of the wave dummy takes into account the temporal evolution of the intercept between 2008 and 2013. This implies that only the change in the average deprivation level is captured, but not the possible evolution of the relation between income/controls and deprivation, which are estimated using the pooled sample including both the 2008 and 2013 samples. This is a strong assumption, which allows us to disentangle the evolution of predicted effects due to the change in the level/distribution of social transfers from possible changes in the income elasticity. The 2013 dummy helps control for the United Kingdom's break in the data, but the impact of the break in data collection may be more complex. It thus requires extra caution when interpreting the results for the United Kingdom.

The high-income dummy is significant and negative in all countries, indicating that such households have a lower risk of deprivation. Without the inclusion of this variable, the income elasticity would be higher in all four countries, which could result in a much larger predicted effect of transfers on material deprivation for lower-income households, who are at higher risk of material deprivation. The very-low-income dummy is significant and positive in all countries, indicating that such households have a higher risk of deprivation. This relatively small number of observations has a disposable income well below the country's relative poverty line and, if excluded, exerts a downward influence on the income elasticity: without the inclusion of this variable, the income elasticity would be considerably lower. The high-transfers income dummy is significant and positive in all countries, indicating that such households have a higher risk of deprivation.

The coefficients of the other control variables have the expected signs and tend to vary in significance and magnitude across countries. In addition to the usual control variables (demographics, citizenship, economic status), literature review suggests the inclusion of controls regarding non-income financial resources, in-kind transfers, costs of living, and special needs. Due to data limitations, our preferred model specification may not sufficiently control for differences in wealth (such as assets, savings, and borrowing) and in-kind transfers (such as access to subsidized goods and services). Differences in wealth and in-kind transfers can

**Table 4.4.** Income Elasticity of Material Deprivation: Comparison of Ordinary Least Squares (OLS) and Negative Binomial (NB) Estimators

| | Germany | | Greece | | Poland | | United Kingdom | |
|---|---|---|---|---|---|---|---|---|
| | — Dependent variable: Number of deprivations | | | | | | | |
| Independent variables | OLS | NB | OLS | NB | OLS | NB | OLS | NB |
| Log income | -0.569*** | -0.505*** | -0.868*** | -0.434*** | -0.739*** | -0.404*** | -0.165*** | -0.331*** |
| **Household** | | | | | | | | |
| • Observed in wave 2013 | 0.042** | 0.029 | 0.037 | 0.060*** | -0.283*** | -0.143*** | 0.254*** | 0.271*** |
| • High income | -0.073** | -0.668*** | -0.310*** | -0.461*** | -0.178*** | -0.275*** | -0.152*** | -0.221*** |
| • Lowest income percentile | 1.025*** | 1.023*** | 0.861*** | 0.714*** | 0.592*** | 0.487*** | 0.425** | 0.588*** |
| • High nonpension transfers income | 0.448*** | 0.307*** | 0.234*** | 0.079*** | 0.308*** | 0.106*** | 0.532*** | 0.343*** |
| Number of observations | 25,903 | 25,903 | 13,840 | 13,840 | 26,835 | 26,835 | 19,000 | 19,000 |
| (Pseudo) $r^2$ | 0.4822 | 0.2122 | 0.4855 | 0.1806 | 0.4411 | 0.1651 | 0.5141 | 0.2258 |
| p-value (p-test of α) | | 0 | | 0 | | 0 | | 0 |

*Notes:* p-value: 10% (*), 5% (**), and 1% (***). Estimated in Stata using a NB regression model (nber) and controlling for survey design (svy). For OLS, we report $r^2$, and for NB, pseudo $r^2$.

*Source:* Authors' computation, UDB August 2010 and March 2015.

explain why people with the same income experience different levels of material deprivation. While our model likely captures some of these effects through the debt burden (access to borrowing), home ownership, and other controls associated with higher wealth (high disposable income, education), the lack of better proxies may affect the estimated income elasticity to an unknown degree.

In conclusion, the income elasticity of material deprivation presented in Table 4.4 suggests that, depending on the Member State, a 1% increase in (transfer) income reduces the number of material deprivations of a household by an order of 0.33 to 0.51 (at average income). As described above, we use this elasticity to estimate the effect of transfers on the number of deprivations and on the EU's SMD rate.

## Effect of Transfers on the Number of Deprivations

Table 4.5 summarizes the average reduction in the number of material deprivations for the sample as a whole and several subpopulations. In this exercise, the well-being levels of those not receiving transfers remain unchanged while the estimated effect on transfer recipients increases as the amount of transfers received increases. In Germany (2008), transfers reduce the average number of deprivations by 1.8 for the population as a whole and by 2.2 for those individuals living in households receiving transfers. Pensions (old age and survivor) have the largest effect, reducing deprivations among transfer recipients by 4.4. Social insurance transfers (unemployment, sickness, and disability) and household transfers (family, housing, and social assistance) reduce deprivations by 1.1 and 0.3 in the group of (all) transfer recipients.

The disaggregation of effects by post-transfers deprivation levels is interesting because it informs us about the likelihood that transfers reduced the SMD rate. Because the severe deprivation threshold is set at four deprivations, it is particularly households reporting one, two, or three deprivations (after transfers) that are more likely to have been lifted out of SMD due to a transfer. For households reporting four or more post-transfers deprivations, the transfers they receive (if any) are clearly insufficient to avoid severe deprivation, but they nonetheless may have reduced the number of deprivations suffered. Table 4.5 shows that, on average, transfers have larger effects on households with lower levels of material well-being. Taking again Germany in 2008, transfers reduce on average the number of deprivations by 3.1 among recipients reporting four or more post-transfers deprivations, 2.3 among recipients reporting 1 to 3 deprivations, and 2.0 among recipients reporting no deprivation. This pattern is observed for all countries when focusing on the combined effect of all transfers and all nonpension transfers. It suggests that transfers are progressively distributed over the material deprivation distribution.[6] Looking at the effects further disaggregated by type of transfer, we see that pensions have a higher impact than nonpension transfers (such as household transfers and social insurance) in most countries and for all deprivation levels, except in the United Kingdom for the severely deprived, where nonpension transfers have the largest impact. Social

**Table 4.5.** Average Effect of Transfers on the Number of Deprivations

| | 2008 | | | | | 2013 | | | | |
| | All transfers | Pensions | All nonpension transfers | Social insurance | Household transfers | All transfers | Pensions | All nonpension transfers | Social insurance | Household transfers |
|---|---|---|---|---|---|---|---|---|---|---|
| **Total population** | | | | | | | | | | |
| Germany | 1.8 | 1.3 | 0.5 | 0.2 | 0.1 | 1.9 | 1.4 | 0.4 | 0.2 | 0.1 |
| Greece | 1.2 | 1.0 | 0.1 | 0.1 | 0.0 | 2.1 | 1.6 | 0.3 | 0.2 | 0.1 |
| Poland | 1.4 | 0.9 | 0.3 | 0.2 | 0.1 | 1.3 | 1.0 | 0.2 | 0.1 | 0.1 |
| United Kingdom | 1.4 | 0.7 | 0.5 | 0.1 | 0.3 | 1.6 | 0.8 | 0.6 | 0.1 | 0.4 |
| **Receivers of transfers** | | | | | | | | | | |
| Germany | 2.2 | 4.4 | 0.8 | 1.1 | 0.3 | 2.3 | 4.8 | 0.8 | 0.9 | 0.3 |
| Greece | 2.2 | 2.6 | 0.4 | 0.5 | 0.2 | 3.3 | 3.8 | 0.9 | 1.3 | 0.5 |
| Poland | 1.9 | 2.3 | 0.7 | 0.8 | 0.4 | 1.9 | 2.3 | 0.6 | 0.6 | 0.4 |
| United Kingdom | 1.8 | 2.4 | 0.8 | 0.4 | 0.5 | 2.1 | 2.6 | 1.2 | 0.7 | 0.7 |
| **Receivers of transfers, 0 material deprivations (after transfers)** | | | | | | | | | | |
| Germany | 2.0 | 4.5 | 0.1 | 0.3 | 0.0 | 2.2 | 4.9 | 0.2 | 0.4 | 0.1 |
| Greece | 2.0 | 2.5 | 0.1 | 0.2 | 0.0 | 3.5 | 4.1 | 0.2 | 0.4 | 0.1 |
| Poland | 1.5 | 2.0 | 0.2 | 0.3 | 0.1 | 1.8 | 2.3 | 0.1 | 0.2 | 0.1 |
| United Kingdom | 1.4 | 2.5 | 0.2 | 0.2 | 0.1 | 1.8 | 2.7 | 0.2 | 0.3 | 0.1 |

**Receivers of transfers, 1 to 3 material deprivations (after transfers)**

| | | | | | | | | | | |
|---|---|---|---|---|---|---|---|---|---|---|
| Germany | 2.3 | 4.5 | 1.2 | 1.3 | 0.3 | 2.4 | 4.7 | 1.5 | 0.9 | 0.4 |
| Greece | 2.3 | 2.5 | 0.3 | 0.5 | 0.0 | 3.2 | 3.7 | 0.5 | 0.9 | 0.2 |
| Poland | 1.8 | 2.4 | 0.4 | 0.6 | 0.2 | 1.8 | 2.3 | 0.4 | 0.5 | 0.2 |
| United Kingdom | 2.3 | 2.1 | 1.3 | 0.4 | 0.8 | 2.1 | 2.3 | 1.2 | 0.5 | 0.7 |

**Receivers of transfers, 4 or more material deprivations (after transfers)**

| | | | | | | | | | | |
|---|---|---|---|---|---|---|---|---|---|---|
| Germany | 3.1 | 3.2 | 2.8 | 2.3 | 1.3 | 3.5 | 3.3 | 3.1 | 1.9 | 1.5 |
| Greece | 2.8 | 3.0 | 1.1 | 1.0 | 0.9 | 3.4 | 3.8 | 2.1 | 2.5 | 1.6 |
| Poland | 2.4 | 2.7 | 1.5 | 1.5 | 1.1 | 2.4 | 2.5 | 1.5 | 1.4 | 1.2 |
| United Kingdom | 3.0 | 1.4 | 2.7 | 1.0 | 1.9 | 3.4 | 1.8 | 3.2 | 1.4 | 2.2 |

*Note:* Numbers are rounded to one decimal point.

*Source:* Authors' computation, UDB August 2010 and March 2015.

insurance and household transfers have a very weak impact for people with zero (post-transfers) deprivation. Among those suffering from intermediate-level deprivation (1 to 3 deprivations), the impact of social insurance and household transfers is larger in Germany (1.5 in 2013) and the United Kingdom (1.2 in 2013) but remains limited in Poland and Greece (0.4 or 0.5). For those suffering from severe post-transfers deprivations, the impact of nonpension transfers is lower in Poland and Greece than in the United Kingdom and Germany. In the United Kingdom, household transfers have a larger impact than social insurance, while in Germany social insurance has a larger impact.

The importance of transfers as an instrument for reducing material deprivation seems to have increased since 2008. The reductions in the number of material deprivations seem to have increased for most countries. In Greece, where (before and after transfers) material deprivation rates have seen the strongest increase since 2008, it is particularly pensions that had a stronger impact on material deprivation (from 2.6 in 2008 to 3.8 in 2013). However, those benefiting from pensions in 2013 are less likely to be among the most deprived in Greece. In 2013, pensions decreased the number of deprivations among the nondeprived by 4.1, but only by 3.7 and 3.8 for those with respectively one to three or four and more deprivations. Also in the United Kingdom, where SMD increased only modestly (at least until 2011), transfers have gained importance since 2008. The United Kingdom is well known as a welfare state in which targeted transfers are relatively important, and it is particularly the household-level transfers that have the largest reduction effects among the more deprived people in the United Kingdom. Particularly among those with four or more deprivations, the effects of these transfers has increased (from 1.9 to 2.2). In Poland, where severe material deprivation steadily declined, the overall reduction effect of transfers among the severely deprived remained constant (2.4).

The increased importance of transfers is likely due to the reduced overall earnings of households in recession-hit countries, which, in a model that uses the logarithm of income as an explanatory variable, implies that a 1-EUR transfer to a low-income household has a larger effect on deprivation than a 1-EUR transfer to a high(er)-income household. Another factor could be that the volume of transfers has increased. Table 4.2 suggests that this factor may play a role in the United Kingdom and Germany but less so in Greece.

## The Effect of Transfers on the AROP and SMD Rates

Tables 4.6 and 4.7 present the impact of social transfers on the SMD rate and compare it with the effect on the EU's AROP rate. The rates before transfers are much higher than those after transfers for both indicators (Table 4.6). The rates before all transfers range from 40% to 53% for AROP and 22% to 42% for SMD. The rates after transfers range from 16% to 23% for AROP and 5% to 20% for SMD. The percentage point reduction in AROP rate, however, is consistently higher than that for the SMD rate. Thus, in an absolute sense, transfers seem

**Table 4.6.** At-risk-of-poverty (AROP) Rate and Severe Material Deprivation (SMD) Rate Before Transfers and After Transfers (%)

| | | AROP rate | | SMD rate | |
|---|---|---|---|---|---|
| | | **2008** | **2013** | **2008** | **2013** |
| Germany | All transfers | 43.4 | 43.2 | 26.2 | 26.0 |
| | Pensions | 35.0 | 35.6 | 20.5 | 21.0 |
| | All nonpension transfers | 24.3 | 24.2 | 10.6 | 9.9 |
| | Social insurance | 19.7 | 19.6 | 8.4 | 7.4 |
| | Household transfers | 20.9 | 21.3 | 6.9 | 6.8 |
| | After transfers | 15.6 | 16.1 | 5.5 | 5.4 |
| Greece | All transfers | 41.6 | 53.4 | 24.7 | 42.2 |
| | Pensions | 38.9 | 49.5 | 22.3 | 38.9 |
| | All nonpension transfers | 23.5 | 28.0 | 12.3 | 21.6 |
| | Social insurance | 22.3 | 25.7 | 12.1 | 21.4 |
| | Household transfers | 21.6 | 25.5 | 11.8 | 20.8 |
| | After transfers | 20.3 | 23.1 | 11.2 | 20.3 |
| Poland | All transfers | 44.1 | 43.0 | 31.5 | 25.8 |
| | Pensions | 36.7 | 38.1 | 27.9 | 23.0 |
| | All nonpension transfers | 25.1 | 23.0 | 19.7 | 13.3 |
| | Social insurance | 21.7 | 20.8 | 19.0 | 12.7 |
| | Household transfers | 20.3 | 19.5 | 18.3 | 12.2 |
| | After transfers | 16.9 | 17.3 | 17.8 | 11.9 |
| United Kingdom | All transfers | 40.1 | 45.2 | 21.8 | 26.2 |
| | Pensions | 32.8 | 32.7 | 13.2 | 17.6 |
| | All nonpension transfers | 28.0 | 30.1 | 9.9 | 14.6 |
| | Social insurance | 21.7 | 20.1 | 5.2 | 9.4 |
| | Household transfers | 25.8 | 27.9 | 7.7 | 12.1 |
| | After transfers | 18.9 | 15.9 | 4.5 | 8.3 |

*Source*: Authors' computation, UDB August 2010 and March 2015.

to reduce AROP rates more than SMD rates. In Germany, for instance, total transfers reduce income poverty by 27 (2013) and 28 (2008) percentage points, but they reduce the SMD rate by 21 percentage points (both years). However, the AROP rates are also consistently higher than the SMD rates for these four countries, implying that it is also important to compare the impact in relative terms by calculating the percentage reduction in income poverty and material deprivation rates (Table 4.7). In this relative sense, the impact of transfers is not always higher for AROP than for SMD. For example, in Germany, the percentage decline in the SMD rates is higher than for the AROP rates for most transfer categories. Household-level transfers are the exception, with a higher relative reduction in

**Table 4.7.** Percentage Reduction in At-risk-of-poverty (AROP) Rate and Severe Material Deprivation (SMD) Rate

| | | AROP rate | | SMD rate | |
|---|---|---|---|---|---|
| | | 2008 | 2013 | 2008 | 2013 |
| Germany | All transfers | 64.1 | 62.7 | 79.0 | 79.2 |
| | Pensions | 55.4 | 54.8 | 73.2 | 74.3 |
| | All nonpension transfers | 35.8 | 33.5 | 48.1 | 45.5 |
| | Social insurance | 20.8 | 17.9 | 34.5 | 27.0 |
| | Household transfers | 25.4 | 24.4 | 20.3 | 20.6 |
| Greece | All transfers | 51.2 | 56.7 | 54.7 | 51.9 |
| | Pensions | 47.8 | 53.3 | 49.8 | 47.8 |
| | All nonpension transfers | 13.6 | 17.5 | 8.9 | 6.0 |
| | Social insurance | 9.0 | 10.1 | 7.4 | 5.1 |
| | Household transfers | 6.0 | 9.4 | 5.1 | 2.4 |
| Poland | All transfers | 61.7 | 59.8 | 43.5 | 53.9 |
| | Pensions | 54.0 | 54.6 | 36.2 | 48.3 |
| | All nonpension transfers | 32.7 | 24.8 | 9.6 | 10.5 |
| | Social insurance | 22.1 | 16.8 | 6.3 | 6.3 |
| | Household transfers | 16.7 | 11.3 | 2.7 | 2.5 |
| United Kingdom | All transfers | 52.9 | 64.8 | 79.4 | 68.3 |
| | Pensions | 42.4 | 51.4 | 65.9 | 52.8 |
| | All nonpension transfers | 32.5 | 47.2 | 54.5 | 43.2 |
| | Social insurance | 12.9 | 20.9 | 13.5 | 11.7 |
| | Household transfers | 26.7 | 43.0 | 41.6 | 31.4 |

*Source*: Authors' computation, UDB August 2010 and March 2015.

the AROP rate. In Greece, the relative reduction is higher for AROP rates with social insurance and household transfers in both years. For pensions, the relative reduction is also higher for the AROP rate in 2013 but in 2008 it was similar to that of SMD rate. In Poland, the relative reductions by transfers on the AROP rate are consistently higher than those on SMD. In the United Kingdom, the relative reduction by pensions on SMD rates is higher than that on AROP in both years, while the relative reductions by social insurance and household transfers were higher for SMD rates in 2008 but lower in 2013.

The tables confirm once again that, in Greece and Poland, the impact of transfers other than pensions is weak, on the income poverty rate and on the SMD rate. Moreover, while Table 4.5 suggests that the reduction effect of transfers on the average number of deprivations may have become larger since the Great Recession (with the exception of Poland), Table 4.7 shows no consistent change in percentage reductions in SMD rates between 2008 and 2013. For Germany and Greece, the percentage reduction in SMD rates are of similar magnitude in both years for all transfer definitions; for pensions in Greece the effect seems larger in 2013; for pensions and household transfers in the United Kingdom the effect seems smaller in 2013. One interpretation could be that, while transfers improve material well-being for a broad population, they may not, or insufficiently, reach a smaller, and more vulnerable, group with higher deprivation levels (pre-transfers). However, it is also possible that changes in the design and generosity of transfers are influenced by simultaneous changes in the demography and economy.

## CONCLUSION

Social transfers are a very influential policy instrument in the fight against poverty and social exclusion. This chapter set out to fill in a gap in the analysis of poverty and social policy, namely the degree to which social transfers reduce material deprivation. This gap also has obvious political salience, because the SMD rate is one of three indicators by which the EU monitors progress toward the Europe 2020 social inclusion goal. In the spirit of the commonly agreed EU indicator measuring the impact of social transfers on income poverty, we developed and tested a regression-based technique to estimate the effect of social transfers on the EU material deprivation indicator. Subsequently, we analyzed the impact of transfers on the average number of deprivations in the population and on the EU SMD rate, also comparing absolute and relative changes in deprivation with those achieved in terms of the EU income poverty rate.

We estimated the income elasticity of material deprivation using a NB regression model. We found that a 1% income transfer (at average income) reduces the number of material deprivations by an order of 0.51 in Germany, 0.43 in Greece, 0.40 in Poland, and 0.33 in the United Kingdom. Thus, in contrast to the effect on income poverty, where a 1-EUR transfer to the income poor increases their aggregated income by 1 EUR, the effect on material deprivation is by definition indirect. Whereas cash transfers and income are both measured in monetary terms, material deprivation is not solely the result of a lack of financial resources, of which income is merely one. Indeed, material deprivation is also influenced by accumulated debt/wealth, access to nonfinancial resources, such as in-kind transfers, and specific needs of the household (child care, health, housing).

The impact of social transfers is substantial, reducing the average number of material deprivations among recipients by 2.2 in Germany and Greece, by 1.9 in Poland, and by 1.8 in the United Kingdom. The impact is larger for recipients who are less well off. The impact of social transfers on SMD is also large, with reductions ranging from 13 to 22 percentage points. In comparison, the reductions in AROP rates are larger, ranging from 26 to 30 percentage points. In percentage terms, however, the reduction in rates is not necessarily larger for the income poverty indicator than for the material deprivation indicator; this depends on the country and the type of transfers. This is not surprising. First, income poor and materially deprived populations only partially overlap. The income poverty indicator misses out some of the well-being effects of transfers that reach materially deprived, although not income poor, households. Second, differences in the design of transfers (i.e., the level of targeting, targeting method, flat-rate benefit) imply that some groups are more likely to receive (more generous) transfers than others. Thus, a specific transfer may have a comparative advantage in reducing material deprivation relative to income poverty (and the other way around). It is less clear whether the Great Recession and austerity have changed the role of transfers: transfers resulted in larger reductions in the average number of deprivations among transfer recipients in 2013 but we found no consistent change in percentage reductions in SMD rates between 2008 and 2013.

In sum, the estimates in this chapter show that social transfers reduce not only income poverty but also (substantially) the extent and depth of material deprivation. Changes in social transfers therefore have a twofold effect on the Europe 2020 social inclusion target.

The method presented in this chapter is still under development. It will need to be refined and expanded to all EU countries. However, the results presented here already highlight the importance of measuring the impact of social transfers on material deprivation, and they show how this approach usefully complements the current EU approach consisting of looking only at income poverty before and after transfers. The method presented here relies on the robustness of the estimation of the income elasticity of material deprivation. On the basis of sensitivity analyses, we describe how the choice of the regression techniques and the selection of control variables/subpopulations of interest influence the estimation of income elasticity. Further research is needed to assess if the uncertainty around the income elasticity of material deprivation can be further reduced. Just as the wage elasticity of labor supply is different for persons with different incomes, genders, and family situations, our checks suggest that the income elasticity of material deprivation may be different for specific population groups, such as pensioners. Moreover, while there are theoretical and empirical grounds to prefer a NB regression to an OLS estimator, there are alternative maximum likelihood-based estimators, such as ordered logit models and zero-inflated regression models, that merit further analysis and testing. A dynamic specification based on individual changes in income and material deprivation (i.e., using panel data) would provide a relevant benchmark for comparison as well. Moreover, the issue of how to account for the evolution of the income elasticity over time also merits attention. Finally, testing the method on data that have better information on specific needs, financial resources, and access to in-kind transfers would allow testing for the magnitude of the omitted variable bias of the specification used here.

Another challenge, which we could not tackle here, is to test the estimation method in the context of a dynamic simulation model and/or a model that would take account of the interrelationships among the different transfers in a complex tax-transfer system. The behavioral assumptions underlying the estimates in this chapter result in inflated effects of transfers on poverty and material deprivation.

Not taking into account the interactions within a tax-transfer system can lead to both under- and overestimation of the effects of transfers on poverty.

## ACKNOWLEDGMENTS

The approach in this chapter was pioneered in ImPRovE working paper 13/13 (Notten, 2013) and in Notten (2015) and was further tested and refined here. This project was undertaken under affiliation with the University of Ottawa as part of research project proposal 210/2014-EU-SILC. The responsibility for all conclusions drawn from the data lies entirely with the authors. We would like to thank John Hills, David Gordon, Tim Goedemé, Brian Nolan, and Ainslie Cruickshank for their valuable feedback.

## NOTES

1  Data from the 2008 wave of EU-SILC were the most recent data available. For more information on EU-SILC, see the Eurostat website. See also Di Meglio, Dupré, Montaigne, & Wolff (2017).
2  "If wanted" refers to the fact that it is not by choice that the household does not have the item but because the household does not have it for financial reasons.
3  This choice offers the best approximation, because the effects of the crisis on economic growth started in 2008. The income reference period of EU-SILC 2008 is 2007 for Germany, Poland, and Greece (2008 for the United Kingdom), and the deprivation reference period is either the present or the past 12 months.
4  The exact cut-off is country-specific and is set at the first decile for which the proportion of households with at least one deprivation is less than its share in the overall population: the top 30% for Germany and Greece, the top 20% (2008) and 30% (2013) for Poland, and the top 40% for the United Kingdom.
5  ImPRove Working Paper 16/17 by Notten and Guio (2016) provides more results on this and alternative model specifications. It also summarizes the assumptions behind the model and discusses their potential implications.
6  It is not a perfect indicator, though, as we disaggregate by the number of deprivations after transfers rather than before transfers.

## REFERENCES

Aaberge, R., Langørgen, A., & Lindgren, P. (2017). The distributional impact of public services in European countries. In A. B. Atkinson, A.-C. Guio, & E. Marlier (Eds.), *Monitoring social inclusion in Europe*. Luxembourg: Office for Official Publications of the European Communities (OPOCE).

Angrist, J. D., & Pischke, J.-S. (2009). *Mostly harmless econometrics. An empiricist's companion*. Princeton, NJ: Princeton University Press.

Battiston, D., Cruces, G., Lopez-Calva, L. F., Lugo, M. A., & Santos, M. E. (2013). Income and beyond: Multidimensional poverty in six Latin American countries. *Social Indicators Research, 112*(2), 291–314.

Bossert, W., & D'Ambrosio, C. (2014), Proximity-sensitive individual deprivation measures. *Economics Letters, 122*(2), 125–128.

Bourguignon, F., & Chakravarty, S. R. (2003). The measurement of multidimensional poverty. *Journal of Economic Inequality, 1*, 25–49.

Brandolini, A., Magri, S., & Smeeding, T. M. (2010). Asset-based measurement of poverty. *Journal of Policy Analysis and Management, 29*(2), 267–284.

Breunig, R., & McKibbin, R. (2011). The effect of survey design on household reporting of financial difficulty. *Journal of the Royal Statistical Society: Series A (Statistics in Society), 174*(4), 991–1005.

Cancian, M., & Meyer, D. R. (2004). Alternative measures of economic success among TANF participants: Avoiding poverty, hardship, and dependence on public assistance. *Journal of Policy Analysis and Management, 23*(3), 531–548.

Di Meglio, E., Dupré, D., Montaigne, F., & Wolff, P. (2017). Investing in European social statistics: EU-SILC. In A.B. Atkinson, A.-C. Guio, & E. Marlier (Eds.), *Monitoring social inclusion in Europe*. Luxembourg: Office for Official Publications of the European Communities (OPOCE).

Eurostat. (2017). *At-risk-of-poverty rate before social transfers*. http://ec.europa.eu/eurostat/web/products-datasets/-/tessi230

Figari, F. (2012). Cross-national differences in determinants of multiple deprivation in Europe. *Journal of Economic Inequality*, 10 (3).

Figari, F., Paulus, A., & Sutherland, H. (2015). Microsimulation and policy analysis. In B. A. Anthony & B. François (Eds.), *Handbook of income distribution* (Vol. 2, pp. 2141–2221). Oxford, England: Elsevier.

Fusco, A., Guio, A., & Marlier, E. (2010). Characterizing the income poor and materially deprived. In A. Atkinson & E. Marlier (Eds.), *Income and living conditions in Europe* (pp. 133–153). Luxembourg: Eurostat.

Fusco, A., Guio, A., & Marlier, E. (2011). *Income poverty and material deprivation in European countries* [Working Paper No 2011-04]. Luxembourg: CEPS/INSTEAD.

Garfinkel, I., Rainwater, L., & Smeeding, T. M. (2006). A re-examination of welfare states and inequality in rich nations: How in-kind transfers and indirect taxes change the story. *Journal of Policy Analysis and Management, 25*(4), 897–919.

Guio, A. (2009). *What can be learned from deprivation indicators in Europe?* [Methodologies and working papers]. Luxembourg: European Commission. Retrieved from http://epp.eurostat.ec.europa.eu.proxy.bib.uottawa.ca/cache/ITY_OFFPUB/KS-RA-09-007/EN/KS-RA-09-007-EN.PDF

Guio, A. -C., Gordon, D., & Marlier, E. (2012). *Measuring material deprivation in the EU: Indicators for the whole population and child-specific indicators*

[Eurostat Methodologies and working papers]. Luxembourg: Office for Official Publications of the European Communities (OPOCE).

Hilbe, J. (2011). *Negative binomial regression* (2nd ed.). New York, NY: Cambridge University Press.

Huston, A. C., & Bentley, A. C. (2010). Human development in societal context. *Annual Review of Psychology, 61*, 411–437.

Marlier E., Atkinson, A. B., Cantillon, B., & Nolan B. (2007). *The EU and social inclusion: Facing the challenges.* Bristol, England: Policy Press.

Muffels, R., & Fouarge, D. (2004). The role of European welfare states in explaining resources deprivation. *Social Indicators Research, 68*(3), 299–330.

Nelson, K. (2012). Counteracting material deprivation: The role of social assistance in Europe. *Journal of European Social Policy, 22*(2), 148–163.

Nolan, B., & Whelan, C. T. (2010). Using non-monetary deprivation indicators to analyse poverty and social exclusion in rich countries: Lessons from Europe? *Journal of Policy Analysis and Management, 29*(2), 305–325.

Notten, G. (2013). *Measuring performance: Does the assessment depend on the poverty proxy?* [ImPRovE Working Paper 13/13]. Antwerp, Belgium: Herman Deleeck Centre for Social Policy, University of Antwerp.

Notten, G. (2015). How poverty indicators confound poverty reduction evaluations: The targeting performance of income transfers in Europe. *Social Indicators Research, 127*(3), 1–37.

Notten, G., & Guio, A.C. (2016). *The impact of social transfers on income poverty and material deprivation* [ImPRovE Working Paper 16/17]. Antwerp, Belgium: Herman Deleeck Centre for Social Policy, University of Antwerp.

Paulus, A., Sutherland, H., & Tsakloglou, P. (2010). The distributional impact of in-kind public benefits in European countries. *Journal of Policy Analysis and Management, 29*(2), 243–266.

Perry, B. (2015). *The material wellbeing of New Zealand households: Trends and relativities using non-income measures, with international comparisons.* Wellington, NZ: Ministry of Social Development.

Ringen, S. (1988). Direct and indirect measures of poverty. *Journal of Social Policy, 17*(03), 351–365.

Saunders, P., & Wong, M. (2011). Using deprivation to assess the adequacy of Australian social security payments. *Journal of Poverty and Social Justice, 19*(2), 91–101.

Sen, A. K. (1999). *Development as freedom.* New Delhi, India: Oxford University Press.

Townsend, P. (1979). *Poverty in the United Kingdom: A survey of household resources and standards of living.* Harmondsworth, England: Penguin.

Wu, C., & Eamon, M. K. (2010). Does receipt of public benefits reduce material hardship in low-income families with children? *Children and Youth Services Review, 32*(10), 1262–1270.

# 5

# POLICY AND POVERTY IN SEVEN EUROPEAN UNION COUNTRIES IN THE LISBON DECADE

## THE CONTRIBUTION OF TAX–BENEFIT POLICY CHANGES

**John Hills, Alari Paulus, Holly Sutherland, and Iva Tasseva**

## INTRODUCTION

A wide range of factors influence poverty and overall income distribution. Many of the factors, such as demographic change or the distribution of work across households, are not under the direct control of policymakers or amenable to short-term public policy intervention, although active labor-market policy and in-work benefits aimed at making work pay do affect labor-market behavior (Cantillon & Vandenbroucke, 2014, p. 321). In assessing the performance of government policy in terms of (income) poverty or inequality reduction, it is important to isolate the impact of the most relevant factors that policymakers can control. This chapter assesses one effect—how changes to the system of cash income protection and direct personal taxes and social contributions over the period 2001–2011 affected household incomes and poverty, with other factors held constant.

This period is particularly salient because, at its starting point, the Lisbon Strategy in 2000 placed a particular emphasis on reducing poverty and social exclusion, and the Open Method of Coordination was established to improve national policymaking toward this common goal (Cantillon & Vandenbroucke, 2014). However, the hoped-for comprehensive "decisive impact on the eradication of poverty" (European Council, 2000) did not occur, and poverty levels in some countries rose rather than fell. The explanations for this are many and various (Nolan et al., 2014).

Many things—not least, the initial period of growth and then the effects of the crisis itself—affected incomes and employment, and hence poverty, over this decade (see Chapters 2 and 6 of this volume). Our aim is to abstract from these wider (in some cases, very large) economic changes, as well as those arising from demographic and other population changes, to focus on the direct redistributive effects of policy. Furthermore, we abstract from the automatic stabilizing effects of policies when economic or demographic changes affect entitlements to benefits or liabilities for taxes. For instance, when unemployment rises and more households are without market incomes, the system automatically has a more redistributive effect. Rather, we focus on the effects of changes in policies, relative to a base case scenario, and on whether the changes themselves were poverty-reducing.[1] Overall, our analysis should help with understanding the different routes taken by European Union (EU) governments in the decade following the Lisbon Treaty and why, in a period of growth, progress in poverty reduction was often disappointing, as well as how some countries were able to counter increases in poverty after the onset of the crisis.

We estimate the effect of policy changes on income distribution using microsimulation techniques, following the decomposition framework formalized in Bargain and Callan (2010).[2] The decomposition method separates the direct policy effect from other effects (i.e., changes in population characteristics, such as the employment rate, fertility, and household structure). We apply this method to seven EU countries in 2001–2011 using the tax–benefit microsimulation model EUROMOD. The countries that we cover are Belgium, Bulgaria, Estonia, Greece, Hungary, Italy, and the United Kingdom, which vary not only in the size and the type of welfare state but also in their experience of very different kinds of economic change and policy reforms in the period considered.[3] We consider separately the period before the economic crisis (2001–2007) and the years covering its start (2007–2011), simulating the effects of the policy systems that each country had in place in 2001, 2007, and 2011 on a fixed population, with the characteristics and distribution of market incomes as they were in a particular year, 2007. In comparing policy systems from different points in time, decisions must be made about the adjustment of monetary levels of policy parameters (e.g., benefit payments or tax thresholds) to allow for changes in prices and incomes. We discuss the issue of how to index the counterfactual policy systems, and we make use of three alternative options in our analysis, each with a distinct interpretation (but we present some detailed results only against one or two counterfactuals).

We find that the effect of policy changes on poverty often depends on the choice of counterfactual indexation against which policies are assessed. Nevertheless, our robust findings are that, compared to the 2001 system, the 2011 policy system is more effective in reducing the risk of poverty against a floating poverty threshold in Belgium, Estonia, and the United Kingdom. However, policy changes were clearly poverty-increasing in Hungary. Overall policy effects in Greece and Italy were smaller. Because of the large difference in the price and income changes in Bulgaria, the size of the policy effect varied substantially with the choice of the counterfactual indexation.

The chapter is structured as follows. The next section explains the tax–benefit microsimulation model EUROMOD and the data used in the analysis and discusses the counterfactual indexation against which changes in the policy parameters are assessed. In the following section, we present our main findings for the effects of policy change on aggregate incomes and the government's fiscal position, on different parts of the income distribution, on poverty rates, and on different age groups. The next section examines in more detail which policy instruments contributed to the patterns shown in each country. This is followed by the summary and conclusion.

## METHODS AND DATA

We use the tax–benefit microsimulation model EUROMOD to assess household disposable income under the different policy scenarios. EUROMOD simulates direct personal tax and social insurance contribution liabilities and cash benefit entitlements for all EU member states based on the national tax–benefit policy rules for a given year and information available in household microdata (see Sutherland & Figari, 2013). The microdata the model makes use of are from nationally representative samples of households from the EU Statistics on Income and Living Conditions (EU-SILC) and the Family Resources Survey (FRS) for the United Kingdom. In this analysis, we use data with an income reference period in 2007. The data contain detailed information on individual and household characteristics as well as income by source. For most direct taxes and benefits, we recalculate (simulate) individual household liabilities and entitlements in accordance with reported market incomes and other circumstances. However, the data do not allow us to make detailed simulations of individual entitlements for items such as contributory benefits, disability benefits, or old-age pensions, which depend on factors such as past employment records. For these, we use the receipts reported in the underlying surveys. We then approximate 2011 (2001) systems by updating (backdating) entitlements observed for 2007 with a factor reflecting the indexation rule of benefit entitlements (including statutory index- ation and ad hoc changes) or the growth in the average entitlement (if informa- tion on the former is not available).[4] Therefore, the overall simulation results we show take account of changes in the generosity of all kinds of benefits and pensions and in rules governing their relationship to household incomes or com- position (but not to changes in conditions related to past employment records).

In order to compare policies from two years, we use an adjustment factor to index the policy parameters with monetary values (e.g., benefit amounts and tax thresholds) for the differences in nominal levels over time and against which the actual changes to the parameters are assessed. We follow the main approaches most often used in the previous literature.

First, using the market income index (MII) adjusts benefit amounts and tax thresholds by the growth in average market income (primarily in the form of wages).[5] MII-based indexation implies that the overall balance between cash benefits and household taxes would be broadly unchanged and the system would be fiscally neutral, as well as neutral between households, regardless of whether they rely on market income or public support. It would thus generally not have effects on disposable income inequality or on relative poverty measures. On the other hand, at times of economic downturn, MII indexation implies that benefit amounts and tax thresholds could be decreased in both nominal and real terms, which could weaken further the position of the most vulnerable at times of hard- ship and could imply rising poverty against a fixed (anchored) threshold.

Second, indexation by the consumer price index (CPI) adjusts benefit amounts and tax thresholds in line with inflation. CPI-based indexation avoids erosion in their real values throughout the business cycle. However, because real market incomes are likely to grow over time, CPI-based indexation is not usu- ally sufficient to maintain the level of public cash support (for benefit recipients) relative to market incomes (of, for example, wage earners) and so would not be neutral in terms of inequality and relative poverty.[6]

In the initial analysis (see Figures 5.3 and 5.4 below) we also use a third in- dexation scenario, with the indexation factor equal to 1, to compare the nominal levels of benefits and tax thresholds in the two periods.

We therefore examine the effect of policy changes over the period 2001–2011 relative to growth in average market incomes, in real terms and in nominal terms. The changes that we capture include actual indexation practice, which may or may not conform to one of the indexation assumptions, together with reforms to the structure of tax–benefit systems or individual taxes and benefits. Due to the very different movements in prices and incomes in the countries considered over this period, as shown in Figure 5.1, the assumption about what index to use in constructing the counterfactual can make a critical difference to the conclusions

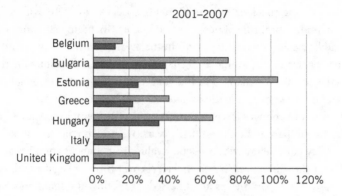

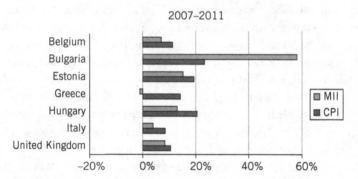

**Figure 5.1.** Percentage change in market incomes (MII) and prices (CPI) in 2001–2007 and 2007–2011. *Source*: The MII is calculated using the tax–benefit microsimulation model EUROMOD to derive the change in average market income. The 2007 values are taken from the input dataset and the 2001 and 2011 values are obtained by updating (or backdating) 2007 incomes with separate factors by income source reflecting their average growth. (See EUROMOD Country Reports for more information on market income updating and the specific CPI sources.) The charts are drawn to different scales, but the interval between gridlines on each of them is the same.

that are drawn about the policy effect. For instance, between 2001 and 2007 in Estonia, benefit amounts and tax thresholds indexed by the CPI would have increased by about 25%, but if they were indexed by MII, they would have more than doubled. By contrast, in Greece between 2007 and 2011, income rose less than prices, so MII indexation would have meant a small cut in nominal values and a larger one in real values.

## RESULTS ACROSS THE INCOME DISTRIBUTION

As explained above, our results isolate the effects of *changing policies* on household incomes by calculating what they would have looked like in 2007 if, instead of the actual 2007 tax and transfer systems, alternative policy systems based on those from 2001 and 2011 had been in place (indexing monetary parameters).

We start by considering the scale and direction of change in aggregate household disposable income due to the policy changes. If a country is reducing the net yield from its tax and transfer system, and so households as a whole are gaining, it may be easier to reduce poverty at the same time. By contrast, if changes generate net revenue and contribute to improving the public finances, achieving a poverty-reducing effect at the same time may be harder. Next, we examine how this aggregate change is distributed across the income distribution, dividing the population into decile groups according to their 2007 incomes.[7] We can then understand how incomes have changed at the bottom of the distribution compared with the middle, and hence how poverty measures using thresholds based on median incomes might be affected. The poverty rate is measured as the percentage of the population with household income below 60% of the median, where the threshold changes according to the median under the policy scenario that is used.[8] We then show the relative movements in incomes by age group due to the policy changes (assuming that household income from all sources is shared equally among all those living together). Finally, we give a country-by-country commentary, highlighting the sources of the larger changes revealed by the analysis.

## Aggregate Effects

The percentage change in household disposable income due to policy changes is shown in Figure 5.2. The diamonds in the diagram show to what extent changes in the tax and transfer systems in 2001–2011 contributed to the average net gain or loss for households, and the bars show the overall net effect split into the two periods, 2001–2007 and 2007–2011.

Focusing first on the comparisons using the MII indexation counterfactual in the left panel, what is most striking is how much households in Greece lost on average over the decade compared to the 2001 system uprated in line with market incomes—around 6% in the first period and 5% in the second. Households as a whole were also net losers between 2001 and 2007 from policy change in Italy and the United Kingdom, and (to a small extent) in Bulgaria. In Belgium and Estonia, there were gains to households as a whole—and so a net fiscal cost. In Hungary, there was a negligible change in aggregate household income in the first period, but between 2007 and 2011 there was a big gain on average for households in Hungary and small gains in the other countries, except Italy and Greece.

By comparison with a price-linked base, the right panel suggests that Belgium, Bulgaria, Estonia, and Hungary were more generous to households (raising less net revenue), and the United Kingdom's changes can be classed as almost neutral.

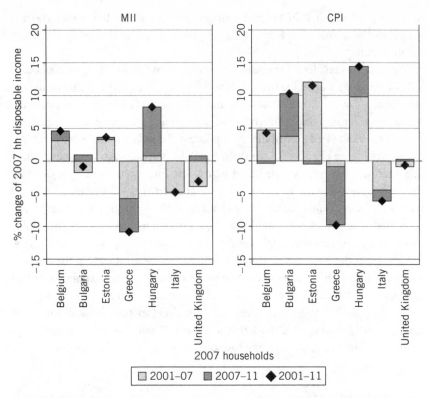

**Figure 5.2.** Effect of policy changes 2001–2011 relative to MII and CPI indexation on household disposable income. *Note*: 2001 and 2011 policy parameters are adjusted to the 2007 levels using market income (MII) or prices (CPI). The 95% confidence intervals for the total change in 2001–2011 are very narrow and not visible in the figure. *Source*: Authors' calculations using EUROMOD version F6.36.

## Distributional Effects by Income Group

How these aggregate effects are distributed by level of household income can be seen in Figures 5.3 and 5.4, showing the impact of policy changes on successive tenths of the income distribution ordered by disposable incomes in 2007. Figure 5.3 shows the impact of changes between 2001 and 2007, and Figure 5.4 shows those between 2007 and 2011. These figures show, in addition to the effects of policy changes relative to MII and CPI indexation, the effects assuming that the counterfactual policies were constant in nominal terms. As explained above, the policy effects are measured using a fixed market income distribution and demographic composition.

In the first period (Figure 5.3), policy effects in nominal terms (the dotted lines) increased household incomes across the distribution in all countries, except for top income groups in Italy and the United Kingdom. Apart from Greece and Hungary, with relatively flat profiles, the changes were also proportionally larger for lower income groups. Results based on the CPI counterfactual indexation

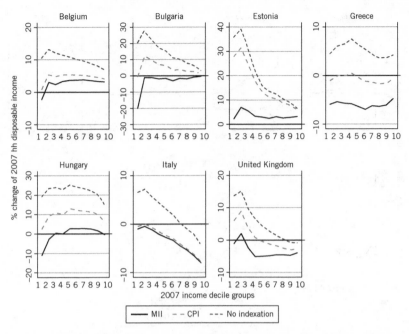

**Figure 5.3.** Effect of policy changes on average disposable income by income decile groups, 2001–2007. *Note*: Income deciles are derived based on 2007 household equivalized disposable incomes. The charts are drawn to different scales, but the interval between gridlines on each of them is the same. *Source*: Authors' calculations using EUROMOD version F6.36.

(the dashed lines) show, however, that policy changes were not everywhere sufficient to keep up with price increases. They were even less generous relative to
changes in market incomes (the solid lines), with a positive effect for all income
groups only in Estonia (and for all except the bottom group in Belgium). The
effects (with MII) were progressive in Estonia, Italy, and the United Kingdom,
but they were regressive for Belgium (at the bottom), Bulgaria, and Hungary.

It is important to note, however, that these results reflect the choice of ranking
the households from poorest to richest by their income in 2007, the base for our
simulations. Those at the bottom in 2007 include those who arrived there following policy changes in earlier years. If, instead, households are ranked in terms
of incomes under 2001 systems, the policy effect can appear more progressive, as
losers in the earlier years would be included higher up the distribution.[9]

In the second period (Figure 5.4), the effects in nominal terms were still
positive, although to a lesser extent. Even after the crisis, nearly all the countries avoided nominal cuts in benefits and tax thresholds. The exception was
Greece, where policy changes reduced nominal incomes. As in the earlier period, policy changes could not match the price increases in some countries,
and gains were lower or losses were greater against a CPI-linked base. Against
a market income–linked base, some of the countries appear more generous (as

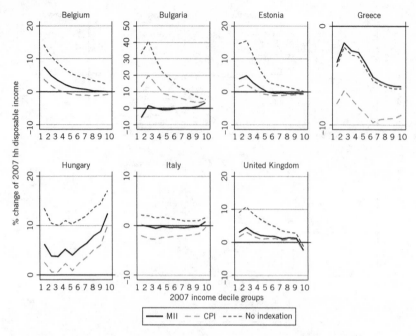

**Figure 5.4.** Effect of policy changes on average disposable income by income decile groups, 2007–2011. *Note:* Income deciles are derived based on 2007 household equivalized disposable incomes. The charts are drawn to different scales, but the interval between gridlines on each of them is the same. *Source:* Authors' calculations using EUROMOD version F6.36.

real incomes were falling). On this basis (the solid lines), reforms were progressive in Belgium, Estonia, Greece, and the United Kingdom and neutral in Italy, but they were regressive in Bulgaria and Hungary.

The panels show that the seven countries made different distributional choices from one another in the generally good times before 2007 and in the generally bad times after it.

## Effects of Policy Reform on Poverty

Closely related to these distributional patterns were the effects of reforms on poverty. Table 5.1 summarizes the effects of changing policy in the seven countries and the two periods on poverty rates measured against a poverty threshold that moves with changes in policies. The change in the poverty rate is measured in percentage points. A positive change indicates an increase in poverty, while a negative change shows a drop in poverty. Figure 5.5 summarizes the effects over the whole decade.

It is again striking how varied the experiences of the seven countries were, both over the 10 years as a whole and over the separate periods. Measured compared to a MII-indexed counterfactual, policy reforms over the last decade had poverty-reducing effects in Estonia (4 percentage points), the United

**Table 5.1.** Poverty Thresholds and Poverty Rates

| Policy system | Poverty threshold | | | Poverty rate | | |
|---|---|---|---|---|---|---|
| | 2001 | 2007 | 2011 | 2001 | 2007 | 2011 |
| Country | MII indexation | | | | | |
| Belgium | 858 | 887 | 899 | 11.1 | 11.6 | 9.5 |
| Bulgaria | 220 | 215 | 215 | 22.0 | 21.1 | 21.2 |
| Estonia | 4,196 | 4,312 | 4,329 | 21.5 | 19.5 | 17.9 |
| Greece | 589 | 556 | 530 | 20.2 | 20.0 | 19.6 |
| Hungary | 50,316 | 51,697 | 53,619 | 10.7 | 12.9 | 13.6 |
| Italy | 798 | 774 | 771 | 19.0 | 17.8 | 17.8 |
| UK | 695 | 660 | 675 | 19.8 | 16.8 | 16.3 |
| | CPI indexation | | | | | |
| Belgium | 842 | 887 | 880 | 11.5 | 11.6 | 9.9 |
| Bulgaria | 205 | 215 | 235 | 24.8 | 21.1 | 19.2 |
| Estonia | 3,796 | 4,312 | 4,281 | 26.4 | 19.5 | 18.7 |
| Greece | 562 | 556 | 504 | 20.6 | 20.0 | 19.9 |
| Hungary | 45,231 | 51,697 | 51,858 | 11.9 | 12.9 | 13.8 |
| Italy | 794 | 774 | 755 | 19.1 | 17.8 | 18.0 |
| UK | 668 | 660 | 669 | 20.8 | 16.8 | 16.5 |

*Notes:* 2001 and 2011 policy parameters are adjusted to the 2007 levels using MII or CPI. Poverty threshold is 60% of median equivalized household income, shown in monthly terms and in the national currency, and is measured under each scenario (varying with the effect of policy changes).
*Source:* Authors' calculations using EUROMOD version F6.36.

Kingdom (3 percentage points), Belgium (2 percentage points), and Italy (1 percentage point). In comparison with a price-indexed counterfactual scenario, policy changes reduced the risk of poverty in six out of the seven countries, the most in Estonia (8 percentage points), Bulgaria (6 percentage points), and the United Kingdom (4 percentage points), and in each case with the greatest effects between 2001 and 2007. With economic and employment growth, it was easier for these countries to increase the values of cash benefits that are received by those on low incomes more rapidly than price inflation and even than growth in market incomes, for instance, or to reduce taxes for those with low incomes. The changes meant that poverty was lower than it would otherwise have been. In contrast, in Hungary, compared to both 2001 MII- and CPI-indexed counterfactuals, poverty was higher with 2011 policies (by 3 percentage points and 2 percentage points, respectively).

More generally, the extent to which policy changes had an impact on poverty depended on their impact on those at the bottom of the distribution relative to those at the median. Compared to both price- and income-linked bases, the early

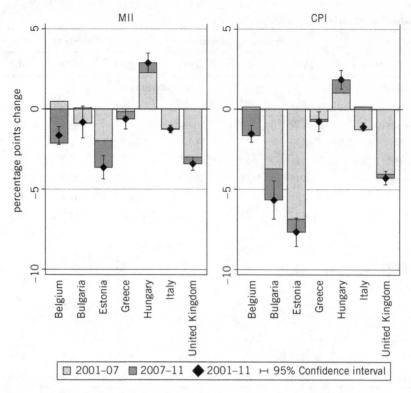

**Figure 5.5.** Effect of policy changes 2001–2011 on the poverty rate. *Note*: The 2001 and 2011 policy parameters are adjusted to 2007 levels using growth in market income (MII) or CPI; poverty is measured using 60% of median equivalized household income under each scenario as the poverty line. Standard errors for confidence intervals are calculated using the delta method. *Source*: Authors' calculations using EUROMOD version F6.36.

period policy changes generally favored those with lower incomes compared to the median, apart from in Belgium and Hungary and for those with the very lowest incomes in Bulgaria (Figure 5.3). In the later period, policies favored the bottom over the middle again in Estonia, Greece, and the United Kingdom, and also in Belgium. Policies were again poverty-increasing in Hungary and neutral in Italy. In Bulgaria, the assessment of the distributional effect of policy changes in both periods depends on the indexation assumption: the policy effect was largely distributionally neutral compared to MII indexation but poverty-decreasing compared to CPI indexation.

The scale of the reductions in poverty due to policy changes, shown in Table 5.1 and Figure 5.5, can be compared with the average net effects of policy on all households in the two periods shown in Figure 5.2. Here, we focus on the comparisons using the MII indexation counterfactual.

While households in Greece lost considerably on average over the decade, this contribution to public finances was accompanied by a small poverty-reducing effect: the tax and transfer system was changed in ways that helped public finances, but this was done without the changes' contributing to greater poverty when measured against a floating poverty line. However, as is clear from Table 5.1, this threshold fell considerably; measured using a fixed threshold, the effect of policies was to increase poverty (see Hills, Paulus, Sutherland, & Tasseva, 2014).

Households as a whole were also net losers from policy change between 2001 and 2007 in Italy and the United Kingdom, and the balance of their reforms also had a poverty-reducing effect. The Estonian case in this period was different, with a gain to households as a whole—and so a net fiscal cost—accompanying the poverty-reducing effect of policy. In Belgium in this period, there was also a gain to households as a whole but the policy changes had a small poverty-increasing effect. In Hungary, there was a negligible change in aggregate household income but with a large upward effect on poverty.

In the period 2007–2011, there was a big gain on average for households in Hungary but a small poverty-increasing effect of policy.

One immediate lesson is that there have been periods when some governments reformed their tax and transfer systems in ways that generated net revenue by comparison with un-reformed (but income-adjusted) systems, but they carried out those reforms in a way that had a poverty-reducing effect, or at least a neutral one. In some other countries, although policy reforms resulted in gains in average household income, they left the bottom end of the distribution worse off compared to the median income.

## The Effects of Structural Reforms and Indexation Policies on Poverty Rates

In our analysis we can further divide policy reforms into two parts—those due to what we describe as "structural" reforms (such as changes in percentage rates of tax or means-testing structures) and those due simply to ways in which the uprating of benefit levels and tax brackets differed from the comparator "neutral" indexation rate. Figure 5.6 shows (by comparison with a market income–linked base) that, in the first period, it was structural reforms that had poverty-increasing effects in Hungary, but poverty-reducing ones in Italy and the United Kingdom. By contrast, it was uprating by more than market income growth that was poverty-reducing in Estonia and Bulgaria. In the second period, the main poverty-reducing effects came from uprating that was more generous than income indexation in Belgium, Estonia, and the United Kingdom, rather than from the net effect of structural reforms (indeed, structural reforms were poverty-increasing overall in the United Kingdom). However, uprating policies were poverty-increasing in Hungary (and to a small extent in Bulgaria).

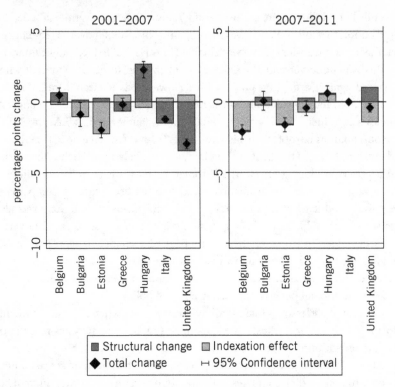

**Figure 5.6.** Effects of policy changes against a market income-indexed counterfactual on floating poverty rates: structural change and indexation effect, 2001–2007 and 2007–2011. *Note:* The 2001 and 2011 policy parameters are adjusted to 2007 levels using MII; 60% of median equivalized household income is used as a poverty line for the floating poverty. Standard errors for confidence intervals are calculated using the delta method. *Source:* Authors' calculations using EUROMOD version F6.36.

## Effects of Policy Reforms by Age Group

Given the ways in which the crisis has in many countries disproportionately affected young people, especially within the labor market, the incidence of the effects of policy reforms by types of people is also of interest, and in particular whether younger people have been favored over older people, or vice versa. Different criteria are often applied to transfers and taxes for pensioners from other parts of the tax and transfer systems. Figure 5.7 (for 2001–2007) and Figure 5.8 (for 2007–2011) show the age effects for the two time periods.[10]

Note that here the age groups are those of individuals but incomes are still those of the household in which they live (adjusted for household size, and assuming equal sharing). Thus, changes that affect, for instance, transfers for children will have an impact on the age group containing children and on the age groups containing their parents. Similarly, if elderly people live in households also containing younger people, changes to public pensions are taken as affecting all household members, not just the pensioners themselves.

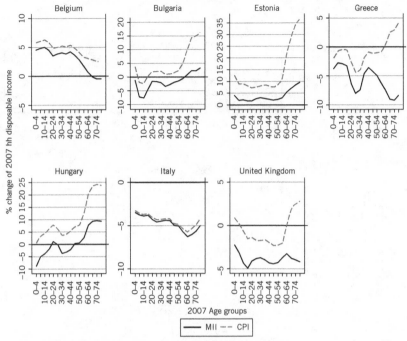

**Figure 5.7.** Effect of policy changes relative to MII and CPI indexation on average disposable income by age groups, 2001–2007. *Note:* Individuals are grouped in 5-year age categories based on 2007 population. The eldest group contains individuals of 80 or more years old. The charts are drawn to different scales, but the interval between gridlines on each of them is the same. *Source:* Authors' calculations using EUROMOD version F6.36.

Figure 5.7 shows some immediate contrasts in the first period. The countries divide into three groups.

In Bulgaria, Estonia, and Hungary, policies measured relative to MII indexation were tilted toward those age 60 or more. In Estonia, that meant that the largest gains went to older people; in Hungary, children and middle-aged people lost, but older people gained substantially; in Bulgaria, the effect was neutral for those age 60 to 64 and positive but small for those age 65 or more, with everyone else losing out. The same patterns are much more pronounced compared to CPI indexation, showing gains across all age groups in the three countries (apart from children age 5 to 14 in Bulgaria, who were worse off relative to both MII and CPI indexation).

In Belgium and Greece, and less sharply in Italy, the changes in the first period were tilted against older people, with no gains or larger proportionate losses for those over 60. Greece is the only country where the direction switches with the counterfactual: the elderly gained and other age groups lost out compared to CPI indexation, but the elderly lost most relative to market income indexation.

In the United Kingdom, the distribution of losses from policy change was fairly age-neutral, although with somewhat smaller losses for the youngest

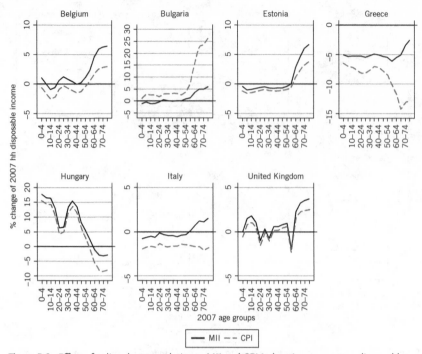

**Figure 5.8.** Effect of policy changes relative to MII and CPI indexation on average disposable income by age groups, 2007–2011. *Note*: Individuals are grouped in 5-year age categories based on 2007 population. The eldest group contains individuals more than 80 years old. The charts are drawn to different scales, but the interval between gridlines on each of them is the same. *Source*: Authors' calculations using EUROMOD version F6.36.

children. With CPI indexation, the effect had a U-shape across age groups, with the elderly and the youngest having small gains, and others experiencing small losses.

The patterns in the second period shown in Figure 5.8 were again different between the countries and, in some cases, from the pre-crisis period.

In Estonia again and also in Belgium, policy reforms were tilted toward the elderly, in both cases because of more favorable indexation than income growth (now negative in real terms). Reforms were largely neutral for people less than 60 years old with MII indexation, although revealing small losses compared to CPI indexation.

In Bulgaria, as in the earlier period, pensions increased faster than the growth in prices and faster than market incomes, which generated income gains for the elderly (age 60+)—especially large with CPI indexation. Policies were neutral for those less than 60 years old compared to MII indexation but resulted in small income gains compared to CPI indexation.

In Italy and the United Kingdom, reforms generated small gains for older people, while in Greece losses were smaller for older people than others. With CPI indexation, preferential treatment of elderly people disappears in Italy and even takes the opposite direction in Greece.

However, in Hungary, there was a sharp reversal of the balance of reforms by age, relative to the earlier period, with substantial gains for children and younger adults, but large losses for older people.

Overall, there were striking differences by age among the countries and between the two time periods in the impact of policy change. Older people were favored in Bulgaria, Estonia, and Hungary in the earlier period and in Belgium, Bulgaria, Estonia, Italy, and the United Kingdom in the second period. But older people were the most adversely affected in Greece and Italy in the first period and—in a striking reversal—in Hungary in the second period.

## FEATURES OF REFORM IN EACH COUNTRY

The broad impacts of the reforms in each country described above come from very varied changes within the separate components of their tax and transfer systems. It is helpful to understand the choices that led to these variations. This section describes the key features of those changes (for simplicity concentrating on comparisons with an income-indexed base), drawing on the analysis of the impact of policy reforms across income and age groups presented above, as well as information on the types of policy change having an impact by income group, which is provided in Figures A5.1 and A5.2 in the Appendix.

### Belgium

The overall regressive effects of Belgium's policy changes between 2001 and 2007 in this analysis arose from large losses in the bottom decile group due to reductions in means-tested benefits and gains in the other decile groups due to tax cuts, leading to an increase in disposable income on average. Policy changes in the first period were targeted at the population under age 65, while the effect on the elderly was neutral on average. Policy changes increased median income more than incomes at the bottom, and poverty increased slightly, as noted earlier.[11]

The period 2007–2011 shows exactly the opposite, with clearly progressive gains primarily through public pensions being kept ahead of market incomes (which were falling in real terms), and a relative increase of non-means-tested benefits raising incomes for the two bottom decile groups. Policy changes decreased poverty—by more than in any other country—in the second period.

## Bulgaria

Bulgaria's policy changes in the first period were also regressive, with the largest losses concentrated on the bottom decile group due to means-testing the universal child benefit and substantial cuts in benefit values relative to market incomes. The losses resulting from the child-benefit reform persisted up to the richest income decile group and were only partly offset by the increase in public pensions and means-tested benefits, which were indexed above income growth. Nevertheless, this was associated with only a small impact on the poverty rate because the main losses were to those already in poverty, rather than on its margins.

Other changes that translated into income losses affecting all income groups were the result of increased rates of employee social insurance contributions, partly offset for all income groups, apart from the lowest, by reduced income tax rates.

In the second period, the net effects of the policy changes were also regressive, but less sharply so. In 2008, Bulgaria replaced a progressive income taxation system with a flat tax with no tax exemption, which led to increases in average tax rates across the whole income distribution, with the exception of the top two income deciles. For the poorest group, this was combined with losses from means-tested benefits (due to indexation below income growth), which were partly offset by the increase in public pensions ahead of market incomes. Again, families with children were most affected by the changes, with elderly people relatively well protected.

## Estonia

By contrast, Estonia's reforms between 2001 and 2007 were (mostly) progressive, resulting from improved public pensions (from indexation) affecting the bottom half of the distribution, at the same time as the flat income tax rate was lowered by 4 percentage points, which benefited the top half of the income distribution almost as much. Households with elderly members unsurprisingly gained most from the pension changes, and lost least from higher social insurance contributions, accounting for the sharp tilt in gains toward older people.

In the second period, the dominant feature was again more generous public pensions in the context of falling real incomes. For higher income groups, the negative effects of higher social insurance contributions outweighed benefits from lowering the income tax rate further, and the top half of the distribution lost overall. The end result was progressive changes overall, tilted toward those of 60 or more years old, and contributing to lower poverty than there would otherwise have been.

The main driver of the overall poverty-reducing impact over the decade as a whole—the largest among the seven countries—was therefore the way in which public pensions were indexed more rapidly than income growth, both before and after the crisis, but also due to pensioners' being more concentrated around the poverty line. In the first period, there was a significant net cost of the reforms as a whole, equivalent to 3% of household income overall. In the second period, they had a neutral effect (compared to the 2007 system indexed to income growth).

## Greece

In the first period, the losses across the income distribution stemmed from a combination of increases in social insurance contributions and taxes as well as indexation of public pensions (the latter spread remarkably equally across the income distribution) that was lower than income growth. The means-tested benefit for large families was made universal in 2002, which explains the drop in disposable income due to means-tested benefits for lower income groups, offset by an increase in their disposable income due to non-means-tested benefits, shown in Figure A5.1. The larger population coverage of the universal benefit moderated losses for the lowest income groups a little.

The second period was dominated by tax changes that reduced incomes fairly evenly across the income distribution. The structural components of this were regressive, while the indexation effect (in the presence of falling average market income) offset this at the bottom, leaving a neutral effect overall. There were some relative gains for the bottom half of the income distribution from means-tested benefits, non-means-tested benefits, and public pensions falling less than market incomes, at the same time as reductions in the value of public pensions for those in higher income groups. Together, these produced the progressive revenue-raising effect and a small contribution to the lowering of poverty across the 10 years as a whole.[12]

## Hungary

The regressive effect of policy change from 2001 to 2007 in Hungary resulted from means-tested benefit losses for the bottom two income decile groups, losses from social insurance contributions across the distribution, and pension and tax reforms benefiting the top half of the distribution. Overall, the bottom tenth were 10% worse off than they would have been with an unchanged but income-linked system, but the top half gained (apart from the top tenth). Households with elderly members were the biggest gainers from the reforms. Overall, the changes had a significant effect, leading to the largest increase in poverty (measured with the floating poverty line) among the countries in the first period.

The substantial changes between 2007 and 2011 were due to a "flat tax" reform that brought its greatest benefits to the highest income groups (with the higher rate reduced in 2009–2010 and then abolished entirely) and a substantial positive effect from public pension changes relative to market incomes, offset by certain pensions' being brought into tax. It was the regressive nature of the tax reforms in the later period, combined with the reductions in the relative value of means-tested benefits for nonpensioners in the earlier period, that meant that policy changes overall had the effect of increasing poverty over the decade as a whole.

## Italy

Between 2001 and 2007, policy change in Italy was dominated by revenue-raising and progressive structural tax changes, with little else changing apart from the indexation of public pensions' falling behind market incomes, resulting in small losses to all income groups.

Between 2007 and 2011, the very limited effect of policy change for all income groups was the result of the offsetting effects of public pension indexation that was more generous than a link to incomes, together with tax-bracket indexation that was less generous. The scale of the effects on all groups was much more modest than for any of the other countries in the post-crisis period, reflected in negligible effects on poverty rates.

## United Kingdom

Increased generosity of means-tested benefits for households in the first three decile groups (as a result of a structural reform associated with the "new tax credits" introduced by the Blair government) meant that the reforms overall were progressive. In other respects, all income groups were affected by increased taxes and reductions in the relative value of both public pensions and non-means-tested benefits. This combination contributed to reducing poverty.

In the post-crisis period from 2007 to 2011, the reforms overall had a progressive effect, with the lowest income groups gaining most proportionately from indexation of public pensions and means-tested benefits that was more generous than overall income growth (partly offset by structural reforms, including higher taper rates for tax credits, which reduced their reach up the income distribution). At the same time, the top income group lost from the addition of a top income tax rate and an increase in social insurance contribution rates for higher earners. This meant the reforms contributed to a modest downward effect on poverty.

## CONCLUSIONS

In this chapter, we assess the direct effect of tax–benefit policy changes on the distribution of household disposable income, and on poverty in particular, in seven EU countries from 2001 to 2011. We further split the period into two, using 2007 as the midpoint to investigate policy effects before and since the start of the Great Recession. The assessment of policy effects relies on constructing counterfactual income distributions (using the microsimulation method), where the choice of an appropriate indexation factor for monetary benefit and tax parameters (to adjust the counterfactual for changes in nominal levels over time) can be—as we demonstrate—important for the outcome.

Our main empirical findings are the following. In terms of relative poverty (i.e., shifting poverty lines), policy changes had a poverty-increasing effect only in Hungary. Except in Belgium, policies after the crisis achieved less in terms of poverty reduction than in the pre-crisis period. This is problematic because it implies the reduction of social support at the time when it was needed the most. It also points toward the need to achieve more under favorable economic conditions in order to be better prepared for more challenging economic periods.[13] On the other hand, there were periods when governments reformed their systems, resulting in net revenue but in a way that avoided increasing relative poverty. Examples include Greece in both periods and the United Kingdom in the first period. There are also examples where policy changes that reduced revenue also resulted in higher poverty (Hungary).

Overall, there were striking differences by age group among the countries and between the two time periods in the impact of policy change. Older people were favored (or less severely affected) in Bulgaria, Estonia, and Hungary in the period before 2007, and in Belgium, Bulgaria, Estonia, Italy, and the United Kingdom after 2007. But older people were the most adversely affected in Greece and Italy in the first period and—in a striking reversal—in Hungary in the second period.

There are two important caveats. First, we assessed policy effects conditional on 2007 (i.e., midperiod) market incomes (and their distribution) and population structure. Using data from another point in time would not necessarily produce the same results. Second, we focus on direct effects only and leave aside behavioral adjustments (e.g., labor supply) to policy changes. This might be an important omission if the policy changes introduced in the period were specifically designed to alter the incentive to take paid work or to work longer hours, for example.

Looking across our results, what is most striking is how varied and complex the differences were among countries in their use of fiscal instruments and in their effects. For policymaking, this illustrates the freedom of action policymakers have, even when they are trying to achieve similar changes in their fiscal positions. The period from 2001 to 2011 was not a "lost decade," as some have suggested, because policy changes did in fact have poverty-reducing effects in most of the countries that we examined. The caveats about lack of comparable poverty estimates for the period 2001–2011 notwithstanding, the available evidence[14] suggests that, out of the seven countries, poverty rose over the period in five countries and fell only slightly in two (Estonia and United Kingdom). Only in Hungary can some of the observed increase in poverty be explained by government action through tax–benefit policy changes. In the other countries, poverty would have risen by more (or fallen by less) had policies remained as in 2001. This suggests that the underlying income distribution became more unequal. Even in the good years before the crisis, welfare states had to work harder in order to keep poverty rates in check. As a corollary, to move toward achievement of poverty-reduction targets, greater efforts would be required.

From a policy point of view, there is a clear need to understand the important influence of indexation of policies on the outcomes in terms of poverty and inequality and relative gains and losses by social and demographic groups. Especially in times of economic volatility, whether policies should keep pace with market incomes, with prices, or with some other economic variable is an important issue for consideration and open debate. Indexation by the growth in market incomes keeps public support in line with changes in private incomes, and hence relative poverty using a floating threshold constant, although this may imply that benefit levels are cut in times of economic hardship.

Indexation of policies by changes in the price level means that public support may lag behind market incomes in times of growth but protects living standards in periods when real (market) incomes are falling, also offering greater automatic stabilization. If short-term fiscal considerations make this impossible, then, as our analysis shows for some countries, it is still possible to structure policy changes to provide relative protection for those on low incomes.

From an analytical point of view, our detailed analysis of the nature of the policy changes reveals that what can look like similar net effects of policy on inequality and poverty can result from very different patterns of change across the income distribution as a whole, and they are often the result of structural reforms and indexation policies that act in opposite directions. In turn, what lies behind these changes can reflect the net effect of complex changes to different aspects of taxes and transfers that need to be seen together to understand the overall balance of policy change.

## NOTES

The authors thank Bea Cantillon, Paola De Agostini, Francesco Figari, Tim Goedemé, Péter Hegedüs, Chrysa Leventi, Péter Szivos, Dieter Vandelannoote, and Toon Vanheukelom for their help and comments on earlier versions of this chapter, as well as acknowledge the contribution of all past and current members of the EUROMOD consortium. The process of extending and updating EUROMOD is financially supported by the Directorate General for Employment, Social Affairs and Inclusion of the European Commission [Progress Grant No. VS/2011/0445]. The analysis here uses microdata from EU-SILC made available by Eurostat under contract EU-SILC/2011/55, national EU-SILC data for Bulgaria, Estonia, Greece, and Italy, made available by the respective National Statistical Offices, and (for the United Kingdom) the Family Resources Survey data made available by the Department of Work and Pensions via the U.K. Data Archive.

1  For similar approaches, see, for example, Decoster, Perelman, Vandelannoote, Vanheukelom, and Verbist (2015) for a longer period in the case of Belgium, or De Agostini, Paulus, and Tasseva (2016) for a wider range of countries for the period since 2008.

2  For more discussion of the method used, as well as a formal description of the decomposition and more detailed empirical results, see Hills et al. (2014). The results here for Bulgaria have been revised since the earlier version.

3  For illustration, examples of policy reforms included the replacement of progressive income taxation with a flat income tax in Bulgaria and Hungary, introduction of contributory maternity and unemployment benefits in Estonia, the complete revision of the income tax schedule in Greece, and reforms to in-work benefits and tax credits in the United Kingdom and to income tax and family allowances in Italy.

4  See EUROMOD Country Reports for more information: https://www.euromod.ac.uk/using-euromod/country-reports/.

5  See Hills et al. (2014), Table 1 and associated notes and discussion, for the values and derivation of these indices.

6  If, for instance, benefit parameters are held constant in nominal terms, this will create losses in real terms or relative to market incomes (conditional on positive growth in prices and market incomes), and this will be shown when looking at effects using the CPI- and MII-indexed counterfactuals. As explained above, we abstract from changes in the underlying distribution of incomes. If, in reality, market income inequality rose less or more than the increase in the progressivity of the simulated policies, one would observe an increase or a decrease in the poverty-reducing capacity of the simulated policies.

7  Disposable income is defined as the sum of gross market income and cash benefits, net of direct taxes and employee/self-employed social insurance contributions. Throughout, it is adjusted for differences in household size and composition using the modified Organisation for Economic Cooperation and Development (OECD) equivalence scale.

8  Results using a fixed poverty line are available in Hills et al. (2014).

9  For presentation of distributional results over the whole 2001–2011 period ranked by initial incomes and by 2011 incomes, see Hills et al. (2014), Appendix 3. For instance, using the ranking by 2001 incomes, the reforms in Belgium and the United Kingdom are uniformly progressive, but when ranked by 2011 incomes, the bottom groups gain less than others (or lose in the United Kingdom).

10  Figures 17 to 20 in Hills et al. (2014) split these results between structural reforms and indexation effects.

11  It is interesting to compare these results with those derived for Belgium using similar methods in a more detailed study for the longer period, 1992–2012, contained in Decoster et al. (2015). Those results are based on the population structure and income distribution as it was in 2009, rather than 2007, as used here. They also include changes in indirect taxes, which we do not. Importantly, they show the distributional results of the changes ranking households by simulated incomes for the first year they cover, 1992. Looking at the distributional effects of policy for the sub-periods we cover, those for 2007–2012 show a similar picture as ours for 2007–2011. However, their results for 2001–2007 show a positive (progressive) effect for their bottom decile group—but that is for households that *would have been* in the bottom group under the 1992 system, not all those who would necessarily have been at the bottom under later systems, such as the 2007 system, which we use for ranking (which shows a loss

in that period for our bottom group). These results are not contradictory, but reflect difference choices for the comparison being made.

12 It should be noted that, when measured in absolute terms against a fixed poverty threshold, policy changes had large negative effects on poverty in Greece (a 3 to 4 percentage point increase in the rate).

13 See Marchal, Marx, and Van Mechelen (2016) for an examination of what happened to minimum income floors given by social assistance in 23 countries after the crisis. They found that, generally, social assistance benefit trends did not deviate much from pre-crisis growth levels. Yet retrenchment did occur through more technical measures, the combined impact of which was significant in some countries.

14 Hills et al. (2014), Appendix 1.

## REFERENCES

Bargain, O., & Callan, T. (2010). Analysing the effects of tax-benefit reforms on income distribution: A decomposition approach. *Journal of Economic Inequality*, 8(1), 1–21.

Cantillon, B., & Vandenbroucke, F. (2014). *Reconciling work and poverty reduction: How successful are European welfare states*. Oxford, England: Oxford University Press.

De Agostini, P., Paulus, A., & Tasseva, I. (2016). *The effect of changes in tax-benefit policies on the income distribution in 2008–2015* [EUROMOD Working Paper EM6/16]. Colchester, England: ISER, University of Essex.

Decoster, A., Perelman, S., Vandelannoote, D., Vanheukelom, T., & Verbist, G. (2015). *A bird's eye view on 20 years of tax-benefit reform in Belgium* [EUROMOD Working Paper EM10/15]. Colchester, England: ISER, University of Essex.

European Council. (2000). *Lisbon European Council Presidency Conclusions 23–24 March*. Brussels, Belgium, European Council.

Hills, J., Paulus, A., Sutherland, H., & Tasseva, I. (2014). *A lost decade? Decomposing the effect of 2001–11 tax-benefit policy changes on the income distribution in EU countries* [ImPRovE Working Paper 14/03]. Herman Deleeck Centre for Social Policy, University of Antwerp: Antwerp, Belgium.

Marchal, S., Marx, I., & Van Mechelen, N. (2016). Minimum income protection in the austerity tide. *IZA Journal of European Labor Studies*, 5, 4.

Nolan, B., Salverda, W., Checchi, D., Marx, I., McKnight, A., Tóth, I. G., & van de Werfhorst, H. G. (2014). *Changing inequalities and societal impacts in rich countries: Thirty countries' experiences*. Oxford, England: Oxford University Press.

Sutherland, H., & Figari F. (2013). EUROMOD: the European Union tax-benefit microsimulation model. *International Journal of Microsimulation* 6(1), 4–26.

# APPENDIX

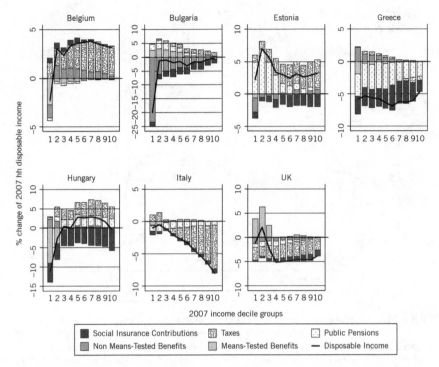

**Figure A5.1.** Effect of policy changes relative to MII indexation on average disposable income by income components and income decile groups, 2001–2007. *Note*: Income decile groups are derived based on 2007 household equivalized disposable incomes. The charts are drawn to different scales, but the interval between gridlines on each of them is the same. *Source*: Authors' calculations using EUROMOD version F6.36.

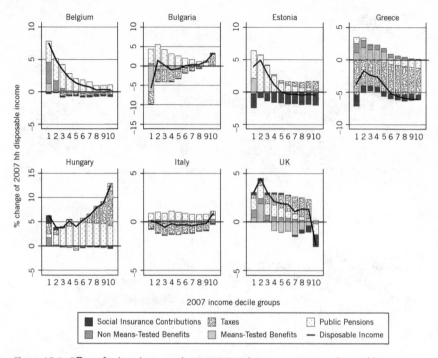

**Figure A5.2.** Effect of policy changes relative to MII indexation on average disposable income by income components and income decile groups, 2007–2011. *Note*: Income deciles are derived based on 2007 household equivalized disposable incomes. The charts are drawn to different scales, but the interval between gridlines on each of them is the same. *Source*: Authors' calculations using EUROMOD version F6.36.

# 6

# DISTRIBUTIVE EFFECTS OF THE CRISIS IN THE EUROPEAN PERIPHERY

## Manos Matsaganis and Chrysa Leventi

## INTRODUCTION

In recent years, the world economy has been in turmoil. The global financial crisis of 2007–2009 was followed by the sovereign debt crisis of 2011–2013, interrupted by a modest recovery. Several authors have labeled this the Great Recession (Jenkins, Brandolini, Micklewright, & Nolan, 2013), because it affected large areas of the globe and because its duration and depth exceeded those of previous downturns. In Europe, the combined GDP of the 27 European Union (EU) Member States contracted by 4.5% in 2009 relative to the year before. The European economy subsequently recovered somewhat, but once again registered negative growth in 2012 and stagnated in 2013. On the whole, by 2013, the European economy had shrunk by 1.2% relative to its 2008 level.

In this context, an abundance of research has accumulated on the macroeconomic effects of the Great Recession, and there is growing debate about how fiscal consolidation packages have contributed to these effects. Nevertheless, our understanding of how individual tax and benefit policies have interacted with wider developments in the economy nationally, as well as how their combined effect has translated to changes in inequality and poverty, remains fairly limited. Given the political importance (and policy relevance) of the question, this is unfortunate. Effective policymaking requires access to reliable and timely analysis at the micro-level, assessing how the material circumstances of different population groups were affected by the crisis, establishing the extent to which changes in the distribution of incomes can be attributed to government policy rather than to developments in the wider economy, and disaggregating the distributional impact of the policy mix adopted in each country into progressive and regressive policy measures.

This chapter aims to provide an assessment of the distributional implications of the Great Recession in seven EU countries in the period 2009–2013. Using a microsimulation model, we quantify the impact of tax–benefit policies (such as fiscal consolidation measures undertaken in several countries) and of developments in the wider economy (such as losses in jobs and earnings) on the income distribution. Moreover, we estimate how the burden of the crisis has been shared across income groups, as well as how the differential impact of the crisis has altered the composition of the population in poverty.

The countries examined are Greece, Spain, Italy, Latvia, Lithuania, Portugal, and Romania. Our choice was driven by the significantly different ways the crisis unfolded in each country. In a single year (2009), Latvia and Lithuania lost as much as 18% and 15% of their respective GDPs. The Romanian economy shrank by 8% in the period 2008–2010. While these economies eventually recovered, further south the crisis was more protracted. In Spain, the size of the contraction in 2007–2013 was around 6%, in Portugal it was 7%, and in Italy it was almost 9%, while in Greece the size of the economy declined by nearly 24% (Eurostat, 2014).

This chapter adds to the existing literature in two ways. On the one hand, it clarifies the distinction between the distributional effects of tax and benefit policies and those of wider developments that lie largely beyond the direct control of policymakers. On the other hand, it identifies policy measures whose first-order effect on the distribution of incomes has been inequality-reducing, in contrast with other policies having an inequality-increasing impact. Our findings have important implications for the design of equitable fiscal consolidation programs.

The chapter begins with a review of the literature on the distributional consequences of a crisis and on the contribution of fiscal consolidation to the intensity of recessions, including key findings of microsimulation studies. The next section explains our methodology. This is followed by our estimates of the distributional effects of the Great Recession in seven EU countries. The chapter ends with a summary of the most important findings and with reflections on the policy implications of the research.

## LITERATURE REVIEW

### Interactions of Austerity with Growth
There can be little doubt that fiscal consolidation interacts with growth. On the one hand, austerity policies cause aggregate demand to fall and therefore lead firms catering to the domestic market to reduce output, cut salaries, and lay off

personnel. On the other hand, a recession weakens the deficit-reducing potential of austerity policies and may lead to calls for the adoption of harsher measures.

This raises the question of how austerity contributes to the intensity of the recession. This is at the heart of the controversy about "fiscal multipliers"—that is, the output loss associated with fiscal consolidation. The issue gained increasing importance in the wake of the current crisis and initiated a heated debate. On the whole, international organizations, such as the International Monetary Fund (IMF) and the Organisation for Economic Co-operation and Development (OECD), now accept that they have underestimated the size of fiscal multipliers and have overestimated growth prospects (IMF, 2012; OECD, 2014a). In contrast, the European Commission has suggested that forecast errors may be due to the negative response of investors to heavily indebted countries, rather than due to an underestimation of the fiscal multiplier (European Commission, 2012), while the European Central Bank has argued that the medium- and long-term effects of fiscal consolidation more than compensate for any short-term output losses (European Central Bank, 2012).

In general, the relationship between changes in government expenditure and growth is nonlinear. The actual effect will depend on a variety of factors. To start with, fiscal multipliers tend to be larger when the economy is in recession (Auerbach & Gorodnichenko, 2012; Corsetti, Meier, & Müller, 2012; Eyraud & Weber, 2013). Also, output losses will be greater when efforts to improve fiscal balances take place simultaneously across several countries, because this will create negative spillover effects via international trade channels (Goujard, 2013).

On the other hand, the policy mix of fiscal consolidation packages may also matter, although the evidence is ambiguous. Some authors (Alesina & Ardagna, 2012; Alesina, Favero, & Giavazzi, 2012; Romer & Romer, 2010) have argued that declines in public spending may lead to stronger economic growth than is the case with tax increases, while others (Ball, Furceri, Leigh, & Loungani, 2013; Jordà & Taylor, 2013) have found that the medium-term relationship of spending cuts with GDP growth is negative. Finally, the size of the multiplier will also depend on the characteristics of the economy under consideration (Favero, Giavazzi, & Perego, 2011). As argued by Alcidi and Gros (2012), output losses after fiscal consolidation will be inversely related to the savings rate, the average (effective) tax rate, and the degree of trade openness.

## Interactions of Austerity (and Growth) with Inequality

While economic crises are widely considered to cause poverty and inequality to rise, establishing their distributional effects is less straightforward than appears at first sight. Their consequences may vary substantially, depending on the interaction between the earnings of those directly affected by the crisis, the sociodemographic structure of the population, the income and employment status of household members not directly affected, and the capacity of the tax–benefit system to absorb macroeconomic shocks (Atkinson, 2009; Nolan, 2009).

Empirical evidence has shown that austerity does not necessarily have to be regressive. A recent survey of fiscal consolidation in 29 countries in the period 1971–2009 by Kaplanoglou, Rapanos, and Bardakas (2013) concluded that "ameliorating the effects of adjustment, by supporting the weaker parts of society . . . may provide the double dividend of enhancing the probability of success of the adjustment and of promoting social cohesion." Similarly, a study of fiscal consolidation in 18 countries in the period 1970–2010 by Agnello and Souza (2012) found that income inequality may actually decline. However, an analysis of 173 episodes of fiscal consolidation in 17 countries over the past 30 years by Ball, Leigh, and Loungani (2011) showed that, on balance, adjustment costs were not shared equally, with lower-income groups experiencing heavier losses, and wages declining more than profits.

The size and makeup of fiscal consolidation may be crucial in determining the distributional impact of the adjustment. Agnello and Souza (2012) found that the decline in income inequality following episodes of fiscal consolidation tended to take place where the policy mix relied more heavily on tax increases than on spending cuts. Ahren, Arnold, and Moeser (2011) showed that progressive taxation and generous unemployment benefits can smooth the distributional impact of a financial crisis and fiscal consolidation.

In other words, an insidious trade-off may be at work: progressive policies, such as raising personal income taxes, may reduce inequality at the cost of damaging long-term growth, while regressive policies, such as raising indirect taxes, may have the opposite effect (OECD, 2013). In view of that, and given that negative (or anemic) growth tends to cause inequality to increase, the static effects of austerity policies may be at odds with their dynamic effects. On the whole, little is known about the combined (static and dynamic) effect of individual policy measures. However, Woo, Bova, Kinda, and Zhang (2013), having analyzed consolidation programs in 17 countries in the period 1978–2009, concluded that spending cuts increase inequality more than tax increases do. Crucially, the authors identified unemployment as an important channel through which consolidation causes inequality to increase.

## Estimating Distributional Effects via Microsimulation

Microsimulation has been extensively used as a tool for assessing the distributional impact of the recent economic downturn, for examining the effects of various austerity measures, and for projecting the shape of the income distribution in future years.

In a single-country setting, Ireland in 2009–2010, Callan, Nolan, and Walsh (2011) assessed the impact of public-sector pay cuts. They were found to be progressive relative to a counterfactual of a universal 4% cut in pay rates in both the public and private sectors. Nolan, Callan, and Maître (2013) expanded that analysis to include the overall distributional impact of tax and welfare changes over the period 2009–2011, and again they found the result to be highly progressive. Brandolini, D'Amuri, and Faiella (2013) argued that, in Italy, the impact of the recent recession on inequality and poverty has been fairly limited, despite the considerable fall in average income. For Greece, Leventi and Matsaganis (2013) estimated how the burden of the crisis was shared across the population in 2009–2012. Their findings suggest that the main driver of growing inequalities appears to have been the recession, especially rising unemployment, rather than austerity policies per se. In Cyprus, Koutsampelas and Polycarpou (2013) assessed the distributional effects of the austerity measures introduced in 2011–2012. Their analysis showed that most of the first-order effects of adjustment fell upon households located at the middle and upper part of the income distribution. In the United Kingdom, the effects of recent (and forthcoming) tax and benefit reforms were analyzed by Browne and Levell (2010), Brewer, Browne, and Joyce (2011), Brewer, Browne, Hood, Joyce, and Sibieta (2013), and Joyce and Sibieta (2013). Their findings suggest that the timing and size of the impact of the recession vary widely across income groups.

In a comparative setting, Avram et al. (2013) simulated the distributional effects of fiscal consolidation measures up to 2012 in nine EU countries. The study showed that the burden of austerity was shared differently in these countries: in Greece, Spain, Italy, Latvia, Romania, and the United Kingdom, the rich lost a higher proportion of their incomes than the poor, whereas in Estonia, the opposite seemed to be the case. Finally, Bargain, Callan, Doorley, and Keane (2013) examined the distributional impact of the economic crisis in France, Germany, the United Kingdom, and Ireland in the period 2008–2010. They found that, in the United Kingdom, France, and especially Ireland, policy reactions contributed to stabilizing or even reducing inequality and relative poverty.

## METHODOLOGY

### Departures from Previous Research

Given that microsimulation studies contribute to a policy debate that is more evidence-based than is usually the case, it is hardly surprising that their findings have generated considerable interest, nor that they have been extensively discussed in publications by international organizations, including the European Commission (2013), the OECD (2014b), and the IMF (2014). Nevertheless, they have also been open to misinterpretation, which is unfortunate in a politically contested field.

For example, Avram et al. (2013) evaluated the distributional effects of policy changes from 2009 to 2012 on the assumption that 2009 policies were implemented on the 2012 market income distribution. This is a crucial assumption. When assessing the distributional impact of tax and benefit policies, the choice of the underlying (market) income distribution may not matter much most of the time. However, at times of major changes, it will matter a lot. Also, as the literature reviewed above suggests, tax and benefit policies affect market incomes and are in turn affected by them. This is both because dynamic effects of austerity on inequality via growth are significant and because policymakers, when determining the content of tax and benefit policies in the coming year(s), tend to take into account the state of the economy and income distribution in the current year.

On the whole, ignoring interactions between policies and changes in market incomes leaves out an important part of the picture. This is clearly acknowledged in many of the previously mentioned microsimulation studies, whose authors take pains to explain that the estimated effects of austerity policies on inequality are first-order only. Nevertheless, the distinction is often muddled when their findings are reported by others. For example, a recent review of the evidence by the IMF (2014, p. 51) contended that "microsimulation studies indicate that these fiscal adjustments relied on progressive measures," even as it noted that "these studies focus exclusively on the impact of spending and tax consolidation measures on household disposable income and consumption, and do not assess the impact of these measures on market income."

Our approach departs from the approach in the study by Avram et al. (2013), where broader developments (such as changes in the labor market) are carefully accounted for as part of the general economic context but are explicitly excluded from the scope of the fiscal consolidation measures being assessed; in this study, we attempt to explore how individual tax–benefit policies have interacted with wider developments in the economy and how the combined effect of both has translated to changes in inequality and poverty. This study also differs from the methodology of Brandolini et al. (2013), where changes in the income distribution are exclusively driven by flows into and out of employment, assuming that market incomes and pensions have not changed during the period under examination.

In this chapter, we model the distributional effects of the crisis in the period 2009–2013 on a year-by-year basis, rather than cumulatively. Also, we assess first-order policy effects between two consecutive years (say $t-1$ and $t$), rather than between the start and the end of a longer period. Moreover, we locate first-order policy effects within the full distributional impact of the crisis, rather than abstracting from that. Finally, unlike most of the studies reviewed above, we attempt to distinguish between inequality-reducing and inequality-enhancing items within the same policy package.

## Modeling the Distributional Effects of the Crisis and Austerity

In principle, as economic activity slows down, policymakers may react by taking countercyclical measures to reduce taxes or increase public spending. Alternatively, if the space for expansionary policies is limited, they may attempt procyclical fiscal consolidation. Consequently, the distribution of incomes will change in two different ways: first, as a result of changing tax and benefits and, second, as a result of developments in the wider economy, such as losses of jobs and earnings in the private sector, where the contraction in activity will inevitably cause market incomes to fall.

Drawing on the decomposition approach developed by Bargain and Callan (2010), we can approximate the first-order distributional effects of policies by simulating a hypothetical counterfactual scenario, capturing the effect of changes in policies on the income distribution as observed before the policies are actually implemented (i.e., typically at the time policy changes are announced or legislated). Since this is the only distribution known to policymakers when they take decisions on policy changes, we believe that estimating this hypothetical scenario is of interest and relevance.

More formally, household disposable income (HDI) in our counterfactual scenario is constructed on the basis of:

1. Individuals' labor-market status, as in year $t-1$
2. Market incomes (other than public-sector pay), as in year $t-1$
3. Tax and benefit polices, as in year $t$.

This is then compared to the situation where all variables are set, as in year $t-1$. This is equivalent to assuming that government policies in a given year alter public-sector pay, public pensions, taxes, and benefits, but leave nominal pretax market incomes and employment levels as in the year before.

Note that, in our counterfactual scenario, we do not allow for monetary parameters of taxes and benefits to grow from one year to another. This is in contrast with what was assumed by Hills et al. (2014; see Chapter 5 above), where different counterfactual indexation scenarios were assessed, with more emphasis put on indexing policy parameters relative to average market income growth or Consumer Price Index (CPI). The main reason for opting for zero growth in policy parameters was that no official indexation was applicable during the period considered in most of our seven countries (or even if there was, it was put on hold as a way of bolstering public finances).

The broader distributional effects of the crisis between years $t$ and $t-1$ (capturing all together the effects of changes in policies, market incomes, and employment status) are modeled by comparing the distribution of HDI in year $t$ to the distribution in year $t-1$.

Also, we use the shorthand term *first-order effects* to warn against identifying the effects of our hypothetical scenario with the (unobservable) contribution of changes in government policies to changes in the income distribution. Note that this scenario does not coincide with first-order effects of government policies as commonly understood (i.e., as assessed on the income distribution observed after the policies are actually implemented). It follows that assessments of the progressiveness of fiscal consolidation packages might differ depending on the choice of the underlying income distribution. Our choice is driven by the fact that the income distribution of year *t* is not available to policymakers at the time policy decisions are made.

## Model and Data

We rely on the European tax–benefit model EUROMOD. The model uses survey data on gross incomes, labor-market status, and other characteristics of individuals and households, which it then applies to the tax and benefit rules in place in order to simulate direct taxes, social insurance contributions (SIC), and entitlements to cash benefits. The components of the tax–benefit system that cannot be simulated are read off the data. EUROMOD has been validated at both the micro-level and the macro-level and has been tested in several applications. For a comprehensive overview, see Sutherland and Figari (2013).

The underlying microdata for all countries are drawn from the 2010 European Union Statistics on Income and Living Conditions (EU-SILC). Updating incomes from the EU-SILC income reference period (2009) to the latest policy year (2013) is performed by using factors based on the available administrative or survey statistics. Specific updating factors are derived for each income source, reflecting the change in their average amount between the income data reference period and the target year.

Changes in labor-market status were taken into account following the approach adopted in Leventi et al. (2013). This approach can be briefly summarized as follows. Observations are selected on the basis of conditional probabilities of being employed. A logit model is used for estimating probabilities for working-age individuals (age 16 to 64) in the EUROMOD input data. The weighted total number of observations that are selected to go through transitions based on their probabilities corresponds to the relative net change in employment levels by age group, gender, and education, as shown in the macro-level Labor Force Survey (LFS) statistics. Annual LFS employment rates are used for 2010–2012, and an average of 2012Q3–2013Q2 for 2013. Changes from short-term to long-term unemployment are also modeled based on a selection procedure similar to the one described above.

Simulations are then carried out on the basis of the tax–benefit rules in place on June 30 of each policy year. Since EU-SILC provides no information on consumption, changes in indirect taxation are beyond the scope of this analysis. In order to enhance the accuracy and credibility of our estimates, we made an effort to address the issues of tax evasion (e.g., in Greece and Italy) and benefit non-take-up (e.g., in Greece).

## RESULTS

### Income Changes by Decile

Has the Great Recession made the rich richer (and the poor poorer)? This is an important question with obvious political implications. Rather disappointingly to those hoping for a simple answer, it all depends on how the income distribution is analyzed. Specifically, one of the effects of a crisis is that different social categories and income groups are affected differently. Over time, a considerable amount of re-ranking within the income distribution takes place, as a result of which composition of income deciles changes.[1]

Changes associated with re-ranking were most pronounced in Greece (where 65% of the population changed income decile between 2009 and 2013), followed by Portugal and Spain (where that proportion was around 35%). By comparison, in Italy, only 18% of the population were found in a different decile in 2013 relative to 2009. In the Baltic countries, around a quarter of the population changed income decile between 2009 and 2013, while in Romania only one sixth changed.

In terms of composition, in 2013 relative to 2009, the poorest 20% of the Greek population contained more unemployed workers (29% vs. 10%), fewer elderly persons (10% vs. 18%), and more city dwellers (40% vs. 35%). The bottom quintile also numbered more unemployed workers in Portugal (19% vs. 13%) and in Spain (16% vs. 8%), and to a lesser extent in Italy (8% vs. 5%) and Romania (3% vs. 0%). Moreover, it included more residents of rural areas in Latvia (63% vs. 61%) and more children in Lithuania (24% vs. 22%). Other changes were marginal.

The effects of re-ranking in real disposable household income are shown in Figure 6.1. These can be seen clearly in Greece, the country where income losses have been most dramatic. When deciles are fixed in 2009 (i.e., not allowing for re-ranking), we find that by 2013 those in the poorest 10% of the population in 2009 had lost a smaller-than-average proportion of their income (34% vs. 36% in real terms). On the other hand, if deciles are recalculated each year (i.e., allowing for re-ranking), we find that the income of those in the poorest 10% of the population in 2013 had fallen by as much as 69% relative to the income of their counterparts in 2009 (i.e., those who occupied the lowest income decile in that year).

A similar pattern prevailed in Spain, Italy, and Lithuania. In all of these countries, those in the bottom decile in 2009 had by 2013 lost a smaller proportion of their income than those in the top decile in 2009. Nevertheless, allowing for re-ranking, the poorest 10% of the population in 2013 found themselves much poorer than the poorest 10% in 2009. True, the richest 10% of the population

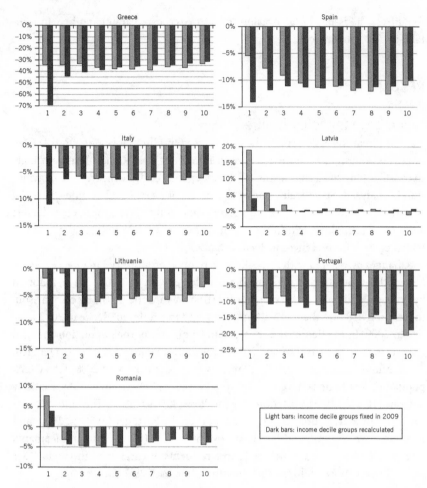

**Figure 6.1.** Changes in disposable income by decile (2009–2013): re-ranking effects.
*Note*: Household disposable income (HDI) is measured in real terms, averaged for each decile.
It is equivalized according to the OECD modified equivalence scale. The dark bars show change
in disposable income between 2009 and 2013 when the composition of deciles is allowed to
change (i.e., by calculating average income per decile for 2009 and 2013, allowing for re-ranking,
and then estimating the difference), while the light bars show average change in disposable
income when deciles are fixed on the basis of the 2009 income distribution. The charts
are drawn to different scales, but the interval between gridlines is the same on each chart.
*Source*: EUROMOD version G1.0.

in these countries were also less rich in 2013 than the richest 10% were in 2009.
However, the decline of the poorest decile was greater than it was for the richest
decile.

The pattern was slightly different in Portugal (where income changes allowing
for re-ranking were similar for the top and bottom deciles), and more radically
so in Romania and especially Latvia, where the poorest deciles actually gained in

real terms in 2009–2013. Even there, the relative gain was greater when deciles were fixed in 2009 than when they were recalculated each year.

Clearly, the above findings reflect changes in the composition of the population in poverty. Those already in poverty before the crisis (e.g., pensioners in southern Europe) were not fully protected, but generally lost less than the average citizen (at least in monetary terms). On the other hand, those falling below the poverty line during the crisis (e.g., unemployed youth) did so because they lost a far greater proportion of their income.

Hence, it becomes apparent that, in countries like Greece, Portugal, and Spain (where a considerable amount of re-ranking took place), the assessment of the progressivity or otherwise of policies may differ significantly according to whether they are assessed on the distribution of market incomes at the beginning or at the end of the period under consideration. For example, a policy change affecting pensioners in Greece will look much more progressive (or less regressive) if it is assessed on the 2013 distribution than if it is assessed on the 2009 income distribution.

## Disentangling the First-Order Effects of Tax–Benefit Policies

Have adverse distributional changes taken place because of the austerity policies introduced by governments? Or, as sometimes is argued, in spite of these policies? In other words, have fiscal consolidation packages been designed to minimize the impact of the recession on the weakest groups in society? Again, the political importance of this question is obvious. Can it be answered?

As a matter of fact, it can—provided we keep in mind that, as discussed previously, we only estimate first-order effects. In Figures 6.2 and 6.3 we estimate the yearly changes in poverty and inequality caused by policies alone (including those of austerity, where applicable) vs. full effects (including those of the wider recession, again where applicable). Poverty is defined as "anchored" (i.e., by reference to a relative poverty line fixed to its 2009 level in real terms). The rational for opting for an anchored poverty line rather than a floating one was that, at times of rapid change in living standards like the ones considered here, individuals may compare their condition not so much with that of "the average person" in the society in which they live, but with their own condition in a previous period.

As seen in Figure 6.2, results varied significantly among countries. Our estimates suggest that, in Greece, about half of the total increase in anchored poverty in 2010 and 2011 can be attributed to the first-order effect of austerity policies; in 2012 and 2013, austerity policies explain a much smaller proportion of the total poverty increase (13% and 33%, respectively). In Spain, policies alone had an important poverty-reducing effect in 2010. On the contrary, in 2011 they explained almost 65% of the total increase in anchored poverty. In 2012–2013, the implemented policy changes seem to not have contributed to the overall rise in poverty.

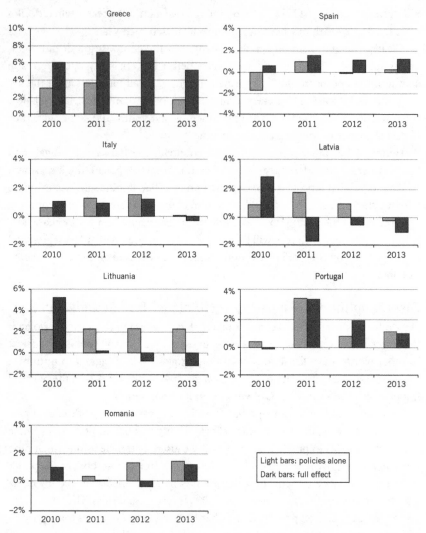

**Figure 6.2.** Year-on-year changes in anchored poverty rates in percentage points: tax and benefit policies alone vs. full effect. *Note:* "Policies alone" shows the first-order effect of changes in tax and benefit policies in year *t* on the income distribution in year *t* – 1 (i.e., before their interaction with wider changes in the economy). "Full effect" shows changes in income distribution in year *t* relative to year *t* – 1. Anchored poverty rate defined as proportion of population below a fixed poverty threshold, set at 60% of the 2009 median equivalized disposable income, adjusted for inflation. Standard error estimates, based on the Taylor linearization using the DASP module for Stata, are available upon request. *Source*: EUROMOD version G1.0.

In Italy (all years except 2010) and Portugal (all years except 2012), the first-order effect of tax–benefit policies was to raise anchored poverty more than the combination of policies and the changes in the wider economy did, with the latter effect being often negative (i.e., poverty-reducing). That was even more

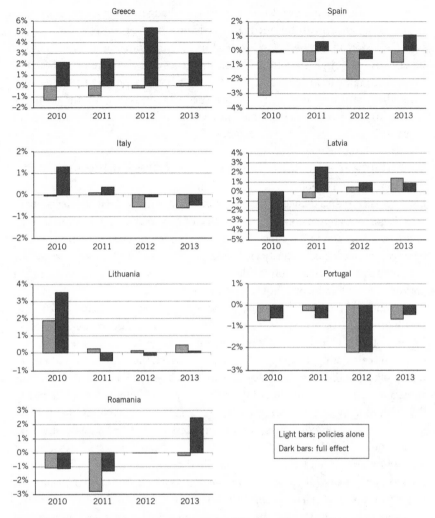

**Figure 6.3.** Year-on-year changes in the Gini index (%): tax and benefit policies alone vs. full effect. *Note*: "Policies alone" shows the first-order effect of changes in tax and benefit policies in year $t$ on the income distribution in year $t - 1$ (i.e., before their interaction with wider changes in the economy). "Full effect" shows changes in income distribution in year $t$ relative to year $t -$ 1. Standard error estimates, based on the Taylor linearization using the DASP module for Stata, are available upon request. *Source*: EUROMOD version G1.0.

the case in the two Baltic republics (especially from 2011 onward) and Romania (throughout the period).

Inequality effects, presented in Figure 6.3, were subtly different. In Greece and Spain, the first-order effect of the policies pursued seems to have mostly compressed the income distribution, while the combined effect of policies with broader economic developments appears to have made it consistently more unequal, with that pattern being stronger in Spain than in Greece. The picture was similar in Italy, Portugal, and Romania, where changes in inequality were generally not as great, with the inequality-reducing (first-order) effect of policies being occasionally strong (as in Portugal in 2012 or Romania in 2011). On the other hand, policy changes in the Baltic countries seem to have contributed to higher inequality in Lithuania in 2010 (i.e., just after the peak of the recession), while the first-order effect in Latvia was inequality-reducing. As the economy recovered, policy reversals in both Baltic countries seem to have driven increases in inequality.

## Identifying the Effect of Individual Policies on Inequality

That some austerity policies per se (as distinct from the wider recession) may have actually reduced inequality seems at odds with established views about what is going on in the countries most affected by the crisis. In fact, our finding seems to be the combined effect of two opposing tendencies: some policies distributed the burden of austerity fairly and/or affected groups located toward the top of the income distribution, while other policies cut incomes across the board and/or affected low-income households more.

In order to reduce complexity, we group tax–benefit policies under four headings: public-sector pay, taxes and SIC, pensions, and other social benefits.[2] We then formally assess the first-order impact of each policy bundle on inequality by calculating the percentage change between the value of the Gini index if the policy bundle in question had remained as in year $t-1$ relative to its actual value after the implementation of the policy in year $t$. Note that, as explained in the methodology section, we are opting for a fixed nominal counterfactual scenario, that is, we do not index policy parameters relative to average market income growth or CPI. Positive (negative) values indicate that, *ceteris paribus*, the policy in question rendered the income distribution less (more) equal. We use the term *progressive* (or *regressive*) interchangeably with *inequality-reducing* (or, respectively, *inequality-enhancing*). The results are shown in Table 6.1.

It can be seen clearly that the impact of many policy changes, although no doubt significant for the groups affected, was actually negligible in terms of the distribution of incomes as a whole. The partial exceptions were as follows.

Cuts in public-sector pay seem to have been progressive, especially in Greece (in particular in 2010 and 2013). This was also the case in Portugal (in 2011–2012) and the Baltic republics (in 2010). The reversal of pay cuts in Portugal (2013) and Latvia and Lithuania (since 2011) seems to have had a regressive effect. This effect mostly stems from the fact that, as a combination of steady employment and assortative mating, civil servants tend to be located in the upper end of the income distribution. In 2009, 77% of civil servants in Portugal and 66% in Greece were located in the top three income deciles, while in Latvia and Lithuania the corresponding figures were 48% and 53%, respectively.

The first-order effect of changes in direct taxes and SIC seemed mostly to have rendered the income distribution less unequal. This was especially so in Portugal

**Table 6.1.** Inequality Effects of Policy Changes

| | Change in the value of the Gini index (%) | | | |
|---|---|---|---|---|
| | **2010** | **2011** | **2012** | **2013** |
| **Greece** | | | | |
| • Public-sector pay | −0.57 | −0.10 | −0.31 | −0.52 |
| • Taxes/SIC | −0.84 | −0.13 | 0.07 | 0.98 |
| • Pensions | −0.30 | −0.06 | −0.41 | 0.90 |
| • Other social benefits | 0.35 | −0.16 | 0.25 | −1.47 |
| **Spain** | | | | |
| • Public-sector pay | −0.12 | −0.12 | −0.23 | — |
| • Taxes/SIC | −0.47 | 0.04 | −1.11 | −0.02 |
| • Pensions | −0.06 | −0.04 | −0.04 | −0.02 |
| • Other social benefits | −0.30 | −0.01 | −0.23 | 0.07 |
| **Italy** | | | | |
| • Public-sector pay | 0.06 | 0.00 | 0.02 | 0.01 |
| • Taxes/SIC | 0.01 | −0.52 | −0.42 | 0.00 |
| • Pensions | 0.00 | 0.00 | −0.01 | 0.00 |
| • Other social benefits | −0.04 | −0.06 | −0.06 | −0.20 |
| **Portugal** | | | | |
| • Public-sector pay | — | −0.53 | −1.04 | 0.96 |
| • Taxes/SIC | −0.39 | −1.93 | −0.60 | −3.67 |
| • Pensions | −0.16 | −0.01 | −1.15 | 0.69 |
| • Other social benefits | −0.18 | 1.97 | −0.13 | 1.15 |
| **Latvia** | | | | |
| • Public-sector pay | −0.95 | 0.43 | 0.39 | 0.15 |
| • Taxes/SIC | −0.98 | −0.32 | 0.01 | 0.42 |
| • Pensions | — | — | — | — |
| • Other social benefits | −2.58 | −0.56 | 0.14 | 0.86 |
| **Lithuania** | | | | |
| • Public-sector pay | −0.50 | 0.24 | 0.19 | 0.36 |
| • Taxes/SIC | 0.19 | 0.01 | 0.00 | 0.00 |
| • Pensions | — | — | 0.00 | −0.05 |
| • Other social benefits | 2.57 | −0.04 | 0.35 | −0.02 |
| **Romania** | | | | |
| • Public-sector pay | N/A | N/A | N/A | N/A |
| • Taxes/SIC | 0.04 | −3.25 | 0.14 | 0.01 |
| • Pensions | −0.11 | −0.12 | −0.11 | −0.13 |
| • Other social benefits | −1.25 | 0.82 | −0.02 | −0.01 |

*Note*: The table shows the percentage change between the counterfactual value of the Gini index if the policy in question had remained as in year $t-1$ relative to its actual value after the implementation of each policy in year $t$. Positive (negative) values indicate that the policy rendered the income distribution less (more) equal, not taking into account second-order effects of the policy in question. — = no policy changes between the two years. N/A = the policy change was not modeled in EUROMOD.

*Source*: EUROMOD version G1.0.

in 2011, and even more so in 2013, and in Romania in 2011 (due to the abolishment of SIC for self-employed workers with annual earnings below 4 average gross wages), as well as in Greece (2010), Spain (2010 and 2012), Italy (2011), and Latvia (2010). On the contrary, the 2013 tax and SIC changes in Greece appeared to have had the opposite effect.

Pension cuts and related policies seem to have had a progressive first-order distributional impact in Portugal, and also to a lesser extent in Greece (in 2010 and 2012). This effect mostly resulted from the actual design of the policies, which partly or fully protected those on low incomes. On the other hand, the across-the-board abolition of the flat-rate holiday allowance that took place in Greece in 2013 appears to have had significantly regressive effects.

Good examples of changes in social benefits having a progressive distributional effect were the improvements in minimum income and unemployment benefits in Latvia (2010), the introduction of a comprehensive child-benefit scheme in Greece (2013), and the increase in the minimum income guaranteed in Romania (2010). By contrast, reductions in the generosity of minimum income in Portugal (in 2011 and 2013) obviously had a regressive impact. The same held for reductions in unemployment insurance benefit and changes in eligibility conditions and means-testing of child allowance in Lithuania (2010) and reductions in unemployment benefit and changes in family allowances and heating benefit in Romania (2011).

## CONCLUSIONS

We set out to estimate the distributional impact of the Great Recession in seven European countries. Our results can be summarized as follows.

On the whole, the Great Recession seems to have changed the composition of the population in poverty.[3] Those at the bottom of the income distribution are younger than before the crisis, and they are more likely to be unemployed (or on low pay) than pensioners. As a result of that, income changes are less pronounced when deciles are fixed as in 2009 than when they are recalculated each year. Indeed, allowing for re-ranking makes it more evident that those in the bottom of the income distribution today are considerably poorer than those occupying the same position before the outbreak of the current crisis.

We have attempted to clarify the various interactions between austerity, recession, and inequality. Specifically, tax–benefit policies act both directly (through their effect on the distribution of incomes as observed before the policies are actually implemented) and indirectly (through their effects on aggregate demand, and hence on jobs and wages). As a result of these interactions, the full effects of tax–benefit policies cannot be reduced to the first-order effects estimated here.

Having said that, isolating the effects on poverty and inequality of tax and benefit policies per se from the total impact of the crisis is of interest, as it may help identify policies that minimize adverse distributional effects while reducing budget deficits. In fact, some of the policies seem to have had a more progressive first-order effect than others. This may be because special care was taken to make a particular policy "fair" by design, as in the case of changes in income tax, cuts in pension benefits that partly or fully exempted those on low incomes, and improvements in means-tested social benefits. Alternatively, the progressive effect may stem from the fact that those adversely affected tended to be located toward the top of the income distribution, as in the case of public-sector pay cuts in Greece and Portugal, which is consistent with findings from Ireland (Callan et al., 2011; Nolan et al., 2013).

While the impact of policies on inequality can be described as moderate (or even equality-enhancing), this is far from saying that fiscal adjustment programs have been a success in overall distributional terms. Our estimates suggest that, in most of the countries examined, poverty increased, and the policies implemented accounted for a major part of that increase. In some cases, the first-order effect of policies raised anchored poverty more than the combined effect of policies and changes in the wider economy did, with the effect of the latter being often poverty-reducing.

A certain amount of caution is called for when interpreting our results. The main issues, related either to our approach or to our assumptions, are briefly discussed below.

First, greater care is warranted when analyzing the distributional impact of government policies vis-à-vis developments in the wider economy. In particular, changes in minimum wage legislation are bundled here together with changes in private-sector earnings attributed to these wider developments, although they are typically the result of government policy. Moreover, no adjustments were made to account for demographic changes between 2009 and 2013 because no major shifts are likely to happen in such a short period. However, where the recent crisis has led to increases in migration flows (such as Latvia and Lithuania), the results will have to be interpreted with extra caution.

Accounting for tax evasion and benefit non-take-up is limited to some of the countries under consideration. Clearly, a more uniform treatment of these issues would enhance the comparability of our findings. Finally, while austerity policies may adversely affect what was once called the "social wage," in-kind benefits are not taken into account.

While we are fully aware of these caveats, we are confident that our research offers a good approximation of the first-order distributional impact of austerity policies and the wider recession in the seven countries considered. Given the topicality of the questions addressed and the public interest in the answers, we believe that work based on microsimulation is much preferable to waiting until future waves of official statistics are released. Furthermore, if the research question involves identifying the effect of different changes taking place at the same time and distinguishing between progressive and regressive items within the same policy package, there is no alternative to microsimulation.

In this chapter we note that the static effects of fiscal consolidation policies may be at odds with their dynamic effects. Clearly, however, we still know too little to quantify the size and direction of the second-order effects of austerity on inequality via growth. More research into that interaction would enable us to identify policies that promote both growth and equality, even when the room for fiscal policy remains limited.

## NOTES

We thank Andrea Brandolini, Francesco Figari, Tim Goedemé, Isabelle Maquet, Alari Paulus, and Holly Sutherland for insightful discussions of earlier versions of the chapter. We are also grateful for valuable comments from Bea Cantillon, John Hills, Gilles Mourre, Karel Van den Bosch, and other participants at a meeting in Brussels (November 2013) and a conference in Antwerp (April 2014), where previous versions were presented. Moreover, we are indebted to Jekaterina Navicke and Olga Rastrigina, without whom our labor-market adjustments would not have been possible. Finally, we thank Eurostat for access to microdata from EU Statistics on Incomes and Living Conditions (EU-SILC), made available under contracts EU-SILC/2011/55 and EU-SILC/2011/32, as well as ISTAT for the Italian version of the EU-SILC (IT-SILC), the Lithuanian Department of Statistics for the national version of the EU-SILC (PGS), and ElStat for access to the Greek SILC Production Database (PDB). Our research is financially supported by the European Union 7th Framework Programme (FP7/ 2012–2016) under Grant Agreement N. 290613 (ImPRovE project). The views expressed in this paper are those of the authors. The usual disclaimer applies.

1 Note that the re-ranking captured in this work is due to (a) simulated policy changes, (b) income updating from EU-SILC 2010 income reference period (i.e., 2009) to the target year (i.e., 2013), and (c) modeled changes in individuals' labor-market status.

2 For a detailed description of policy changes between 2009 and 2013, see Matsaganis and Leventi (2014).

3 Note that the aspects of the Great Recession that have been taken into account in this study are changes in (a) taxes and benefits, (b) market incomes, and (c) people's employment status. For more information, see the section "Model and Data."

## REFERENCES

Agnello, L., & Souza, R. (2012). Fiscal adjustments and income inequality: A first assessment. *Applied Economics Letters, 19*(16), 1627–1632.

Ahren, R., Arnold, J., & Moeser, C. (2011). *The sharing of macroeconomic risk: Who loses (and gains) from macroeconomic shocks?* [OECD Economics Department Working Paper 877]. Paris, France: Organisation for Economic Co-operation and Development.

Alcidi, C., & Gros, D. (2012). *Why is the Greek economy collapsing? A simple tale of high multipliers and low exports* [CEPS Commentary (December 21, 2012)]. Brussels, Belgium: Centre for European Policy Studies.

Alesina, A., & Ardagna, S. (2012). *The design of fiscal adjustments* [NBER Working Paper 18423]. Cambridge, Massachusetts: The National Bureau of Economic Research.

Alesina, A., Favero, C., & Giavazzi, F. (2012). *The output effects of fiscal consolidations* [NBER Working Paper 18336]. Cambridge, Massachusetts: The National Bureau of Economic Research.

Atkinson, A. B. (2009). Stress-testing the welfare state. In B. Ofstad, O. Bjerkholt, K. Skrede, & A. Hylland (Eds.), *Rettferd og politikk: Festskrift til Hilde Bojer på 70- årsdagen (Justice and politics: Festschrift for Hilde Bojer on her 70th birthday)*. Oslo, Norway: Emiliar Forlag.

Auerbach, A., & Gorodnichenko, Y. (2012). Measuring the output responses to fiscal policy. *American Economic Journal—Economic Policy, 4*, 1–27.

Avram, S., Figari, F., Leventi, C., Levy, H., Navicke, E., Matsaganis, M., . . . Sutherland, H. (2013). *The distributional effects of austerity measures: A comparison of nine EU countries* [EUROMOD Working Paper EM2/13]. Colchester, England: ISER, University of Essex.

Ball, L., Furceri, D., Leigh, D., & Loungani, P. (2013). *The distributional effects of fiscal austerity* [IMF Working Paper 13/151]. Washington, DC: International Monetary Fund.

Ball, L., Leigh, D., & Loungani, P. (2011). Painful medicine. *Finance and Development, 48*(3), 20–23.

Bargain, O., & Callan T. (2010). Analysing the effects of tax-benefit reforms on income distribution: A decomposition approach. *Journal of Economic Inequality, 8*(1), 1–21.

Bargain, O., Callan, T., Doorley, K., & Keane, C. (2013). *Changes in income distributions and the role of tax-benefit policy during the great recession: An international perspective* [IZA Discussion Paper 7737]. Bonn, Germany: IZA Institute of Labor Economics.

Brandolini, A., D'Amuri, F., & Faiella, I. (2013). Country case study—Italy. In S. P. Jenkins, A. Brandolini, J. Micklewright, & B. Nolan (Eds.), *The Great Recession and the distribution of household income*. Oxford, England: Oxford University Press.

Brewer, M., Browne, J., & Joyce, R. (2011). *Child and working-age poverty from 2010 to 2020* [IFS Commentary C121]. London, England: Institute for Fiscal Studies.

Brewer, M., Browne, J., Hood, A., Joyce, R., & Sibieta, L. (2013). The short- and medium-term impacts of the recession on the UK income distribution. *Fiscal Studies, 34*(2), 179–201.

Browne, J., & Levell, P. (2010). *The distributional effect of tax and benefit reforms to be introduced between June 2010 and April 2014: A revised assessment* [IFS Briefing Note 108]. London, England: Institute for Fiscal Studies.

Callan, T., Nolan, B., & Walsh, J. (2011). The economic crisis, public sector pay, and the income distribution. In H. Immervoll, A. Peichl, & K. Tatsiramos (Eds.), *Who loses in the downturn? Economic crisis, employment and income distribution. Research in Labor Economics*, (32), 207–225.

Corsetti, G., Meier, A., & Müller, G. (2012). What determines government spending multipliers? *Economic Policy, 27*(72), 521–556.

European Commission. (2012). *European economic forecast, Autumn 2012* [European Economy 8/2012]. Luxembourg: Publications Office of the European Union.

European Commission. (2013). *EU employment and social situation quarterly review (March 2013)*. Luxembourg: Publications Office of the European Union.

European Central Bank. (2012). *Monthly bulletin, December 2012*. Frankfurt, Germany: European Central Bank.

Eurostat. (2014). Online statistics database (accessed March 2014). Luxembourg: Eurostat.

Eyraud, L., & Weber, A. (2013). The challenge of debt reduction during fiscal consolidation [IMF Working Paper 13/67]. Washington, DC: International Monetary Fund.

Favero, C., Giavazzi, F., & Perego, J. (2011). Country heterogeneity and the international evidence on the effects of fiscal policy. *IMF Economic Review, 59*(4), 652–682.

Goujard, A. (2013). Cross-country spill-overs from fiscal consolidation [OECD Economics Department Working Paper 1099]. Paris, France: Organisation for Economic Co-operation and Development.

Hills, J., Paulus, A., Sutherland, H., & Tasseva, I. (2014). A lost decade? Decomposing the effect of 2001–11 tax-benefit policy changes on the income distribution in EU countries [ImPRovE Discussion Paper No. 14/03]. Antwerp, Belgium: Herman Deleeck Centre for Social Policy, University of Antwerp.

International Monetary Fund. (2012). *World economic outlook: Coping with high debt and sluggish growth*. Washington, DC: International Monetary Fund.

International Monetary Fund. (2014). *Fiscal policy and income inequality*. Washington, DC: International Monetary Fund.

Jenkins, S. P., Brandolini, A., Micklewright, J., & Nolan, B. (2013). *The Great Recession and the distribution of household income*. Oxford, England: Oxford University Press.

Jordà, Ò., & Taylor, A. M. (2013). *The time for austerity: Estimating the average treatment effect of fiscal policy*. Paper presented at the NBER Summer Institute. Cambridge, Massachusetts: The National Bureau of Economic Research.

Joyce, R., & Sibieta, L. (2013). Country case study—UK. In S.P. Jenkins, A. Brandolini, J. Micklewright, & B. Nolan (Eds.), *The Great Recession and the distribution of household income*. Oxford, England: Oxford University Press.

Kaplanoglou, G., Rapanos, V. T., & Bardakas, I. C. (2013). *Does fairness matter for the success of fiscal consolidation?* [Economics Discussion Report 2013/6]. Athens, Greece: Department of Economics, University of Athens.

Koutsampelas, C., & Policarpou, A. (2013). *Austerity and the income distribution: The case of Cyprus* [EUROMOD Working Paper EM4/13]. Colchester, England: ISER, University of Essex.

Leventi, C., & Matsaganis, M. (2013). *Distributional implications of the crisis in Greece in 2009–2012* [EUROMOD Working Paper EM14/13]. Colchester, England: ISER, University of Essex.

Leventi, C., Navicke, J., Rastrigina, O., Sutherland, H., Ozdemir, E., & Ward, T. (2013). *Now casting: Estimating developments in the risk of poverty and income distribution in 2012 and 2013* [Social Situation Monitor Research Note 1/2013]. Brussels, Belgium: Directorate-General for Employment, Social Affairs and Inclusion, European Commission.

Matsaganis, M., & Leventi, C. (2014). Distributive effects of the crisis and austerity in seven EU countries [ImPRovE Discussion Paper No. 14/04]. Antwerp, Belgium: Herman Deleeck Centre for Social Policy, University of Antwerp.

Nolan, B. (2009). *Background note for roundtable discussion on monitoring the effects of the financial crisis on vulnerable groups.* Paris, France: Organisation for Economic Co-operation and Development.

Nolan, B., Callan, T., & Maître, B. (2013). Country case study—Ireland. In S. P. Jenkins, A. Brandolini, J. Micklewright, & B. Nolan (Eds.), *The Great Recession and the distribution of household income.* Oxford, England: Oxford University Press.

Organisation for Economic Co-operation and Development (OECD). (2013). *How much scope for growth and equity-friendly fiscal consolidation?* [OECD Economics Department Policy Notes 20]. Paris, France: Organisation for Economic Co-operation and Development.

Organisation for Economic Co-operation and Development (OECD). (2014a). *OECD forecasts during and after the financial crisis: A post mortem* [OECD Economics Department Policy Notes 23]. Paris, France: Organisation for Economic Co-operation and Development.

Organisation for Economic Co-operation and Development (OECD). (2014b). *Society at a glance 2014: The crisis and its aftermath.* Paris, France: Organisation for Economic Co-operation and Development.

Romer, C. D., & Romer, D. H. (2010). The macroeconomic effects of tax changes: Estimates based on a new measure of fiscal shocks. *American Economic Review, 100*(3), 763–801.

Sutherland, H., & Figari, F. (2013). EUROMOD: The European Union tax-benefit microsimulation model. *International Journal of Microsimulation, 6*(1), 4–26.

Woo, J., Bova, E., Kinda, T., & Zhang, Y. S. (2013). *Distributional consequences of fiscal consolidation and the role of fiscal policy: What do the data say?* [IMF Working Paper 13/195]. Washington, DC: International Monetary Fund.

# 7

# DO EMPLOYMENT-CONDITIONAL EARNINGS SUBSIDIES WORK?

## Lane Kenworthy

**C**ash transfers and tax credits to people in paid work but with low earnings are increasingly prominent in affluent countries. The United States and the United Kingdom began using employment-conditional earnings subsidies in the 1970s, and in recent decades most of the other rich longstanding democratic countries have adopted some version of them, including Australia, Austria, Belgium, Canada, Denmark, Finland, France, Germany, Ireland, Japan, Korea, the Netherlands, New Zealand, Portugal, and Sweden.

These programs aim to reduce poverty and to increase employment. How effective are they?

## EMPLOYMENT-CONDITIONAL EARNINGS SUBSIDIES

While all employment-conditional earnings subsidies have in common that eligibility is contingent on paid work, they can vary along a number of dimensions (Immervoll & Pearson, 2009; Organisation for Economic Co-operation and Development (OECD), 2009, 2010).

- Is the subsidy limited (targeted) to those with low earnings or income? Or is it available to everyone in employment (universal)?
- Is the benefit amount determined by individual earnings or by household earnings?

154

- Is eligibility for the subsidy conditional on a minimum number of hours of employment (such as 15 per week)? Or is any paid work sufficient?
- Is eligibility conditional on the presence of children?
- Is eligibility conditional on employment in a particular industry or sector, such as household services?
- Is the subsidy paid in cash, as a tax reduction, as a tax credit, or in kind (access to services or housing)? And if the subsidy is a tax credit, is it refundable? That is, if the individual or household owes less tax than the amount of the subsidy, do they receive the difference in cash?
- Is there a "phase-in" range where the amount of the subsidy increases as earnings rise?
- Is there a "phase-out" range where the amount of the subsidy decreases as earnings rise?
- Is the subsidy "permanent" with no limit on the length of eligibility? Or is it temporary—e.g., limited to a year or two after transition from social assistance or unemployment benefit into employment?
- Is the subsidy paid on a regular basis (biweekly, monthly) or as a once-a-year lump sum?

There are many possible combinations of these features. The focus here is on what might be called the "Anglo" version: a refundable tax credit or cash transfer with phase-in and phase-out ranges. Ireland, New Zealand, the United Kingdom, and the United States have a relatively large subsidy of this type, and Canada has a moderately generous one.

In most other nations that have an employment-conditional earnings subsidy, the subsidy is smaller. It takes the form of a tax reduction or tax credit, in some cases temporary, in some cases limited to particular sectors of the economy, and in some instances tied to other benefits, such as unemployment compensation or social assistance. A common strategy for such subsidies has been to reduce employee social contributions (payroll tax payments) for employees in low-wage jobs. For example, in the early 2000s Belgium put in place a reduction in social security contributions for low-wage workers and then added a refundable tax credit (Marx, Vanhille, & Verbist, 2012). Germany has gone farthest in this direction, introducing a large reduction in employee tax payments in the 1990s and 2000s while simultaneously creating a new category of workers who can be paid lower wages. A notable exception to this pattern is Sweden, which in 2007 introduced a large tax credit with no phase-out. Sweden's credit costs approximately 2.4% of GDP, compared to 1.0% for the U.K. Working Tax Credit and 0.3% for the U.S. Earned Income Tax Credit (EITC).

## THE ANGLO VERSION: LARGE REFUNDABLE TAX CREDIT OR CASH TRANSFER WITH PHASE-IN AND PHASE-OUT RANGES

In the rich English-speaking countries, unions and collective bargaining are comparatively weak, so individuals and households at the low end are more vulnerable to economic pressures than in many other affluent nations. Each of these nations has a statutory minimum wage, and each also has a subsidy that boosts the income of low-earning households. Ireland and New Zealand have relatively generous subsidies, Canada introduced a moderately generous one in 2007, and Australia has a small one. The best known and most extensively studied are the U.S. EITC and the U.K. Working Tax Credit (now Universal Credit), and they are the main focus here.

The U.S. EITC was created in 1975. The EITC subsidizes earnings by as much as 45%. It is paid to households rather than to individuals. As of 2014, households with at least one employed adult and earnings below $55,000 are eligible. The credit is refundable; if it amounts to more than the household owes in federal income taxes, the household receives the difference as a cash refund. It therefore functions like a cash benefit.

The amount of the subsidy increases with earnings up to a certain level, then plateaus, and then decreases with earnings. Figure 7.1 shows the benefit level for households with varying marital status and number of children.

An important feature of the EITC, clearly visible in Figure 7.1, is that the benefit amount is very small for a household with no children. A household with one child can receive more than $3,000, but the maximum for a childless household is just $500. Childless households account for 25% of EITC recipients, but they

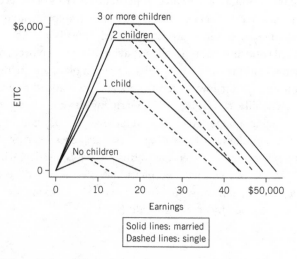

**Figure 7.1.** U.S. Earned Income Tax Credit benefit structure. *Note:* The benefit levels shown are for 2014. *Source:* Tax Policy Center, "Earned Income Tax Credit Parameters."

receive only 5% of total EITC payments. The credit thus creates little employment incentive for childless adults, and it provides very little income support if they are employed.

Another key feature is that most recipients receive the credit in a single lump-sum once a year (in April, when income tax reports are filed in the United States). This may affect its attractiveness to recipients, the degree to which it incentivizes employment, and the ways recipients spend the benefit money (Barrow & McGranahan, 2002; Smeeding, Phillips, & O'Connor, 2002; Sykes, Križ, Edin, & Halpern-Meekin, 2014).

The average amount recipient households get is $2,300 per year. As Figure 7.2 shows, this amount increased sharply between 1987 and 1996 (Nichols & Rothstein, 2015). Since then it has been flat.

Nearly one in four Americans receives the EITC. This share rose sharply between the late 1980s and the mid-1990s and again in the 2000s, as Figure 7.3 indicates. The increases were a result of changes in eligibility criteria, increases in the benefit amount, and stagnant wage levels for Americans on the lower rungs of the wage ladder.

About half of the U.S. states and a few cities have their own EITC (Center on Budget and Policy Priorities, 2014b). Many of the state and local EITCs are quite small, but some supplement the national EITC by as much as 40%.

The United Kingdom was the first country to have an employment-conditional earnings subsidy (Blundell, Duncan, McCrae, & Meghir, 2000; Brewer, 2001; Dilnot & McCrae, 2000). The Family Income Supplement, created in 1971, provided a means-tested benefit to adults with a dependent child when the adult

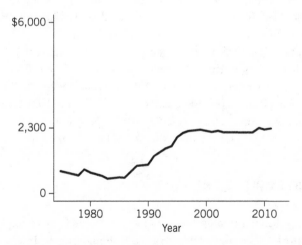

**Figure 7.2.** U.S. Earned Income Tax Credit (EITC) benefit amount. *Note:* Average EITC per recipient family, in 2011 dollars. Inflation adjustment is via the CPI-U-RS. The top value on the vertical axis, $6,000, is the maximum value of the credit. *Source:* Tax Policy Center, "Historical EITC Recipients," using Internal Revenue Service data.

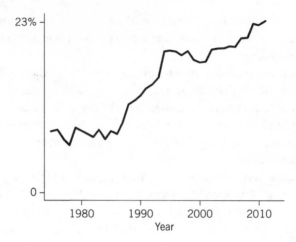

**Figure 7.3.** U.S. Earned Income Tax Credit (EITC) recipients as a share of the U.S. population. *Note:* These numbers are estimates, calculated using the number of EITC recipient households, the average number of persons per U.S. household, and the U.S. population. *Source:* Tax Policy Center; U.S. Census Bureau.

worked 24 hours or more per week. In 1988, the program name was changed to Family Credit. In the early 1990s, the hours requirement was reduced to 16 per week and a child-care disregard was added.

In 1999, the Labor government replaced the Family Credit with the Working Families Tax Credit, substantially expanding eligibility and increasing the benefit amount. These changes had large effects on program use and generosity. Within four years, the average benefit level increased by nearly half and the number of recipients doubled. In 2003, the credit was extended to childless households and the program name was changed to Working Tax Credit.

In 2012, the U.K. government began a process of merging the Working Tax Credit and five other government benefits into a single Universal Credit (Elming et al., 2015; Finch, Corlett, & Alakeson, 2014; Pareliussen, 2013). The new credit simplifies the application process, creates a single rate of reduction in benefits as earnings increase, and enables benefit access for people working fewer than 16 hours per week. There also is a reduction in the benefit amount.

## EFFECT ON EMPLOYMENT

An earnings subsidy increases the financial incentive in favor of employment for persons at the low end of the labor market. It should thereby increase the share of people who are employed and the number of hours worked by those in employment. This is particularly true for those in the phase-in and flat ranges of the subsidy (see Figure 7.1).

For people in the phase-out range, the employment incentive is weaker. In the United States, imagine a person with one child who is employed at a wage of $15 per hour. If the person works full-time year-round, her earnings would be approximately $30,000 ($15 per hour multiplied by 2,000 hours). Such a person is in the phase-out range of the EITC; her credit will decrease as her earnings increase (Figure 7.1). If she reduces her work hours, she will receive a larger EITC payment, which will offset some of the lost earnings, and this will give her more time to spend with her child. For some people, this will make it attractive to work fewer hours. For similar reasons, in a low-earning household with two employed adults, the phase-out of the earnings subsidy may induce the second earner to cut back on work hours or leave employment altogether.

## Within-Country Evidence

Most studies of the U.S. EITC conclude that it increases employment (Blank, Card, & Robbins, 2000; Chetty, Friedman & Saez, 2013; Chyi, 2012; Eissa & Hoynes, 2006; Hoffman & Seidman, 2003; Hotz & Scholz, 2003; Leigh, 2010; Meyer, 2010; Meyer & Rosenbaum, 2002). These studies typically use sophisticated econometric analysis, but a simple way to see the EITC's impact is to compare the employment trend for single women with low education and one or more children—a group for whom the EITC is likely to exert considerable pull—to the employment trend for other comparable women. Figure 7.4 does this. The two comparison groups are single women with the same education and no children and single women with children and a little more education. During the economic downturns in the early 1990s and early 2000s and in the rest of the

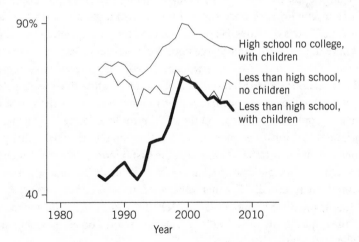

**Figure 7.4.** Employment rate: U.S. nonmarried women. *Note*: The vertical axis does not begin at zero. *Source*: Meyer, B. D. (2010). The effects of the Earned Income Tax Credit and recent reforms. In J. D. Brown (Ed.), *Tax policy and the economy*, Table 6, using Current Population Survey data. National Bureau of Economic Research.

2000s, the employment rates for all three groups moved in the same direction and at a similar pace, which suggests that these comparison groups are useful.

Figures 7.2 and 7.3 show that the chief expansions of EITC eligibility and benefit amount occurred between 1987 and 1996, so we would expect the biggest effect on employment during this period. Consistent with this expectation, Figure 7.4 shows that the employment rate among nonmarried U.S. women with children and less than a high school education increased sharply in the late 1980s, whereas that wasn't true for similarly educated women without children or for women with children and a bit more education.

From 1993 to 2000, the employment rate for all three groups increased, but the pace of increase was by far the greatest for women with children and less than a high school education. This, too, is consistent with the expectation. Note also that the pace of increase for this group was just as rapid from 1993 to 1996 as from 1997 to 2000, which suggests that it wasn't solely the 1996 welfare reform that was driving the increase in the latter years.

Studies of the U.K. Working Families Tax Credit and Working Tax Credit have tended to yield a similar conclusion of positive employment effects (Blundell, Brewer, Haan, & Shephard, 2009; Blundell & Shepard, 2011; Blundell et al., 2000; Brewer, 2001, 2009; Brewer, Duncan, Shephard, & Suarez, 2006; Francesconi & van der Klaauw, 2007; Gregg, Harkness, & Smith, 2009; Gregg, Hurrell, & Whittaker, 2012).[1]

Studies based on interviews and other qualitative research strategies tend to support the finding from quantitative analyses that employment-conditional earnings subsidies boost employment (Millar, 2008; Sykes et al., 2014).

If employment-conditional earnings subsidies do increase employment, is it by encouraging people to enter employment, or do they primarily encourage people to remain in employment once there? Mead (2014) argued that, in the case of America's EITC, it is the latter. He noted that until recently, quantitative empirical studies have not tended to find a large impact of financial incentives on the quantity of employment of low-income women. In addition, the fact that the EITC is paid out in a once-a-year lump sum might limit its attractiveness to potential jobseekers, since the payout occurs months in the future rather than right away. Also, many people don't know about the EITC prior to entering employment.

Thus, the EITC makes employment attractive enough financially that people with jobs stay in them rather than quit at the first opportunity (see also Dickens & McKnight, 2008), but it doesn't increase the likelihood that a person will enter employment initially. For that, other incentives or constraints are needed. Mead (2014, pp. 30–31) quoted Jason DeParle, a journalist who looked carefully at the impact of the mid-1990s U.S. welfare reform on employment among low-skilled women:

I haven't heard people on welfare say the credit pushed them to go to work. My sense is that the hassle factor of welfare is much more powerful in pushing them off the rolls (and consequently into jobs) than the vaguer promise of later wage subsidies.

On the other hand, that's not to say that they don't think about the EITC. They are hugely aware of it, especially after they start working. It's a big part of their survival strategy. It no doubt reinforces the desirability of work (or, phrased the opposite way—it plays a huge role in blunting the harshness of the low-wage economy). In enabling people to buy cars, keep up with the rent, etc., it may even make work possible. Without it, many fewer people might be willing to stay in the workforce.

So that's why I say I accept the point that it raises work rates. . . . My impression is that it's not the thing that initially gets welfare recipients working. The first is the hassle of the welfare system. My sense is the EITC then plays an important secondary role, in stabilizing them economically and rewarding them psychologically.

If this is correct, the impact of an employment-conditional earnings subsidy on employment will be strongest when it is combined with other activation efforts that push or pull people into paid work.

## Cross-Country Evidence

Can we see an employment-boosting effect of employment-conditional earnings subsidies if we compare across countries? If the subsidies have a large impact, the United Kingdom and the United States should have a high employment rate compared to other rich nations, and they should compare favorably when we look at change in the employment rate over time.

Figure 7.5 shows employment rates in 21 rich countries since the 1970s. The employment rates for the United Kingdom and the United States are shown with thick lines, those for 18 other countries with thin lines, and the rate for Canada with a dashed line. There is little support in this picture for a conclusion that employment-conditional earnings subsidies significantly boost employment. The United Kingdom began the period in the middle of the pack. Its employment rate increased steadily, but not much faster than that of a number of other countries that don't have a large earnings subsidy. The United States also began in the middle of the pack. In the 1980s it jumped up, with rapid employment growth, but in the 1990s the pace of increase slowed, and in the 2000–2007 business cycle there was no increase. By 2007, the peak business cycle year prior to the 2008 economic crash, a number of other nations had caught up to the United States.

These countries differ in lots of ways that might affect employment (Kenworthy, 2008). Canada is probably the closest comparison case to the United Kingdom and the United States—the most similar in labor-market regulation, union strength, taxation, and social policy. Canada's employment rate is the bold, dashed line in Figure 7.5. Canada didn't have an employment-conditional earnings subsidy prior to 2007, yet its employment performance was quite similar to

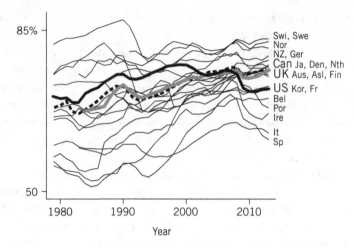

**Figure 7.5.** Employed persons aged 25 to 64 as a share of the population age 25 to 64.
*Notes:* The vertical axis does not begin at zero. Swi is Switzerland; Swe is Sweden; Nor is Norway; NZ is New Zealand; Ger is Germany; Can is Canada; Ja is Japan; Den is Denmark; Nth is Netherlands; UK is United Kingdom; Aus is Austria; Asl is Australia; Fin is Finland; US is United States; Kor is South Korea; Fr is France; Bel is Belgium; Por is Portugal; Ire is Ireland; It is Italy; Sp is Spain. *Source:* OECD, stats.oecd.org.

that of the United Kingdom and the United States. This, too, doesn't support the notion that earnings subsidies have a large impact on employment.

Perhaps an impact will be seen if we narrow the lens a bit. One group that an employment-conditional earnings subsidy should be especially likely to attract into employment is those who have little education and are in prime parenting years. Their lack of education means their labor-market prospects are limited, and as parents they typically qualify for the largest subsidy amount. Figure 7.6 shows employment rates among persons age 35 to 44 who have less than a secondary education. These data are available only beginning in 2000. Here, too, we see don't see an indication that U.K.- and U.S.-type employment-conditional earnings subsidies have a large employment-boosting effect. The United Kingdom's employment rate begins in the middle of the pack, and it subsequently moves toward the bottom. The United States starts low and doesn't improve its position. Canada is similar.

Another potentially informative indicator is the share of working-age households without an employed adult.[2] The United Kingdom's employment-conditional earnings subsidy was significantly increased in 1999 and 2003, and Gregg and colleagues (2012) showed that, over the ensuing decade, the share of workless households fell more rapidly in the United Kingdom than in France, Ireland, Italy, the Netherlands, or Spain. But this is a small set of comparison countries. The OECD has compiled data on workless households for a larger set of nations, although only beginning in 2007. Figure 7.7 shows that, on this

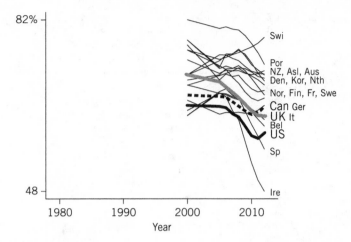

**Figure 7.6.** Employment rate among persons age 35 to 44 with less than secondary education. *Note*: The vertical axis does not begin at zero. Asl is Australia; Aus is Austria. *Source*: OECD, *Education at a Glance*, 2014, table A5.3a.

indicator, the United States and the United Kingdom perform decently, but their record isn't outstanding.

Overall, the evidence suggests that an employment-conditional earnings subsidy tends to boost employment in U.S.- and U.K.-type economies, but the labor-market institutions of those two countries, including their earnings subsidies (and low wages and limited regulations), don't appear to yield superior employment performance compared to the institutions of many other rich nations.

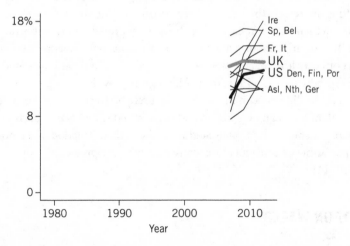

**Figure 7.7.** Workless households, as a share of adults in households with no employed adult. *Note*: Adults are the population age 15 to 74. Households composed solely of students or nonemployed people age 65 and over are excluded. *Source*: OECD, *Society at a Glance*, 2014, Figure 1.5, using data from the European Labour Force Survey and the U.S. Current Population Survey.

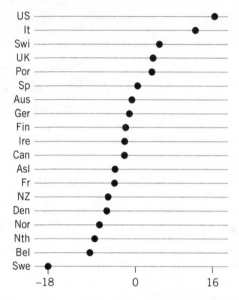

**Figure 7.8.** Employment rate: difference between low-education immigrants and low-education native-born among persons age 15 to 64, 2009–2010. *Note*: Low education refers to less than upper secondary completion. *Source*: OECD, *Settling In: OECD Indicators of Immigrant Integration*, 2012, Figure 6.2.

A U.K.- or U.S.-style labor market may, however, be better at incorporating low-skilled immigrants. Such immigrants face not only skill deficits but also, in many cases, language barriers and employer worries about their likelihood of quitting to return to their country of origin. Countries with a low wage floor supplemented by an earnings subsidy may provide more opportunity for less-skilled immigrants to get a foothold in the formal labor market, because with labor costs lowered, employers don't need to be quite as concerned about workers' productivity and turnover. Although it provides only a crude test, we can look at the difference in the employment rate between foreign-born persons with less than secondary education and similarly educated native-born persons. As Figure 7.8 shows, the United States and the United Kingdom are among the better performers on this measure, consistent with the prediction (for more, see OECD, 2014).

## EFFECT ON WAGES

An employment-conditional earnings subsidy might cause wage levels to fall. In the presence of the subsidy, employers may offer a lower wage than they other-wise would, and workers may be willing to accept a lower wage. Also, the sub-sidy may increase the supply of less-educated people seeking jobs, and without an increase in employer demand for such workers, this rise in supply is likely to push wages down.

What do we know about the impact of employment-conditional earnings subsidies on low-end wages? Because we lack cross-nationally comparable data on low-end wage levels, evidence here is confined to within-country studies.

Rothstein (2011) simulated a variety of potential effects of the U.S. EITC on the wages of persons with low skills. He concluded that, under assumptions consistent with existing estimates of labor supply and wage responses to tax changes, part of the EITC benefit goes to workers, and part goes to employers in the form of reduced wage payments.

Leigh (2010) used variation in state EITCs across the United States to estimate the impact on wages. He also examined variation in the national EITC across gender-age-education groups. He, too, concluded that the EITC tends to reduce wages. Households with children receive a net income boost, according to Leigh's estimates, because the value of the credit they receive more than offsets the decrease in earnings due to lower wages (see also Neumark & Wascher, 2001). But households without children are likely to suffer a drop in income, since for them the EITC benefit is too small (see Figure 7.1) to offset the reduction in wages.

Azmat (2006) examined the impact of the 1999 increase in the U.K.'s Working Families Tax Credit and concluded that about 20% went to employers via reduced wages. Gregg and Harkness (2003) also found a reduction in wages, although only for nonrecipients of the credit.

Is the over-time trend in low-end wages in the United States consistent with the notion that the EITC has a small negative effect on wage levels? Figure 7.9 shows inflation-adjusted hourly wages at the tenth percentile of the wage ladder since the late 1970s. The EITC was significantly expanded in generosity and

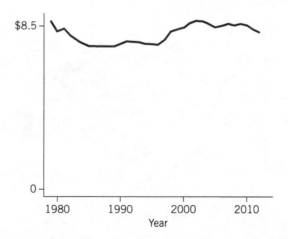

**Figure 7.9.** U.S. tenth-percentile wage (hourly wage), in 2012 dollars. *Note:* Inflation adjustment is via the CPI-U-RS. *Source:* Economic Policy Institute, stateofworkingamerica.org/data.

coverage between 1987 and 1996 (see Figure 7.2 and Figure 7.3), and the tenth-percentile wage level was flat during those years. This seems supportive of the wage-reduction hypothesis.

Then again, U.S. wages at the tenth percentile were flat or declining during most of the period since the late 1970s, not just when the EITC was expanding. Moreover, there are many causes of U.S. wage stagnation other than the EITC. One contributor is the flat statutory minimum wage (see below), but there is much more, including the shift of employment from manufacturing to services, increased product market competition, firms' heightened options for replacing workers (with machines or low-cost laborers abroad), shareholder pressure for constant cost-cutting, weakened labor unions, and a rise in low-skill immigration (Kenworthy, 2014).

Overall, the evidence suggests that a U.S.- or U.K.-style employment-conditional earnings subsidy may reduce wages somewhat, but more research is needed on this question.

A high wage floor reduces the likelihood that a U.S.- or U.K.-style employment-conditional earnings subsidy will cause low-end wages to fall. Figure 7.10 shows trends in the statutory minimum wage in the affluent nations that have one. The comparatively low minimum wage in the United States and its lack of increase over time may help explain why the U.S. EITC has reduced low-end wages according to the studies noted above.

For a U.S.- or U.K.-style employment-conditional earnings subsidy, there is another reason why a moderately high wage floor probably is preferable to a low floor. If the minimum wage is low, the amount of the subsidy will need to be large in order to accomplish the desired poverty reduction. Suppose policymakers want to keep the subsidy confined to households with low earnings. The phase-out rate—the slope of the lines on the right side in Figure 7.1 (above)—will

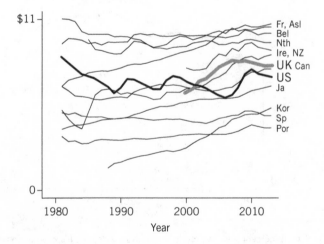

**Figure 7.10.** Statutory hourly minimum wage (U.S. PPPs) *Source*: OECD, stats.oecd.org.

then become quite steep, which will create a strong incentive for households in the phase-out range to reduce employment hours. If policymakers instead are willing to extend eligibility for the subsidy further up the income ladder, this problem can be avoided, but then the budgetary cost of the subsidy will rise, perhaps dramatically.

An additional consideration is that the wage floor acts as a ceiling on the level of government benefits likely to be made available to those who are working-age but not employed (Cantillon, Collado, & Van Mechelen, 2015). This, too, suggests that a high wage floor is an important complement to an employment-conditional earnings subsidy.

## EFFECT ON HOUSEHOLD INCOMES

Employment-conditional earnings subsidies can affect the incomes of low-end households in four ways. First, there is the direct impact of the subsidy. The U.S. EITC adds an average of $2,300 to the pretransfer-pretax incomes of recipient households (Figure 7.2 above). In doing so, it raises the incomes of 1% to 3% of the population from below the U.S. government's poverty line to above the line (Center on Budget and Policy Priorities, 2014a; Meyer, 2010; Scott & Crandall-Hollick, 2014). A similar story holds for the United Kingdom (Brewer, Browne, Joyce, & Sibieta, 2010; Hills, 2013).

Because it is targeted to low-earning households rather than to low-earning individuals, a U.S.- or U.K.-style earnings subsidy is more efficient at boosting household incomes than an increase in the minimum wage (Hotz & Scholz, 2003; Marx, Vanhille, & Verbist, 2012; Neumark & Wascher, 2001). This may or may not be true of an earnings subsidy that goes to individuals rather than to households, such as those in Germany, Belgium, and Sweden.

Second, if the subsidy increases employment in low-end households, as the bulk of research reviewed above suggests it does, it will increase market (pretransfer-pretax) incomes. The poverty-reducing effect of higher employment can vary, however, depending on the magnitude of the increase and depending on whether employment also is increasing around the median (Cantillon & Vandenbroucke, 2013; Kenworthy, 2011a; Marx, Vandenbroucke, & Verbist, 2012).

Third, an employment-conditional earnings subsidy may reduce wage levels. In this scenario, much of the subsidy ends up in the pockets of employers rather than workers. Any reduction in poverty is largely illusory, because in the absence of the subsidy, wages would be higher and fewer households would have market incomes below the poverty line. As noted above, the limited research on this question suggests that a U.S.- or U.K.-style subsidy may indeed result in lower wage levels but that overall it does boost the incomes of low-end households.

Fourth, an employment-conditional earnings subsidy may allow for larger out-of-work benefits in a country with a low wage floor. As noted above, the wage floor acts as a benefit ceiling, as policymakers won't want benefits to the unemployed to exceed earnings for those employed full-time year-round. If low earnings are boosted by a subsidy, the benefit level for those out of work can be higher. Given that there will always be a nontrivial fraction of the working-age population who for one reason or another are not employed—illness, disability, family constraints, structural or frictional unemployment, and so on—this is an important consideration for those concerned about the incomes of households at the low end (Cantillon et al., 2015; Kenworthy, 2011a).

Figure 7.11 shows country trends in the inflation-adjusted income of households at the tenth percentile. (In most of the rich countries, net government transfers are larger than earnings in the bottom decile, and then earnings become more and more important as we move above the tenth percentile; see Kenworthy, 2011a, Figure 2.2; Kenworthy, 2011b, Figure 2). Despite America's enormous wealth, the income of tenth-percentile U.S. households is in the middle of the pack. And the income was essentially flat over this period of several decades, so the U.S. position compared to other countries slipped a bit. The United Kingdom began as one of the poorest performers. It did well between the mid-1990s and the mid-2000s but still ended up below the best performers.

As noted above, Canada is probably the best comparator nation for the United States and the United Kingdom, as its labor market regulations and social policies are broadly similar and for most of this period it didn't have an employment-conditional earnings subsidy. The United States and the United Kingdom haven't done better than Canada at achieving high household incomes for those at the

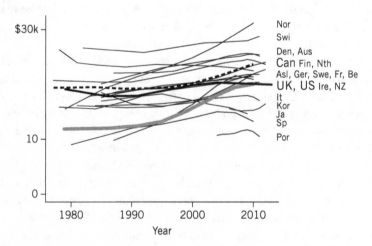

**Figure 7.11.** Tenth-percentile household income. *Notes*: Posttransfer–posttax household income. The incomes are adjusted for household size and then are rescaled to reflect a three-person household, are adjusted for inflation, and are converted to U.S. dollars using purchasing power parities (PPPs). k = thousand. Asl is Australia; Aus is Austria. The lines are LOESS curves. *Source*: Luxembourg Income Study, "LIS Key Figures"; OECD, stats.oecd.org.

low end. And while the United Kingdom was successful at increasing those incomes, the United States was not.

Figure 7.12 shifts from an absolute measure of well-being to a relative one. It shows country trends in the relative poverty rate, with the poverty line set at 60% of each nation's median income. The United States had the highest relative poverty rate at the beginning of the period, and its comparative position didn't improve at all. Canada didn't improve either, but it started and ended lower than the United States. The United Kingdom did poorly until the mid-1990s, with relative poverty increasing to nearly America's level. After the mid-1990s, the United Kingdom achieved a sizable decline in relative poverty. The enhanced Working Tax Credit was part of the reason for this success, but the Labor governments during that period also increased a number of other transfers to low-end households (Sefton, Hills, & Sutherland, 2009; Waldfogel, 2010).

We should perhaps adjust the performance of the United States and the United Kingdom somewhat. The union movement in the United States was comparatively weak throughout this period, and its British counterpart was weakening rapidly. As a result, the new economic pressures on low-end workers and households since the 1970s—competition, globalization, computers, robots, the shift from manufacturing to services, financialization—hit with greater force in these two nations than elsewhere. Even if we were to make some adjustment, however, the United States' and the United Kingdom's record in achieving decent and rising incomes for low-end households would look less than stellar.

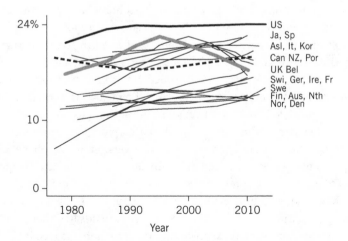

**Figure 7.12.** Relative poverty rate, as share of people in households with an income below 60% of the country median. *Note*: Posttransfer–posttax household income, adjusted for household size. The lines are LOESS curves. Asl is Australia; Aus is Austria. *Source*: Luxembourg Income Study, "LIS Key Figures"; OECD, stats.oecd.org.

## CONCLUSIONS

All of the English-speaking rich nations have a U.S.- or U.K.-style employment-conditional earnings subsidy—a tax credit or cash transfer with a phase-in range and a phase-out range. In Ireland, New Zealand, the United Kingdom, and the United States, the benefit amount is large. In Canada, it is moderate. Only Australia's is small, and that is partly because Australia's minimum wage is by far the highest among these countries.

For this type of economy, in which unions and collective bargaining are comparatively weak and labor-market regulations are limited, the experience of the United States and United Kingdom suggests that an employment-conditional earnings subsidy increases employment among persons at the low end of the labor market. It probably also reduces wage levels, although the evidence on this is thin. Overall, it appears to boost the absolute incomes of low-end households.

On the other hand, the cross-country evidence offers little support for a conclusion that the institutional configuration in these countries—weak unions, limited labor-market regulations, low wage floor, and employment-conditional earnings subsidy—is comparatively effective at generating high and rising employment, high and rising incomes among low-end households, or low and decreasing relative poverty rates. Quite a few other affluent nations have done as well as, or better than, the United States and the United Kingdom over the past generation.

In many other rich countries, unions and collective bargaining are stronger. For such countries, one potential path is Sweden's (Kenworthy, 2015). Sweden has maintained a high wage floor and a compressed wage distribution. It has nonetheless put in place a large employment-conditional tax credit aimed at stimulating employment among the less-educated and supplementing low-end household incomes. Consistent with the bulk of Swedish social programs, the subsidy is universal; there is no phase-out. This makes the program expensive compared to its counterparts in the United States and the United Kingdom, which are targeted to households well below the median income. The Swedish subsidy began in 2007, so we don't yet know much about its impact.

Many other rich nations have introduced employment-conditional earnings subsidies that are smaller than the Anglo version, in size (benefit level), in scope (some are sector-specific), or in duration (some are temporary). There is a good chance some of these subsidies, perhaps most of them, will be expanded. Some countries may do this because the subsidy is an effective policy or because the European Union recommends it. Others may do so in response to an unwanted expansion of low-wage jobs, especially if unions continue to weaken (Cantillon et al., 2015). And others may follow Germany in expanding the subsidy as part of an intentional shift toward the Anglo path (Kenworthy, 2015). A decade ago, Immervoll and Pearson (2009, p. 44) noted that interest in employment-conditional earning subsidies had gone "from polite but slightly suspicious curiosity to urgent consideration." That looks likely to continue.

## NOTES

The author thanks Bea Cantillon and Josefine Vanhille for helpful comments on earlier drafts. The research for this publication has benefited from financial support by the European Union's 7th Framework Programme (FP7/2012-2016) under Grant Agreement N. 290613 (ImPRovE: Poverty Reduction in Europe: Social Policy and Innovation).

1 Sweden's earned income tax credit is much newer, so its effects have been studied less. Karin Edmark and colleagues (2012) found little or no impact on employment rates when comparing across Swedish municipalities, but they concluded that the variation they observed may have been too small to produce noteworthy employment differences. Aaberge and Flood (2013) found a strong positive effect on employment rates and employment hours of single mothers—stronger than for the U.S. EITC. They attributed this, quite plausibly, to the Swedish credit's lack of a phase-out range. Andrén and Andrén (2013) found positive employment effects on single and married women and men.

2 Household joblessness is also affected by household composition. A country with more single-adult households is likely, all else being equal, to have a larger share of jobless households (de Graaf-Zijl & Nolan, 2011).

## REFERENCES

Aaberge, R., & Flood, L. (2013). *U.S. versus Sweden: The effect of alternative in-work tax credit policies on labor supply of single mothers* [Discussion Paper 7706]. Bonn, Germany: Institute of Labor Economics (IZA).

Andrén, D., & Andrén, T. (2013). *Women's and men's responses to in-work benefits: The Influence of younger children* [Working Paper]. Orebro, Sweden: Orebro University School of Business.

Azmat, G. Y. (2006). *The incidence of an earned income tax credit: Evaluating the impact on wages in the UK* [Discussion Paper 724]. London: Centre for Economic Performance, London School of Economics and Political Science.

Barrow, L., & McGranahan, L. (2002). The effects of the Earned Income Tax Credit on the seasonality of household expenditures. In B. D. Meyer & D. Holtz-Eakin (Eds.), *Making work pay: The Earned Income Tax Credit and its impact on America's families* (pp. 329–365). New York, NY: Russell Sage Foundation.

Blank, R. M., Card, D., & Robbins. P. K. (2000). Financial incentives for increasing work and income among low-income families. In R. M. Blank & D. Card (Eds.), *Finding jobs: Work and welfare reform* (pp. 373–419). New York, NY: Russell Sage Foundation.

Blundell, R., Brewer, M., Haan, H., & Shephard, A. (2009). Optimal income taxation of lone mothers: An empirical comparison of the UK and Germany. *Economic Journal, 119*, F101–F121.

Blundell, R., Duncan, A., McCrae, J., & Meghir, C. (2000). The labor market behavior of the Working Families Tax Credit. *Fiscal Studies, 21*, 75–103.

Blundell, R., & Hoynes, H. (2004). Has "in-work" benefit reform helped the labor market? In R. Blundell, D. Card, & R. B. Freeman (Eds.), *Seeking a premier league economy* (pp. 411–460). Chicago, IL: University of Chicago Press.

Blundell, R., & Shephard, A. (2011). Employment, hours of work, and the optimal taxation of low-income families. *Review of Economic Studies, 79*, 481–510.

Brewer, M. (2001). Comparing in-work benefits and the reward to work for low-income families with children in the US and UK. *Fiscal Studies, 22*, 41–77.

Brewer, M. (2009). *How do income-support systems in the UK affect labor force participation?* [Working Paper 2009: 27]. Uppsala, Sweden: IFAU.

Brewer, M., Browne, J., Joyce, R., & Sibieta, L. (2010). *Child poverty in the UK since 1998−99: Lessons from the past decade* [Working Paper 10/23]. London: Institute for Fiscal Studies (IFS).

Brewer, M., Duncan, A., Shephard, A., & Suarez, M. J. (2006). Did Working Families Tax Credit work? The impact of in-work support on parents' labor supply and take-up behavior in Great Britain. *Labor Economics, 13*, 699–720.

Cantillon, B., Collado, D., & Van Mechelen, N. (2015). *The end of decent social protection for the poor? The dynamics of low wages, minimum income packages, and median household incomes* [ImPRovE Working Paper 15-20]. Antwerp, Belgium: Herman Deleeck Centre for Social Policy, University of Antwerp.

Cantillon, B., & Vandenbroucke, F. (2013). *Reconciling work and poverty reduction: How successful are European welfare states?* Oxford, England: Oxford University Press.

Center on Budget and Policy Priorities. (2014a). *New poverty figures show impact of working-family tax credits.* www.cbpp.org.

Center on Budget and Policy Priorities. (2014b). *Policy basics: State earned income tax credits.* www.cbpp.org.

Chetty, R., Friedman, J. N., & Saez, E. (2013). Using differences in knowledge across neighborhoods to uncover the impacts of the EITC on earnings. *American Economic Review, 103*, 2683–2721.

Chyi, H. I. (2012). The 1993 EITC expansion and low-skilled single mothers' welfare use decision. *Applied Economics, 44*, 1717–1736.

De Graaf-Zijl, M., & Nolan, B. (2011). *Household joblessness and its impact on poverty and deprivation in Europe* [GINI Discussion Paper 5].

Dickens, R., & McKnight, A. (2008). *The changing pattern of earnings: Employees, migrants, and low-paid families.* York, England: Rowntree Foundation.

Dilnot, A., & McCrae, J. (2000). The family credit system and the Working Families Tax Credit in the United Kingdom. *OECD Economic Studies, 31,* 2, 69–84.

Edmark, K., Liang, C.-Y., Mörk, E., Selin, H. (2012). *Evaluation of the Swedish earned income tax credit.* Uppsala, Sweden: Institute for Labour Market Policy Evaluation.

Eissa, N., & Hoynes, H. W. (2006). *Behavioral responses to taxes: Lessons from the EITC and labor supply* [NBER Chapters in Tax Policy and the Economy]. Cambridge, MA: National Bureau of Economic Research.

Elming, W., Emmerson, C., Johnson, P., & Phillips, D. (2015). *An assessment of the potential compensation provided by the new "national living wage" for the personal tax and benefit measures announced for implementation in the current parliament.* London, England: Institute for Fiscal Studies.

Finch, D., Corlett, A., & Alakeson, V. (2014). *Universal credit: A policy under review.* London: Resolution Foundation.

Francesconi, M., & van der Klaauw, W. (2007). The socioeconomic consequences of "in-work" benefit reform for British lone mothers. *Journal of Human Resources, 42,* 1–31.

Gregg, P., & Harkness, S. (2003). Welfare reform and lone parents' employment. In R. Dickens, P. Gregg, & J. Wadsworth (Eds.), *The labor market under Labor: The state of working Britain 2003.* Basignstoke, England: Palgrave Macmillan.

Gregg, P., Harkness, S., & Smith, S. (2009). Welfare reform and lone parents in the UK. *Economic Journal, 119,* F38–F65.

Gregg, P., Hurrell, A., & Whittaker, M. (2012). *Creditworthy: Assessing the impact of tax credits in the last decade and considering what this means for universal credit.* London: Resolution Foundation.

Hills, J. (2013). *Labor's record on cash transfers, poverty, inequality, and the lifecycle, 1997–2010* [Working Paper 5]. Centre for the Analysis of Social Exclusion (CASE). London: London School of Economics.

Hoffman, S. D., & Seidman, L. S. (2003). *Helping working families: The Earned Income Tax Credit.* Kalamazoo, MI: Upjohn Institute for Employment Research.

Hotz, V. J., & Scholz, J. K. (2003). The Earned Income Tax Credit. In R. A. Moffitt (Ed.), *Means-tested transfer programs in the United States.* Chicago, IL: University of Chicago Press.

Immervoll, H., & Pearson, M. (2009). *A good time for making work pay? Taking stock of in-work benefits and related measures across the OECD* [OECD Social, Employment, and Migration Working Paper 81]. Paris: OECD.

Kenworthy, L. (2008). *Jobs with equality.* Oxford, England: Oxford University Press.

Kenworthy, L. (2011a). *Progress for the poor.* Oxford, England: Oxford University Press.

Kenworthy, L. (2011b). *When does economic growth benefit people on low to middle incomes—and why? Commission on Living Standards.* London: Resolution Foundation.

Kenworthy, L. (2014). *Social Democratic America.* New York, NY: Oxford University Press.

Kenworthy, L. (2015). *Do employment-conditional earnings subsidies work?* [ImPRovE Working Paper 15-10]. Antwerp, Belgium: Herman Deleeck Centre for Social Policy, University of Antwerp.

Leigh, A. (2010). Who benefits from the Earned Income Tax Credit? Incidence among recipients, coworkers, and firms. *B.E. Journal of Economic Analysis and Policy, 10,* 1–41.

Marx, I., Vandenbroucke, P., & Verbist, G. (2012). Can higher employment levels bring down relative income poverty in the EU? Regression-based simulations of the Europe 2020 Target. *Journal of European Social Policy, 22,* 472–486.

Marx, I., Joseine Vanhille, J., & Verbist, G. (2012). Combating in-work poverty in Continental Europe: An investigation using the Belgian case. *Journal of Social Policy, 41,* 19–41.

Mead, Lawrence M. (2014). Overselling the Earned Income Tax Credit. *National Affairs, 36,* 20–33.

Meyer, B. D. (2010). The effects of the Earned Income Tax Credit and recent reforms. In J. D. Brown (Ed.), *Tax policy and the economy* (pp. 153–180). Cambridge, MA: National Bureau of Economic Research.

Meyer, B. D., & Rosenbaum, D. T. (2002). Making single mothers work: Recent tax and welfare policy and its effects. In B. D. Meyer & D. Holtz-Eakin (Eds.), *Making work pay: The Earned Income Tax Credit and its impact on America's families* (pp. 69–115). New York, NY: Russell Sage Foundation.

Millar, J. (2008). Making work pay, making tax credits work: An assessment with specific reference to lone-parent employment. *International Social Security Review, 61*(2), 21–38.

Neumark, D., & Wascher, W. (2001). Using the EITC to help poor families: New evidence and a comparison with the minimum wage. *National Tax Journal, 54,* 281–318.

Nichols, A., & Rothstein, J. (2015). *The Earned Income Tax Credit (EITC)* [Working Paper 21211]. Cambridge, MA: National Bureau of Economic Research.

Organisation for Economic Co-operation and Development (OECD). (2009). Is work the best antidote to poverty? *OECD Employment Outlook.* Paris, France: Organisation for Economic Co-operation and Development.

Organisation for Economic Co-operation and Development (OECD). (2010). *Employment-conditional benefits.* www.oecd.org.

Organisation for Economic Co-operation and Development (OECD). (2014). Labor market integration of immigrants and their children: Developing, activating, and using skills. *International Migration Outlook*. Paris, France: Organisation for Economic Co-operation and Development.

Pareliussen, J. K. (2013). Work incentives and universal credit: Reform of the benefit system in the United Kingdom. Economics Department Working Paper 1033. Paris, France: Organisation for Economic Co-operation and Development.

Rothstein, J. (2011). Is the EITC as good as an NIT? Conditional cash transfers and tax incidence. *American Economic Journal: Economic Policy*, 2, 177–208.

Scott, C., & Crandall-Hollick, M. L. (2014). *The Earned Income Tax Credit (EITC): An overview*. Washington, DC: Congressional Research Service.

Sefton, T., Hills, J., & Sutherland, H. (2009). Poverty, inequality, and redistribution. In J. Hills, T. Sefton, & K. Stewart (Eds.), *Towards a more equal society? Poverty, inequality, and policy since 1997*. Bristol, England: Policy Press.

Smeeding, T. M., Ross Phillips, K. R., & O'Connor, M. A. (2002). The Earned Income Tax Credit: Expectation, knowledge, use, and economic and social mobility. In B. D. Meyer & D. Holtz-Eakin (Eds.), *Making work pay: The Earned Income Tax Credit and its impact on America's families* (pp. 301–328). New York, NY: Russell Sage Foundation.

Sykes, J., Križ, K., Edin, K., & Halpern-Meekin, S. (2014). Dignity and dreams: What the Earned Income Tax Credit (EITC) means to low-income families. *American Sociological Review*, 80(2), 243–267.

Waldfogel, J. (2010). *Britain's war on poverty*. New York, NY: Russell Sage Foundation.

Woolley, F. (2012, November 3). Five years of the Working Tax Credit [Web log post]. Retrieved from http://worthwhile.typepad.com/worthwhile_canadian_initi/2012/11/five-years-of-the-working-income-tax-benefit.html

# PART 3

## NEW POLICY PARADIGMS

WHAT CAN BE EXPECTED?

# 8

# IMPROVING POVERTY REDUCTION

## LESSONS FROM THE SOCIAL INNOVATION PERSPECTIVE

**Stijn Oosterlynck, Andreas Novy, Yuri Kazepov, Pieter Cools, Tatiana Saruis, Bernhard Leubolt, and Florian Wukovitsch**

This chapter starts from an increasingly widespread concern about the effectiveness of mainstream policies to combat poverty and to foster social cohesion. As demonstrated in detail in other chapters of this book (Gábos, Branyczki, Binder, and Tóth in Chapter 2 and Cantillon and Marchal in Chapter 12), there has been a standstill or even setbacks in attaining the ambitious objectives of the fight against poverty in Europe. In this chapter, we look at the potential of social innovations as effective policies and actions to reduce poverty. We focus on innovations that mobilize an unconventional mix of actors and apply multifaceted approaches to respond to social needs that are not adequately met by macro-level welfare policies. We argue that interstitial and innovative initiatives can expand our understanding of poverty and policies to combat it.

The chapter begins with an overview of the history and definitions of social innovation, deepening the understanding of social innovation as a contested quasi-concept. It has a long history as an academic concept and a shorter history as an important concept in current European policies to combat poverty. In the second section, which is mainly based on a broad literature review (Oosterlynck et al., 2013), we focus on three often neglected issues in strategies to reduce poverty: the multidimensional and relational character of poverty, the importance of place-based developments and their multilevel governance embeddedness, and the issue of participation and empowerment. In the last section, we present preliminary lessons for effective strategies to combat poverty based on our detailed case-study analyses performed in the context of the ImPRovE project.

## SOCIAL INNOVATION AS A QUASI-CONCEPT[1]

Important concepts for policymaking, such as social capital, sustainable development, or social cohesion, are always normative, hybrid, and contested terms. The same goes for "social innovation," which Jenson and Harrisson (2013) consider a "quasi-concept."

Social innovation as a phenomenon can be traced back at least to the social movements and economic cooperatives that innovated social policies in the 19th century (Martinelli, 2010) and re-emerged in the context of the democratization and civil rights movements in the 1960s, whereas academic discussion dates back at least to the 1970s (Moulaert, MacCallum, & Hillier, 2013, pp. 15–17). We, therefore, proceed inductively by first describing the new phenomenon of diverse forms of societal self-organization, followed by the historical embedding of two opposing approaches to social innovation. At the end of this section, the academic discussion is introduced to better grasp this quasi-concept.

### The Emergence of a "New" Phenomenon

We consider social innovation an exciting empirical phenomenon of diverse initiatives, projects, and programs to address unmet social needs: from re-use social enterprises to intercultural learning initiatives and Housing First.[2] Civil society organizations, social entrepreneurs, and sometimes also local governments have started to take up increasingly active roles in defining, designing, funding, and implementing projects to combat poverty. Andreotti et al. (2012) identified the improved ability to decode complex social needs, the diversification of competences and types of intervention which have all increased legitimacy through participatory arrangements.[3] However, we are cautious here neither to present social innovation as a new paradigm for providing welfare and social protection nor to assume a normative standpoint with respect to the "assumed" superiority of social innovation initiatives.

These initiatives seldom emerge unrelated to contextual specificities. In general, they are inserted in specific opportunity structures that provide a political-cultural context prone to self-initiative or take up innovations from a specific policy field that have been applied successfully at other places (as in the case of Housing First) or at other times (as in the case of the cooperative movement from the 19th century). For this reason, each social initiative derives its novel nature from the institutional context in which it takes place (Moulaert, 2009; Oosterlynck et al., 2013). A particular phenomenon can be a revival of an "old" practice in a different, contemporary context or the transfer of an established practice to another (spatial or institutional) context. Novelty is a characteristic not of the social action itself but of its relationship to a certain institutional context. It is about the introduction of an alternative way of addressing certain social problems or needs. Therefore, we are interested in social initiatives that are new with regard to established social and anti-poverty policies in particular welfare states. By reconstructing the historical context in which the most recent revival of social innovation took place, we attempt to identify their core contributions to the ongoing restructuring of the welfare states across Europe. Both a bottom-up and a top-down approach to social innovation can be observed.

## Bottom-up Initiatives for Civic Empowerment

Contemporary social innovation initiatives have part of their roots in the civil rights and democratization movement, perhaps most well-known for the events of May 1968 (Chambon, David, & Devevey, 1982; Moulaert, 2010), when a multiclass civil rights movement in the United States perceived the strong link between civic and social rights and their joint violation. This resulted in severe social struggles, urban riots, and political turmoil, first in the United States and then spreading to Europe. The broad grassroots movement not only was opposed to economic power but also criticized progressive organizations and even welfare institutions as oppressive as well (Fraser, 2013), aiming at overcoming the disempowering effects of bureaucratic, standardized, and centralized welfare institutions on citizens. This New Left philosophy, built around notions like empowerment, autonomy, participation, self-governance, and cultural recognition (Chambon et al., 1982), had an anti-systemic standpoint based on an anti-centralist philosophy, assuming that an affluent society should be governed in more participatory ways and recognize diversity.

Historically, European welfare states were, despite their differences (Arts & Gelissen, 2002), based on relatively stable, culturally homogeneous nation-states, national socioeconomic development models, and quite standardized social risks. The nation-state bureaucracies directly addressed emerging social needs or offered a multilevel welfare mix within a clearly delimited national territory, through expanding entitlements and benefit generosity. This was facilitated after World War II through a broad commitment to an inclusive full-employment strategy and the increase of public expenditure backed up by economic growth (Judt, 2010; Streeck, 2013). Since the mid-1970s, deep structural changes undermined the societal consensus of postwar welfare capitalism, modified the ways social risks were produced, undermined the functioning of consolidated welfare institutions and the effectiveness of social policies and the existing re-distributive mechanisms (Bonoli, 2005; Castel, 2003; Taylor-Gooby, 2005). Criticism focused on the bureaucratic and authoritarian features of welfare institutions, due to their causing—in rather strong words—"institutional pollution" (Chambon et al., 1982, p. 67). The pillorized welfare regimes were criticized for their institutional rigidities, because both state bureaucracies and established civil society organizations were perceived as slow and ineffective.

Social innovations popped up as creative and bottom-up responses to the perceived limitations of welfare regimes.

## Top-Down Discourses on an "Enabling Welfare State"

Over the past decades, non-economic policy fields have increasingly been under pressure to legitimize their functionality with respect to economic competitiveness (Jessop, 2002; Moulaert & Nussbaumer, 2005). One emblematic example of this is the subordination of the agenda of territorial and social cohesion under the imperatives of competitiveness (Ache & Andersen, 2008; Novy, Coimbra Swiatek, & Moulaert, 2012). It is as part of this overall policy shift that social innovation has become an important policy term in Europe (Sabato, Vanhercke, & Verschraegen, 2015). It made its first appearance in European institutions when the European Commission launched its Renewed Social Agenda in July 2008 in an attempt to deal with the failure of the social objectives of the Lisbon Agenda, which before then had been one-sidedly focused on job creation and economic growth (Euractiv, 2009). It was strongly supported by the former president of the European Commission, Manuel Barroso (2004–2014), becoming part of Europe 2020 as well as Horizon 2020 (Jenson & Harrisson, 2013, p. 7). By launching and promoting the social innovation agenda—given its limited competences—the European Commission confirmed itself in an apparently paradoxical position in the social policy field. It does not directly act at the macro-level of defining social citizenship or universal social rights at the European level, but it supports decentralized initiatives that seem to be promising and innovative.

In 2010, the Bureau of European Policy Advisors (BEPA), an internal think tank, published a report on social innovation. According to BEPA, the intention of social innovation was to create an "enabling welfare state" that uses the creativity and personal commitment of citizens. This apparent necessity is given because of tight budgetary constraints on European governments (BEPA, 2010, p. 7) and the widespread lack of willingness to progressively tax increasingly concentrated and unevenly distributed wealth and income (Piketty, 2014). Under these policy constraints, social innovation was offered as a new paradigm for social intervention (Barroso, 2011; BEPA, 2010). Assuming that traditional methods of service provision have failed, the BEPA report called for the "recognition of the innovation capacity of public services and the dynamics of a user-based, demand-pull approach in which social innovation is supported and promoted" (BEPA, 2010, p. 27). It thereby reframes local social innovation in an attempt to offload public responsibilities to civil society and local actors. This puts a particular spin on place-based and decentralized initiatives and results in policies that are often at odds with the historical roots of social innovation (as described in this chapter) as well as universalist macro-policies to reduce poverty (as described in many other chapters in this book).

Similar arguments have been made on the national level, most notably in the Netherlands and the United Kingdom. In 2013, the Dutch King Willem Alexander announced the end of the welfare state and welcomed its successor, the "participation society," in which citizens are expected to take over care tasks formerly executed by public institutions. Former U.K. Prime Minister Cameron launched the "Big Society Initiative," stating that, "in the past, the left focused on the state and the right focused on the market. We're harnessing that space in between—society—the 'hidden wealth' of our nation" (David Cameron, Speech on the Big Society, Milton Keynes, May 23, 2011). While Europe has not recovered from the crisis of 2008, neither economically nor socially, the policy orientation has remained path-dependent—deepening neoliberal restructuring of social welfare, if possible, with the help of civic initiatives (Ishkanian & Szreter, 2012). In fact, social innovation is "increasingly embraced as a 'new' approach to solving the crisis of the welfare state, by creating new jobs in the 'cheap' social economy and reorganizing the welfare system through commodification and privatization" (Moulaert et al., 2013, p. 17).

## Academic Debates on Social Innovations to Combat Poverty and Social Exclusion

Depending on the approach used to consider social innovation, either bottom-up or top-down, other characteristics of the quasi-concept can be highlighted. European policymaking is strongly based on the BEPA definition of social innovation (Oosterlynck & Cools, 2012). With the support of the British Young Foundation, social innovations are defined as "innovations that are social in both their ends and their means" (BEPA, 2010, p. 9; The Young Foundation, 2006). More specifically, social innovation is about new ideas (products, services and models) that simultaneously meet social needs (more effectively than alternatives) and create new social relationships or collaborations (The Young Foundation, 2006, p. 9). The BEPA definition takes into account that social innovation is a contested quasi-concept but entails a focus on both process and product, which has been a recurring feature (see Schumpeter, 1942).[4] Jenson and Harrisson (2013, p. 18) also perceive a clear focus on processes and the way civil society contributes to the satisfaction of social needs.

In the academic debate, however, the concept of social innovation has a much longer history than the top-down and managerial approach. The concept was notably popular with intellectuals of the student movement in the 1960s and 1970s, resulting in the journal *Autrement* as a key voice of grassroots critics, such as Pierre Rosanvallon and Jacques Attali. Their concerns were "different types of collective actions and social transformations that would lead us from a top-down economy and society into a more bottom-up, creative and participatory society" (Moulaert et al., 2013, p. 15). This broader approach to economics and macro-structures was taken over by Chambon et al. (1982) and later on by Moulaert and colleagues (MacCallum, Moulaert, Hillier, & Vicari, 2009; Moulaert, Martinelli, Swyngedouw, & Gonzalez, 2010).

Moulaert and his colleagues explicitly refer to the older traditions and stress the importance of power relations in social innovation. They claim that social innovation has three basic components: the satisfaction of basic social needs (content dimension), the transformation of social relations (process dimension), and the increase of sociopolitical capabilities and access to resources (empowerment dimension linking process and content; Moulaert et al., 2005). Empowerment as a process of overcoming repression and privilege entails conflicts between opposing groups and interests. This approach is clearly distinguishable from the focus of social policy on technocratic interventions mainly aimed at cost-efficient allocation of monetary resources, thereby neglecting social relationships and the modes of governance that underpin these interventions (see Klein, Fontan, Harrisson, & Lévesque, 2012, for the example of Québec).

## NEGLECTED ISSUES IN STRATEGIES TO REDUCE POVERTY

Clearly, there is tension between the older, market-critical, bottom-up approach and the more recent, market-friendly, top-down approach to social innovation with their different, in part even antagonistic, understanding of welfare and poverty-reduction strategies. While the former insists on a broad and systemic analysis and long-term social transformation, the latter sees social innovations as short-term, cost-efficient measures to reduce poverty. This section identifies issues that are often inadequately conceptualized in mainstream social policies. First, we sharpen the understanding of poverty and "social needs" as multidimensional and relational (redefining the content dimension of social innovation). Second, we insist that place-based approaches offer important innovations, yet have to be reconceptualized within a multilevel governance perspective (redefining the process dimension of social innovation). Third, we insist on a power-sensitive analysis of poverty and stress the crucial role of participation in combating poverty (redefining the role of power in social innovations).

### Poverty as Multidimensional and Relational

A multidimensional understanding of poverty was present from the beginning of the modern poverty discussion.[5] It seems to be a truism to perceive poverty as multidimensional and relational, as was well reflected in Adam Smith's famous dictum "to appear in public without shame" (quoted in Sen, 2010, p. 52). Indeed, the multidimensional and relational nature of poverty is acknowledged in European policymaking. Nevertheless, concrete policies increasingly focus on a restrained, short-term-focused understanding of poverty as remaining below a certain monetary threshold. Reducing poverty not only requires optimizing monetary transfers, but also includes questions of how to organize social interventions for people in poverty that are empowering, participatory, recognize diversity, and improve people's autonomy.

In this context, the discourse on social innovation attaches itself to a broader definition of poverty in terms of a set of processes of social exclusion in various spheres of life that hinders people's full participation in society. Stressing transformation of social relations draws attention to the institutional embedding of the multiplicity of social exclusion processes that crystallize into a condition of poverty or impoverishment (Vranken, 2001). Furthermore, insisting on the relational aspects of poverty implies a reorientation of research on poverty reduction toward a stronger focus on governance issues. In particular, we have identified specific governance challenges in dealing with poverty, covering issues of upscaling and mainstreaming, active and passive subsidiarity, and the task of striking a balance between equality and diversity (ImPRovE Social Innovation Team, 2013).

Given the focus of social innovation on the transformation of social relations, rather than merely income transfers, one should not always expect an immediate effect in terms of income. The contribution of social innovation is to be considered potentially broadening what constitutes poverty and hence anti-poverty strategies. Of crucial importance is the current threat of social and territorial cleavages in Europe, because reducing poverty is strongly linked to fostering social cohesion as a way of "living together differently" (Patsy Healey in Novy et al., 2012, p. 1874). This has implications for the effectiveness of cash transfers versus in-kind service provisioning, which allows for multidimensional interventions to foster cohesion. As our case-study research has shown, this often requires long-term and multidimensional support by social workers and other professionals in building capacity and social competences beyond combating short-term monetary deprivation.

## Place-Based Development and Multilevel Governance

The stress on integrating actions and interventions through a focus on place follows, among others, from the awareness of the spatial concentration of poverty and social exclusion (Fainstein et al., 1992; Marcuse, 1989; Mollenkopf & Castells, 1991; Wilson, 1987). Deindustrialization (Silver, 1993) and the resultant full-fledged urban crisis (Theodore & Peck, 2011) have led to an upsurge in socially innovative neighborhood development strategies (Christiaens, Moulaert, & Bosmans, 2007; Moulaert et al., 2010). They often opposed top-down solutions as well as the ways in which bureaucratic welfare states have compartmentalized social needs in a range of institutionally separated policy sectors. Social innovations emerge from the everyday life context of citizens and have a bottom-up character (Fontan & Klein 2004; Moulaert, 2009). Therefore, place-based interventions are well placed to overcome sectorial policy divides (Moulaert, 2002).

For many members of disadvantaged groups, the neighborhood is the predominant place of daily experiences, and hence—according to most social innovators—might be a privileged scale at which experienced but unmet needs of disadvantaged groups can be satisfied. As a consequence, research focuses on the individual and the meso-level (Jenson & Harrisson, 2013, pp. 28–31). In many cases, the sense of a shared environment is strong and is one of the few remaining bases for broad and inclusive participation, solidarity, and collective mobilization (Moulaert et al., 2010). In local welfare studies, local public institutions are considered best suited to promote and support social innovation in the fight against poverty and social exclusion, because they are closest to the citizens and their needs (Andreotti et al., 2012). This highlights the role of local actors and networks in detecting, fostering, and stimulating social innovations.

The ongoing process of territorial reorganization of welfare policies ("vertical subsidiarization" and devolution) and their increasing localization in terms of capacities and responsibilities (Andreotti & Mingione, 2014; Kazepov, 2010) created potential openings for socially innovative local actors and networks. Decentralization is an ambiguous process. It can be seen as the spatial component of a neoliberal agenda of liberalization and privatization, in which the central level is undercut precisely because it is the level on which socioeconomic development is most strongly regulated (Brenner, 2004). Alternatively, decentralization may promote democracy, by facilitating social participation, creating social networks (Fung & Wright, 2001), mobilizing new resources, and adapting interventions to local specificities. As a consequence of this process, regional and municipal authorities have become more proactive actors in providing welfare, while national and supranational institutions have in most cases mainly had roles of coordination, territorial redistribution, and rights homogenization. An important risk entailed by this process of vertical subsidiarization is the fragmentation of policies and territories and the consequent diversification of citizenship rights (Kazepov, 2010).

Parallel—and related to—processes of vertical subsidiarization is the trend toward horizontal subsidiarization. The increasing number of actors involved in social policy design, management, funding, and implementation created an increasingly complex welfare mix (Ascoli & Ranci, 2002). Horizontal subsidiarization leads to mixed networks of public institutions and a host of (new or less established) civil society organizations as well as for-profit firms. This process can occur at various territorial levels, from national to local. In our cases, localized mixed networks were drawing on combinations of different points of view, competencies, skills, and tools for needs' analysis, approaches, and resources. By doing so, they aimed to be more effective and efficient in realizing de-standardized and complex interventions, responding to needs' individualization and cultural differentiation and calls for choice, activation, and participation. By including the actors upon whom decisions will be implemented, the policymaking process acquires new legitimation. The actors also reinforce the social "tissue" while working, activating social participation and thus building, generating, and consolidating social relationships to face and prevent poverty and social exclusion (Kazepov, 2008, 2010).

Over the last decades, the vertical and horizontal subsidiarization of national welfare regimes has been increasingly shaped by neoliberalization and the pressures deriving from fiscal austerity (Peck, 2004). Scarcity and retrenchment of services is shaping the social policy debate, opening room to maneuver for cheaper or more effective service providers. The ensuing spatio-institutional transformation of the welfare state multiplies the potential "points of contact" with local social innovations. The current opening up of the welfare mix creates opportunities for (from the perspective of social policy) unconventional civil society organizations, social entrepreneurs, and local public institutions to be involved in the provision of welfare. This further opens up the system to place-based socially innovative actors. It does not, however, predetermine that these contacts will be forged and institutionalized—other actors, such as multinational for-profit service providers, may take over this task (see Ishkanian & Szreter, 2012, on the United Kingdom's Big Society agenda).

## Participation

Poverty involves not only material well-being but also sociopolitical capabilities and access to resources. Moulaert et al. (2005) called this the empowerment dimension of social innovation that links process and content. Following the same type of reasoning, Fraser insisted that full participation in society depends on a just economic (re)distribution, as well as on cultural recognition and political representation (Fraser, 2012). People can be hindered from fully participating in society due to their lack of financial and material resources, but also due to discrimination on the basis of cultural background as well as underrepresentation in public institutions and decision-making bodies. Transferred to the field of social innovation, this means that innovations are particularly focused on attempts to sensitize and to complement the redistributive and protective policies of the welfare state with concerns of representation and recognition. The heated public debate in Europe on migration, refugees, and Islam shows that there is a very strong link between multilayered social inequality and intercultural tensions that threaten social cohesion. This represents a key sociocultural challenge for European policymaking in general: How to live together differently on a continent that has always been a melting pot of cultures and people. What are the common norms, laws, and rules that all have to obey? How can a governance system be organized so that all inhabitants "have the opportunity to be different and yet be able to live together"? (Mikael Stigendal in Novy et al., 2012, p. 1874).

In dealing with these policy challenges, social innovation accords a central role to civil society (whether social movements, NGOs, third-sector organizations, or volunteers),[6] social entrepreneurs, and local governments (as the traditional barrier against the centralization of state power). From this point of view, social innovation not only aims at supporting weaker individuals and groups but also aims at transforming social relationships through participation, raising awareness about social inequalities, and intercultural learning. In the final section, we present preliminary empirical evidence of the need for participatory governance models. Once policies to reduce poverty focus on the multifaceted dimensions of poverty, fostering participation is a key ingredient in integrated approaches to social inclusion and social cohesion.

## PRELIMINARY LESSONS FOR STRATEGIES TO COMBAT POVERTY

This final section presents preliminary lessons from our fieldwork[7] investigating specific socially innovative initiatives (see Table A8.1 in the appendix). First, we link social innovations aimed at reducing poverty to the broader concern of fostering social cohesion. Second, we present bottom-linked approaches as attempts to overcome the dualism of micro versus macro as well as bottom-up versus top-down. Finally, we insist on the importance of collective empowerment as a means for tackling the structural causes of poverty.

### Context-Sensitive Strategies to Foster Social Cohesion

In the preceding section, we show the importance of taking a multidimensional and relational approach to reducing poverty seriously. In our case studies,[8] concerns about recognition and diversity have popped up as key long-term objectives, which may enter into conflict with short-term success rates.

For example, for intercultural training programs to be successful, they have to be context sensitive and accept the respective sociocultural differences. Two Swedish cases on activation and social inclusion of immigrant citizens, Rätt Steg and Språk-stödjande insatser (see Table A8.1, Case Studies 25 and 27), show that standardized welfare measures cannot be effective without taking into account both cultural and linguistic differences, but also the complex mix of individual needs and specificities. The projects combine social and activation measures, courses on the Swedish language, society, and job regulations, and intercultural mediation in training and internship activities.

An obstacle in another project, Romane Buca in Sundbyberg (Case Study 24), was that the municipality of Stockholm refused to re-adapt the timing of income support to the duration of the vocational training proposed by the Folk Schools. The reason was that the municipal rules do not allow provision of benefits for more than four months and, following a principle of equality, regular adult education is provided with the same conditions for everybody. However, Roma adults, cumulating multidimensional disadvantages due to secular discrimination, require long-term pathways integrating education programs and other social, cultural, and economic measures. The problem was resolved with a national intervention that provided social welfare measures for the time of the experimentation. In all these cases, the innovative initiatives were aimed at building a specific balance between the traditional universalistic approach of the Swedish welfare system with social, economic, and cultural target groups' and individuals' specificities.

In times of austerity, passive subsidiarity is a very real threat to a multidimensional approach for reducing poverty and, thereby, to social cohesion in general. Activities to sustain social capital and foster multidimensional individual capabilities have been the first to come under severe pressure. Context-sensitive policymaking valorizing the multidimensional and relational character of poverty—which might enhance success—is not available at zero costs. If public authorities want to sustain social cohesion, they have to be aware of this. The simple delegation of the problems without adequate resources (passive subsidiarity) cannot be the answer to lack of public funds in one of the richest regions of the world.

An exemplary case of passive subsidiarity is the Ánde Škola initiative (Case Study 2). The start-up phase of the project about Roma children's education and social inclusion realized in Lecce (Italy) by the Association Alteramente was financed by the Puglia Region with EU funds. The municipal social services' employees and school teachers consider the project a sort of "service for services," which helps them to better do their own jobs. Nevertheless, it was never supported by the municipality of Lecce and the schools; both claimed lack of resources as the main impediment. After the regional funds expired, the project continued thanks to a crowdfunding campaign and the contribution of Roma parents, but without public support. Other examples in which a state avoids its responsibility are to be found in Hungary, where socially innovative projects are either funded privately or via European funds (Case Studies 6 and 17).

An example in which a trend toward more active subsidiarity can be observed is the initiative Tutti a casa, a Housing First–inspired project realized in Bologna, the first application of this approach to homelessness in Italy (Case Study 22). At the beginning of the experiment, the municipality was skeptical and not supportive, and the Association Piazza Grande undertook the initiative. After good results were obtained, the municipality became the most important partner in the initiative. In the end, it decided to close its old shelter in order to direct resources to the realization of its own Housing First project. In this example, the municipality shifted from passive to active subsidiarity and direct investment in a socially highly innovative initiative.

Local social innovations are often tied better into the life-world of people living in poverty and address multiple forms of exclusion and deprivation in an integrated and customized way. To find such context-sensitive solutions for governance challenges requires good public service and infrastructures that can substitute viable civic organizations, which tend to be lacking in peripheral regions (Putnam, 1993). In many cases, social innovations have taken over broader responsibilities than their contractual obligations in order to foster a web of local public and civic organizations to sustain social cohesion (as, for instance, in the Italian Tradate Solidale, Case Study 23).

## Bottom-Linked Social Innovations

The focus on multilevel governance is the best entry point for overcoming the dualism of micro versus macro as well as top-down and bottom-up. The limits of conventional top-down approaches, with their focus on the national state, have led to increasing interest in bottom-up approaches. But poverty has structural causes and relates to supra-local dynamics, which cannot be dealt with only locally. Indeed, a welfare regime positioned to deal with the challenges of the 21st century has to foster empowerment by context-sensitive forms of welfare mix that mobilize the respective strengths of different actors. An example of governance misalignment affecting the ability to deal with structural causes of social problems emerges from the case study on SEI (Case Study 24), the help desk on over-indebtedness in Venice, Italy. The cooperative for ethical finance Mag Venezia offers citizens free support on social, economic, and legal difficulties created by the indebtedness problem. The cooperative acts on individual problems together with the local welfare system, but it has neither the will nor the competence to deal with the structural, always multiscalar, causes of current private household indebtedness.

Active subsidiarity offers a better institutional setting for increasing individual capabilities as well as dealing with poverty as multidimensional. This is illustrated by a comparison of two networks of work-integration social enterprises that organize the re-use of household materials, namely De Kringwinkel in Flanders (Case Study 8) and the Furniture Re-use Network in the United Kingdom (Case Study 19). In Flanders, the socially innovative model benefited from relatively generous subsidized employment schemes and supportive waste-reduction policies, which allowed for successful mainstreaming and professionalization of the initiative. It also enabled the re-use initiative to develop long-term and tailored working and support relationships with the long-term unemployed. In Flanders, these support services are developed fairly uniformly across the territory. In the United Kingdom, the employment schemes do not exist and waste reduction is not supported systematically by the state. Consequently, re-use organizations have little choice but to engage with the target population in short-term and narrowly focused trajectories. At the same time, the increased competition at the local level results in large differences in availability of schemes across the country.

These cases show that the most effective initiatives are those that link top-down and bottom-up and include local and national, as well as European and global, strategies. The initiatives are therefore best characterized as bottom-linked. The "'bottom-linked' approach to social innovation . . . recognizes the centrality of initiatives taken by those immediately concerned, but stresses the necessity of institutions that would enable, gear, or sustain such initiatives through sound, regulated, and lasting practices and clearer citizen rights guaranteed by a demo-cratic state-functioning" (Moulaert, 2010, p. 9). Many of the more mature social innovations point toward the importance of active subsidiarity, in which central governments provide logistical and financial support. From the bottom-linked perspective, it is relevant to point out that, in Flanders, the umbrella organiza-tions of the re-use sector have been much more involved in the development of employment and waste-reduction policies. The Brazilian case study on the multilevel governance of recycling by including MNCR (national movement of collectors of recyclable material) points out the merits of active and coordi-nated subsidiarity (Case Study 20). In contrast with the U.K. initiative in re-use and its reliance on market-friendly solutions (Case Study 19), Brazilian gov-ernment programs on the municipal and the national level have been set up to stimulate the collective action of hitherto marginalized people. In addition to fostering the provision of an important environmental service, along with so-cial inclusion, processes of empowerment have been promoted. Public funds are crucial for promoting activities of long-term common interest, especially in the environmental field.

In short, the examples acknowledge the importance of adequate institutional and governance dynamics to overcome current shortcomings in social policies. Furthermore, a multi-level perspective goes beyond the nation-state—centered mainstream approach to social policy without falling into the localist trap in-duced by passive subsidiarity. We argue for a different agenda from the current one, which tends to focus on social innovation as a vehicle to offload public responsibilities on volunteers, civil society, and social entrepreneurs. To use social innovations in an instrumental way to reduce costs or to contribute to renewed economic growth is explicitly not an agenda focused on retooling the welfare state, but rather on undermining it. Effective and efficient multilevel gov-ernance of fiscal responsibilities is a prerequisite for empowerment. This includes rethinking how service provision is organized, how social support is delivered, and what role people in poverty themselves play in the development, design, and implementation of actions, initiatives, and policies targeted at them. This leads to the final and perhaps most important lesson for the future of social innovation as well as social policy.

## Empowering Social Innovation?

In principle, social innovations to reduce poverty have always insisted in empowering the poor as citizens, not just as clients. A focus on empower-ment is important in all analyses of social innovation. However, there are huge differences in definitions and policy implications. In the more recent initiatives we analysed, empowerment is conceptualized as individual capacity-building fostering human capital. These projects are executed within the market-friendly framework of an enabling state that supports citizens in asserting themselves on the labor market. Policies in line with this social investment perspective aim at individual empowerment in the sense of capacity building. This is very clear in some of the ESF-funded cases, such as the Inspire!NEET Programme in North London (Case Study 31) and Ten for Cooking (Case Study 7), a training scheme for people on minimum subsistence income in Leuven, Belgium. These initiatives are very much concerned with clients' backgrounds and ambitions and, therefore, constitute a really multidimensional and relational approach to combating poverty. However, the current dominance of labor-market-participation outcome criteria and payment-by-result funding narrows processes of empowerment to "enhancing employability" and shows a tendency to instrumentalize non-economic dimensions to this end. Furthermore, many of the research projects on social innovation funded by the EC-Framework Programme are deliberately individual (micro) or institutional (meso); (Jenson & Harrisson, 2013, pp. 28–31).

Historically, local social innovations have stressed autonomy, participation, empowerment, and cultural recognition as important dimensions of social inclusion and hence values to be strived for by all societal institutions, including the welfare state. Social innovations were seen as attempts at (macro-)systemic change. In general, they emerged or were linked to social movements and were deeply skeptical about market solutions. These approaches have remained strong, especially in times of crisis. The Spanish case study SIDH (Housing Debt Intermediation Service, Case Study 29) was set up by public institutions to respond to the pressure of the anti-eviction movement PAH, which protests against evictions due to indebtedness. It highlighted the collective dimension of the problem and convinced the municipalities, under the pressure of public opinion, to promote collaboration among local, provincial, and regional public organizations. This allowed the creation of a service that offers not only information and advice but also legal assistance and mediation between users and financial institutions, with the aim of maintaining people in housing.

The Brazilian case study UNMP—MCMV-E (National Popular Housing Movement, included in the national housing program Minha Casa Minha Vida—Entidadeds) is another important example (Case Study 21). The housing movement (UNMP) has voiced demands for public housing initiatives since the 1980s, while also having been engaged in direct political action (squatting, linked to collective self-management of the houses, and political and social education of its members). In 2009, the national government set up an ambitious program to construct a million houses to fight the economic crisis. Due to strong political pressure by social movements, 1% of the resources were devoted to MCMV-E, which has become the first large-scale housing program in which social movements have been responsible for all stages—planning, acquisition of land, project elaboration, and selection of prospective residents. MCMV-E opened space for social and political experimentation by offering organizational and financial resources, which permitted the involved actors to put in practice their ideas of self-management and thereby fostered political empowerment.

Both cases show the crucial role of political representation and the pressure from below to force public authorities to recognize emerging social needs. If the current high levels of unemployment and poverty persist, it would not be surprising if forms of social innovation based on grassroots mobilization once again rejuvenate the social policy field in Europe.

## CONCLUSION

In the context of an increasing concern with the effectiveness of mainstream policies to combat poverty, this chapter looks at the potential of social innovations as effective policies and actions to reduce poverty. Starting from a brief overview of the history and definitions of social innovation, we distinguish two approaches to social innovation: a bottom-up approach focused on local initiatives for civic empowerment and a top-down approach to social innovation centered on an "enabling welfare state." Since the former concept of social innovation has a much longer history in the academic debates, we chose to adopt it over the latter top-down and managerial approach. We then argue that socially innovative initiatives thus defined significantly expand our understanding of poverty and policies to combat it. They do so by highlighting that poverty is multidimensional and relational, that place-based but multiscalar strategies are adequate in addressing it, and that participation and empowerment are required to increase the sociopolitical capabilities and access to resources of people living in poverty. Local social innovations thus offer an alternative to the focus of social policy on technocratic interventions mainly aimed at the cost-efficient allocation of monetary resources, thereby neglecting social relationships and governance dynamics. Social innovations cannot substitute for effective central measures of social protection and redistribution, but—as the lessons drawn from empirical research in the final section of the paper illustrate—they show that effective implementation needs adequate context-sensitive governance models. These preliminary lessons for socially innovative strategies to combat poverty are based on 31 detailed case-study analyses of social innovations in eight different countries and five types of welfare regimes. The first lesson concerns the importance of context-sensitivity for anti-poverty strategies to adequately address concerns about recognition and diversity. We also show that local social innovations develop networks of local organizations that have the capacity to reinforce social cohesion. The second lesson is that bottom-linked approaches to social innovation are an effective way to combine the strengths of bottom-up and top-down approaches. The third lesson is focused on empowerment and insists on the importance of collective forms of empowerment as a means for tackling the structural causes of poverty, despite the notable tendency to see empowerment as individual capacity-building to foster human capital.

## NOTES

1 The research on which this chapter is based was financially supported by the European Union 7th Framework Programme (FP7/2012–2016) under Grant Agreement N. 290613 (ImPRovE project).

2 Housing First is a new approach to homelessness in which homeless people get immediate and unconditional access to permanent housing in order to stabilize their living conditions (see Tsemberis, 2010).

3 For critical reflections and potential risks, see Anheier (2005), Anheier and Seibel (1990), Ascoli and Ranci (2002), and Kazepov (2010).

4 Economically inspired definitions of social innovation tend to stress the product over the process dimension. Pol and Ville, for example, argue than an innovation is a social innovation "if the implied new idea has the potential to improve either the quality or the quantity of life" (Pol & Ville, 2009). Because contemporary interest in social innovation is to an important extent informed by a critique on the dominant economically and technologically determinist models of innovation, which either ignore social processes altogether or treat them in an instrumental way (Moulaert & Sekia, 2003), we here prefer definitions of social innovation that include an important focus on social processes and relations. Mumford, for example, defines social innovation as "the generation and implementation of new ideas about how people should organize interpersonal activities, or social interactions, to meet one or more common goals" (Mumford, 2002, p. 253).

5 In Townsend's (1979) seminal contribution to the debate, poverty was also not seen as exclusively related to the scarcity of monetary resources. Although monetary resources play a major role, poverty is instead considered to be a complex, multidimensional, and cumulative problem, depending on a mix of contextual conditions (e.g., labor market and social policies), individual characteristics (and family background), life and work trajectories, and social networks.

6 It is important to point out here that civil society involvement is not at all a new feature of welfare states (even more so, it is a defining feature of corporatist welfare states). The reference here is to new civil society organizations (e.g., new social movements), older civil society organizations that were not yet involved in macro-level social policies, or new forms of involvement of civil society organizations that are already involved in macro-level social policies. What is different as well is that these new linkages between state institutions and civil society organizations are not structured in ideological pillars.

7 For our fieldwork, we adopted a comparative case-oriented approach, studying 31 cases of social innovations in five different types of welfare regimes (liberal, corporatist, universalistic, familistic, and transitional). The case studies were equally distributed over the fields of labor-market activations, housing,

and education for ethnic minorities and covered eight different countries (Belgium, the United Kingdom, Hungary, Brazil, Spain, Sweden, Italy, and Austria). We used multiple sources of information: secondary data sources, such as archival records, documents, and policy reports, and qualitative (non-numeric) and quantitative (numeric) data and information collected in the field of research, mainly through open-ended interviews and focus groups.

8   For more information, see the appendix, which lists all the case studies, their countries, and their policy fields.

9   All case study reports can be downloaded via the following link: http://improve-research.eu/?page_id=2507

## REFERENCES

Ache, P., & Andersen, H. T. (2008). Introduction. In P. Ache, H. T. Andersen, T. Maloutas, M. Raco, & T. Tasan-Kok (Eds.), *Cities between competitiveness and cohesion—Discourses, realities and implementation* (pp. 3–18). Berlin: Springer.

Andreotti, A., & Mingione, E. (2014). Local welfare systems in Europe and the crisis. *European Urban and Regional Studies, 23*(3), 252–266.

Andreotti, A., Mingione, E., & Polizzi, E. (2012). Local welfare systems: A challenge for social cohesion. *Urban Studies, 49*(9), 1925–1940. doi:10.1177/0042098012444884.

Anheier, H. K., & Seibel, W. (1990). *The third sector: comparative studies of nonprofit organizations.* Berlin: De Gruyter.

Anheier, H. (2005). *Nonprofit organisations. Theory, management, policy.* London: Routledge.

Arts, W., & Gelissen, J. (2002). Three worlds of welfare capitalism or more? A state-of-the-art report. *Journal of European Social Policy, 12*(2), 137–158. doi:10.1177/0952872002012002114

Ascoli, U., & Ranci, C. (Eds.) (2002) *Dilemmas of the welfare mix: the new structure of welfare in an era of privatization.* Berlin: Springer.

Barroso, J. M. (2011). *Europe leading social innovation* (p. 5). Brussels, Belgium: Social Innovation Europe Initiative.

Bonoli, G. (2005). The politics of the new social policies: providing coverage against new social risks in mature welfare states. *Policy & Politics, 33*(3), 431–449.

Brenner, N. (2004). *New state spaces: Urban governance and the rescaling of statehood.* Oxford, England: Oxford University Press.

Bureau of European Policy Advisors (BEPA). (2010). Empowering people, driving change: Social innovation in the European Union. Brussels, Belgium: European Commission.

Castel, R. (2003). *From manual workers to wage laborers. Transformation of the social question*. New York, Transaction Publishers.

Chambon, J.-L., David, A., & Devevey, J.-M. (1982). *Les innovations sociales*. Paris, France: Presses Universitaires de France.

Christiaens, E., Moulaert, F., & Bosmans, B. (2007). The end of social innovation in urban development strategies? The case of Antwerp and the neighbourhood development association "Bom." *European Urban and Regional Studies, 14*, 14.

Euractiv. (2009, January 21). Brussels promotes "social innovation" to tackle crisis. *Euractiv.* https://www.euractiv.com/section/social-europe-jobs/news/brussels-promotes-social-innovation-to-tackle-crisis/ [last accessed on 9 July 2018]

Fainstein, S., & Harloe, M. (1992). *Divided cities: New York and London in the contemporary world*. Oxford: Blackwell.

Fontan, J.-M., & Klein, J. L. (2004). La mobilisation du capital socio-territorial: le cas du technopôle Angus. *Lien Social et Politiques, 52*, 139–149.

Fraser, N. (2012). Marketization, social protection, emancipation: toward a neo-Polanyian conception of capitalist crisis. In C. Calhoun & G. Derluguian (Eds.), *Business as usual: the roots of the global financial meltdown* (pp. 137–158). New York: New York University Press.

Fraser, N. (2013). A triple movement? Parsing the politics of crisis after Polanyi. *New Left Review, 81*, 119–132.

Fung, A., & Wright, E. O. (2001). Deepening Democracy: Innovations in Empowered Participatory Governance. *Politics & Society, 29*(1), 5–41.

ImPRovE Social Innovation Team. (2013). Governance challenges for successful local forms of social innovation. http://improve-research.eu/?page_id=170

Ishkanian, A., & Szreter, S. (2012). *The Big Society debate: A new agenda for social welfare?* Cheltenham, England: Edward Elgar.

Jenson, J., & Harrisson, D. (2013). Social innovation research in the European Union: Approaches, findings and future directions—Policy Review. Brussels, Belgium: European Commission.

Jessop, B. (2002). *The future of the capitalist state*. Cambridge, England: Polity Press.

Judt, T. (2010). *Ill fares the land*. London, England: Penguin Books.

Kazepov, Y. (Ed.) (2008). *Cities of Europe. Changing contexts, local arrangements and the challenge to urban cohesion. Studies in urban and social change*. Oxford: Blackwell Publishing.

Kazepov, Y. (2010). *Rescaling social policies: Towards multilevel governance in Europe*. Farnham, England: Ashgate.

Klein, J.-L., Fontan, J.-M., Harrisson, D., & Lévesque, B. (2012). The Québec system of social innovation: A focused analysis on the local development field. *Finisterra, XLVII*(94), 9–28.

MacCallum, D., Moulaert, F., Hillier, J., & Vicari, S. (Eds.). (2009). *Social innovation and territorial development*. Aldershot, England: Ashgate.

Marcuse, P. (1989). 'Dual city': a muddy metaphor for a quartered city. *International Journal of Urban and Regional Research, 13*(4), 697–708.

Martinelli, F. (2010). Historical roots of social change: Philosophies and movements. In F. Moulaert, E. Swyngedouw, F. Martinelli, & S. Gonzalez (Eds.), *Can neighbourhoods save the city? Community development and social innovation* (pp. 17–48). Abingdon, England: Routledge.

Mollenkopf, J., & Castells, M. (Eds.) (1991). *Dual city. Restructuring New York.* New York: Russell Sage Foundation.

Moulaert, F. (2002). *Globalization and integrated area development in European cities.* Oxford, England: Oxford University Press.

Moulaert, F. (2009). Social innovation: Institutionally embedded, territorially (re)produced. In D. MacCallum, F. Moulaert, J. Hillier & S. Vicari Haddock (Eds.), *Social innovation and territorial development.* Surrey: Ashgate Publishing Limited.

Moulaert, F. (2010). Social innovation and community development: Concepts, theories and challenges. In F. Moulaert, F. Martinelli, E. Swyngedouw, & S. Gonzalez (Eds.), *Can neighbourhoods save the city?* (pp. 4–16). London, England: Routledge.

Moulaert, F., MacCallum, D., & Hillier, J. (2013). Social innovation: Intuition, precept, concept, theory and practice. In F. Moulaert, D. MacCallum, A. Mehmood, & A. Hamdouch (Eds.), *The international handbook of social innovation: Collective action, social learning and transdisciplinary research* (pp. 13–24). Cheltenham, England: Edward Elgar.

Moulaert, F., Martinelli, F., Swyngedouw, E., & Gonzalez, S. (2005). Towards alternative model(s) of local innovation. *Urban Studies, 42*(11), 1169–1990.

Moulaert, F., Martinelli, F., Swyngedouw, E., & Gonzalez, S. (2010). *Can neighbourhoods save the city?* Abingdon, England: Routledge.

Moulaert, F., & Nussbaumer, J. (2005). The social region—Beyond the territorial dynamics of the Learning Economy. *European Urban and Regional Studies, 12*(1), 45–64.

Moulaert, F., & Sekia, F. (2003). Territorial innovation models: A critical survey. *Regional Studies, 37*(3), 289–302.

Mumford, M. D. (2002). Social innovation: Ten cases from Benjamin Franklin. *Creativity Research Journal, 14*(2), 253–266.

Novy, A., Coimbra Swiatek, D., & Moulaert, F. (2012). Social cohesion: A conceptual and political elucidation. *Urban Studies, 49*(9), 1873–1889.

Oosterlynck, S., & Cools, P. (2012). Lokale initiatieven als bouwstenen van sociale innovatie. In D. Dierckx, S. Oosterlynck, J. Coene, & A. Van Haarlem (Eds.), *Armoede en Sociale Uitsluiting Jaarboek 2012* (pp. 195–212). Leuven, Belgium: Acco.

Oosterlynck, S., Kazepov, Y., Novy, A., Cools, P., Barberis, E., Wukovitsch, F., Saruis, T., Leubolt, B. (2013). The butterfly and the elephant: Local social innovation, the welfare state and new poverty dynamics [ImPRovE Discussion

Paper No. 13/03]. Antwerp, Belgium: Herman Deleeck Centre for Social Policy, University of Antwerp.

Peck, J. (2004). Geography and public policy: Constructions of neoliberalism. *Progress in Human Geography, 28*(3), 392–405.

Piketty, T. (2014). *Capital in the twenty-first century.* Cambridge: Harvard University Press.

Pol, E., & Ville, S. (2009). Social innovation: Buzz word or enduring term? *Journal of Socio-Economics, 38*(6), 878–885.

Putnam, R. D. (1993). *Making democracy work. Civic traditions in modern Italy.* Princeton, NJ: Princeton University Press.

Sabato, S., Vanhercke, B., & Verschraegen, G. (2015). *The EU framework for social innovation–Between entrepreneurship and policy experimentation* [ImPRovE Working Paper 15/21]. http://improve-research.eu/?page_id=37

Schumpeter, J. A. ([1942] 1994). *Capitalism, socialism and democracy.* London: Routledge.

Silver, H. (1993). National conceptions of the new urban poverty: Social structural change in Britain, France and the United States. *International Journal of Urban and Regional Research, 17*(3), 336–354.

Streeck, W. (2013). *Gekaufte Zeit. Die vertagte Krise des demokratischen Kapitalismus.* Berlin, Germany: Suhrkamp.

Taylor-Gooby, P. (Ed.) (2005). *Ideas and Welfare State Reform in Western Europe.* Basingstoke: Palgrave/Macmillan.

The Young Foundation (2006). *Social silicon valleys. A manifesto for social innovation: what it is, why it matters and how it can be accelerated.* London: The Basingstone Press.

Theodore, N., & Peck, J. (2011). Framing neoliberal urbanism: Translating "commonsense" urban policy across the OECD zone. *European Urban and Regional Studies.* doi:10.1177/0969776411428500

Townsend, P. (1979). *Poverty in the United Kingdom,* London: Allen Lane and Penguin Books.

Tsemberis, S. (2010). *Housing First: The Pathways Model to End Homelessness for people with mental illness and addiction.* Center City, MN: Hazelden Publishing.

Vranken, J. (2001). Unravelling the social strands of poverty: Differentiation, fragmentation, inequality and exclusion. In H. T. Andersen & R. Van Kempen (Eds.), *Governing European cities* (pp. 71–91). Aldershot, England: Ashgate.

Wilson, W. J. (1987). *The Truly Disadvantaged: The Inner City, the Underclass, and Public Policy.* Chicago: University of Chicago Press.

# APPENDIX

**Table A8.1.** Overview of Case Studies[9]

| Case study number | Country | Field | Code | Name of socially innovative initiative | Authors |
|---|---|---|---|---|---|
| 1 | Austria | IE | 1AT-IE | Vielfalter | Wukovitsch, Weinzierl, & Novy |
| 2 | Italy | IE/R | 2IT-IE/R | Ánde Škola | Kazepov, Saruis, & Civino |
| 3 | Italy | HH | 3IT-HH | Io Cambio Status | Kazepov, Saruis, Colombo, & Civino |
| 4 | Italy | AL | 4IT-AL | Over-indebtedness Help Desk | Kazepov, Saruis, Colombo, & Civino |
| 5 | Austria | HH | 5AT-HH | Housing First Vienna | Wukovitsch, Novy, & Weinzierl |
| 6 | Hungary | HH | 6HU-HH | Housing First Hungary | Bernát & Tamás Kubik |
| 7 | Belgium | AL | 7BE-AL | Ten for Cooking | Cools & Oosterlynck |
| 8 | Belgium | AL | 8BE-AL | De Kringwinkel | Cools & Oosterlynck |
| 9 | Belgium | IE | 9BE-IE | Domo vzw Leuven | Cools & Oosterlynck |
| 10 | Austria | AL | 10AT-AL | ERfA—Sewing Workshop | Weinzierl & Novy |
| 11 | Austria | IE | 11AT-IE | HIPPY—Home Instruction for Parents of Pre-School Youngsters | Weinzierl, Wukovitsch, & Novy |
| 12 | Austria | AL/R | 12AT-AL/R | THARA | Wukovitch, Novy, & Weinzierl |
| 13 | Belgium | HH | 13BE-HH | Energy for All | Cools & Oosterlynck |
| 14 | United Kingdom | HH | 14UK-HH | Camden Housing First | Cools & Oosterlynck |
| 15 | Hungary | AL | 15HU-AL | Charity Shops | Bernát & Vercseg |
| 16 | United Kingdom | IE/R | 16UK-IE/R | The MigRom Project | Cools & Oosterlynck |
| 17 | Hungary | IE/R | 17HU-IE/R | Study Halls | Vercseg & Bernát |
| 18 | Belgium | HH/R | 18BE-HH/R | The Emmaüs Monastery Housing First Experiment | Cools & Oosterlynck |
| 19 | United Kingdom | AL | 19UK-AL | The Furniture Re-use Network | Cools & Oosterlynck |

(continued)

**Table A8.1.** Continued

| Case study number | Country | Field | Code | Name of socially innovative initiative | Authors |
|---|---|---|---|---|---|
| 20 | Brazil | AL | 20BR-AL | Movimento Nacional dos Catadores de Materiais Recicláveis | Tatagiba & Teixeira |
| 21 | Brazil | HH | 21BR-HH | União Nacional por Moradia Popular/Minha Casa Minha Vida—Entidades | Tatagiba & Teixeira |
| 22 | Italy | HH | 22IT-HH | Tutti a casa | Kazepov, Saruis, Colombo, & Civino |
| 23 | Italy | AL | 23IT-AL | Tradate Solidale | Kazepov, Saruis, Colombo, & Civino |
| 24 | Sweden | IE/AL/R | 24SE-IE/AL/R | Romane Buca in Sundbybergs | Kazepov, Civino, Saruis, & Colombo |
| 25 | Sweden | AL | 25SE-AL | Sprakstödjande Insatser | Kazepov, Civino, Saruis, & Colombo |
| 26 | Sweden | HH | 26SE-HH | Housing First Stockholm | Kazepov, Colombo, Saruis, & Civino |
| 27 | Sweden | AL | 27SE-AL | Rätt Steg | Kazepov, Colombo, Saruis, & Civino |
| 28 | Sweden | HH | 28SE-HH | UngBo 12 | Kazepov, Saruis, Colombo, & Civino |
| 29 | Spain | HH | 29ES-HH | SIDH | Kazepov, Colombo, Saruis, & Civino |
| 30 | Spain | IE | 30ES-IE | Caixa ProInfancia | Kazepov, Colombo, & Saruis |
| 31 | United Kingdom | IE/AL | 31UK-IE/AL | Inspire! ESF NEET programme | Cools & Oosterlynck |

*Note*: IE = inclusive education; HH = housing and homelessness; AL = activation and labor market; R = Roma.

# 9

# SOCIAL INVESTMENT AT CROSSROADS

## "THE THIRD WAY" OR "THE ENLIGHTENED PATH" FORWARD?

**Axel Cronert and Joakim Palme**

## INTRODUCTION

The European Union (EU) discourse on social policy has become increasingly focused on "capacitating strategies" that are associated with what is now commonly called social investment. Over the past decades, social investment has been identified as a strategy to promote not only equality of opportunity but also social inclusion, not least by preparing people for enduring participation in changing labor markets. A key idea underlying the social investment strategy is that the goals of increasing employment and reducing poverty are reconcilable. In 2005, when the President of the European Commission José Manuel Barroso defined his and the Commission's goals of the European Social Model (ESM) in terms of "equality of opportunity" and "social inclusion," the social investment strategy appeared to be a logical policy choice. Since then, the concept of social investment has gained further traction at the EU level, manifested among other things in the EU's "future agenda," Europe 2020, and in particular the launching of the Social Investment Package (SIP) by the European Commission in 2013 and the subsequent engagement in the follow-up of that initiative in, for example, the European Semester.

While social investment at the EU level has become a popular policy concept, the extent to which a social investment approach has been adopted by
the EU Member States "varies very widely" (Bouget, Frazer, Marlier, Sabato, &
Vanhercke, 2015, p. 6). What is clear, however, is that in recent years, the social
investment agenda has attracted much scholarly attention, including criticism
from a number of perspectives. Perhaps most notably, analysts have questioned
whether social investment–oriented policies achieve their intended distributional consequences, and raise doubts about the idea that the goals of increasing
employment and reducing poverty are reconcilable (Cantillon, 2011; Cantillon
& Vandenbroucke, 2014).

Here we recollect parts of the criticism on social investment and explore how
it applies differently to two different versions of the social investment approach
identified in the literature (e.g., Morel, Palier, & Palme, 2012): the "Nordic approach" (Esping-Andersen, Gallie, Hemerijck, & Myles, 2002)—which might
also be labeled the "Enlightened Path," both because it has been informed
by the social sciences and because the high tax road it entails is narrow and
demanding—and the "Third Way" pioneered by Giddens (1998).

The tension between these two approaches can be traced back to the late
1990s and to the development of the Lisbon agenda adopted in 2000. The Lisbon
agenda served as the context for the important contribution of Esping-Andersen
and colleagues in their report to the Belgian Presidency of the EU during the fall
of 2001, later published with the title *Why We Need a New Welfare State* (Esping-
Andersen et al., 2002). Although the approach promoted in the report has many
similarities with Giddens's (1998) Third Way—not least, the focus on the supply
side of the labor market and on investments in skill formation—it clearly defined
an alternative approach to social investment.

In a discourse where scholars fail to distinguish between these approaches
to social investment, this chapter aims to clarify how they differ in their understanding of what constitute productive and unproductive social expenditures,
the roles they ascribe to social policy and to civil society actors, their view
of equality, and how they appear to want to strike a balance between rights
and responsibilities (Andersson, 2009; Morel et al., 2012). We do this by, first,
tracing the origins of the two approaches. This clarification paves the way for
an analysis of how the two approaches relate differently to the concerns about
the redistributive effects of social investments and about the trade-off between employment and equality. Thereafter follows an examination of policy
developments in the Swedish welfare state to illustrate the tension between
the two approaches. As the subtitle implies, we see this chapter as a contribution to the policy discussion by identifying the choice between two competing
versions of the social investment approach, a choice that matters for how well

countries can deliver on the goals of both employment creation and poverty reduction.

## THE TWO APPROACHES TO SOCIAL INVESTMENT

### The Origins of the Nordic Approach to Social Investment

The origins of the social investment approach in its Nordic flavor can be traced back to the 1930s, to the Great Depression, and to what in Sweden came to be called the "Crisis in the Population Question" (i.e., the falling birth rates). In the midst of these crises, Alva and Gunnar Myrdal, a pedagogue and an economist, began to develop an approach to social policy aimed at supporting production and reproduction, which opened up an investment perspective on social policy (Morel et al., 2012). Decreasing birth rates were seen as an economic problem, in the context of increasing costs for households raising children, and with social consequences for those who could not afford to have children. Myrdal and Myrdal advocated policies that would combine direct economic support to families with children and indirect support for housing, as well as the provision of opportunities for female labor-force participation. The population question was formulated not only in terms of the "quantity" but also in terms of the "quality" (health and education) of the population—the social conditions for human capital formation.

The Myrdals, who became two of the most important Swedish policy intellectuals of the 20th century, were also concerned with economic growth and productivity. This is also true for the post-World War II continuation of the social investment approach in Sweden. Part of this continuation is closely intertwined with the Myrdals, even if the actual policy implementation came with a delay of (about four) decades. Part of it developed in a different context and by other actors in the labor movement, namely the trade union economists Gösta Rehn and Rudolf Meidner (Morel et al., 2012). The Rehn–Meidner model of economic policy was designed to support a kind of Schumpeterian creative destruction and transformation of the economy, while at the same time promoting "social construction" by means of selective but encompassing active labor market policy (ALMP) measures, including retraining of the labor force to make workers fit for the new economic structures. These investments in education and training of the labor force can no doubt be labeled "social" due to their distributional properties and inclusive effects (cf. Nelson & Stephens, 2012). The Rehn–Meidner model was also underpinned by a centralized, egalitarian wage policy, meant to shift resources toward the more productive sectors of the economy while stimulating consumer demand and, in turn, labor demand and employment (Kangas & Palme, 2005).

The expansion and universalization of the education system that began in the late 1950s and continued gradually throughout the postwar period were also clearly "social" in nature (Lindensjö & Lundgren, 2014). Next, beginning in the 1960s, the approach was complemented with adult education, which first appeared under the label "lifelong education." This further geared the regular education systems toward combining social and economic objectives. This also fed into a broader discussion of the role of education for societal development in the Organisation for Economic Co-operation and Development (OECD), now with the label of "lifelong learning," which eventually gained ground in the EU context (Jakobi, 2006).

While Keynesianism grew in importance and dominated as an economic paradigm in the Western Hemisphere until the late 1970s, it may be argued that following Keynes's primary concerns, the function of public spending was mainly a macroeconomic balancing mechanism rather than an instrument for reducing inequalities (cf. Sen, 2009) or an instrument for "social investment." The focus on female labor-market participation and gender equality in Sweden is something that belongs to the Myrdal imprint on the Swedish version of Keynesianism rather than (male) mainstream Keynesianism (Hobson, 2006). Gradually since the 1970s, the various components of what can be labeled the "dual-earner model" came into place, including separate taxation of spouses' incomes to improve incentives for a second earner and expansion of cradle-to-grave social services enabling women to combine family responsibilities with paid work in the expanding public sector as well as in the private sector. These services were vital to enable individuals and society to harvest the investment in women's human capital that had taken place during the first postwar decades and that would continue to expand (Palme, 1999).

Two other important features of the Nordic approach to social investment are the idea that widespread employment and decent wages are the best guarantees for avoiding poverty and other socioeconomic ills, and the notion of complementarities between "demanding" and "enabling" social policies to this end. Thus, clarifying the responsibility for individuals to search for, to move to, and to take up new employment, i.e., demanding social policies, became integral to the Nordic social investment approach as a complement to education and training programs, i.e., enabling social policies (Palme, 1999). In the realm of labor-market policy, the basic formula—at least before the crisis of the 1990s—was to allocate 75% of the overall expenditure to "active" labor market measures, i.e., ALMP, and 25% to "passive" measures, i.e., unemployment benefits (OECD, 2016). Still, social transfers were acknowledged as a potential productive factor and as an important tool for preventing poverty and inequality as well as depletion of human capital, and it was recognized that unemployment benefits may serve to reward formal labor-force attachment, to improve matching, to cater to macroeconomic stabilization, and to promote economic restructuring (Palme, Nelson, Sjöberg, & Minas, 2009). Family-related benefits are important for reducing child poverty and are even a precondition for social investments oriented toward children; parental leave insurance provides a second income for families with infants, and child-care benefits allow for a second earner in families with small children (Ferrarini, 2006).

In sum, from the 1930s onward, well into the postwar period, the social policy agenda formulated in Sweden was based on the core assumption that the trade-off between equality and efficiency can be bridged by social policies that also have economic objectives and by economic policies that also have social objectives. Thus, fighting poverty was about enhancing the productivity and employment of the population, and countercyclical policies were about fighting poverty and inequality. Redistribution was seen as an irrigation system (G. Myrdal), not a leaky bucket (Okun; cf. Korpi, 1985). The goal was equality and not merely poverty reduction (Erikson, 1993), and equality not only between social classes but also between the two genders. The means were universal and lifelong education, cradle-to-grave social services (particularly child care, but also elderly care), ALMP (particularly training and mobility grants), combined with earnings-related sickness insurance and parental leave benefits, as well as unemployment benefits to avoid human capital depletion and to cushion job transitions, and centralized wage bargaining to promote wage compression. At this point, it should be noted that wage bargaining structures do not figure as prominently as they deserve in the social investment literature. In this chapter, we take steps to remedy this omission.

## The Nordic Approach Meets the Third Way

The description above serves to facilitate the distinction between the Nordic approach to social investment—reflected in the work of Esping-Andersen and colleagues (2002) – and Giddens's (1998) Third Way. As mentioned above, the approaches differ in their understanding of what constitute productive and un-productive social expenditures, in the roles they ascribe to social policy and to civil society actors, in their view of equality, and how they appear to want to strike a balance between rights and responsibilities (Andersson, 2009; Morel et al., 2012). Where Giddens emphasized the moral hazards and unproduc-tive character of unemployment benefits and similar cash transfers, Esping-Andersen saw the productive values of such programs. Where Giddens valued the incentives created by inequalities, Esping-Andersen problematized the effects of lack of equality. Where Giddens promoted a "positive welfare society," the Nordic approach emphasized the role of the state. With respect to rights and responsibilities, Andersson (2009), on a discursive level, identified illuminating differences between the two approaches by comparing Swedish Social Democrats and New Labour in the United Kingdom. One way to interpret her rich analysis is to say that, whereas New Labour, inspired by the Third Way, tilted the balance between rights and responsibilities in the direction of responsibilities, in Sweden that kind of tilt did not occur until the Social Democrats lost the election in 2006.

It has to be recognized, though, that during the New Labour government, a number of significant real-world policy advancements took place. Investments in education increased substantially and more so than in most other countries in the Western Hemisphere. Poverty rates were also reduced following a number of changes in the tax-transfer system accompanied by employment growth. Particularly female employment was facilitated by expansion of child-care programs (Stewart, 2009; Stewart & Obolenskaya, 2016). Yet, traditional social insurance programs were left on a minimal level (Palme et al., 2009) signaling the political priority order for this kind of social policy instrument. This feature, in addition to the lack of a wage-formation model that would directly prevent in-work poverty, distinguished New Labour's model from a more fully fledged Nordic-style social investment package.

Although the polysemic nature of the concept of "social investment" (Jenson, 2010) has enabled it to accommodate these rather different approaches to social and labor-market policy reform, it is important for researchers to keep the two apart analytically, both when describing and explaining policy developments and when assessing the achievements and shortcomings of the social investment approach. However, this is not to argue that the two approaches are fixed or frozen—quite the contrary. On the one hand, in the post—New Labour era, the United Kingdom has seen a rhetorical move toward a Nordic-style emphasis on the quality of social services, lifelong learning, and quality of jobs (cf. Diamond & Liddle, 2012). On the other hand, as elaborated in the fourth section of this chapter, there has been a real move by the Swedish regime toward the Third Way. As regards the debates about the potential effect of social investment policies on poverty and inequality, it is important to keep the analytical distinctions between the approaches clear. In what follows, we elaborate further on these debates.

## SOCIAL INVESTMENT, REDISTRIBUTION, AND THE TRADE-OFF BETWEEN EMPLOYMENT AND EQUALITY

In recent scholarly debates on the merits of the social investment approach, it is the distributive consequences of its policy recipe—and in particular its consequences for poverty—that have received the most skepticism. Two other important strands of criticism concern its (lack of) commitment to equalizing power relations between women and men (see Jenson, 2009) and its inherent trade-off between imposing negative economic incentives and establishing a close monitoring of people's willingness to work (see Vandenbroucke & Vleminckx, 2011). With regard to its detrimental effect on poverty, a number of factors have been brought up that are held to be intrinsic to the social investment approach. However, some of these concerns primarily have bearing on either the particular principles or policy prescriptions linked to the Third Way approach, or the consequences of "activation" reforms introduced across Europe over the past two decades, most of which have had very little investment content (De la Porte & Jacobsson, 2012).

First, it has been suggested that, because the consumption of those public services that are associated with the social investment approach are typically work-related, such services have a less redistributive profile than traditional cash transfers, giving way to "Matthew effects" (Cantillon, 2011). Second, it has been suggested that the shift on the political agenda from passive income-support policies to active investment policies has resulted in a reallocation of resources away from the more redistributive policy areas to the less so. Third, it has been argued that the discursive emphasis on "making work pay" has justified, and perhaps even necessitated, a re-commodification of citizens by means of retrenchment of benefits, with detrimental consequences for the more vulnerable (Vandenbroucke & Vleminckx, 2011). Fourth, it has been argued that, while on an aggregate level these consequences could have been mitigated in case the policies were successful in moving unemployed people into employment, the proportion of people living in jobless households has hardly decreased in the EU in the wake of the employment and inclusion strategies, despite rising overall employment rates.

Turning first to the redistributive profile of the services, most evidence so far seems to suggest that, on an aggregate level, social investment-oriented services are redistributive in an egalitarian direction—although findings vary with respect to the extent. For instance, Esping-Andersen and Myles (2009, p. 654) found that services are generally redistributive but less so than some cash transfers, whereas Verbist and Matsaganis (2014) found that the poverty-reducing effect of services is much larger than the same effect of cash transfers in the working-age population. Using concentration coefficients, they show that this is true because, although the design of cash transfers in most cases make them more oriented toward lower income groups, services are much more important in size. Nelson and Stephens (2012) find that a range of social investment–oriented services are positively related to the consequent level of general skills—especially in the bottom half of the skill distribution—and to both employment levels in general and employment in knowledge-intensive services.

Perhaps more importantly, however, the distributional profile of services seems to depend on the design of specific policies, the context in which they are introduced, and how they are combined to achieve institutional complementarities. With respect to child-care policies, for instance, Vaalavuo (2011) found that in only a few countries, the top income quintiles benefit disproportionally from child-care services, likely due to higher take-up. Comparing child-care provision in Flanders and Sweden, Van Lancker and Ghysels (2012) argued that the larger redistributive effect found in the Swedish case can be explained by the guaranteed and sufficient access to the services and the higher employment level among low-skilled women in Sweden.

With respect to ALMP, Gingrich and Ansell (2015), as well as Cronert (2017), argued that these do not have predefined distributional profiles but can be targeted at different groups by different actors. Accordingly, Cronert (2017) found that left-wing governments are more prone to expand programs targeted exclusively at those who are unemployed or at risk of losing their jobs, whereas no partisan difference was found for programs meant to increase labor-force participation among groups outside of the labor force (i.e., those not previously in employment or actively seeking employment). This is consistent with Gingrich and Ansell's (2015) argument that right-wing governments are more likely to expand ALMP programs in those institutional contexts—characterized by lower employment-protection legislation and lower union influence—where they are more likely to be targeted at individuals outside of the labor force.

In order to understand the distributional effects of services, we also need to consider the revenue side of the programs in the analysis, as was observed by Åberg (1989), was illustrated by Rothstein (1998), and more recently was emphasized by Whiteford (2008).

In sum, existing evidence seems to suggest that, in general, the distributional profile of social investment-oriented services, as defined in the previous section, is a function of their content and targeting, and of the national context in which they are implemented (Gingrich & Ansell, 2015; Vandenbroucke & Vleminckx, 2011), but that their potential is there. With Vandenbroucke and Vleminckx (2011), we argue not only that Matthew effects of services can be countered by a quasi-universal provision, combined with labor-market conditions that enhance female employment at all skill levels, but also that such a policy design represents a step toward an "enlightened" social investment path.

The second and the third concerns, labeled resource-competition and re-commodification by Vandenbroucke and Vleminckx (2011), warrant a recollection of the distinction between the Nordic and the Third Way approaches to social investment. Whereas for Giddens (1998) welfare-state restructuring is indeed about enacting a shift from "passive" to "active" social policies, the Nordic approach stresses that "social promotion" must be combined with "social protection" (Hemerijck, 2012). Thus, on an ideational basis, the resource-competition and re-commodification critiques are primarily relevant to the Third Way approach. Granted, both approaches explicitly favor labor market participation (market work). However, following Esping-Andersen, we reserve the concept of de-commodification to what social protection does in terms of changing the bargaining power of workers and thus labor relations; presumably allowing de-commodified workers "to walk tall and look the employers in the eye", to paraphrase Pettit (2012). Re-commodification, therefore, should not be equated to the kind of market work that is decent, reasonably well paid, and adequately insured, but should be reserved to describe circumstances of "any" jobs with inadequate insurance and/or in-work poverty.

Turning to the empirical thrust of the resource-competition critique, Vandenbroucke and Vleminckx (2011) concluded their analysis of change in social expenditure over two decades in 14 countries by noting that "if there was pressure on traditional redistributive budgets because of competing claims, it came more from healthcare (and in a number of countries from old age spending) than from the new [social investment–oriented] programs," and by pointing out that "in most countries long-term evolutions are in play, rather than a sudden policy change prompted by the [social investment–oriented] Lisbon agenda" (2011, p. 460). Along the same lines, the results from Nikolai's (2012) and Vandenbroucke and Diris' (2014) studies of long-term social expenditure contradict the idea of a shift from passive to active spending. Vandenbroucke and Vleminckx (2011) did not rule out, however, that given the context of relatively tight budgetary constraints for many European governments, the "making work pay" component of social investment may have justified and reinforced pressures for retrenchment in the field of unemployment benefits. We agree, and as elaborated in the concluding section, budgetary constraints do appear to make combined expansions of social investments and social protection difficult in many European countries. Thus, it may be possible to avoid the "employment/poverty/budgetary constraints" trilemma only in the longer run and only if spending is both progressive and capability-enhancing (cf. Cantillon & Vandenbrouke, 2014).

When addressing the fourth concern, the poverty-reducing capacity of social investment policies, and more specifically, the "employment vs. poverty trade-off," it is again important to distinguish between the Nordic and the Third Way approaches to social investment. We agree that an even distribution of work is key to poverty reduction (Cantillon, 2011; de Beer, 2007), and we see that as another reason to stress the importance of providing enabling services, such as child care, to households with low work-intensity. But that might not be enough to escape the trade-off. Atkinson (2010) outlines two potential strategies for achieving high employment among workers with low productivity: lowering the cost of job creation (which generally requires mobilization of public resources) and reducing reservation wages by reducing the generosity of social protection. While the second strategy is less expensive, it may come at the cost of increasing the number of working poor (i.e., if reservation wages are set below the poverty line). The German experience since the Hartz reforms in the first half of the 2000s and the introduction of low-paid "mini-jobs" might illustrate this strategy. Between 2000 and 2010, employment in the age group 20 to 64 increased by a notable 6.1 percentage points (Eurostat, 2016b). In 2010, however, the overall at-risk-of-poverty rate at 50% (60%) of the median income was 9.6% (16.4%), which corresponds to a 26% (29%) increase over the period (Luxembourg Income Study, 2015).

Presented to Atkinson's dilemma—which bears resemblance to those earlier phrased by Esping-Andersen (1993) and Iversen and Wren (1998)—most proponents of social investment would probably argue that the trade-off can be mitigated to the extent that investments in human capital and in universal education systems, combined with targeted ALMP, succeed in raising productivity in the lower end of the distribution. Second, proponents of the Nordic approach would go on to point out that the extent to which increased employment leads to increased poverty is likely to depend on the degree of wage compression. If statutory or collectively bargained entry-level wages are high relative to the median wage, the prevalence of in-work poverty is likely to be limited. Whereas the influential trilemma of the service economy (Iversen & Wren, 1998) has it that, in the post-industrial era, wage compression inhibits employment growth in the first place, proponents of the Nordic approach would tend to agree more with the revised version of the trilemma offered by Wren, Fodor, & Theodoropoulou (2013), which suggests that "the possibility exists for high-productivity, internationally traded service sectors to take over from manufacturing sectors as the dynamic drivers of employment expansion in the post-industrial economy, reducing the need to rely on low relative wages at the bottom of the earnings distribution to facilitate private service employment expansion" (2013, p. 109). Anyhow, the main point here is that, to the extent that employment increases, it should primarily fail to decrease poverty if taking place in a context of high wage dispersion.

To sum up this section, we argue that the distinction between the Nordic approach and the Third Way approach to social investment is important to bear in mind when assessing the critiques directed at the social investment perspective, especially with respect to the complementarity between social investments and social protection for promoting high employment and low poverty. To further illustrate this point, the next section demonstrates how the distinction between the two approaches can be used to describe the changes in the Swedish social investment state that have taken place over the past three decades.

## SOCIAL INVESTMENT TRENDS IN SWEDEN: FROM THE ENLIGHTENED PATH TO THE THIRD WAY?

In the mid-1980s—around the time that our historical outline of the development of the Nordic approach to social investment ends—Sweden clearly had the most pronouncedly social investment–oriented social expenditure profile among the European countries (Meeusen & Nys, 2012). As suggested by Vandenbroucke and Diris (2014), these past investments probably help explain why, until recently, the country has also had a comparably good poverty record. The policy developments that took place over the three decades that followed suggest that, gradually over the period, and more distinctly during the last decade, Sweden has turned away from the Nordic approach, toward a Third Way approach. In our understanding, this shift is also important for understanding the substantial increase in the relative at-risk-of-poverty rate after transfers in Sweden since the mid-2000s, reported in Figure 9.1 as well as by Gabos et al. in Chapter 2 of this volume.

Consider first some changes in social expenditure, discussed in greater detail in Palme and Cronert (2015). Whereas total social expenditures were at remarkably similar levels in relation to GDP in the mid-1980s and the early 2010s, there have been important changes in the composition of spending—away from human capital investment and social protection, toward promotion of labor-force participation. Among social investment–oriented policies, parental leave, elderly care, and child-care services have increased, whereas ALMP has seen a steady and sizable drop. In parallel, there has been a profound shift of focus of the ALMP portfolio, from skill formation toward employment assistance (or "work first" policies). Training programs decreased from 0.7% of GDP to 0.1% of GDP, whereas employment incentives and labor-market services—aimed at promoting labor-market entry—increased from 0.6% to 0.9% of GDP. The latter types now account for 75% of the ALMP portfolio.

With respect to public spending on regular education in Sweden, the overall levels as share of GDP have remained relatively stable since the mid-1990s, but because enrollment has increased, the education system has, in a sense, been diluted (Palme and Cronert, 2015). Thus, human capital investment effort, measured as spending per student, has gradually dropped for all

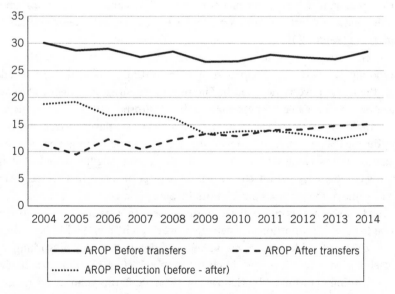

**Figure 9.1.** At-risk-of-poverty (AROP) rates before and after transfers in Sweden, 2004–2014. *Note:* "AROP Before transfers" and "AROP After transfers" refer to the AROP rate at the 60% threshold, before and after social transfers (excluding pensions). "AROP Reduction (before – after)" is the difference between the two rates. The trends are similar if we consider the Poverty Reduction Index used by Gabos et al. in Chapter 2 of this volume. *Source:* Eurostat (2016a).

school types except preschool (age 1 to 6), and especially so for tertiary education. Last, with respect to social protection, expenditures on unemployment compensation, early retirement, social assistance, paid sick leave, and family allowances are down 25% in relation to GDP since 1985. Importantly, this trend is a matter of not only shrinking caseloads but also the decreased adequacy of the social protection systems. Replacement rates have dropped sharply since the early 2000s in the case of unemployment benefits, and more gradually since the early 1990s in the case of social assistance benefits (Kuivalainen & Nelson, 2012). These developments are also reflected in the decreasing poverty-reducing capacity of social transfers reported in Figure 9.1, as well as in Gabos et al. in Chapter 2 of this volume.

In addition, the Swedish social investment state has been affected by changes in three areas not reflected in the expenditure data, namely, the demanding dimension of ALMP, minimum wages, and tax policy. First, whereas the enabling dimension of the Swedish ALMP regime—expressed, for instance, in terms of the share of the ALMP portfolio that is devoted to labor-market training programs—has been pulled back, its demanding dimension—that is, the requirements placed on jobless individuals—has clearly been strengthened. Overall, early enrollment in ALMP programs—notably in low-cost job-search assistance programs but also in costlier wage-subsidy programs—has increased; the overall share of registered unemployed who are enrolled in a program was up from 42% in 1999 to 60% in 2013 (Cronert, 2015). In addition, the strictness of the sanctions imposed on unemployment benefit recipients if they fail to comply with the program requirements or reject a suitable job offer have been increased stepwise since the mid-1990s (Knotz, 2016).

Given these changes, as well as the growing social expenditure aimed at promoting labor-force participation, it is interesting to note that, in parallel with the rising poverty depicted in Figure 9.1, overall employment in Sweden has grown by a notable 2.5 percentage points (Eurostat, 2016b). At first glance, these trends seem to indicate that an "employment vs. poverty" trade-off is in play during the period. As mentioned above, such a trade-off might occur in two scenarios: if new employment primarily takes place among households that are already comparably "work-rich," or if it takes place at wages that are below the poverty line or the previous out-of-work income packages.

The first scenario is contradicted in the present case, as employment growth seems to have disproportionately benefited "work-poor" households. Indeed, between 2004 and 2014, Sweden saw a 26% reduction in the share of working-age households with very low work intensity, from 8.5% to 6.3% (Eurostat, 2016a), and according to estimates by Gabos et al. (Chapter 2, this volume) for roughly the same period, the reduction of jobless households has translated into a slight reduction of the relative poverty rate.

The second scenario is disputed by the development of minimum wages in recent decades. In Sweden, minimum wages are not regulated by law, but they are subject to sector-specific negotiations between employers and trade unions. Settlements on minimum wages are found in the numerous collective agreements, which in total cover approximately 90% of the Swedish workers. Whereas workers who are not covered by a collective agreement are typically not entitled to occupational pensions and other benefits, their wages tend to match collectively agreed levels. Data for seven of the largest collective agreements indicate that, in each settlement, gross real minimum wages have grown faster than the real median disposable income over the past two decades. These agreements are signed by unions that make up about 74% of the total membership of the Swedish Confederation of Trade Unions (LO). Data from Skedinger (2010) and complemented by the authors show an average 2.3% annual growth rate of gross real minimum wages, while the real median disposable income grew 1.5% annually over the period 1995–2011 (Statistics Sweden, 2016).

For a single-person household, this implies a reduction in the share of annual full-time work at minimum wage needed to yield a disposable income that exceeds the 60% of median poverty line from 98% to 76% between 2000 and 2011. This has contributed to a decrease in the relative at-risk-of-poverty rate before social transfers, as shown in Figure 9.1. Taken together, these observations challenge the notion of an employment vs. poverty trade-off in the Swedish case and suggest that the explanations for the rising relative poverty have to be sought elsewhere.

In addition to the deterioration of social protection discussed above, some recent tax reforms are likely to have contributed to the rising relative poverty rates. Perhaps most significant is the Jobbskatteavdrag, a general, non-means-tested earned income tax credit (EITC) first introduced in 2007. The general application of the EITC to all workers notably bears the imprint of the Nordic principle of universalism. However, it clearly resembles those EITCs previously introduced in the United Kingdom and the United States, in the sense that it constitutes "fiscal social policy" (i.e., the use of the tax system to promote social purposes), and because it discriminates specifically between the working and nonworking populations. Expanded four times since its introduction, the EITC has substantially reduced income taxes for workers across the wage distribution (OECD, 2014), albeit with larger relative reductions for workers with lower incomes. While these reforms have increased disposable income for all working persons, and arguably increased employment and extended the tax base (cf. Kenworthy, Chapter 7 in this volume), they are "far from self-financed" (Ericson, Flood, & Wahlberg, 2009, p. 1), and consequently, resources available for potentially more "pro-poor" expenditure have significantly decreased. Also, by design, the EITC does not apply to income from pensions and other social benefits. As a result, disposable income for the nonworking population has decreased relative to the median disposable income, which in turn has mechanically pushed a reasonably large number of them below the relative at-risk-of-poverty threshold. This notion is in line with the finding by Gabos and colleagues (Chapter 2, this volume) that the rise in poverty risk in Sweden over the years in which the EITC was expanded was primarily located among jobless households (Halleröd, Fritzell, Palme, & Schön, 2015).

To sum up, this survey shows that, despite a largely unchanged level of total social expenditure, Sweden has seen a clear recasting of its social and labor-market policy portfolio. Policies to promote labor-force participation and to "make work pay"—such as child-care and elderly-care services, employment assistance programs, benefit sanctions, and the EITC—have been expanded, whereas the human capital investment content of the policy portfolio has been diluted and the social protection systems for the working-age population have been weakened. This can best be described as a movement away from the Nordic social investment approach that identified Sweden in the postwar era, toward a Third Way approach to social investment. Considering that social protection cutbacks and in-work benefits are distinctive to the Third Way approach to social investment, it also suggests that it is not the social investment agenda per se— through any inherent employment vs. poverty trade-off—but the shift from the Nordic approach to the Third Way approach that emerges as the more plausible explanation for the observed rise in relative poverty in Sweden.

## CONCLUSION

The results presented in this chapter highlight the importance for scholars of social investment to distinguish between its two dominant approaches, not only for identifying differences among countries but also within countries over time— as illustrated by the Swedish case. A recent example points to the failure of the field to establish a consensus on this distinction. In a thoughtful study on the conditionality of the effect of increasing unemployment on poverty, Rueda initially equated "activation" and "social investment" (2012, p. 364), and he later concluded that his results

> clearly illustrate that the best way to control or even reverse the effects of unemployment on poverty is for welfare states to increase the generosity of their unemployment benefits at the same time that they increase their levels of ALMP. This is *not* a prescription of the workfare-social investment framework and, more important, it is not a prescription that is easy to implement in times of crisis. (Rueda, 2012, p. 382; emphasis added)

While Rueda's second point is certainly true, the critique he directed toward the prescriptions of the social investment approach should reasonably be targeted to its Third Way interpretation rather than to the approach in its entirety. Interestingly, the recipe that Rueda found most efficient in mitigating poverty effects of unemployment is precisely the balanced approach to social investment promoted by Esping-Andersen et al. (2002), Vandenbroucke and Vleminckx (2011), and Morel et al. (2012), in which social protection and social promotion are combined. This suggests that the tension between old and new forms of social policies is less clear than assumed by the critics of the social investment perspective, and that it may actually be dissolved by a proper policy design. Another point that deserves to be emphasized is the role of wage-bargaining institutions and adequate minimum wages, which appear to have been largely neglected in previous literature on social investments. Together with the chapters by Collado et al., Vandelannoote and Verbist, and Cantillon et al. in this volume, we take steps to highlight the importance of adequate minimum wages for successful poverty prevention.

Turning from ideas to practice, our findings may also shed some new light on two contested empirical issues concerning the social investment approach, at least with respect to the case of Sweden: the alleged trade-off between spending on social protection and social promotion, and the economic sustainability of the social investment state. Streeck and Mertens (2011) studied long-term trends in expenditure on "soft public investment"—which is essentially equivalent to social investment—in Sweden, Germany, and the United States. Identifying a long-term, negative trend in each of the cases, they suggested that fiscal stress and political austerity have caused, and will continue to cause, a downward pressure on collective investment, which might in the end realize a "convergence on the lowest possible level" (2011, p. 25). When it comes to the Swedish case, we are not convinced that this observed downward trend is inevitable. In any event, it is evident that the fiscal conditions of Swedish public finances over the past ten years—marked by a severe financial crisis—did allow for a planned tax revenue cut amounting to 3.5 times the size of the national budget for ALMP. This, we suggest, indicates that the steps recently taken, away from the Enlightened Path of social investment toward the Third Way, are not singlehandedly a result of economic necessity or any inescapable trade-off between poverty reduction today and investments for tomorrow, but also a matter of political choice. Hence, for Sweden, getting back on the track of the Enlightened Path requires a reversal of policy priorities, and it demands what should openly be declared as massive investments.

The scope for political choice is more limited in countries in Southern Europe, and Ireland for that matter, which have been experiencing a sovereign debt crisis in the wake of the global financial crisis. In line with Streeck and Mertens (2011), we can expect that the scope for action is similarly restricted in other European countries, strained by a combination of the increasing burden of entitlements of an aging population and sharpened tax competition. However, as evidenced in Hills et al. and Matsaganis et al. (in this volume), the policy responses even among the most crisis-stricken countries in the EU have differed—with varying repercussions for social outcomes. This suggests that it may actually be possible for many EU Member States to choose an Enlightened Path forward, only that it perhaps is more narrow and demanding than ever.

## NOTE

The authors thank the participants at the ImPRovE meeting in Antwerp in April 2014, a workshop within the project "Global economic crisis, institutional change and inequality in comparative perspective" (VR Dnr 2012-5503), at Uppsala University in June 2014, and the CROP/WCFIA/CES workshop on Social Inclusion and Poverty Eradication, at Harvard University in November 2016, and in particular the é, and John Hills—as well as Peter A. Hall for useful comments on previous versions of the chapter. The research for this chapter has benefited from financial support by the European Unioneditors of this volume—Bea Cantillon, Tim Goedem's 7th Framework Programme (FP7/2012-2016) under Grant Agreement N. 290613 (ImPRovE: Poverty Reduction in Europe: Social Policy and Innovation; http://improve-research.eu).

## REFERENCES

Åberg, R. (1989). Distributive mechanisms of the welfare state—A formal analysis and an empirical application. *European Sociological Review, 5,* 167–182.

Andersson, J. (2009). *The library and the workshop.* Stanford, CA: Stanford University Press.

Atkinson, A. B. (2010). Poverty and the EU: The new decade [Macerata Lectures on European Economic Policy]. Macerata, Italy: Universita degli Studi di Macerata.

Bouget, D., Frazer, H., Marlier, E., Sabato, S., & Vanhercke, B. (2015). *Social investment in Europe: A study of national policies.* Brussels, Belgium: European Social Policy Network.

Cantillon, B. (2011). The paradox of the social investment state: Growth, employment and poverty in the Lisbon era. *Journal of European Social Policy, 21*(5), 432–449.

Cantillon, B., & Vandenbroucke, F. (2014). *Reconciling work and poverty reduction: How successful are European welfare states?* Oxford, England: Oxford University Press.

Cronert, A. (2015). *Arbetsförmedlingen och arbetskraftsförmedlingen— Missbedömd eller dömd att misslyckas?* Stockholm, Sweden: Landsorganisationen i Sverige.

Cronert, A. (2017). Unemployment reduction or labor force expansion? How partisanship matters for the design of active labor market policy in Europe. *Socio-Economic Review.*

de Beer, P. (2007). Why work is not a panacea: A decomposition analysis of EU-15 countries. *Journal of European Social Policy, 17*(4), 375–388.

De la Porte, C., & Jacobsson, K. (2012). Social investment or recommodification? Assessing the employment policies of the EU member states. In N. Morel, B.

Palier, & J. Palme (Eds.), *Towards a social investment welfare state?* Bristol, England: The Policy Press.

Diamond, P., & Liddle, R. (2012). Aftershock: The post-crisis social investment welfare state in Europe. In N. Morel, B. Palier, & J. Palme (Eds.), *Towards a social investment welfare state?* Bristol, England: The Policy Press.

Ericson, P., Flood, L., & Wahlberg, R. (2009). *SWEtaxben: A Swedish tax/benefit micro simulation model and an evaluation of a Swedish tax reform* [IZA Discussion Paper No. 4106]. Bonn, Germany: Institute for the Study of Labor (IZA).

Erikson, E. H. (1993). *Childhood and society.* New York, NY: Norton.

Esping-Andersen, G. (1993). *Changing classes: Stratification and mobility in post-industrial societies.* London, England: Sage.

Esping-Andersen, G., Gallie, D., Hemerijck, A., & Myles, J. (2002). *Why we need a new welfare state.* Oxford, England: Oxford University Press.

Esping-Andersen, G., & Myles, J. (2009). Economic inequality and the welfare state. In W. Salverda, B. Nolan, & T. M. Smeeding (Eds.), *The Oxford handbook of economic inequality.* Oxford, England: Oxford University Press.

Eurostat. (2016a). *EU statistics on income and living conditions (ilc_li02, ilc_li06, ilc_li10, and ilc_lvps03).* www.ec.europa.eu/eurostat

Eurostat. (2016b). *EU labour force survey (lfsa_ergan).* www.ec.europa.eu/eurostat

Ferrarini, T. (2006). *Families, states and labour markets: Institutions, causes and consequences of family policy in post-war welfare states.* Cheltenham, England: Edward Elgar.

Giddens, A. (1998). *The Third Way: The renewal of social democracy.* Cambridge, England: Polity Press.

Gingrich, J., & Ansell, B. (2015). The dynamics of social investment: Human capital, activation, and care. In P. Beramendi, S. Häusermann, H. Kitschelt, & H. Kriesi (Eds.), *Towards a social investment welfare state?* Cambridge, England: Cambridge University Press.

Halleröd, B., Fritzell, J., Palme, J., & Schön, P. (2015). *ESPN country profile: Sweden.* Brussels, Belgium: European Commission.

Hemerijck, A. (2012). Two or three waves of welfare state transformation? In N. Morel, B. Palier, & J. Palme (Eds.), *Towards a social investment welfare state?* Bristol, England: The Policy Press.

Hobson, B. (2006). The evolution of the women friendly state: Opportunities and constraints in the Swedish welfare state. In S. Hassim & S. Razavi (Eds.), *Gender and social policy.* Basingstoke, England: Palgrave.

Iversen, T., & Wren, A. (1998). Equality, employment and budgetary restraint: The trilemma of the service economy. *World Politics, 50*(4), 507–546.

Jakobi, A. (2006). *The worldwide norm of lifelong learning: A study of global policy development* (Doctoral dissertation), Bielefeld, Germany: Bielefeld University.

Jenson, J. (2009). Lost in translation: The social investment perspective and gender equality. *Social Politics: International Studies in Gender, State & Society, 16*(4), 446–483.

Jenson, J. (2010). Diffusing ideas for after neoliberalism: The social investment perspective in Europe and Latin America. *Global Social Policy, 10*(1), 59–84.

Kangas, O., & Palme, J. (2005). *Social policy and economic development in the Nordic countries.* Basingstoke, England: Palgrave.

Korpi, W. (1985). Economic growth and the welfare state: Leaky bucket or irrigation system? *European Sociological Review, 1*(2), 97–118.

Knotz, C. (2016). *Forcing the unemployed to work: Essays on the politics of unemployment benefit reform in affluent democracies* (Doctoral dissertation). Lund, Sweden: Lund University.

Kuivalainen, S., &Nelson, K. (2012). Eroding minimum income in the Nordic countries and abroad? Reassessing the typical character of Nordic social assistance. In J. Kvist, J. Fritzell, B. Hvinden, & O. Kangas (Eds.), *Changing social equality—The Nordic welfare model in the 21st Century.* Bristol, England: The Policy Press.

Lindensjö, B., & Lundgren, U. P. (2014). *Utbildningsreformer och politisk styrning.* Stockholm, Sweden: Liber förlag.

Luxembourg Income Study (LIS). (2015). *Luxembourg Income Study inequality and poverty key figures: Germany 2000, 2010.* www.lisdatacenter.org

Meeusen, L., & Nys, A. (2012). *Are new social risk expenditures crowding out the old?* [CSB Working Paper 12/08]. Antwerp, Belgium: Herman Deleeck Centre for Social Policy, University of Antwerp.

Morel, N., Palier, B., & Palme, J. (2012). *Towards a social investment welfare state?* Bristol, England: The Policy Press.

Nelson, M., & Stephens, J. D. (2012). Do social investment policies produce more and better jobs? In N. Morel, B. Palier & J. Palme, (Eds.), *Towards a social investment welfare state?* Bristol, England: The Policy Press.

Nikolai, R. (2012). Towards social investment? Patterns of public policy in the OECD world. In N. Morel, B. Palier, & J. Palme (Eds.), *Towards a social investment welfare state?* Bristol, England: The Policy Press.

Organisation for Economic Co-operation and Development (OECD). (2016). *Social expenditure database.* stats.oecd.org

Organisation for Economic Co-operation and Development (OECD). (2014). *Taxing wages: Comparative tables.* stats.oecd.org

Palme, J. (1999). *Den nordiska modellen och moderniseringen av de sociala trygghetssystemen i Europa: i korthet.* Copenhagen, Norway: Nordic Council of Ministers.

Palme, J., & Cronert, A. (2015). *Trends in the Swedish social investment welfare state: 'the Enlightened Path' or 'the Third Way' for 'the lions'?* [ImPRovE

Working Paper no. 15/12]. Antwerp, Belgium: Herman Deleeck Centre for Social Policy, University of Antwerp.

Palme, J., Nelson, K., Sjöberg, O., & Minas, R. (2009). *European social models, protection and inclusion.* Stockholm, Sweden: Institute for Futures Studies.

Pettit, P. (2012). *On the people's terms.* Cambridge, England: Cambridge University Press.

Rothstein, B. (1998). *Just institutions matter.* Cambridge, England: Cambridge University Press.

Rueda, D. (2012). West European welfare states in times of crisis. In N. Bermeo & J. Pontusson (Eds.), *Coping with crisis.* New York, NY: Russell Sage Foundation.

Sen, A. (2009). Capitalism beyond the crisis. *The New York Review of Books, 56*(5).

Skedinger, P. (2010). Sweden: A minimum wage model in need of modification. In D. Vaughan-Whitehead (Ed.), *The minimum wage revisited in the enlarged EU.* Cheltenham, England: Edward Elgar.

Statistics Sweden. (2016). *Data on Consumer Price Index (KPI) and disposable income per consumption unit (HEK).* www.scb.se

Stewart, K. (2009). "A scar on the soul of Britain": Child poverty and disadvantage under New Labour. In J. Hills, T. Sefton, & K. Stewart (Eds.), *Towards a more equal society? Poverty, inequality and policy since 1997.* Bristol, England: The Policy Press.

Stewart, K., & Obolenskaya, P. (2016). Young children. In R. Lupton, K. Stewart, T. Burchardt, J. Hills, & P. Vizard (Eds.), *Social policy in a cold climate: Policies and their consequences since the crisis.* Bristol, England: The Policy Press.

Streeck, W., & Mertens, D. (2011). *Fiscal austerity and public investment: Is the possible the enemy of the necessary?* [MPIfG Discussion Paper 11/12]. Cologne, Germany: Max Planck Institute for the Study of Societies.

Vaalavuo, M. (2011). *Towards an improved measure of income inequality: The impact of public services on income distribution—An international comparison (Diss.).* Florence, Italy: European University Institute.

Van Lancker, W., & Ghysels, J. (2012).Who benefits? The social distribution of subsidized childcare in Sweden and Flanders. *Acta Sociologica, 55*(2), 125–142.

Vandenbroucke, F., & Vleminckx, K. (2011). Disappointing poverty trends: Is the social investment state to blame? *Journal of European Social Policy, 21*(5), 450–471.

Vandenbroucke, F., & Diris, R. (2014). Mapping at-risk-of-poverty rates, household employment and social spending. In B. Cantillon & F. Vandenbroucke (Eds.), *Reconciling work and poverty reduction: How successful are European welfare states?* Oxford, England: Oxford University Press.

Verbist, G., & Matsaganis, M. (2014). The redistributive capacity of services in the European Union. In B. Cantillon & F. Vandenbroucke (Eds.), *Reconciling work and poverty reduction: How successful are European welfare states?* Oxford, England: Oxford University Press.

Whiteford, P. (2008). How much redistribution do governments achieve? The role of cash transfers and household taxes. *Growing Unequal?* Paris, France: Organisation for Economic Co-operation and Development.

Wren, A., Fodor, M., & Theodoropoulou, S. (2013). The trilemma revisited: Institutions, inequality, and employment creation in an era of ICT-intensive service expansion. In A. Wren (Ed.), *The political economy of the service transition.* Oxford, England: Oxford University Press.

# PART 4

## TOWARD A DECENT SOCIAL FLOOR FOR ALL EUROPEANS

# 10

# THE END OF CHEAP TALK ABOUT POVERTY REDUCTION

## THE COST OF CLOSING THE POVERTY GAP WHILE MAINTAINING WORK INCENTIVES

**Diego Collado, Bea Cantillon, Karel Van den Bosch, Tim Goedemé, and Dieter Vandelannoote**

## INTRODUCTION

Previous research has calculated the cost of closing the gap between the incomes of poor families and poverty thresholds (Cantillon, Van Mechelen, Pintelon, & Van den Heede, 2014; Vandenbroucke, Cantillon, Van Mechelen, Goedemé, & Van Lancker, 2013). These studies usually find that the amounts required to close the poverty gap in the developed welfare states of Northern and Western Europe are sizable, although they seem generally not beyond the capacity of these welfare states to generate. For example, they were between 1.9% and 2.7% of total population incomes in 2009 in the countries we studied, namely, Belgium, Denmark, and the United Kingdom. However, given that in many European countries the incomes of low-earnings households are below the at-risk-of-poverty threshold, such a measure in itself would result in considerable "unemployment traps." Any realistic proposal to eliminate poverty should ensure that in-work income exceeds out-of-work income, in order to maintain sufficient work incentives. Hence, in this chapter we calculate the cost of closing the poverty gap for the entire population (including those retired from the labor market) while maintaining current average financial participation incentives at the bottom of the income distribution.

Results of our calculations suggest that the amounts needed to close the poverty gap in these countries while maintaining financial work incentives are around twice the budget needed just to lift all disposable household incomes to the poverty threshold. This highlights that the eradication of poverty in Europe would require substantial additional income redistribution. These findings point to the need to reconnect the discourses about poverty reduction, on the one hand, with those on rising income inequality, downward pressures on low wages, and the issue of adequate work incentives, on the other hand.

The chapter is structured as follows. The next section details the policy context. The third section discusses the data and methods used. This is followed by the results and then the conclusion.

## POLICY CONTEXT: A SOCIAL TRILEMMA

We argue that the structural forces underlying the inadequacy of social protection can be understood as a "social trilemma" (Cantillon & Vandenbroucke, 2014). As a consequence of mounting pressures on segments of the labor market with low productivity, resulting from skill-biased technological change and increased global competition, it might have become difficult to achieve adequate income protection for those out of work while preserving current financial work incentives, without increasing social spending for both those in and out of work.[1,2]

In the past decades, the first 15 countries that joined the EU (EU15) seem to have struggled with a social trilemma so conceived. On the one hand, there were attempts to increase employment by reducing and tightening social protection for jobless households (Atkinson, 2010; Bartels & Pestel, 2016). For example, in the 2000s, in just about half of the countries considered by Cantillon, Marchal, and Luigjes in Chapter 12 in this volume, the minimum social floor for jobless households was raised in relation to poverty thresholds. On the other hand, "gross-to-net" efforts for households through cash transfers and tax credits to low wage earners were increased in most countries (Immervoll, 2007; Marchal & Marx, 2015; Marx, Marchal, & Nolan, 2013). Consistent with this, there is evidence that, before the crisis, in the richest EU countries, decreases in the number of jobless households were generally compensated by increases in poverty among the households that remained jobless. In some countries, this was also accompanied by increased poverty among working households (see Chapter 2 by Gábos et al. in this volume; Corluy & Vandenbroucke, 2014). This suggests that gross-to-net efforts might have been insufficient (Cantillon, Collado, & Van Mechelen, 2015). Furthermore, while the magnitude of these trends strongly differed across countries and time, not a single EU15 country achieved simultaneously an expansion in employment, a reduction in poverty, and a decrease of spending on cash transfers (Cantillon & Vandenbroucke, 2014). This chapter provides further evidence to illustrate the complexity of simultaneously achieving all three objectives of the social trilemma. Our hypothesis is that significant spending is necessary to reduce relative income poverty without substantially reducing current work incentives.

## METHODS AND DATA

### Estimating the Cost of Reducing Poverty

Previous research has already calculated the cost of closing the poverty gap. In this chapter, we improve on these studies by estimating the cost of closing the poverty gap while maintaining average labor-market participation incentives at the bottom of the income distribution. The latter is defined as the three bottom deciles of equivalized household income. If governments closed poverty gaps regardless of the labor-market status of household members, the difference between household incomes when members work and do not work would probably be reduced or even eliminated. Because some individuals might withdraw from the labor market when work incentives are reduced in this way, the true cost of closing the poverty gap is probably higher than was suggested by previous calculations that did not take work incentives into account. For this reason, we complement the calculation of the cost of closing the poverty gap as follows. When a household member works, we add a top-up beyond the poverty threshold necessary to maintain the difference between household incomes in this situation and in the situation in which the household member would not work. We refer to the total amount spent in excess of the poverty threshold as "overspill," and to the cost of closing the poverty gap allowing for overspill as the "poverty fill with overspill."

The specific way in which we allow for overspill is the following. The poverty gap measures the difference between the poverty line and the incomes of poor households. The amount needed to fill the poverty gap can thus be calculated by subtracting from the poverty line all of the household incomes, regardless of their composition in terms of earned and non-earned components. We allow for overspill by subtracting only part of earned income. Since the overspill is equal to the nonsubtracted earned income, the subtracted percentage is referred to as the withdrawal rate (see Equation 1).

$$Poverty\ fill\ with\ overspill = Max\,(0, poverty\ line - y_{net\ non\text{-}earned}$$
$$- y * withdrawal\ rate) \qquad (1)$$

Ideally, we would set the withdrawal rate as low as possible to ensure work incentives are sufficiently high. However, this would entail a high budgetary cost. For this reason, we take the existing situation in each country as national benchmark and aim to maintain the current level of participation incentives for low-income households. Given the very simple design of our exercise, it is not possible to keep participation incentives at the same level for each individual or household separately, so we focus on the average level of participation incentives for the three bottom (equivalized household income) deciles.

Earned and non-earned incomes are considered net, meaning that taxes and social contributions (including tax credits) levied on each source of income are subtracted from the respective gross components. The at-risk-of-poverty threshold is equal to 60% of median equivalized household income using the modified Organisation for Economic Co-operation and Development (OECD) scale and remains fixed throughout the exercise. An important limitation of the study is that we do not specify where the resources to close the poverty gap with overspill would come from, except that we assume implicitly that it would not directly affect the incomes of households in the bottom of the income distribution. Total costs are presented as a proportion of total net (non-equivalized) population incomes to give an indication of the effort needed in relation to the remaining tax base. Another limitation is that we do not take into account any second-order effects (e.g., behavioral reactions, general equilibrium effects, etc.) when estimating the cost of closing the poverty gap with overspill.

Figure 10.1 exemplifies what closing the poverty gap, allowing for some overspill, would mean in terms of disposable household income, considering one-person households only. The x-axis represents current disposable income ("current income"), while the income after closing the poverty gap with overspill ("after income") is represented on the y-axis. Households with current income below B (the at-risk-of-poverty threshold) and no earnings end up at the level of the poverty line (line A–B), while households with the same level of income but only earnings move to the line A–C, as earnings are withdrawn from the poverty line at a rate less than 100%. The triangle A–B–C represents the amount of overspill: part of the resources that would be allocated above the poverty line, including resources for households that were not below the threshold to begin with (those in the area between B and C). For all households to the right of C (the break-even point), the overspill is zero and after income is always equal to current income.

As shown in the two charts in Figure 10.1, the withdrawal rate defines the steepness of the line A–C and the amount of overspill. It also determines where in the current income distribution the intersection point C is located, above which no household would benefit from overspill. At a withdrawal rate of 40%, the triangle A–B–C is larger than at a withdrawal rate of 60%, implying greater costs. On the other hand, households with earnings below C end up with a

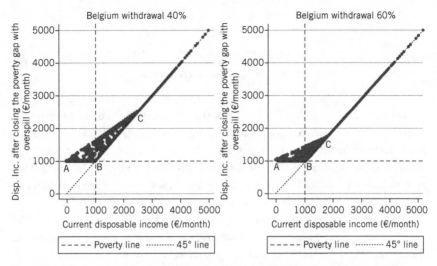

**Figure 10.1.** The impact on disposable household incomes of closing the poverty gap while allowing for overspill. Scatterplot of disposable household income of single-person households with positive disposable incomes, before and after filling the poverty gap with overspill, Belgium 2011. *Source*: EUROMOD simulated data for 2011.

higher after income, implying that incentives to work would be stronger. In this way, the steepness and the intersection point defined by different withdrawal rates represent the trade-off between work incentives and financial costs. Our methodology then boils down to (a) finding the withdrawal rate that maintains average participation incentives at the bottom of the income distribution and (b) calculating the financial cost of closing the poverty gap with that amount of overspill.

## Measuring Work Incentives

Financial work incentives are usually measured in two ways: participation tax rates (PTRs) and effective marginal tax rates (EMTRs; Immervoll, Kleven, Kreiner, & Saez, 2007; OECD, 2005, 2009, 2014a). PTRs are used to measure the financial incentive to start working, in comparison to not working at all. This is often called the incentives at the extensive margin. It is also possible to look at the intensive margin on the basis of EMTRs, a measure of the financial incentive to work more hours. In this chapter, we are primarily concerned with participation incentives, because the population below the poverty line includes many jobless households and because changes in participation in many cases have a larger impact on household income. Also, behavioral responses at the extensive margin tend to be larger than at the intensive margin (Bargain, Orsini, & Peichl, 2014). This does not mean that the intensive margin is not relevant or that EMTRs would not be affected if the poverty gap were closed as explained in Equation 1, to which we come back at the end of the chapter.

The general formula of PTRs is expressed in Equation 2:

$$PTR = 1 - \frac{(hh.\ netinc.\ in\ work) - (hh.\ netinc.\ out\ of\ work)}{individual\ gross\ wage\ in\ work} \qquad (2)$$

PTRs can be understood as the inverse of (i.e., one minus) the gain in household disposable income when a household member is working, relative to the household income when that member is not working, expressed as a proportion of the individual gross wages of that member. Alternatively, PTRs can be interpreted as how much household gross income is taxed away when a person enters or stays in the labor market, be it explicitly through income taxes and social insurance contributions or implicitly through the loss of benefits. We use this specific measure to represent the financial incentives constraint of the social trilemma. Bartels and Pestel (2016) showed that, at least in Germany, PTRs indeed change the likelihood of a person's taking up employment, which supports their usage in this context.

To calculate the PTR of each person available for work, the disposable household income both in and out of work must be calculated. To do so, in each status we verify the benefits households and their members are entitled to and calculate the corresponding taxes and social contributions. PTRs are calculated only for persons available for, or actually doing, paid work (thus excluding pensioners, students, and those who are disabled or sick), living in households composed of either couples or singles, with or without dependent children. The reason for selecting this subsample[3] is that PTRs assume that decisions to work are based on pooled household incomes, an assumption that is difficult to make for other household types (e.g., how do households with two working parents and a working child pool their incomes?). Although we examine PTRs within this subsample, and therefore other groups are not considered when finding the withdrawal rate that maintains incentives, the cost of closing the poverty gap with overspill using that withdrawal rate is calculated and is presented for the full population. Note also that PTRs take into account household incomes but they represent an individual measure of incentives. Therefore, we calculate PTRs separately for each partner in a couple, one time modifying the labor income of one partner, keeping constant the labor income of the other partner, and then vice versa.

Some additional assumptions and calculations must be made for each labor-market status.

1. Calculating in-work incomes of persons currently out of work: It is necessary to make a prediction about the hourly wage that these persons would receive if they were working. This is done by a so-called Heckman selection model in which we use information about people

currently in work to estimate an hourly wage for persons currently not working. A Heckman selection model is used to control for sample selection bias given that those currently in work might have unobserved characteristics different from those currently out of work. We assume that persons currently out of work would work full-time (38 hours) and for the whole year.

2. Calculating out-of-work incomes of persons currently out of work: For those recorded in the dataset as recipients of an unemployment benefit, we simulate the amount of this benefit. We use simulated rather than observed amounts to make sure they are comparable to the necessarily simulated benefits for those currently in work (step 4). As unemployment benefits are earnings-related in Belgium and Denmark (but not in the United Kingdom) and in order to be consistent with the previous step, for the simulation we utilize the predicted hourly wage recalculated to a full-time full-year basis. We assume that this wage equals the wage received in the previous year, so we adjust it (downward). For persons who are recorded in the dataset as not receiving an unemployment benefit, we verify whether their households are entitled to social assistance.

3. Calculating in-work incomes of persons currently in work: To make PTRs comparable between those not working and those working part-time (or more than full-time) or only a part of the year, observed wages of people in work are also recalculated to a full-time full-year basis.

4. Calculating out-of-work incomes of persons currently in work: We verify whether these persons would be eligible to receive an unemployment benefit, using different assumptions regarding work history.[4] The amount of this benefit is calculated on the basis of their observed wage. To be consistent with previous steps, this wage is recalculated to a full-time full-year basis, adjusted to the previous year, and, if a person is not eligible for unemployment benefit, we verify whether the household is entitled to social assistance.

Given these assumptions, we probably underestimate the size of the PTRs. Extra details on PTRs calculations and results of the Heckman selection model are available in the online Addendum.[5]

## Data and the Microsimulation Model
In order to calculate the cost of closing the poverty gap (with some overspill), we make use of the EU Statistics on Income and Living Conditions (EU-SILC) data (wave 2012 version 3). Income data refer to the year before the survey year (except for the United Kingdom, where it refers to the survey year), whereas information on the household composition refers to the survey year.

For calculating PTRs, information is required on incomes both in and out of work, while we can observe only one. For this reason, we simulate in- and out-of-work incomes (see previous discussion) by making use of the microsimulation model EUROMOD.[6] With EUROMOD, it is possible to calculate net incomes, given people's gross wage and household characteristics. Because simulated data have the drawback of assuming full compliance with taxes and take-up of benefits, we only use it to calculate PTRs (and not to calculate budgetary costs).

We consider the fiscal and social policies of 2011. In the case of the United Kingdom, EUROMOD estimations rely on the Family Resources Survey (FRS) data of 2012/2013, rather than EU-SILC 2012 data. Because FRS monetary values correspond to 2012, they are (downward) adjusted in EUROMOD. As aforementioned, when we estimate work incentives using simulated data, we assume full take-up of benefits. This means that we estimate the hypothetical budget constraint as imposed by the tax–benefit system, regardless of whether people make full use of it. Negative self-employment incomes are bottom coded to zero in EUROMOD. In the nonsimulated data that we use to calculate budgetary costs, we also bottom code to zero negative self-employment incomes and, in contrast to Eurostat practice, we do not include the imputed value of company cars as part of disposable income in order to be consistent with the EUROMOD simulated datasets.

Equation 1 describes how we calculate the cost of closing the poverty gap with overspill, distinguishing between earned and non-earned income components (see Table A10.1 and Table A10.2 in the Appendix). Allocating taxes and social contributions to either earned or non-earned income is not always possible unambiguously. In those cases, we allocate them proportionally to gross earned and non-earned incomes.[7] In addition, in the EU-SILC data, some earned and non-earned components are included in the same variable. For instance, in the United Kingdom, tax credits are included in the same variable as social assistance. This implies that, in the EUROMOD data, the U.K. tax credits are correctly treated as earned income when calculating financial incentives, whereas in the EU-SILC data they are considered non-earned income when calculating financial costs. Consequently, for cases in which earned income components are included in a variable referring to non-earned income, we are underestimating the financial cost, because in that case they are fully withdrawn.

## RESULTS

We begin by showing in Figure 10.2 the impact on participation incentives of using different withdrawal rates when closing the poverty gap with overspill. It is important to remember that earned income components are withdrawn at a rate of less than 100% when filling the poverty gap, whereas non-earned components—for example, unemployment benefits and social assistance—are

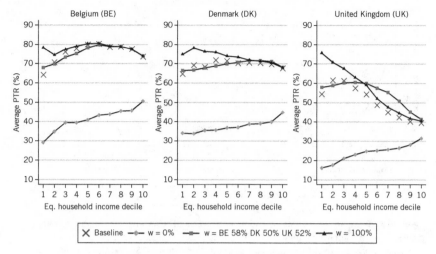

**Figure 10.2.** Participation incentives when closing the poverty gap applying different withdrawal rates (w), 2011. *Source*: EUROMOD simulated data for 2011.

fully withdrawn. Thus, as the withdrawal rate is increased, the difference between in- and out-of-work incomes after closing the poverty gap with overspill would become smaller—which increases PTRs (cf. Equation 2).[8] Withdrawal rates of 58%, 50%, and 52% maintain current average PTRs for the first three income deciles in Belgium, Denmark, and the United Kingdom, respectively.

At the same time, since higher withdrawal rates imply less overspill (cf. Figure 10.1), those higher rates represent a lower budgetary cost. Figure 10.3 shows that closing the poverty gap while not withdrawing at all earned income would cost more than 30% of total population incomes, while closing the poverty gap without taking into account work incentives (i.e., a withdrawal rate of 100%) would amount to less than 5% of total population incomes.

Now we present the cost and the impact on incentives of lifting all incomes just up to the poverty line, compared to including the extra expenditure (over-spill) needed to maintain participation incentives at the bottom of the income distribution. Table 10.1 shows estimates of the poverty headcount rate, the cost of closing the poverty gap,[9] and the average PTRs in the first three equivalized household income deciles. The first column presents the current situation—that is, without closing the poverty gap. The second column shows the cost (in relation to total net population incomes) of closing the gap only up to the poverty line. This is equivalent to applying a withdrawal rate of 100%, thus reducing or eliminating work incentives for persons in households that were below the poverty line. The third column includes the overspill needed to maintain the average PTRs in the first three income deciles at their present level.

If we compare the current situation in the first column of Table 10.1 with the cost of lifting incomes up to the poverty threshold in the second column, we

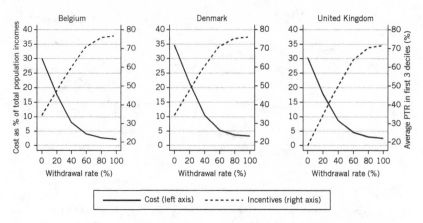

**Figure 10.3.** Trade-off between participation incentives and costs when closing the poverty gap with overspill applying different withdrawal rates, 2011. *Note*: Costs are estimated as a proportion of current total (non-equivalized) population incomes. *Source*: EU-SILC 2012 data and EUROMOD simulated data for 2011.

**Table 10.1.** Cost of Closing the Poverty Gap and PTR (in %)

| Country | Indicator | Current scenario | Closing poverty gap with withdrawal = 100% | Closing poverty gap with withdrawal = BE 58%, DK 50%, UK 52% |
|---|---|---|---|---|
| BE | Poverty | 15.0 | | |
| | | [14.0,16.0] | | |
| | Cost | | 2.2 | 4.2 |
| | | | [1.9,2.5] | [3.8,4.6] |
| | Bottom PTRs | 70.2 | 76.9 | 70.4 |
| | | [69.2,71.3] | [76.1,77.8] | [69.8,70.9] |
| DK | Poverty | 12.9 | | |
| | | [11.7,14.0] | | |
| | Cost | | 3.2 | 7.1 |
| | | | [2.4,3.9] | [6.2,8.0] |
| | Bottom PTRs | 66.9 | 76.1 | 67.0 |
| | | [65.2,68.6] | [74.7,77.5] | [66.4,67.5] |
| UK | Poverty | 15.4 | | |
| | | [14.6,16.2] | | |
| | Cost | | 2.5 | 5.7 |
| | | | [2.2,2.8] | [5.4,6.1] |
| | Bottom PTRs | 58.9 | 71.7 | 59.0 |
| | | [58.2,59.5] | [71.1,72.3] | [58.6,59.3] |

*Note*: Bottom means are average in the first three equivalized household income deciles. Costs are estimated as a proportion of current total (non-equivalized) incomes. In square brackets, 90% confidence intervals (CI). CI of poverty estimates take into account the sample design of EU-SILC (Goedemé, 2013; Zardo Trindade & Goedemé, 2016), while for PTRs in the UK we assume random sampling due to lack of sample design variables in the simulated data based on FRS.

*Source*: EU-SILC 2012 data and EUROMOD simulated data for 2011.

see that Denmark presents the lowest poverty headcount but the highest budgetary cost,[10] which implies that poverty is less frequent but deeper in Denmark. However, if households composed solely of students are removed, the estimate of the cost of closing the poverty gap in Denmark would be just 1 percentage point higher than in the United Kingdom. Belgium presents a higher poverty headcount but the lowest estimate for the cost of closing the poverty gap, while poverty estimates are slightly worse in the United Kingdom, although these differences are not statistically significant.

When we analyze participation incentives, we see that Belgium combines the lowest cost estimate for closing the poverty gap (without overspill) with the highest current PTRs. The United Kingdom presents a slightly higher cost estimate combined with the lowest PTRs, while Denmark has the highest cost estimate but in-between PTRs. It is interesting to mention that, when calculating the in-work components of the formula for PTRs, in the United Kingdom, the high average ratio of net in-work incomes to gross wages is achieved with the lowest effective taxation (i.e., balance between taxes and benefits) on low gross incomes. Effective taxation on low incomes in the United Kingdom actually does not affect the ratio between in-work incomes and gross wages, compared to decreases of 16% and 27% in Belgium and Denmark, respectively.

The cost of closing the poverty gap displayed in column 2 of Table 10.1 does not take work incentives into account. As already mentioned and as indicated in the same column, in this case, PTRs would worsen. Since some households might work less or not at all after these changes, the estimates at a withdrawal rate of 100% are very likely an underestimation of the true cost of closing the poverty gap. As a consequence, if we want to close the poverty gaps while maintaining existing average participation incentives at the bottom of the income distribution, we need to allow an important overspill above the poverty line to working households. Due to different poverty gaps and participation incentives created by tax–benefit systems, these overspill costs vary considerably between countries. In the third column, the cost includes the overspill needed to maintain the average PTRs in the first three income deciles at their present level. This is achieved with the withdrawal rates (presented in Figure 10.2) of 58% in Belgium, 50% in Denmark, and 52% in the UK. In Belgium, closing the poverty gap while keeping average PTRs unchanged at the bottom of the income distribution would come at a lower budgetary cost (4.2% of total net population incomes) compared to Denmark (7.1%) and the United Kingdom (5.7%).[11] The source of funding is left unspecified, so any effects of increased taxes or contributions needed to finance the closing of the poverty gap and the overspill are not taken into account.

The budgetary cost would be the lowest in Belgium because currently this country presents the lowest cost of lifting incomes up to the poverty line and a comparatively low difference between the in- and out-of-work incomes involved in the calculations of PTRs. As we close the poverty gap, the overspill needed to maintain low PTRs for working families is consequently relatively limited—and can be achieved with a relatively high withdrawal rate. The opposite is the case for the United Kingdom, where the difference between in- and out-of-work incomes is the largest. Denmark presents the highest cost due to the relatively large cost of lifting incomes up to the poverty line and also because, despite not having the strongest work incentives, it would allocate the largest amount to overspill. As earnings are not fully withdrawn, having a higher density of earnings below the break-even point implies that filling the poverty gap is more costly.

The effort required to close the poverty gap maintaining existing participation incentives thus depends importantly on the current incentives and the earnings distribution in each country, which vary substantially. It is interesting to see in Figure 10.3 that, at each level of PTRs, the withdrawal rate needed implies a cost that is always the highest in Denmark and the lowest in the United Kingdom. For example, achieving in all countries average PTRs of 50% at the bottom of the income distribution (without taking behavioral reactions into account) requires withdrawal rates that imply costs of roughly 15%, 20%, and 10% of total population incomes in Belgium, Denmark, and the United Kingdom, respectively.

Similarly, in Figure 10.4 we look at the costs of closing the poverty gap in each country to achieve its own and other countries' PTRs. For instance, the required withdrawal rate for the United Kingdom to close the poverty gap without changing its average PTR of 59% in the bottom deciles is 52%. For Belgium and Denmark, reaching the PTR of the United Kingdom would only be achieved at a withdrawal rate of 37%, and therefore would be associated with substantially

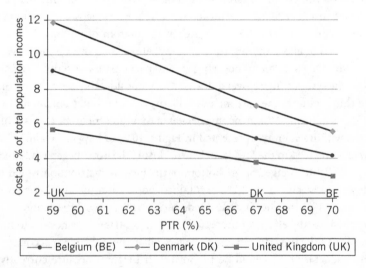

**Figure 10.4.** The cost of closing the poverty gap to achieve other countries' average participation tax rates (PTR) at the bottom of the income distribution. *Note:* Costs are estimated as a proportion of current total (non-equivalized) population incomes. Country labels on top of x-axis indicate current PTRs in the respective country. BE = Belgium, DE = Denmark, UK = United Kingdom. *Source:* EU-SILC 2012.

higher costs. The reason is that, to reach this PTR, substantially more re-sources should flow to working (poor and nonpoor) households in Belgium and Denmark than flow with current systems. In other words, the United Kingdom is already making a gross-to-net (wage) effort that the other countries would need to make if they wanted to achieve stronger participation incentives. Defining the appropriate level of incentives for each country is beyond the scope of this paper. However, it is clear that sizable incentives, as measured by the PTRs, are not a precondition for high employment rates: Denmark has high PTRs and the United Kingdom has low ones, but both have high employment levels. This suggests that, in some countries, the magnitude of work incentives could be reconsidered.

We should mention that, keeping work incentives at the extensive margin at the same level does not imply that those at the intensive margin will also remain constant. To measure incentives in the intensive margin, EMTRs follow the same logic as PTRs but, instead of a change in incomes from not working to working, we use a marginal change in hours equal to 5%—that is, they represent how much of a person's gross income is taxed away when she works more hours.[12] If governments were to close the poverty gap allowing for overspill, because they would withdraw part of earned income, this would lower the current marginal gain of working more hours, increasing EMTRs. That being said, the effect of closing the poverty gap is different across countries due to important differences in current EMTRs. Average EMTRs in the lowest three income deciles are 45% in Belgium, 40% in Denmark, and 63% in the United Kingdom. Closing the pov-erty gap while allowing overspill to maintain average PTRs in the lowest three deciles of the income distribution would increase EMTRs to 68% in Belgium, to 67% in Denmark, and to 70% in the United Kingdom. The divergent results of our estimates at both the intensive and the extensive margin reflect the very different nature of current tax–benefit systems. The current U.K. tax and benefit system somewhat resembles the way we simulate filling the poverty gap with overspill: the United Kingdom already imposes low PTRs and high EMTRs at the bottom of the income distribution. If Belgium and Denmark want to increase work incentives at the extensive margin in the same way, this would come at the cost of worsening incentives to work more hours (higher EMTRs). Although there is a growing agreement that labor-force participation is more responsive to taxes and transfers than hours worked,[13] especially at the bottom of the income distribution (Bargain et al., 2014; Eissa, Kleven, & Kreiner, 2008; Immervoll et al., 2007), this points to an additional trade-off.

## CONCLUSION

Poverty reduction requires substantial additional welfare-state efforts. In this chapter, we calculated the cost of closing the poverty gap while adding an earnings-based top-up beyond the poverty threshold to maintain current average participation incentives at the bottom of the income distribution. We found that this cost would be around two times the cost of just lifting all incomes to the level of the poverty threshold. The cost would be the lowest in Belgium because Belgium combines a relatively small poverty gap with low work incentives. The cost is higher in the United Kingdom because of the very large differences between in- and out-of-work incomes in that country. Surprisingly, Denmark presents the highest cost, due to a relatively big poverty gap and a higher density of in-work incomes in the vicinity of the poverty threshold (incomes that would need to be lifted to keep work incentives). If, instead of just maintaining participation incentives, we want to increase them, the cost would be considerably higher in countries where these incentives are lower, such as Belgium and Denmark. One should keep in mind as well that a top-up decreasing in earnings inevitably diminishes the marginal gain of working more hours at the intensive margin. In general, our analysis not only points at the high cost of poverty reduction but also signals difficult trade-offs between the cost of social spending, guaranteeing decent incomes for the poor, and work incentives for both those out of work and those in work. However, results vary enormously between countries, reflecting differences in tax–benefit systems and in the wage distribution.

On a broader level, our results illustrate the complexity of countries' attempts to simultaneously achieve the objectives of what can be considered a social trilemma—poverty reduction, employment growth, and budgetary restraint. Although our analysis is static, our results can be seen as a first minimum estimate of the cost of, and the trade-offs involved in, a strategy balancing social protection and financial work incentives. Ultimately, the magnitude of the efforts required both in terms of the budgets involved and the design of smart policies, point to the fact that anti-poverty strategies inevitably have to address the drivers of rising income inequality and downward pressures on the bottom end of the labor market.

## NOTES

We are grateful to the members of the ImProvE Consortium who have commented on previous presentations of this paper, including John Hills, Holly Sutherland, Chrysa Leventi, Iva Tasseva and Alari Paulus. The results and conclusions are the authors' and not those of Eurostat, the European Commission, or any of the national statistical authorities whose data have been used. We utilize EUROMOD version G2.75++. EUROMOD is maintained, developed, and managed by the Institute for Social and Economic Research (ISER) at the University of Essex, in collaboration with national teams from the EU member states. We are indebted to the many people who have contributed to the development of EUROMOD and to the European Commission for providing financial support for it. Belgian SILC data is made available by the FOD Economie under the confidentiality contract number E8/DG/2016/000912 and by the approval of the privacy commission number STAT-MA-2016-007 of June 14, 2016. Family Resources Survey data is made available by the Department of Work and Pensions via the U.K. Data Archive. The results and their interpretation are the authors' responsibility. The research for this paper has benefited from financial support by the European Commission's 7th Framework Programme (FP7/2012-2016) under Grant Agreement N. 290613 (ImPRovE program; http://improve-research.eu). The authors are solely responsible for any remaining shortcomings and errors.

1 Our trilemma refers to improving the social floor by increasing social transfers while not affecting employment through financial work incentives. Therefore, it does not consider other possible ways out of the trilemma, such as measures affecting gross wages (e.g., higher minimum wages or working hours reallocations), nonmonetary measures, or others.

2 This argument has some parallels with the notion of Iversen and Wren (1998) of a "social service trilemma." These authors argued that advanced democracies facing the objectives of wage equality, employment, and low public outlays for wages, could only pursue two of them as a consequence of their transition into service-dominated economies. Therefore, the resemblance between the trilemmas is the idea of tough political trade-offs among policy objectives related to equality, employment, and spending, whereas the difference rests on the specific policy objectives analyzed and consequently on the mechanisms explaining the trade-offs.

3 People living in households belonging to our subsample are the lowest in the United Kingdom, where they represent 62% of the total population, and the highest in Denmark, where they represent 68%. As a percentage of the people living in households with at least one person available for work, they represent from 77% in the United Kingdom to 93% in Denmark.

4 In Belgium, we assume that the months worked in the current year are representative for the qualifying period; in Denmark, we use an indicator variable included in EUROMOD that reflects the probability of being insured; and in the United Kingdom, we use work history as a proxy for the number of months paying National Insurance contributions.

5 It is presumable that an important portion of the unemployed would not work full-time full-year (FTFY). PTRs for individuals not working FTFY tend to be somewhat higher than for individuals working FTFY (OECD, 2009). Therefore, assuming that potential and current not FTFY workers work FTFY probably replaces their PTRs for lower ones. More details on the PTRs and results of the Heckman selection model are available in the online Addendum: http://www.centrumvoorsociaalbeleid.be/index.php?q=node/6216.

6 EUROMOD is a tax–benefit microsimulation model that operates on microdata and follows the country-specific tax–benefit rules (Figari, Paulus, & Sutherland, 2015; Sutherland & Figari, 2013).

7 The caveat of this approximation is that it does not include different treatments for both types of incomes, which might provoke some misallocations in the hypothetical transfer. These can be caused by, for example, different tax

schedules for each source of income or the fact that some benefits are fully or partially exempted from taxation.

8  For some non-earners in single-earner couples, PTRs can be decreasing in the withdrawal rate (see, for example in Figure 10.2, the top half of the income distribution in the United Kingdom at withdrawal rates of 52% and 100%). This is because, from certain withdrawal rates and above, some single-earner couples would be below the break-even point only when the non-earner partner remains out of work. In those cases, a higher withdrawal rate would lower the overspill and hence the value of the out-of-work option, while the value of the in-work option would stay unaffected, therefore resulting in higher PTRs.

9  Because in the United Kingdom income data refer to the survey year, as sensitivity analysis we calculated the budgetary costs using EU-SILC 2011, and the results were practically the same.

10  Although the cost difference with the United Kingdom is only statistically significant at an 85% confidence level.

11  As a percentage of GDP, amounts are around half: 1.8 in Belgium, 3.3 in Denmark, and 2.9 in the United Kingdom. As a reference, social expenditure on cash benefits as a percentage of GDP in the branches of family (allowances and other), unemployment (compensation and severance pay), and other social policy areas (income maintenance and other) was 5.2% in Belgium and 2.9% in Denmark and the United Kingdom (OECD, 2014b).

12  Relevant assumptions of PTRs for people in work apply to EMTRs. The formula of EMTRs is $1 - \dfrac{y_{+5\%} - y}{g_{+5\%} - g}$.

13  Labor supply elasticities in Bargain et al. (2014) are calculated as the responses in hours to a 1% increase in wages. As a reference, in 1998 in the countries we studied, gross wage elasticities in the first quintile at the extensive margin were on average 0.36 and 0.15 for single and married people, respectively, while they were just 0.02 at the intensive margin for both groups.

## REFERENCES

Atkinson, A. B. (2010, May 29). *Poverty and the EU: the new decade.* Macerata Lectures on European Economic Policy, Universita degli Studi di Macerata. Retrieved from https://core.ac.uk/download/pdf/6565535.pdf

Bargain, O., Orsini, K., & Peichl, A. (2014). Comparing labor supply elasticities in Europe and the United States: New results. *Journal of Human Resources, 49*(3), 723–838.

Bartels, C., & Pestel, N. (2016). Short- and long-term participation tax rates and their impact on labor supply. *International Tax and Public Finance, 23*(6), 1126–1159. doi:10.1007/s10797-016-9400-9

Cantillon, B., Collado, D., & Van Mechelen, N. (2015). *The end of decent social protection for the poor? The dynamics of low wages, minimum income packages and median household incomes* [ImPRovE working paper]. Retrieved from http://improve-research.eu/?wpdmact=processanddid=NzAuaG90bGl uaw==

Cantillon, B., Van Mechelen, N., Pintelon, O., & Van den Heede, A. (2014). Social redistribution, poverty and the adequacy of social protection. In B. Cantillon & F. Vandenbroucke (Eds.), *Reconciling work and poverty reduction: How successful are European welfare states* (pp. 157–184). Oxford, England: Oxford University Press.

Cantillon, B., & Vandenbroucke, F. (2014). *Reconciling work and poverty reduction: How successful are European welfare states?* Oxford, England: Oxford University Press.

Corluy, V., & Vandenbroucke, F. (2014). Individual employment, household employment, & risk of poverty in the European Union: A decomposition analysis. In B. Cantillon & F. Vandenbroucke (Eds.), *Reconciling work and poverty reduction: How successful are European welfare states?* (pp. 94–130). Oxford, England: Oxford University Press.

Eissa, N., Kleven, H. J., & Kreiner, C. T. (2008). Evaluation of four tax reforms in the United States: Labor supply and welfare effects for single mothers. *Journal of Public Economics*, 92(3–4), 795–816. doi:http://dx.doi.org/10.1016/j.jpubeco.2007.08.005

Figari, F., Paulus, A., & Sutherland, H. (2015). Microsimulation and policy analysis. In B. A. Anthony & B. François (Eds.), *Handbook of income distribution* (Vol. 2, pp. 2141–2221). Amsterdam, the Netherlands: Elsevier.

Goedemé, T. (2013). How much confidence can we have in EU-SILC? Complex sample designs and the standard error of the Europe 2020 poverty indicators. *Social Indicators Research*, 110(1), 89–110. doi:10.1007/s11205-011-9918-2

Immervoll, H. (2007). *Minimum wages, minimum labor costs and the tax treatment of low-wage employment* [Discussion Paper Series]. Retrieved from http://www.oecd-ilibrary.org/docserver/download/5l4w2bvsd0nt.pdf?expire s=1458304235andid=idandaccname=guestandchecksum=A997DBA27DC1 39904123EF5B9FAD7315

Immervoll, H., Kleven, H. J., Kreiner, C. T., & Saez, E. (2007). Welfare reform in European countries: A microsimulation analysis. *The Economic Journal*, 117(516), 1–44.

Iversen, T., & Wren, A. (1998). Equality, employment, and budgetary restraint: The trilemma of the service economy. *World Politics*, 50(04), 507–546.

Marchal, S., & Marx, I. (2015). *Stemming the tide: What have EU countries done to support low-wage workers in an era of downward wage pressures?* [IZA Discussion Papers]. Retrieved from http://ftp.iza.org/dp9390.pdf

Marx, I., Marchal, S., & Nolan, B. (2013). Mind the gap: Net incomes of minimum wage workers in the EU and the US. In I. Marx & K. Nelson (Eds.), *Minimum income protection in flux* (pp. 54–80). Basingstoke: Palgrave-Macmillan.

Organisation for Economic Co-operation and Development (OECD). (2005). *OECD employment outlook 2005.* Retrieved from /content/book/empl_ outlook-2005-en http://dx.doi.org/10.1787/empl_ outlook-2005-en

Organisation for Economic Co-operation and Development (OECD). (2009). *OECD employment outlook 2009.* Retrieved from /content/book/empl_ outlook-2009-en http://dx.doi.org/10.1787/empl_outlook-2009-en

Organisation for Economic Co-operation and Development (OECD). (2014a). *In it together: Why less inequality benefits all.* Retrieved from /content/book/ 9789264235120-en http://dx.doi.org/10.1787/9789264235120-en

Organisation for Economic Co-operation and Development (OECD). (2014b). OECD.Stat (database). http://dx.doi.org/10.1787/data-00285-en)

Sutherland, H., & Figari, F. (2013). EUROMOD: The European Union tax-benefit microsimulation model. *International Journal of Microsimulation,* 6(1), 4–26.

Vandenbroucke, F., Cantillon, B., Van Mechelen, N., Goedemé, T., & Van Lancker, A. (2013). The EU and minimum income protection: Clarifying the policy conundrum. In I. Marx & K. Nelson (Eds.), *Minimum income protection in flux* (pp. 271–317). Hampshire, England: Palgrave-Macmillan.

Zardo Trindade, L., & Goedemé, T. (2016). *Notes on updating the EU-SILC UDB sample design variables, 2012 and 2013* [CSB Working Paper]. Retrieved from http://www.centrumvoorsociaalbeleid.be/index.php?q=publicaties/ workingpapers/en

# APPENDIX—INCOME COMPONENTS

Table A10.1. Income Components of Net and Gross Non-earned and Earned Incomes in EUROMOD Datasets

| | Belgium | | | | Denmark | | | | United Kingdom | | | |
|---|---|---|---|---|---|---|---|---|---|---|---|---|
| | Non-earned | | Earned | | Non-earned | | Earned | | Non-earned | | Earned | |
| **Net** | | | | | | | | | | | | |
| | + | Gross | + | Gross | + | Gross | + | Gross | + | Gross | + | Gross |
| | − | Proportional income tax, municipal tax, and maintenance payments | − | Proportional income tax, municipal tax, and maintenance payments | − | Proportional taxes and maintenance payments | − | Proportional taxes and maintenance payments | − | Proportional income tax and maintenance payments | − | Proportional income tax and maintenance payments |
| | − | Investment & property tax, pension, and disability contributions | − | Employee, special, & self-employed contributions | − | Capital & property tax | − | Employee & self-employed contributions | − | Council tax | − | Employee & self-employed contributions |
| | | | + | Work bonus | | | | | | | + | Working tax credit |
| **Gross** | | | | | | | | | | | | |
| | + | Investment income | + | Income from employment and self-employment | + | Investment income | + | Income from employment and self-employment | + | Investment income | + | Income from employment and self-employment |
| | + | Income of children <16 years old | | | + | Income of children <16 years old | | | + | Income of children <16 years old | | |

*(continued)*

**Table A10.1.** Continued

| Belgium | | | Denmark | | | United Kingdom | | |
|---|---|---|---|---|---|---|---|---|
| Non-earned | Earned | | Non-earned | Earned | | Non-earned | Earned | |
| | Gross | | | Gross | | | Gross | |
| + Property income | | | + Property income | | | + Property income | | |
| + Private pension | | | + Private pension | | | + Personal pension | | |
| + Received transfers | | | + Received transfers | | | + Received transfers | | |
| + Benefits | | | + Benefits | | | + Benefits | | |
| | | | | | | + Income from odd jobs | | |

**Table A10.2.** Income Components of Net and Gross Non-earned Income and Net Earned Income in EU-SILC Datasets

| Non-earned | | Earned | |
|---|---|---|---|
| **Net** | | | |
| + | Gross | + | Gross |
| – | Proportional tax on income and social insurance contributions and maintenance payments (HY140G + HY130G) | – | Proportional tax on income and social insurance contributions and maintenance payments (HY140G + HY130G) |
| – | Investment & property tax (HY120G) | | |
| **Gross** | | | |
| + | Investment income (HY090G) | + | Income from employment and self-employment (PY010G + PY050G) |
| + | Income of children <16 years old (HY110G) | | |
| + | Property income (HY040G) | | |
| + | Private pension (PY080G) | | |
| + | Received transfers (HY080G) | | |
| + | Benefits (PYG: 90 + 100 + 110 + 120 + 130 + 140 + HYG: 50 + 60 + 70) | | |

*Note*: The name of the variables in EU-SILC is in parentheses.

# 11

# THE DESIGN OF IN-WORK BENEFITS

## HOW TO BOOST EMPLOYMENT AND COMBAT POVERTY IN BELGIUM?

### Dieter Vandelannoote and Gerlinde Verbist

## INTRODUCTION

Individuals with a low earnings potential or belonging to disadvantaged groups increasingly encounter difficulties in finding a job. They often face low work incentives and have a higher risk of being poor (Immervoll & Pearson, 2009). As a result, policymakers and researchers have suggested several options for making work financially more attractive. The introduction of making-work-pay policies, and more specifically in-work benefits, has been put forward as an important way to increase net incomes without raising gross incomes and the cost of labor for the employer. Other options are to increase minimum wages or to lower the labor cost for the employer by introducing wage subsidies (Immervoll & Pearson, 2009). In this chapter, the focus is on how in-work benefits could be designed in a budget-neutral way, while maximizing work incentives and their poverty-reducing effect.

In-work benefits have received considerable attention from both scholars and policymakers. The United Kingdom (Family Income Supplement, 1970) and the United States (Earned Income Tax Credit, 1975) were the first two countries to implement this type of making-work-pay policy. Various European countries followed their example in recent decades—for an overview, see the Organisation for Economic Co-operation and Development (OECD; 2010), and Chapter 7 of this volume. The effectiveness of in-work benefits regarding employment incentives and poverty reduction depends on many factors, notably the size and design of the benefit, as well as the wider policy and socioeconomic context. The wider context refers to the tax–benefit system as a whole, the prevalence and level of a minimum wage, the existence and extent of child-care provisions, the distribution of incomes and wages, etc. In this chapter, these contextual factors are kept constant by limiting the focus to the design of in-work benefits in one country, Belgium.

The majority of evaluations focus on the United Kingdom and the United States, while in this chapter we look at Belgium, a country with a relatively compressed income and wage distribution (see Marx, Vanhille, & Verbist, 2012). Belgium has a minimum wage, which is an essential condition for the functioning of in-work benefits (i.e., to avoid downward pressure on gross wages). Several studies indicate that a major challenge for Belgium is to improve work incentives at the bottom of the income distribution (Cantillon, Marchal, & Luigjes, 2015; Immervoll & Pearson, 2009). We show how microsimulation techniques can be used to study stylized design changes in a stepwise manner, and we examine which characteristics of an in-work benefit "make it work," in terms of both employment and poverty aims. We find that the details of the design of in-work benefits matter a great deal, as well as the overall budget allocated to them. In addition, at least in the case of Belgium, there appears to be some trade-off between increasing financial work incentives and reducing poverty. Few studies have considered the impact of the design characteristics of in-work benefits in detail (see Liebman, 2002, on the optimal design of the EITC). This chapter is the first, to our knowledge, to study the impact on both employment incentives and poverty outcomes of various designs of in-work benefits. In addition, we provide information on the budgetary impact of taking labor-supply effects into account.

The chapter starts with a review of the literature and identifies the most relevant design characteristics of in-work benefits. We then describe the data and methodology used, explaining the microsimulation approach and how we measure outcomes, notably potential poverty and employment incentive effects. The impact of the design characteristics on both first- and second-order poverty results is then presented. The final section is the summary and conclusion.

## THE EFFECT OF IN-WORK BENEFITS ON POVERTY AND EMPLOYMENT

In-work benefits have received increased attention over the past decades in OECD countries, as a core part of making-work-pay policies. They can be defined as "permanent work-contingent tax credits, tax allowances, or equivalent work-contingent benefit schemes designed with the dual purpose of alleviating in-work poverty and increasing work incentives for low-income workers" (OECD, 2011). Their main objectives can thus be described as, on the one hand, to increase employment by creating additional financial rewards for remaining in work or for taking up a low-paid job and, on the other hand, to increase the income of disadvantaged groups of workers and their families (Immervoll & Pearson, 2009).

The effect of in-work benefits on employment is complex, because the effect may differ at the extensive and intensive margins.[1] Also, different target groups may create conflicting work incentives. Most studies point toward positive effects at the extensive margin. Total employment effects are generally rather small (Immervoll & Pearson, 2009). The most researched examples of in-work benefits are the U.S. Earned Income Tax Credit (EITC) and the U.K. Working (Families) Tax Credit (W(F)TC).[2] For both the EITC (Blank, Card, & Robbins, 2000; Chetty, Friedman, & Saez, 2013; Eissa & Hoynes, 2006) and the W(F)TC (Blundell, Duncan, McCrae, & Meghir, 2000; Blundell & Sheppard, 2012; Brewer et al., 2006), positive employment effects are found at the extensive margin. The evidence at the intensive margin is more mixed. It is indeed possible that in-work benefits may reduce the number of hours worked, as a worker might decide to work fewer hours in order to qualify for the benefit (OECD, 2011; Saez, 2002).

In-work benefits also aim to reduce in-work poverty. However, studies provide mixed evidence and show that the design of the in-work benefit plays a big role, as well as its interaction with the income distribution. There are indications that the poverty impact is largest in countries with dispersed income distributions, as is the case in the United States and the United Kingdom. Far less research has been done on more condensed income distributions, as is the case in Belgium.

In-work benefits are considered to be relatively cost effective. Immervoll, Kleven, Kreiner, and Saez (2007) showed that the cost to taxpayers of redistributing 1 EUR in the form of an in-work benefit can be around 1 EUR, implying an efficiency cost close to zero. This is a remarkable outcome compared to the sometimes large efficiency costs of other redistributive measures.

About half of the OECD countries use one or more permanent[3] in-work benefits (for an overview, see OECD, 2011). These benefits differ from one another in many dimensions (see Immervoll & Pearson, 2009, and Chapter 7 of this volume). In this chapter, we focus on the design characteristics and group them into three different categories:

1. The unit of assessment (individual or household)—Previous studies have indicated the importance of having either the individual or the household as the unit of assessment. An individual-based system is set up with the intention of improving work incentives, while a household-based system has a greater potential for reducing poverty.

2. Income-related characteristics—The benefit may be designed for conditionality on income or earnings levels and may have a phase-in and phase-out range.

3. Employment-related characteristics (e.g., hours of work).[4]

In-work benefits have been studied from theoretical and empirical angles. Optimal taxation theory has provided the most influential theoretical framework. For instance, Saez (2002) derived theoretically that the shape of the optimal tax schedule, as proposed in the standard Mirrlees model, changes when extensive labor-supply reactions are incorporated; subsidizing low-income workers then becomes desirable. In empirical analyses, different tracks have been followed. OECD studies typically use the OECD tax–benefit model with hypothetical families (see Immervoll & Pearson, 2009), while other studies have worked with representative samples of the population, possibly in combination with a tax–benefit microsimulation model (e.g., Bargain & Orsini, 2006; Figari, 2015). The few studies that take an international comparative perspective apply mostly so-called policy swaps, namely introducing in-work benefits applicable in one country into the tax–benefit system of other countries; examples of such studies include Bargain and Orsini (2006) and Marx et al. (2012). The drawback of this approach is that many design features are often changed at the same time. Therefore, in this chapter we focus on a "stepwise" approach in which we change the design of in-work benefits incrementally.

Design characteristics have mainly been discussed from a work-incentive perspective, and far less from their potential influence on poverty reduction. In order to identify the work incentive and poverty impact of the different design characteristics, we introduce a set of stylized in-work benefits. With regard to the poverty impact, we distinguish both first- and second-order effects (i.e., without and with incorporating potential behavioral reactions). We do this on a representative sample of the population, making use of the tax–benefit microsimulation model EUROMOD.

## DATA AND METHODOLOGY

### Data and the Tax–Benefit Model EUROMOD
Our empirical analysis is performed on data from the Belgian Survey on Income and Living Conditions (BE-SILC) of 2012. To assess the impact of design characteristics, we simulate counterfactual scenarios by using a tax–benefit microsimulation model, which allows us to estimate household incomes under different tax options, holding everything else constant, and therefore avoiding endogeneity problems (Figari, Paulus, & Sutherland, 2015). The policy reform simulations are performed using EUROMOD, the multicountry European tax–benefit microsimulation model (Figari et al., 2015; Sutherland & Figari,

2013). We use the policies as simulated in EUROMOD on July 1, 2014, while incomes of BE-SILC 2012 are uprated to 2014 (Hufkens, Spiritus, & Vanhille, 2014). Negative incomes are set to zero.

EUROMOD simulates tax liabilities (direct taxes and social insurance contributions) and cash benefit entitlements on the basis of the tax–benefit rules in place and information available in the underlying dataset. The components of the tax–benefit system that are not simulated due to lack of information in the survey data (e.g., on previous employment) and that are used as input for EUROMOD (e.g., for the calculation of contributory benefits), as well as market incomes, are taken directly from the data. EUROMOD is a static model: the arithmetic simulation of taxes and benefits disregards potential behavioral reactions of individuals (for further information, see Sutherland & Figari, 2013). In order to measure second-order employment effects, we have enriched EUROMOD with labor-supply reactions. We do not consider potential labor demand or general equilibrium effects.

## Incorporating Labor-Supply Reactions: Estimating a Discrete Labor-Supply Model

Labor-supply effects are calculated for four different family types: couples in which one partner is available for the labor market, couples in which both partners are available, single men, and single women. By "available for the labor market" we mean being between 18 and 65 years old, not in education or (pre) retired, not disabled or ill, and not self-employed. This last group is excluded from the sample because labor-supply decisions of self-employed people are possibly very different from those of salaried workers. Also, households with children available for the labor market but still living with their parents are excluded from the sample. Because it is not clear whether these households see their labor-supply decisions as a collective or individual process, their labor-supply decisions may be different from households without working children. Also, other households with more than two persons available for the labor market are excluded from the sample, because it is not clear how these families pool their incomes. Table 11.1 provides descriptive statistics for the different family types. We estimate four separate labor-supply models, one for each group. A discrete labor-supply model (Van Soest, 1995) is implemented (for more details on the model used, see Vandelannoote & Verbist, 2016). We assume that each person can work the number of hours per week desired, thus labor-demand constraints are not taken into account.

BE-SILC 2012 contains information on the weekly number of hours usually worked in the main job, as well as in the second and subsequent jobs. We assume that both males and females face a choice set of five discrete points: not working (0 hours), working short part-time (19 hours), working long part-time (30 hours), working full-time (38 hours), or working more (50 hours).[5] Singles and

**Table 11.1.** Basic Descriptive Statistics of Four Family Types, Belgium 2012

| | Couples, both available | | Couples, one available | Single male | Single female |
|---|---|---|---|---|---|
| | Male | Female | | | |
| Average working time/ week (hours) | 37.0 | 27.0 | 22.3 | 31.2 | 26.0 |
| Average hourly gross wage (EUR) | 20.4 | 17.2 | 17.6 | 18.6 | 17.1 |
| Participation rate (%) | 91.1 | 80.2 | 63.2 | 77.9 | 76.4 |
| Average age (years) | 41.6 | 39.1 | 48.8 | 42.9 | 43.6 |
| Higher education degree (%) | 43.2 | 50.5 | 36.2 | 39.2 | 39.8 |
| Presence of child in the family, age 0-18 (%) | 65.2 | 36.2 | 7.7 | 39.0 | |
| Number of observations | 5,097 | 1,971 | 545 | 1,121 | |

*Note*: For couples where one person is available for the labor market, statistics are shown for this person.
*Source*: Authors' calculations based on EUROMOD (underlying data BE-SILC 2012).

households where one person is available for the labor market can thus choose among five discrete working points. When two persons are available for work in a household, 25 different discrete points are available.

Total disposable household income is calculated for each discrete point, using EUROMOD. Gross earnings from employment are calculated by multiplying gross hourly wages by the respective working hours in each category. Hourly wages are obtained by dividing observed monthly gross income by the actual observed number of hours worked. For individuals for whom no gross earnings are observed and who are available for the labor market, gross hourly wages are calculated on the basis of a Heckman selection model, with separate estimations for men and women (see Vandelannoote & Verbist, 2016). Wages are imputed for 319 men (15% of our subsample) and 569 women (21% of our subsample).

Gross household income is equal to the sum of both labor and nonlabor incomes of all household members. Social security contributions and personal income taxes are deducted from gross income, while social transfers are added to obtain total disposable household income. Social transfers include child, education, and housing benefits. For currently nonworking individuals, the social assistance or unemployment benefit that is reported in the data is included in nonlabor income. For currently working individuals, we construct a counterfactual scenario of not working, in which this individual receives a simulated social assistance benefit (if eligible); this means that we do not simulate an unemployment benefit, as we assume that individuals freely choose whether to work or not (and therefore they are not eligible for unemployment benefits when deciding to stop working). Summary statistics of the budget constraints and details on the

**Table 11.2.** Participation Elasticity and Total Hours Elasticity of the Four Subsamples, Belgium 2012

|  | Couples, both available | | Couples, one available | Single male | Single female |
|---|---|---|---|---|---|
|  | Male | Female |  |  |  |
| Participation elasticity | 0.13 | 0.21 | 0.29 | 0.22 | 0.36 |
| Total hours elasticity | 0.20 | 0.32 | 0.40 | 0.31 | 0.42 |

*Source:* Authors' calculations based on EUROMOD (underlying data BE-SILC 2012).

estimation of the labor-supply functions can be found in Vandelannoote and Verbist (2016). The estimated models fit the data well. Participation and hours elasticities for the four subsamples can be found in Table 11.2. Elasticities for women are higher than those for men, a result often found in the literature (see Bargain, Orsini, & Peichl, 2014). Persons living in a household at the bottom of the income distribution have higher labor-supply elasticities (e.g., for single women, total hours elasticity goes from 0.59 in the first decile to 0.20 in the tenth). Elasticities at the extensive margin (taking up a job or not) are higher than those at the intensive margin (increasing or decreasing the hours worked) for all four subsamples.

## Scenarios for Simulations

Our starting point is the main in-work benefit in Belgium, the work bonus (for an evaluation, see Vanleenhove, 2014). It comes in the form of a reduction of the monthly paid social security contributions for individuals with a low hourly wage, equal to a maximum monthly reduction of 198 EUR in 2014 for an individual working full-time and earning the minimum wage. There is a tapering-out rate of 22%, until the benefit equals zero. A fraction (14.4%) of the benefit is tax deductible. Eligibility for the in-work benefit is not based on total income, which might give an incentive to diminish the hours worked in order to become eligible, but on hourly wage, therefore targeting individuals with a low earnings potential. Moreover, the benefit gives an incentive to work more hours, as the total amount of the benefit linearly increases with the hours worked by the individual. The budget for the Belgian in-work benefit is limited, around 600 million EUR, or 0.16% of GDP, in 2015. Recipients are found mainly in the middle of the income distribution (see Figure 11.1).

Table 11.3 summarizes the alternative scenarios we simulate, focusing on the three different categories of design characteristics: unit of assessment, income-related characteristics, and employment-related characteristics. The first category looks at the distinction between individual- and household-based systems. As this distinction is crucial, it is taken up in all the simulations of alternatives. For the income-related characteristics, we look at the impact of an income

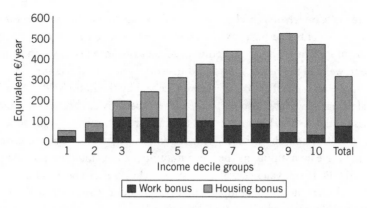

**Figure 11.1.** Distribution of the budget made available for the new in-work benefit (abolishing the housing bonus and work bonus), Belgium 2014. *Source*: Authors' calculations based on EUROMOD (underlying data BE-SILC 2012).

threshold (based on either gross income or hourly wage) and a tapering-out and a tapering-in phase. Regarding the employment-related characteristics, we look at the introduction of an in-work benefit based on hours worked.

The simulations are done in a revenue-neutral setting and are performed step by step in order to test the impact of specific design characteristics. We start with a lump sum for everyone at work. We then make the policy more complex by introducing, consecutively, an income threshold (which is based on the minimum wage level in Belgium), a tapering-out phase, and a tapering-in phase. In

**Table 11.3.** Overview of the Different Simulations

| | Unit of assessment | |
|---|---|---|
| | **Individual** | **Household** |
| **Lump sum: weight**[a] | • Individual | • Modified OECD equivalence scale<br>• [Household]<br>• [Number of household members] |
| **Threshold based on gross income**[a] | • Minimum wage of a full-time worker<br>• [1.5 * minimum wage of a full-time worker] | |
| **Threshold based on hourly wage**[a] | • [12 EUR per hour]<br>• 15 EUR per hour | |
| **Tapering-out based on gross income**[a] | • [rate of 10%]<br>• rate of 30%<br>• [rate of 70%] | |
| **Tapering-in based on gross income**[a] | • rate of 20%<br>• [rate of 30%] | |
| **Tapering-in based on hours worked**[b] | X | |

*Note*: Numbers in brackets are sensitivity checks.
[a] Income-related characteristics; [b] Employment-related characteristics.

order to make our results as "clean" as possible, we introduce the stylized in-work benefits as benefits that have no interactions with other elements of the Belgian tax-benefit system, with the exception of social assistance (as this is income dependent, we take the newly introduced in-work benefit into account when calculating the amount of social assistance received by the household).[6] Besides a central scenario, we have also performed several sensitivity checks to test the robustness of the results. For instance, in the case of the "lump sum" in-work benefit, our central household-based scenario entails a benefit that depends on the household size by multiplying the basic amount of a one-adult household by the modified OECD equivalence scale;[7] sensitivity checks here consist of a scenario where the basic amount is multiplied by 1 ("household") and a scenario where it is multiplied by the number of household members.

Simulations of the existing in-work benefit in Belgium (the work bonus) show that adapting its design has a relatively small impact on poverty and work incentives, due to the relatively small budget that is allocated to this policy measure.[8] Therefore, we consider it more instructive to show the importance of design features if more budget were allocated to this policy. To do so in a budget-neutral way, we "abolish" the housing bonus in the simulations, corresponding to an extra 1.6 billion EUR in 2014. We opted to abolish the housing bonus because it has been criticized on several occasions for its distortionary effects on the housing market (see OECD, 2015), implying that the budget could be put to a better use. Moreover, it mainly benefits richer households (see Figure 11.1), implying that mainly the higher income deciles pay for the new in-work benefit. We now have a budget of 2.2 billion EUR (0.5% of GDP) available for implementing a new in-work benefit. We impose budget neutrality of the different simulations in the first order—that is, without taking possible labor-supply effects into account. We also calculate the budgetary effects of taking account the behavioral effects, thus showing potential changes in revenue resulting from changes in work incentives.

## THE IMPACT OF THE DESIGN CHARACTERISTICS OF AN IN-WORK BENEFIT ON POVERTY

The outcome indicators of the different stylized in-work benefits are: poverty headcount and poverty gap ratio (FGT0 and FGT1; see Foster, Greer, & Thorbecke, 1984), which are first-order effects (i.e., without accounting for potential labor-supply effects); changes in labor supply; poverty headcount and poverty gap, which are second-order effects (i.e., accounting for potential labor-supply changes); and yearly governmental gains or losses due to labor-supply effects.[9] The poverty headcount and poverty gap ratio are shown for individuals between 20 and 64 years old, because they are the main target group for the in-work benefits. The poverty line is defined as 60% of median equivalent disposable income (of the total population). Poverty rates are shown based both on a fixed poverty line[10] and on a poverty line that is recalculated based on the changed income distribution (a so-called floating poverty line).

## First-Order Poverty Effects

We start with a simple design, namely a lump sum in-work benefit granted to every person who works at least one hour per week. This can be given either on an individual or on a household basis. The basic benefit in the individual-based scenario equals 39 EUR per month. In the household-based scenario, the benefit is granted if at least one person in the household is at work; its level depends on the household size: 35.5 EUR per month multiplied by an equivalence scale (i.e., the modified OECD equivalence scale).[11] Compared to a situation without an in-work benefit, the introduction of this benefit has a significant positive effect on both the poverty headcount and poverty gap when using a fixed poverty line; the effect is somewhat stronger for a household-based system compared to an individual-based system (−0.56 and −0.3 percentage points, respectively, for the poverty headcount and −0.17 and −0.12 percentage points, respectively, for the poverty gap ratio; see Table 11.4). An individual-based lump sum is more beneficial for one-person households and for couples where both partners are at work, while a household-based system is better for larger families and for couples where only one partner works. The latter are more often found in the bottom of the income distribution, and hence a household lump sum in-work benefit is somewhat more targeted toward the bottom, resulting in better poverty results. As a sensitivity check for the household-based scenario, we also applied two "extreme" scenarios of equivalence scale, notably using either the number of household members (i.e., multiplying the monthly benefit by household size, thus favoring larger families) or using 1 (i.e., each household receives the same amount). Unsurprisingly, the first system yields better poverty results, although the differences are small.

In a second step, we introduce an income threshold, so that only working individuals or households with a gross income below the threshold receive the in-work benefit. Results are compared with the lump sum simulations. The threshold is set equal to the gross minimum wage of a full-time worker in Belgium (1,502 EUR per month). Using an individual-based threshold, 19% of all working individuals receive the benefit, equal to 203 EUR per month. In the household-based scenario, the threshold is set at 1,502 EUR multiplied by the household's equivalence scale; in this scenario, 20.7% of households with at least one person at work receive the benefit, which amounts to 150 equivalent EUR per month. Introducing an income threshold limits the number of beneficiaries, so that a higher in-work benefit for recipients can be granted, resulting in a significant poverty decrease (using both a fixed and a floating poverty line); the household-based system outperforms the individual one. As a sensitivity check, we multiplied the previous income threshold by 1.5 (2,253 EUR per month),

**Table 11.4.** Individual (IND)- and Household (HH)-Based In-work Benefit: Impact on Poverty Headcount and Poverty Gap,[a] Belgium 2014

| Simulation | Compared to | Poverty headcount, percentage point change | | | | Poverty gap, percentage point change | | | |
| --- | --- | --- | --- | --- | --- | --- | --- | --- | --- |
| | | Fixed | | Floating | | Fixed | | Floating | |
| | | IND | HH | IND | HH | IND | HH | IND | HH |
| **Policies 2014** | | 11.26% | | | | 3.07% | | | |
| No in-work benefit | Policies 2014 | 0.30* | | −0.26* | | 0.08* | | −0.08* | |
| **Lump sum** | | | | | | | | | |
| • Individual | No in-work benefit | −0.30* | | 0.06 | | −0.12* | | 0.01 | |
| • HH equivalence scale | | | −0.56* | | −0.08 | | −0.17* | | −0.02 |
| • HH as one | | | −0.61* | | −0.12 | | −0.17* | | −0.04 |
| • Number of HH members | | | −0.64* | | −0.21* | | −0.19* | | −0.05 |
| **Threshold** | | | | | | | | | |
| • Income (1) | Lump sum | −1.25* | −1.74* | −1.08* | −1.9* | −0.33* | −0.39* | −0.31* | −0.45* |
| • [Income (1.5)] | (equivalence scale for HH) | −0.80* | −0.80* | −0.63* | −0.72* | −0.18* | −0.18* | −0.16* | −0.15* |
| • [Hourly wage 12 EUR] | | −0.86* | | −0.75* | | −0.23* | | −0.22* | |
| • Hourly wage 15 EUR | | −0.58* | | −0.40* | | −0.14* | | −0.12* | |

**Tapering-out**

| | Threshold: income (1) | | | | | | | |
|---|---|---|---|---|---|---|---|---|
| • [10%] | 0.44* | 0.57* | 0.47* | 0.78* | 0.13* | 0.16* | 0.13* | 0.22* |
| • 30% | 0.26* | 0.33* | 0.29* | 0.34* | 0.05 | 0.08* | 0.06* | 0.10* |
| • [70%] | 0.19* | 0.18* | 0.2* | 0.17* | 0.02 | 0.04 | 0.03 | 0.05 |

**Tapering-in**

| | Tapering-out: 30% | | | | | | | |
|---|---|---|---|---|---|---|---|---|
| • 20% | 0.17* | 0.19* | 0.17* | 0.23* | 0.08* | 0.10* | 0.09* | 0.10* |
| • [30%] | 0.17* | 0.18* | 0.17* | 0.18* | 0.05 | 0.06* | 0.05 | 0.06* |
| • Hours worked | 0.03 | 0.03 | | 0.02 | 0.02 | | 0.02 | — |

*Note:* Scenarios between brackets are sensitivity checks. * = statistically significant at 95% confidence intervals of 0.05. Calculations based on method developed by Goedemé et al., 2013.

[a] Working-age adults 20 to 64 years old, first order, fixed and floating poverty line.

*Source:* Authors' calculations based on EUROMOD (underlying data BE-SILC 2012).

resulting in higher eligibility rates of 36.5% of all working individuals and 40.6% of all households with at least one working person. Due to imposed budget neutrality, the level of the in-work benefit is lower than with a tighter income threshold (respectively, 107 EUR and 81 equivalent EUR per month) and consequently the poverty reduction potential is also lower.

Another way of implementing income selectivity is to apply a threshold based on hourly wages; this scenario only makes sense in an individual-based system. With a 15 EUR threshold, 41.9% of all individuals at work are eligible, and they receive 93 EUR per month; the benefit mainly goes to working individuals in the middle of the income distribution, illustrating that individuals with a low hourly wage are not necessarily concentrated in the lowest income deciles. With a 12 EUR threshold, the in-work benefit is somewhat more directed toward lower-income families (27.4% of all individuals at work are eligible, receiving 143 EUR per month). The stricter the hourly wage threshold, the higher the probability of targeting poor individuals and the higher the benefit level can be, which could result in greater poverty reduction. In practice, we find that using a threshold based on either gross income or hourly wage results in comparable results.

In a third step, we introduce a tapering-out phase, meaning that the amount of the in-work benefit gradually diminishes with increasing income, in order to avoid poverty traps resulting from income thresholds. We work with three rates, a central scenario of 30% (i.e., for every gross 1 EUR earned above the income threshold, the in-work benefit diminishes by 0.3 EUR, until it equals zero) and two sensitivity check rates (10% and 70%). When introducing a tapering-out, the base amount of the benefit needs to be lowered to remain budget neutral. In an individual-based system, the basic benefit is reduced from 203 to 180 EUR, 160 EUR or 119 EUR per month with a tapering-out of 70%, 30% or 10%, respectively. In a household-based system, the benefit is reduced from 150 equivalent EUR to 134 equivalent EUR, 122 equivalent EUR or 96 equivalent EUR per month with a tapering-out of 70%, 30% or 10%, respectively. The impact of introducing a tapering-out crucially depends on the choice of the threshold. With a generous threshold, many recipients will receive a relatively low in-work benefit (given the budget neutral environment) and introducing a tapering-out zone will thus have little impact. The exact opposite is true for a tighter threshold. Using an income threshold equal to 1,502 EUR per month, we find that tapering-out leads to an increase in poverty outcomes. The slower one tapers out (i.e., the lower the rate), the stronger the increase in both the poverty headcount and poverty gap, as compared to a scenario without tapering-out.

As a final step, we introduce tapering-in, which aims to avoid having individuals with small incomes benefit from the system; often, these small incomes are the earnings of the second earner in the household, who is in general not considered to be part of the target population for in-work benefits. We work with two rates, a central scenario of 20% (i.e., for every gross 1 EUR one earns, one receives 0.2 EUR until the maximum amount of the in-work benefit is reached) and a sensitivity check rate (30%). For the individual-based system, the maximum amount of the benefit can be raised from 160 EUR per month (no tapering-in) to 184 EUR or 199 EUR, with a tapering-in of 30% or 20%, respectively. For the household-based system, the original benefit of 122 equivalent EUR per month is raised to 128 equivalent EUR or 133 equivalent EUR, with a tapering-in of 30% or 20%, respectively. As for a tapering-out, the impact of a tapering-in depends on the threshold used. With a low threshold, the tapering-in zone is limited and the in-work benefit per person is relatively low (given budget neutrality) and thus generates limited poverty effects. The exact opposite is true for a higher threshold corresponding to a longer tapering-in zone. Introducing a tapering-in phase has a significant negative impact on poverty figures in both an individual and a household-based system. The lower the tapering-in rate, the larger this negative impact.

Tapering-in can also be based on hours worked. Simulations are done for an individual-based system (i.e., someone who works half-time will receive only 50% of the in-work benefit). We do this as an extension of the simulation in which we implement an individual threshold based on hourly wage. We compare our results with a simulation with an individual threshold equal to 15 EUR per hour and a tapering out of 30%. Due to the introduction of a tapering-in based on hours worked, the maximum amount of the benefit can be increased from 83 to 90 EUR per month. The introduction of a tapering-in based on hours worked has a small negative impact on individuals lower in the income distribution. This is due to the fact that part-time workers are more often found in lower income deciles. Hence, poverty changes are negligible.

In sum, in terms of first-order poverty reduction, the most promising design for Belgium would be to use the household as unit of assessment, rather than the individual. A strict income threshold reduces the number of beneficiaries of the in-work benefit, and—for a fixed budgetary cost—increases the amount of the benefit received per person or household, resulting in significant decreases in both the first-order poverty headcount and the poverty gap ratio. Introducing a tapering-out or tapering-in phase leads to higher first-order poverty outcomes.

## The Impact on Work Incentives and the Public Budget

Using the model described in the preceding section, we now look at labor-supply effects of our stylized in-work benefit scenarios. The percentage point changes in the probability of working 0, 19, 30, 38, or 50 hours per week are presented in Tables 11.5a and 11.5b. We also show the potential budgetary impact for the government. Second-order poverty outcomes (i.e., those accounting for potential labor-supply effects) are presented in the next section.

Compared with the situation without an in-work benefit, the introduction of a lump sum in-work benefit generates positive work incentives with stronger outcomes for an individual-based system than for a household-based one (e.g., the share of those working zero hours goes down 0.74 percentage points in an

Table 11.5a. Individual In-work Benefit: Impact on Work Incentives, Belgium 2014

| Simulation | Compared to | Hours worked, percentage point change | | | | | Budgetary cost/gain |
|---|---|---|---|---|---|---|---|
| | | 0 | 19 | 30 | 38 | 50 | Million EUR per year |
| **Policies 2014** | | 21.6% | 11.3% | 10.2% | 44.7% | 12.2% | |
| No in-work benefit | Policies 2014 | 0.54* | 0.03 | -0.1 | -0.48* | 0.01 | -494 |
| Lump sum | No in-work benefit | -0.74* | 0.19* | 0.12* | 0.39* | 0.05 | +300 |
| **Threshold** | | | | | | | |
| • Income (1) | Lump sum | -0.3* | 2.04* | -0.05* | -1.41* | -0.28* | -1,107 |
| • [Income (1.5)] | | -0.22* | 1.26* | 0.27* | -0.92* | -0.4* | -818 |
| • [Hourly wage 12 EUR] | | 0.24* | -0.04 | -0.03 | -0.13* | -0.03 | -31 |
| • Hourly wage 15 EUR | | 0.01 | 0 | 0 | -0.02 | 0.01 | -12 |
| **Tapering-out** | | | | | | | |
| • [10%] | Threshold: income (1) | 0.1 | -0.86* | 0.43* | 0.47* | -0.14* | +248 |
| • 30% | | 0.13* | -0.39* | 0.17* | 0.18* | -0.09 | +97 |
| • [70%] | | 0.17* | -0.25* | 0.08 | 0.06 | -0.06 | +47 |
| **Tapering-in** | | | | | | | |
| • 20% | Tapering-out: 30% | -0.28* | 0.53* | 0.09 | -0.23* | -0.1 | -98 |
| • [30%] | | -0.18* | 0.36* | 0.05 | -0.15* | -0.07 | -75 |
| • Hours worked | | 0.18* | -0.94* | 0.17* | 0.53* | 0.06 | +158 |

*Note:* Scenarios between brackets are sensitivity checks. * = statistically significant at 95% confidence intervals of 0.05. Calculations based on method developed by Goedemé et al., 2013.

*Source:* Authors' calculations based on EUROMOD (underlying data BE-SILC 2012).

Table 11.5b. Household In-work Benefit: Impact on Work Incentives, Belgium 2014

| Simulation | Compared to | Hours worked, percentage point change | | | | | Budgetary cost/gain |
|---|---|---|---|---|---|---|---|
| | | 0 | 19 | 30 | 38 | 50 | Million EUR per year |
| **Policies 2014** | | 21.6% | 11.3% | 10.2% | 44.7% | 12.2% | |
| **No in-work benefit** | Policies 2014 | 0.54* | 0.03 | –0.1 | –0.48* | 0.01 | –494 |
| **Lump sum** | | | | | | | |
| • HH equivalence scale | No in-work benefit | –0.55* | 0.15* | 0.09 | 0.29* | 0.02 | +102 |
| • HH as one | | –0.73* | 0.18* | 0.11 | 0.4* | 0.03 | +147 |
| • Number of HH members | | –0.48* | 0.14* | 0.08 | 0.24* | 0.01 | +77 |
| **Threshold** | | | | | | | |
| • Income (1) | Lump sum (equivalence scale) | 0.63* | 1.36* | –0.33* | –1.21* | –0.46* | –1,551 |
| • [Income (1.5)] | | 0.23* | 0.69* | 0.16* | –0.57* | –0.51* | –1,058 |
| **Tapering-out** | | | | | | | |
| • [10%] | Threshold: income (1) | 0.07 | –0.63* | 0.12* | 0.58* | –0.16* | +304 |
| • 30% | | 0.23* | –0.39* | 0.08 | 0.22* | –0.14* | +101 |
| • [70%] | | 0.28* | –0.3* | 0.06 | 0.11* | –0.14* | +57 |
| **Tapering-in** | | | | | | | |
| • 20% | Tapering-out: 30% | –0.06 | 0.08 | 0.04 | –0.01 | –0.04 | –42 |
| • [30%] | | –0.04 | 0.06 | 0.02 | 0 | –0.03 | –35 |

*Note:* Scenarios between brackets are sensitivity checks. * = statistically significant at 95% confidence intervals of 0.05. Calculations based on method developed by Goedemé et al., 2013.

*Source:* Authors' calculations based on EUROMOD (underlying data BE-SILC 2012).

individual-based system and 0.55 percentage points in a household-based one). This can be explained by the fact that a household-based benefit does not give financial incentives to the second partner in the household to start working or to work more hours. The potential revenue generated is higher with the individual lump sum (+300 million EUR per year) than with a household-based system (+102 million EUR for the central scenario).

Introducing an income threshold has mixed effects on work incentives: at the extensive margin, it becomes more interesting for persons below the income threshold to start working, as the difference in income between not working and working increases (due to the higher basic amount). At the intensive margin, one might expect people deciding to work fewer hours to remain below the income threshold and thus be eligible. In the individual-based scenario, we find a lower probability of working 0 hours and full-time (or more) and an increase in the probability of working part-time. A household-based system appears not to give an incentive for the partner in a couple to start working (the probability of not working increases by 0.63 percentage points). This follows from the fact that total gross household income might surpass the income threshold, resulting in the loss of the in-work benefit. The budgetary cost of introducing an income threshold could be relatively high, in comparison to a lump-sum based system: from 1.1 billion EUR per year in an individual-based system to 1.6 billion EUR per year in a household-based system. Outcomes with a broader income threshold are less pronounced.

One way to avoid possible negative effects on work incentives at the intensive margin is to use a threshold based on gross hourly wages: eligibility is then no longer dependent on the number of hours worked, while maintaining a focus on low wages. When using the 15 EUR per hour threshold, we find no significant changes in work incentives, and consequently, hardly any change in the government budget, in comparison with an individual lump sum in-work benefit. A stricter threshold of 12 EUR has a small negative impact on work incentives; the budgetary consequences remain small.

Two factors influence work incentives when a tapering-out phase is introduced. First, it results in a lower maximum amount of the in-work benefit, creating a negative work incentive at the extensive margin, mainly for persons at the bottom of the income distribution (who have high labor-supply elasticities). We thus see an increase in the probability of working zero hours. Second, it gives an incentive to work more hours, as illustrated by an increase in the probability of working full-time. The lower the tapering-out rate, the stronger these two effects are. Tapering-out generates larger work incentives in a household-based system than in an individual-based system, at both the extensive margin and the intensive margin. The budgetary impact of introducing a tapering-out phase is positive, because the financial gains at the intensive margin are larger than the budgetary losses at the extensive margin.

The impact of introducing a tapering-in phase on work incentives is higher for the individual-based system than for the household-based one, where its impact is not significant. Implementing a tapering-in phase gives an incentive to individuals to increase their working hours when they work only a few hours and are in the tapering-in zone (working more hours not only generates a higher income from work but also a higher in-work benefit). We also notice a work dis-incentive for persons who work full-time: as the maximum amount of the benefit increases due to the introduction of a tapering-in, it becomes more interesting to lower the number of hours at work to become or remain eligible for the in-work benefit. For the government budget, tapering-in results in a cost, due to the fact that the disincentive for full-time workers has a larger impact than the incentives for individuals at the bottom of the hours-of-work distribution. To avoid this net negative work incentive, using a tapering-in based on hours of work appears to be a good solution. It generates a positive incentive at the intensive margin, as the amount of the in-work benefit received increases proportionally. At the ex-tensive margin, however, it becomes less interesting to start working part-time, resulting in an increase in the probability of working zero hours. As the gain at the intensive margin is more important than the loss at the extensive margin, the budgetary impact is positive (158 million EUR per year).

In sum, in terms of work incentives at the extensive margin, an individual-based system seems to work best, and this is enhanced by an income threshold and a tapering-in phase (while a tapering-out and a threshold based on hourly wages are less effective). A household-based system has a much lower effect on work incentives at the extensive margin, and especially the income threshold is counterproductive as it provides a disincentive for nonworking partners in a couple to start working. This finding is in line with the evaluation literature on the U.K. systems. At the intensive margin, the income threshold stimulates part-time work as compared to full-time jobs, as too high earnings may lead to a loss of the in-work benefit. This can (to some extent) be remedied by using a tapering-out phase.

## The Second-order Impact on Poverty

Labor-supply effects may have an impact on disposable income and affect pov-erty outcomes of the in-work benefits. A comparison of Table 11.6 with Table 11.4 shows how poverty outcomes may change when these potential behavioral reactions are incorporated.

Introducing a lump sum in-work benefit has stronger poverty-reducing effects with labor-supply changes than with the first-order impact. For almost all scenarios, we now find significant reductions in poverty, with a stronger effect when measuring with a fixed poverty line than with a floating poverty line. This can be explained by the fact that persons in the bottom of the income distribu-tion could react most strongly to the lump sum in-work benefit (they have the highest labor-supply elasticities). As with the first-order outcomes, household-based systems have a stronger poverty impact than individual-based systems. The simulation with the equivalence scale equal to 1 generates the strongest work

**Table 11.6.** Individual (IND)- and Household (HH)-Based In-work Benefit: Impact on Poverty Headcount and Poverty Gap,[a] Belgium 2014

| Simulation | Compared to | Poverty headcount, percentage point change | | | | Poverty gap, percentage point change | | | |
|---|---|---|---|---|---|---|---|---|---|
| | | Fixed | | Floating | | Fixed | | Floating | |
| | | IND | HH | IND | HH | IND | HH | IND | HH |
| **Policies 2014** | | 11.26% | | | | 3.07% | | | |
| **No in-work benefit** | Policies 2014 | 0.28* | | −0.33* | | 0.18* | | 0.04 | |
| **Lump sum** | | | | | | | | | |
| • Individual | No in-work benefit | −0.65* | | −0.14* | | −0.22* | | −0.11* | |
| • HH equivalence scale | | | −0.65* | | −0.26* | | −0.24* | | −0.13* |
| • HH as one | | | −0.75* | | −0.29* | | −0.27* | | −0.16* |
| • Number of HH members | | | −0.64* | | −0.11 | | −0.23* | | −0.10* |
| **Threshold** | | | | | | | | | |
| • Income (1) | Lump sum (equivalence scale for HH) | −0.05 | −0.57* | −0.18* | −0.88* | −0.06* | −0.13* | −0.09* | −0.22* |
| • [Income (1.5)] | | −0.07 | −0.44* | −0.14* | −0.41* | −0.11* | −0.11* | −0.14* | −0.14* |
| • [Hourly wage 12 EUR] | | −0.76* | | −0.69* | | −0.18* | | −0.17* | |
| • Hourly wage 15 EUR | | −0.56* | | −0.38* | | −0.12* | | −0.11* | |

**Tapering-out**

| | | | | | | | | |
|---|---|---|---|---|---|---|---|---|
| • [10%] | Threshold: income (1) | −0.13 | 0.15* | 0.02 | 0.26* | −0.04 | 0.02 | −0.03 | 0.04 |
| • 30% | | −0.10 | 0.05 | 0.03 | 0.10* | −0.03 | 0.01 | −0.03 | 0.01 |
| • [70%] | | −0.06 | 0.08 | −0.01 | 0.10* | −0.01 | 0.01 | −0.02 | 0.01 |

**Tapering-in**

| | | | | | | | | |
|---|---|---|---|---|---|---|---|---|
| • 20% | Tapering-out: 30% | −0.16* | −0.09 | −0.27* | −0.11* | −0.07* | −0.02 | −0.07* | −0.02 |
| • [30%] | | −0.11 | −0.09 | 0.13* | −0.07 | −0.05 | −0.02 | −0.04 | −0.01 |
| • Hours worked | | 0.04 | 0.04 | −0.06 | −0.06 | 0.01 | 0.01 | 0.01 | – |

*Note:* Scenarios between brackets are sensitivity checks. * = statistically significant at 95% confidence intervals of 0.05. Calculations based on method developed by Goedemé et al., 2013.

[a] Working-age adults 20 to 64 years old, second order, fixed and floating poverty line.

*Source:* Authors' calculations based on EUROMOD (underlying data BE-SILC 2012).

incentives and is relatively more favorable for smaller families; higher in-work benefits result in the strongest impact on household disposable income and poverty outcomes.

The additional poverty impact of introducing an income threshold is much smaller in the second order than in the first order. For an individual-based system, we find significant but small effects for the poverty gap measure only; this system generates work incentives for individuals with a low individual wage, who are mainly found in the middle and higher income distribution, yielding little impact on poverty outcomes. For the household-based system, all changes are significant, but much smaller than in the first order; this is because the household-based system creates negative work incentives for the partner in the household, causing certain households to fall below the poverty line. First-order and second-order poverty outcomes are very similar when using hourly wage for the threshold, which is logical given that this measure has very limited work-incentive effects. From a poverty-reduction perspective, this is probably the most interesting system.

The introduction of a tapering-out has a negative effect on first-order poverty figures. However, when we take second-order effects into account, this negative effect disappears and the poverty impact becomes very limited and mainly insignificant (in both an individual-based and a household-based system).

While a tapering-in phase has a negative effect on first-order poverty figures, we now find a small poverty-reducing effect on both the poverty headcount and poverty gap when we take account of labor-supply reactions. This follows from the fact that persons working a limited amount of hours have an incentive to increase their work hours, resulting in some cases in a disposable income above the poverty line. Second-order poverty results are very limited and not significant when a tapering-in phase based on hours worked is used. One should bear in mind, however, that the results for second-order effects assume that the increased labor supply is met by a similar increase in labor demand.

## CONCLUSION

This chapter focuses on the impact of the design of an in-work benefit on poverty and employment outcomes. We look not only at first-order poverty effects but also at second-order effects, by making use of a discrete labor-supply model to estimate possible work-incentive effects. As this study makes clear, both the size and design matter for work incentives and poverty effects of in-work benefits. Sufficient budget is needed to reach significant changes in outcomes, while the exact specifications of the way in which the benefit is designed are crucial. In line with other studies, we find that an individual-based in-work benefit generates stronger work incentives than a household-based one, as the latter does not give financial incentives to the second partner in the household to start working or to work more hours. In contrast, for poverty-reduction purposes, a household-based benefit seems to be the better alternative. Our results also show the complex interactions between the different outcomes and some trade-offs between employment and poverty objectives, as well as between labor supply outcomes at the intensive and the extensive margin. It is difficult to find a design that performs best in terms of both work incentives and poverty outcomes. According to our results, a system that would reconcile both aims in the most satisfactory way for the Belgian context would be an individual-based system that uses hourly wages as a threshold. This would perform reasonably well in terms of work incentives as well as in reducing poverty. One might consider combining it with a tapering-out and a tapering-in, although second-order poverty outcomes turned out to be limited. The current Belgian system of the work bonus resembles these design characteristics, but it is currently too small to generate substantial effects. Therefore, it might be advisable to raise the budgetary allocation in order to have a stronger employment and poverty impact.

## NOTES

We thank Bea Cantillon, Francesco Figari, Joris Ghysels, and Tim Goedemé, as well as the participants in the ImPRovE project, for their helpful comments and suggestions.

1  The term *employment effects* refers to the impact of policy measures on labor-supply incentives only, because actual employment effects depend on other factors as well (e.g., the demand side of the labor market). Employment impacts at the extensive margin are incentives to take up a job or not, whereas those at the intensive margin are incentives to increase or to reduce working hours.

2  The Family Income Supplement was renamed the Family Credit in 1988, which was in turn replaced by the Working Family Tax Credit (WFTC) in 1999. The WFTC was again renamed and reformed in 2003 into the Working Tax Credit.

3  We consider permanent in-work benefits only. In contrast to one-off or time-limited in-work benefits, the permanent benefits provide a recurrent work incentive and income support.

4  A fourth category is non-employment-related characteristics (e.g., the presence of children). Because these elements are often on the border with other policy domains, we do not consider them here.

5  Not working is 0 to 4 hours per week, short part-time is 5 to 25 hours, long part-time is 26 to 34 hours, full-time is 35 to 44 hours, and overtime is 44 to 60 hours. These points are chosen on the basis of the distribution pattern in the subsamples.

6  In our simulations, we assume full take-up of both in-work and social assistance benefits.

7 The modified OECD equivalence scale assigns a value 1 to the first adult, a value 0.5 to each subsequent adult, and a value 0.3 to each child (individuals less than 14 years old).

8 The results of these simulations are available from the authors upon request.

9 As individuals start working or decide to work more hours, the government has to pay less social benefits and receives more social security contributions and personal income taxes. The opposite is true when negative work incentives are created. Of course, this applies under the assumption that each person can work his or her desired amount of work.

10 Fixed poverty line is calculated with the current policies in place in Belgium in 2014, thus including both the existing work bonus and the housing bonus.

11 The basic amount then differs from the individual-based scenario as we impose budget neutrality.

## REFERENCES

Bargain, O., & Orsini, K. (2006). In-work policies in Europe: Killing two birds with one stone? *Labor Economics, 13*(6), 667–697.

Bargain, O., Orsini, K., & Peichl, K. (2014). Comparing labor supply elasticities in Europe and the United States: New results. *Journal of Human Resources, 49*(3), 723–838.

Blank, R. M., Card, D., & Robbins, P. K. (2000). Financial incentives for increasing work and income among low-income families. In R. M. Blank & D. Card (Eds.), *Finding jobs: Work and welfare reform*. New York, NY: Russell Sage Foundation.

Blundell, R., Duncan, A., McCrae, J., & Meghir, C. (2000). The labor market behavior of the Working Families Tax Credit. *Fiscal Studies, 21*, 75–103.

Blundell, R., & Shephard, A. (2012). Employment, hours of work, and the optimal taxation of low-income families. *Review of Economic Studies, 79*(2), 481–510.

Brewer, M., Duncan, A., Shephard, A., & Suarez, M.J. (2006). Did Working Families Tax Credit work? The impact of in-work support on parents' labor supply and take-up behavior in Great Britain. *Labor Economics, 13*, 699–720.

Cantillon, B., Marchal, S., & Luigjes, C. (2015). *Decent incomes for the poor: Which role for Europe?* [ImPRovE Working Paper 15/20]. Antwerp, Belgium: Herman Deleeck Centre for Social Policy, University of Antwerp.

Chetty, R., Friedman, J. N., & Saez, E. (2013). Using differences in knowledge across neighborhoods to uncover the impacts of the EITC on earnings. *American Economic Review, 103*, 2683–2721.

Eissa, N., & Hoynes, H. W. (2006). *Behavioral responses to taxes: Lessons from the EITC and labor supply* [NBER Chapters in Tax Policy and the Economy]. National Bureau of Economic Research, Cambridge.

Figari, F. (2015). From housewives to independent earners: How the tax system can help women to work in a context of strong familialism. *Journal of Social Policy, 44*(01), 63–82.

Figari, F., Paulus, A., & Sutherland, H. (2015). Microsimulation and policy analysis. In A. B. Atkinson & F. Bourguignon (Eds.), *Handbook of income distribution* (Vol. 2B, pp. 2141–2221). Amsterdam, Netherlands: Elsevier.

Foster, J. E., Greer, J., & Thorbecke, E. (1984). A class of decomposable poverty measures. *Econometrica, 52*(3), 761–766.

Goedemé, T., Van den Bosch, K., Salanauskaite, L., & Verbist, G. (2013). Testing the statistical significance of microsimulation results: A plea. *International Journal of Microsimulation, 6*(3), 50–77.

Hufkens, T., Spiritus, K., & Vanhille, J. (2014). *EUROMOD country report Belgium (BE) 2009–2013*. Institute for Social and Economic Research (ISER), Essex.

Immervoll, H., Kleven, H. J., Kreiner, C. T., & Saez, E. (2007). Welfare reform in European countries: A micro-simulation analysis. *Economic Journal, 117*(517), 1–44.

Immervoll, H., & Pearson, M. (2009). *A good time for making work pay? Taking stock of in-work benefits and related measures across the OECD* [OECD Social, Employment and Migration Working Papers, No. 81]. Paris, France: Organisation for Economic Co-operation and Development.

Liebman, J. (2002). The optimal design of the earned income tax credit. In B. Meyer & D. Holtz-Eakin (Eds.), *Making work pay: The Earned Income Tax Credit and its impact on American families*. New York, NY: Russell Sage Foundation.

Marx, I., Vanhille, J., & Verbist, G. (2012). Combating in-work poverty in continental Europe: An investigation using the Belgian case. *Journal of Social Policy, 41*(1) 19–41.

Organisation for Economic Co-operation and Development (OECD). (2010). *Employment-conditional benefits*. www.oecd.org.

Organisation for Economic Co-operation and Development (OECD). (2011). *Taxation and employment* [OECD Tax Policy Studies, No. 21]. Paris, France: Organisation for Economic Co-operation and Development.

Organisation for Economic Co-operation and Development (OECD). (2015). *OECD economic surveys: Belgium*. Paris, France: Organisation for Economic Co-operation and Development.

Saez, E. (2002). Optimal income transfer programs: Intensive versus extensive labor supply responses. *The Quarterly Journal of Economics, 117*(3), 1039–1073.

Sutherland, H., & Figari, F. (2013). EUROMOD: The European Union tax-benefit microsimulation model. *International Journal of Microsimulation, 1*(6), 4–26.

Vandelannoote, D., & Verbist, G. (2016). *The design of in-work benefits: How to boost employment and combat poverty in Belgium* [ImPRovE Working Paper

No. 16/15]. Antwerp, Belgium: Herman Deleeck Centre for Social Policy, University of Antwerp.

Vanleenhove, P. (2014). *Essays on the effects of the tax-benefit structure on labor supply: Empirical evidence for Belgium* (Doctoral thesis, Katholieke Universiteit Leuven, Leuven, Belgium).

Van Soest, A. (1995). Structural models of family labor supply: A discrete choice approach. *Journal of Human Resources, 30*(1), 63–88.

# 12

# TOWARD ADEQUATE MINIMUM INCOMES

## WHICH ROLE FOR EUROPE?

**Bea Cantillon, Sarah Marchal, and Chris Luigjes**

## INTRODUCTION

In Chapter 3, Goedemé, Trindade, and Vandenbroucke raised two fundamental questions about the role of the European Union (EU) in reducing poverty among European citizens: what is the meaning of solidarity in Europe, and should the EU adopt pan-European solidarity mechanisms? In this chapter, we take a step back. We ask how to give more bite to European social governance and how to further "socialize" the existing Europe 2020 strategy and the European Semester. We argue that binding input governance in the field of minimum income protection is the place to start. As a first step, we propose augmenting the so-called auxiliary output indicators with relevant input indicators.

The outline of the chapter is as follows. In the next section, we discuss the lack of bite of existing output social governance in the EU. We proceed by presenting minimum income protection as a policy area where increased EU social governance is both conceivable and needed. Then we propose including policy indicators in the social governance framework of the EU, in order to render the different policy choices explicit, thereby enabling a more transparent monitoring of policy efforts toward more adequate minimum income protection. We then discuss the data and method on which the proposed indicators build. In the following section, we use these indicators to capture the current variation in levels and trends of minimum incomes, relating them to minimum wages, gross-to-net efforts, and unemployment traps. In the next-to-last section, we consider the instrumental relevance of adequate minimum income packages for poverty reduction. The final section is a summary and conclusion.

## THE LACK OF BITE OF "OUTPUT" GOVERNANCE

Ever since the Treaty of Rome, the underlying assumption of European social governance is that economic integration contributes to economic growth and eventually to the development of inclusive national welfare states. Therefore, EU-level involvement in poverty reduction has remained mainly limited to soft governance initiatives, such as the formulation of nonbinding outcome targets and the monitoring of Member States' progress toward these targets in the Open Method of Coordination (OMC) Social Inclusion and more recently in the revised European Semester.

An ex post evaluation suggests that the founders were not wrong, at least not until the end of the previous century. Despite the absence of a supranational social policy and pan-European solidarity mechanisms, in the post-war period, the old EU Member States have succeeded in developing and enhancing minimum income protection through various instruments, such as minimum wages, social insurance, and social assistance. National welfare states became stronger, and income inequalities and poverty went down. Yet, in recent decades, things have changed thoroughly in crucial areas. In the past, the then European welfare states sailed on the tides of economic growth, strong productivity growth, and equivalent increases of wages. They were pushed forward by strong trade unions and by "the sympathy of the (then) European governments for social aspirations."[1] The EU was homogeneous and labor markets remained largely confined within national borders. Today, these conditions no longer apply.

For one, the current degree of economic and financial integration seriously constrains national choices, in particular within the eurozone. In a monetary union it is no longer possible to adapt exchange rates in order to respond to asymmetric shocks. Therefore, the EU response to the sovereign debt crisis was to strengthen macroeconomic surveillance. New measures, such as the Macroeconomic Imbalance Procedure and the Fiscal Compact, introduced stricter standards for fiscal discipline and reinforced sanction procedures. Likewise, the new overall governance framework of the European Semester adopted this focus (Juncker, Tusk, Dijsselbloem, Draghi, & Schulz, 2015). Clearly, such changes seriously inhibit national welfare states' room to maneuver.

Second, creeping economic integration and continuous expansion have given rise to fears of welfare tourism and social dumping within the EU. Famous cases, such as Rüffert, Laval, and Viking, illustrate how the European Court of Justice (ECJ) challenges nationally based social regulation (Ferrera, 2012, p. 22; Leibfried, 2010). These cases, combined with the 2004 enlargement, have only fostered such fears. This is exemplified by recent proposals to limit exportability of benefits and access to employment-related benefits (Cameron, 2013). Even recent ECJ decisions reflect fears of benefit tourism (Verschueren, 2015).

Third, for a considerable time now, in many countries real wages no longer keep pace with labor productivity growth, putting especially low wages and social protection under strain. This trend manifests itself in all developed nations but may weigh more heavily within the heterogeneous common market of the EU.

Clearly, these developments are testing the limits of social subsidiarity, while common pressures caused by globalization and technological changes preclude the idea that national achievements can be protected by building "firewalls" around welfare states. Hence, a soul-searching exercise on what role the EU should play in facilitating further social development has become a necessity (Vandenbroucke, 2017). Because EU Member States are so heterogeneous, and due to the lack of democratic capacity at the EU level to organize the struggle over scarce resources, it is impossible to think of a social Europe as a supranational welfare state. Rather, as so rightly said by Vandenbroucke and Vanhercke (2014, p. 86), the EU should "support national welfare states on a systemic level . . . and guide the substantive development of national welfare states—via general social standards and objectives, leaving ways and means of social policy to member states." So, the question is, where to start?

## MOVING FROM GOALS TO INSTRUMENTS: THE CASE FOR MINIMUM INCOME PROTECTION SENSU LATO

New ways to think about social Europe should acknowledge the principle of subsidiarity. Yet, social standards and objectives should more forcefully point national welfare states toward more efficient and adequate social protection. They should signal to the EU and the Member States that the most vulnerable must not become the victims of austerity, while—in good times—those at the bottom should be first to benefit from the fruits of economic growth.

For a number of reasons, a broad focus on minimum income protection, including minimum wages, seems to be the place to start. We now know that social investment strategies and employment policies are important, but not sufficient, for poverty reduction (Cantillon & Vandenbroucke, 2014). More specifically, the general conclusion of the contributions to this book is that, if Europe wants to reduce poverty, Member States must simultaneously fight unemployment traps and raise income packages for working and nonworking families at the bottom.

The term *minimum incomes* refers here to the income floor that is in principle guaranteed to all citizens. For a working-age person out of work, this is often the general social assistance benefit (although there are exceptions—see Van Mechelen & Marchal, 2013).[2] For those in work, most EU Member States have legislated minimum wages, which in many cases are increased by in-work and family-related benefits (Marx, Marchal, & Nolan, 2013).

The minimum incomes have repeatedly been a vehicle for proposals for a more caring Europe. On numerous occasions, the European Council, European Parliament, and NGOs alike have pointed toward the importance of minimum income protection for those out of work—see, for instance, the 1992 Council Recommendation "common criteria concerning sufficient resources and social assistance in social protection systems" (92/441/EEC; Council, 1992). However, EU stances on minimum income protection never went further than recommendations, proposals, and resolutions.

Likewise, on several occasions both the European Parliament and the Council of Europe have expressed concerns about minimum wage levels across Europe.[3] In 2013, then Eurogroup president Jean-Claude Juncker advocated an agreement on a European minimum wage, while France and Germany proposed "minimum wage floors, defined at national level that would guarantee a high level of employment and fair wages—leaving the choice between legislation and collective-bargaining agreements" (cited by Vandenbroucke, 2014, p. 22).

Recently, in a resolution on a European Pillar of Social Rights, the European Parliament highlighted "the importance of adequate minimum income schemes for maintaining human dignity and combating poverty and social exclusion, as well as their role as a form of social investment in enabling people to participate in society, and to undertake training and/or look for work." Parliament invited "the Commission and the Member States to assess minimum income schemes in the European Union, including whether the schemes enable households to meet their needs," and it invited "the Commission and the Member States to evaluate on this basis the manner and the means of providing an adequate minimum income in all Member States and to consider further steps in support of social convergence across the European Union, taking into account the economic and social circumstances of each Member State, as well as national practices and traditions." In the same resolution, the Parliament recommended "the establishment of wage floors in the form of a national minimum wage, where applicable, with due respect for the practices of each Member State and after consulting the social partners."[4]

The principle of European standards for national minimum incomes *sensu lato* has the support from the European Commission. Also, the European Trade Union Confederation (ETUC) favors minimum social protection standards, although the unions have not yet reached a consensus on standards for minimum wages (European Trade Union Confederation, 2013).

In the 2008 Active Inclusion Recommendation, the European Commission acknowledged the inherent relationship between minimum wages, social assistance, and work incentives. In this Recommendation, the Commission reinforced the 1992 Council Recommendation with a more focused message on active inclusion by "combining adequate income support, inclusive labor markets and access to quality services" (2008/867/EC).[5] The Commission explicitly linked minimum income protection for those out of work ("those on a large distance from the labor market") to their chances and prospective income on the labor market (European Commission, 2008; Marchal & Van Mechelen, 2017). However, the recommendation did not go beyond very broad and nonbinding general objectives and policy suggestions, and so far it has had only very limited impact (European Commission, 2013; Frazer & Marlier, 2013; Marchal & Van Mechelen, 2017).

Here we argue that, in the spirit of the 2008 Recommendation and the European Pillar of Social Rights, a thorough assessment of minimum income protection necessitates a synthetic view on the income floors for those out of work as well as in work (i.e., including social assistance and minimum wages). Admittedly, poverty reduction is often not considered as the main justification for minimum wages. The impact of minimum wages on poverty is indeed limited, since many minimum wage earners can rely on other household incomes (Eurofound, 2013; Nolan & Marx, 2009). Yet, minimum wages are at least indirectly important: they may serve as a "glass ceiling" to minimum benefits for jobless households because they have an impact on unemployment traps of low-skilled job seekers (Cantillon, Collado, & Van Mechelen, 2015). Policymakers' common sense indeed dictates maintaining a reasonable wedge between minimum income benefits and low wages. Either decision-makers should ensure that wages are sufficiently high at the bottom of the distribution in order to enable adequate out-of-work benefits, or they should boost net take-home pay from low-paying jobs, or they must accept relatively low work incentives conditional on stringent activity requirements and strong active labor-market policies, or they should take all these steps.[6] So conceived, there is an inextricable link between minimum wages, minimum income protection, and work incentives for low-production workers. This is what justifies a broad focus on minimum incomes.

## ADDING "INPUT INDICATORS" TO OUTCOME GOVERNANCE

The OMC Social Inclusion and the social targets in Europe 2020 are based on nonbinding outcome targets that leave it to the Member States to outline national policy strategies. A set of "output" indicators guide the existing outcome governance. Important in the present context is the European poverty line, which is set at 60% of median equivalent income in any given country. Various other indicators build on this notion, including those relating to poverty risks in jobless households and the depth and duration of poverty risks. These income indicators are prominently present within the portfolio of indicators.

The indicators were subsequently refined and enhanced, not least thanks to the excellent work of the Indicators Sub-Group (Marlier, Atkinson, Cantillon, & Nolan, 2007). In addition to the original outcome indicators, designed to measure progress toward the common objectives, a number of policy indicators were introduced. For the purpose of the OMC Social Protection, replacement rates for pensions were included, as was an indicator of the adequacy of social assistance benefits (by comparing them to the relative poverty line), albeit merely as a contextual variable, not as an indicator for the evaluation of anti-poverty strategies.

In the wake of the budgetary eurozone crisis, the EU has increased the policy monitoring of its Member States through the European Semester.[7] Whereas the focus remains on macroeconomic indicators, more recently, the monitoring includes progress toward the Europe 2020 outcome targets, including the poverty-reduction target. In a detailed analysis of recent developments in the EU's institutional architecture for economic and social governance, Zeitlin and Vanhercke (2014, p. 13) argue that "since 2011 there has been a partial but progressive 'socialization' of the European Semester." Obvious examples are the inclusion of auxiliary social outcome indicators in the macroeconomic imbalance procedure, and the separate development of the Social Scoreboard (see also Costamagna, 2013). The Scoreboard monitors progress on five social outcome indicators, including unemployment level and real disposable household income. These recent advances open up an opportunity to include input indicators in the monitoring process, thereby allowing for a first step along the continuum of nonbinding output governance toward input governance.[8]

Including input indicators has also become necessary because some of the country-specific recommendations the Commission voices in the process of the European Semester already point to particular policy tools, such as the level of the minimum wage and the organization of minimum income protection (Council, 2015a, 2015b). However, systematically basing these country-specific recommendations on uniform indicators assessed through a clear analytical grid will render them more forceful as well as more coherent.

The Social Protection Committee recently adopted a Minimum Income Benchmarking Framework. This should be considered a major step forward in socializing the European project. Including carefully selected input indicators in the streamlined EU policy monitoring process, on top of the currently used outcome indicators, has indeed a number of advantages. For one, the EU and the Member States would be rendered accountable for the social quality of economic policies conceptualized as a means of realizing the fundamental social rights of citizens (Vandenbroucke, 2014). The aim should be to support the Member States in finding adequate country-specific economic and social balances and to prevent the poor's becoming the first victims of austerity. Second, adding policy indicators pertaining to minimum income packages to the Social Scoreboard will be helpful to link outcome indicators (i.e., the reduction of at-risk-of-poverty rates and joblessness) to policies. A well-thought-out selection of indicators can bring out different policy mixes, available options, and trade-offs. Without interfering with national authority and policy structures, such contextualized indicators can indicate imbalances in the nexus of minimum wages, work incentives, and minimum incomes for jobless households. In line with the aforementioned initiatives, most in particular the 2008 Active Inclusion Recommendation, this leaves room for subsidiarity, monitoring, and mutual learning, starting from a broad view of the overall quality of social policy.

## THE CONSTRUCTION OF INPUT INDICATORS

Policy indicators should measure policy input alone, not confounded by demographic or other variables. The indicators should inform on the policy design and policy choices regarding the balance of minimum income protection for different target groups, such as working and nonworking households. They should, in line with the 2008 Recommendation, gauge the interrelations and incentive effects at the bottom of the labor market. This can be achieved by indicators based on model-family simulations of income packages. By keeping the definition of the family type constant across countries and over time, shifts in the income package (and its components) are solely based on differences or shifts in policy. Moreover, results are easily comparable across countries, and they are intuitively understandable. An additional advantage of using standard simulations is that data requirements are limited, allowing for a timely release of the indicators. Moreover, a longstanding academic and institutional interest in gathering and refining model-family simulations of minimum income protection guarantees valid indicators (Bradshaw & Finch, 2002; Cantillon, Van Mechelen, Marx, & Van den Bosch, 2004; Eardley, Bradshaw, Ditch, Gough, & Whiteford, 1996; Gough, Bradshaw, Ditch, Eardley, & Whiteford, 1996; Immervoll, 2009; Nelson, 2008; Van Mechelen, Marchal, Goedemé, Marx, & Cantillon, 2011). Likewise, the European Commission has supported various initiatives to ensure comparable model-family simulations of Member States' policies. For instance, the Commission funds an extension of the Organisation for Economic Co-operation and Development (OECD) benefits and wages simulations for the non-OECD EU Member States. The results of these simulations are published by Eurostat. Also, the Commission is currently funding an add-on to the microsimulation tool EUROMOD that will allow for extremely versatile standard simulation possibilities for EU Member States.

Model-family simulations give only a partial picture: the adequacy of minimum income schemes is defined not solely by the level of household income it guarantees. Strict means-tests, work conditions, severe residential requirements, and stigma may limit access in a prohibitive way.[9] This limitation of the indicators should be kept in mind. A more specific drawback of model-family simulations is heavy reliance on the definition of the hypothetical family. Therefore, the model family should be carefully selected.

Here, we define the model family as a single-parent household with two children, in a minimum income situation. We focus on the single-parent case because it is a case where policy choices are straightforward. In the out-of-work case, the household has no income and fully relies on the applicable minimum income protection scheme, as well as other income components insofar as the household is eligible for them. In the in-work case, the single parent is full-time employed at the statutory minimum wage or an equivalent proxy of the wage floor.

The two indicators show the adequacy of the final net income floor for single-parent households out of work and in full-time employment. We include three additional indicators: the financial incentives to work (defined as the income difference between full-time minimum wage employment and net social assistance income), the gross minimum wage, and the gross-to-net welfare effort (calculated as the difference between the minimum wage and the final disposable income), all expressed relative to the EU at-risk-of-poverty threshold. The simulated income packages are extracted from CSB MIPI, a dataset on minimum income protection hosted by the Herman Deleeck Centre for Social Policy at the University of Antwerp, because this dataset specifically contains information on minimum wages.[10]

## DECENT MINIMUM INCOMES FOR THE POOR: A WAKE-UP CALL

We measure the adequacy of minimum income protection by comparing the rights-based net income packages to the EU at-risk-of-poverty threshold. Admittedly, this threshold is defined arbitrarily, while the indicator builds on the assumption that economies of scale at the household level are proportional to the level of household income and are constant across countries. The contextualization of the thresholds by means of the reference budgets presented in Chapter 1 suggests, however, that in many cases the at-risk-of-poverty thresholds underestimate the minimum financial resources that a household requires for adequate social participation. This is especially the case in the poorest EU Member States and for families with children. It is important to keep this in mind when interpreting the results shown in Figure 12.1.

In most cases, the comparison of the social floor with the at-risk-of-poverty threshold shows a substantial inadequacy of net income packages for jobless single parents. However, differences among EU Member States are enormous,

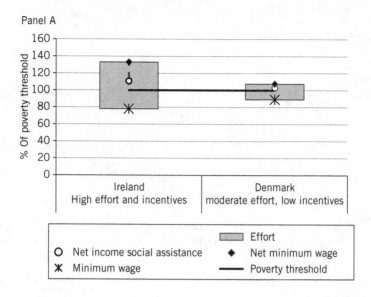

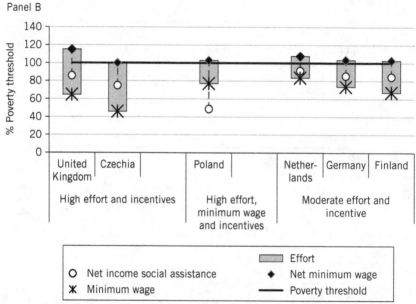

**Figure 12.1.** Balance of minimum income protection packages, relative to at-risk-of-poverty threshold, single parent with two children, 2012. *Panel A:* High road—Adequate minimum income protection packages for in-work and out-of-work status. *Panel B:* Middle road—Adequate minimum income package for a working single-parent family, inadequate out-of-work protection. *Panel C:* Low road—Inadequate minimum income packages, both out-of-work and in-work status. *Panel D:* Low road—Inadequate minimum income packages, both out-of-work and in-work status. *Notes:* Countries are ranked according to the level of the net income at social assistance. Social assistance in Spain (ES) and Italy (IT) is based on legislation in Catalonia and Milan, respectively. No social assistance in Greece (EL). In Denmark (DK), Germany (DE), Finland (FI), Austria (AT), and Italy (IT), no statutory minimum wage existed in 2012. Standard simulations are based on a proxy of the wage floor. Data for Greece (EL) and Bulgaria (BG) include experience-related top-ups. Incentives: income gain when moving from social assistance to full-time minimum wage employment. *Source:* CSB MIPI Version 3/2013 (Van Mechelen et al., 2011); poverty thresholds from Eurostat (2015b).

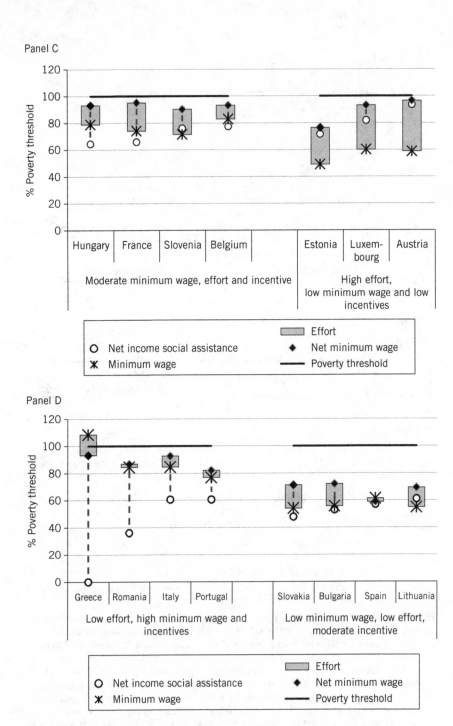

**Figure 12.1.** Continued

ranging from less than 40% of the poverty line in Romania to adequate levels in Denmark. Roughly speaking, net income packages are relatively more generous—although still inadequate—in the richer Member States than in the poorer ones. This is extremely worrying, especially in the poorest EU Member States, where—as shown in Chapter 1—an income at the level of the poverty threshold is too low for simultaneous access to adequate housing and adequate food, even if the income were spent exclusively on these items.

More countries shift to adequate (or nearly adequate) income protection in the case of full-time work at minimum wage. However, the number of countries where full-time employment at the minimum wage level does not guarantee an income above the poverty threshold remains substantial.

This is not surprising given gross minimum wage levels. As a general rule, gross minimum wages largely fall short of protecting single parents with two children. However, there is a large variation in relative values across countries, ranging from a low 46% of the poverty line in the Czech Republic to a high of 84% in Romania.

Most countries provide substantial direct additional income support to single-parent families that rely on a full-time minimum wage (the gray bars in Figure 12.1). The value of these benefits generally surpasses any taxes or contributions. Again, the variation across countries is enormous. Gross-to-net efforts range from a negative 15% of the poverty line in Greece to 54% in the Czech Republic and 50% in the United Kingdom. However, despite these efforts, disposable incomes at a full-time minimum wage protect against poverty in only a limited number of countries (see Panel A and Panel B of Figure 12.1).

Finally, and not unimportantly, there also is a large variation in the wedge between net income at minimum wage and the net social assistance benefit: some countries accept very limited financial work incentives (e.g., Denmark and Austria), while in other countries the financial gains are exceptionally high. In Romania and Poland, the difference between minimum incomes for jobless households (social assistance) and net income at minimum wage is larger than 50% of the poverty line. Other countries have installed financial incentives in a broad range, from 10% to 30% of the poverty threshold.

In Figure 12.1, we bring these indicators together. Countries are divided into three groups, based on the adequacy of their income floors using the poverty threshold as a benchmark. In high-road countries (Ireland and Denmark), the packages for both in-work and out-of-work single-parent households are adequate. In middle-road countries, the guaranteed income package of a working single-parent family exceeds the poverty threshold, but for jobless single-parent families, it is inadequate. In 2012, this was the case in six countries: the United Kingdom, the Czech Republic, Poland, the Netherlands, Germany and Finland. Finally, in the numerous low-road countries, both in-work and out-of-work income protection is inadequate.

Although optimal policy mixes for single-parent households cannot be readily derived—they should take into account such things as the large variation in activation policies (Marchal & Van Mechelen, 2017), the share of low-paid work, additional cost compensations, budget constraints, and other context variables—the presented combined indicators are useful for indicating possible social imbalances. The cross-national comparison of the country-specific relations between the adequacy of minimum incomes, work incentives, minimum wages, and gross-to-net efforts suggests that, in order to make minimum incomes more adequate:

1. Some countries could consider an increase of the gross-to-net effort (e.g., Belgium).
2. Others might rebalance gross minimum wage, minimum income protection, and financial work incentives (e.g., Romania and Poland).
3. In yet another set of countries, there might be room for increasing minimum wages (e.g., Luxembourg).

For many countries, however, raising the net income for those out of work will require an equivalent increase of the net income for those in work, either through a relative increase of gross minimum wages or through bigger gross-to-net efforts.[11]

How did social floors evolve over the past decades? Tables 12.1 and 12.2 show changes for the 1990s and 2000s, respectively. In order to ensure comparability over time, there are some differences with the indicators presented in the preceding section, while some countries are excluded because they lacked a statutory minimum wage (or a proxy for the wage floor) at the beginning of the time period considered.

In the 1990s, in five out of the nine countries included, we observe a deterioration of the adequacy of the minimum social floor for jobless households.[12] Also, minimum wages (or proxies for the wage floor) eroded in the majority of countries relative to the median household income. At the same time, gross-to-net efforts increased. The combination of these trends led to unchanged or increasing financial incentives in most countries.[13]

In the 2000s, the picture is more diffuse. In a majority of countries, net disposable income at minimum wage increased, while in half of the countries, social assistance, too, became more adequate. However, in a sizable number of Member States, including countries where the social floor was low to start with, minimum incomes decreased compared to the poverty threshold. This means that financial incentives in general became stronger, both in countries where they were absent or low to start with, as well as in countries where they initially were quite substantial.

**Table 12.1.** Changes in Indicators Relative to Trends in Living Standards, 1992–2001

| Country | Net disposable income at social assistance | Net disposable income at minimum wage | Minimum wage | Effort | Financial incentive |
|---|---|---|---|---|---|
| Netherlands (NL) | – | – | – | + | + |
| Spain (ES) | – | – | – | = | – |
| Germany (DE) | – | – | – | – | = |
| Luxembourg (LU) | – | + | – | + | + |
| Belgium (BE) | – | + | – | + | + |
| Italy (IT) | + | – | – | + | – |
| Greece (EL) | = | – | – | = | = |
| Portugal (PT) | + | + | – | + | – |
| France (FR) | + | + | + | = | + |
| Austria (AT) | + | + | + | + | = |

*Notes*: More than one percentage point change upward or downward on the indicator over the period. Countries are grouped by decrease or increase in net social assistance and decrease or increase in net disposable income at minimum wage; within those groups, countries are ranked by trends in gross minimum wage. DE, AT, IT: proxy for the wage floor or a low wage. PT: no out-of-work minimum income scheme in 1992. IT and EL: no national minimum income scheme, local scheme of the city of Milan for IT. Living standards in 1992 proxied by 1994 poverty thresholds, adjusted for inflation.

*Source*: CSB MIPI Version 3/2013 (Van Mechelen et al., 2011); poverty thresholds from Eurostat (2015b), consumer price indices from International Labor Organization (2014).

## THE LINK BETWEEN INPUT AND OUTPUT: HOW INSTRUMENTAL IS MINIMUM INCOME PROTECTION FOR POVERTY REDUCTION?

Whereas the principle of guaranteeing adequate minimum incomes should be based on a social rights perspective, the question whether this is relevant in achieving poverty reduction is equally important.

Whereas the expectation of a negative relation between adequate social assistance benefits and poverty makes intuitive sense at the individual level, whether this holds true on the country (macro) level is less straightforward. The link between input and outcome is complex. For one, the focus of our indicators on income neglects equally relevant issues related to non-take-up and eligibility. In addition, minimum income protection is a truly residual scheme that comes into action only after all other social rights are exhausted. The overall generosity of social protection as a whole may be more relevant in this regard. Also, most countries do not guarantee a minimum income floor above the 60% at-risk-of-poverty threshold. Therefore, we should not expect to find meaningful

**Table 12.2.** Changes in Indicators Relative to Trends in Living Standards, 2001–2009/2012

| Country | Net disposable income at social assistance | Net disposable income at minimum wage | Minimum wage | Effort | Financial incentive |
|---|---|---|---|---|---|
| Italy (IT) | − | − | − | + | + |
| France (FR) | − | − | − | + | + |
| Czechia (CZ) | − | − | − | − | + |
| Finland (FI) | − | − | = | − | + |
| Estonia (EE) | − | − | + | − | + |
| Poland (PL) | − | + | − | + | + |
| Sweden (SE) | − | + | − | + | + |
| Lithuania (LT) | = | + | − | + | + |
| Belgium (BE) | + | = | − | + | − |
| Portugal (PT) | + | + | + | + | + |
| Spain (ES) | + | + | + | − | − |
| Luxembourg (LU) | + | + | + | + | + |
| United Kingdom (UK) | + | + | + | = | + |
| Slovenia (SI) | + | + | + | + | + |
| Hungary (HU) | + | + | + | − | = |

*Notes:* More than one percentage point change upward or downward on the indicator over the period. Data are most recent available at time of writing. Countries are grouped by decrease or increase of net social assistance and decrease or increase of net disposable income at minimum wage; within those groups, countries are ranked by trends in gross minimum wage. IT, FI, SE: proxies for the wage floor or a low wage.
*Source:* CSB MIPI Version 3/2013 (Van Mechelen et al., 2011); poverty thresholds from Eurostat (2015b).

correlations between generosity and poverty headcounts based on this threshold. Thus, it might make more sense to expect a relation with the depth of poverty, or severe poverty (for instance, at the 40% at-risk-of-poverty threshold).

In Table 12.3 we present correlations between the input indicators and the share of jobless households, the poverty headcount using the 40% poverty threshold, and severe material deprivation among single-parent families. Some reservations apply: the correlations are based on a small group of cases that in no way can be considered a representative sample of all countries. Moreover, we do not control for other country characteristics. Hence, these correlations can only serve to illustrate potential and tentative relations, and can in no way be interpreted as causal mechanisms.

**Table 12.3.** Exploration of the Instrumental Relevance of Adequate Minimum Income Protection for Single-Parent Households, 2012

|  | Employment | Poverty | |
| --- | --- | --- | --- |
|  | Share of people living in a jobless single-parent household, out of all people living in a single- parent household | At-risk-of-poverty rate of people living in working-age single-parent households (40% AROP) | Severe material deprivation among single-parent households |
| Net social assistance[a] | 0.1347 | −0.7238 | −0.6071 |
| Net minimum wage[b] | 0.4278 | −0.5729 | −0.1531 |
| Minimum wage | 0.3051 | 0.1315 | 0.1823 |
| Gross-to-net effort | 0.2686 | −0.5735 | −0.2007 |
| Financial incentive | 0.1894 | 0.3864 | 0.5907 |

Notes: [a] Net disposable household income at social assistance for a single-parent household with two children. [b] Net disposable household income at full-time minimum wage employment for a single-parent household with two children. Correlations in italics appear to be relatively robust when taking account of influential cases and data variations.

Source: CSB MIPI Version 3/2013 (Van Mechelen et al., 2011), EU-SILC, authors' calculations, Eurostat (2015b).

Taking account of the large impact single-country cases can have, we repeated the exercise for different country groups and data sources (i.e., the OECD Benefits and Wages data; see Cantillon, Marchal, & Luigjes, 2015). The inclusion of the Southern European countries especially led to an overestimation of the correlates between input indicators and poverty outcomes. In light of these robustness checks, the following observations can be made:

- Adequate minimum income protection for out-of-work single-parent households tends to coexist with lower poverty rates among persons living in working-age single-parent households.
- Similarly, adequate minimum income protection for in-work single-parent households tends to correlate with lower poverty rates among persons living in working-age single-parent households.
- There appear to be no consistent correlations between the other input indicators and outcomes.

As said, it is impossible to draw stark conclusions from these correlations. However debatable the exercise may be, at least it does not contradict the assumption of the instrumental relevance of adequate minimum income protection for poverty reduction.

## CONCLUSION

In this chapter, we propose a modest first step in a necessarily much broader soul-searching exercise on the role of the EU in reducing poverty among European citizens. We argue that including carefully selected indicators of minimum income packages *sensu lato* in the streamlined EU policy-monitoring process, on top of the currently used outcome indicators, is the place to start. This would give European social governance more bite, while the social quality of economic policies and anti-poverty strategies would become visible in a more concrete way, starting from the fundamental social rights of citizens. Adding policy indicators pertaining to minimum income packages to the Social Scoreboard will more specifically be helpful to link broadly defined outcome indicators (i.e., the reduction of at-risk-of-poverty rates and joblessness) to policies: the well-thought-out selection of indicators can bring out different policy mixes, available options, and potential imbalances. This would allow for better balanced and more coherent policy recommendations, signal difficult trade-offs, and point to the important efforts to be made, especially within the poorest Member States. Most importantly, augmenting the existing outcome indicators with input indicators as a first step to binding input governance in the field of minimum income protection is a necessity: in nearly all European nations, the comparison of the social floor with the at-risk-of-poverty threshold shows a substantial inadequacy of net income packages for jobless families.

The current work of the Social Protection Committee on the development of a benchmarking framework for minimum income benefits should therefore be considered as a major step forward in the further socializing the European project. By making the goal of guaranteeing adequate minimum incomes to all EU citizens explicit, the admittedly prudent strategy that has been put forward in this chapter will ultimately encourage reflection on whether and how the EU should support the individual Member States to make this goal happen.

## NOTES

The research for this paper has benefited from financial support by the European Union's Seventh Framework Programme (FP7/2012-2016) under grant agreement n° 290613 (ImPRovE: Poverty Reduction in Europe: Social Policy and Innovation; http://improve-research.eu). The authors would like to thank John Hills, Tim Goedemé, Rudi Van Dam and Frank Vandenbroucke, as well as the participants to the May 2015 ImPRovE meeting in Antwerp, for helpful suggestions and comments. The authors are solely responsible for any remaining shortcomings and errors.

1 This was an important argument used in the Ohlin report preparing the Treaty of Rome (International Labor Organization, 1956, pp. 86–87).

2 This is not to say that other income-replacement schemes may not be more empirically relevant, either in size or scope, for unemployed working-age persons. Yet, these do not provide a guaranteed minimum, but depend on contribution records and/or prior work history and wages. A minimum income reflects the absolute floor of what a society deems acceptable protection for persons on either fringe of the labor market, and, moreover, consequently stipulates a minimum floor for the entire building of (replacement and other) incomes.

3 For concrete proposals, see Schulten (2014) and Eurofound (2014).

4 European Parliament resolution of January 19, 2017, on a European Pillar of Social Rights.

5 This recommendation was eventually affirmed by the European Parliament (resolution of 6/5/2009). In 2010, the European Anti-Poverty Network (EAPN) launched The European Minimum Income Network (EMIN)—based on the 2008 Recommendation—and released a draft "Framework Directive on Minimum Income" (Van Lancker, 2010).

6 These are the options for work incentives and legitimacy. Evidently, bringing budgetary concerns into focus further complicates the matter.

7 This is a structured policy-monitoring cycle, with fixed and streamlined reporting and feedback moments.

8 Vandenbroucke, Cantillon, Van Mechelen, Goedemé, and Van Lancker (2013) distinguish between input and output and first-order and second-order governance. Second-order governance merely seeks to influence existing policy structures and objectives, whereas first-order governance aims to encourage, replace, or adjust existing policy strategies more directly. Both governance modes may target policy outputs (social outcomes) or input (policy instruments). Hence, the current OMC Social Inclusion can be firmly categorized as second-order output governance here, as the proposals mentioned above vary from (nonbinding) first- to second-order input governance.

9 Studies that cross-nationally assess these limitations specifically for minimum income protection are rare, but see, for instance, Bargain, Immervoll, and Viitamäki (2010); and Immervoll, Marianna, and Mira d'Ercole (2004); as well as Eurofound (2015) on coverage and non-take-up; Marchal and Van Mechelen (2017) on activity requirements; and De Wilde (forthcoming) on the discretion of case workers.

10 Detailed information on the specific assumptions on minimum wage proxies, household characteristics, treatment of intranational variation, and reference dates is given in Van Mechelen et al. (2011).

11 In Chapter 10, Collado et al. present calculations of the cost of closing the poverty gap while maintaining average financial participation incentives at

the bottom (three equivalized household income deciles) of the income distribution in Belgium, Denmark, and the United Kingdom.

12  Increases were observed only in Vienna, France, Milan, and Portugal.

13  Exceptions are limited to countries with nonrepresentative regional or
local minimum income schemes (Spain and Italy), and Portugal, which
introduced a minimum income scheme in 1996.


## REFERENCES

Bargain, O., Immervoll, H., & Viitamäki, H. (2010). *No claim, no pain: Measuring
the non-take-up of social assistance using register data* [IZA Discussion
Paper 5355]. Bonn, Germany: Institut zur Zukunft der Arbeit.

Bradshaw, J., & Finch, N. (2002). *A comparison of child benefit packages in 22
countries* [Research Report 174]. Norwich, England: U.K. Department for
Work and Pensions.

Cameron, D. (2013, November 26). Free movement in Europe needs to be less
free. *Financial Times.* Retrieved from http://www.ft.com/cms/s/0/add36222-
56be-11e3-ab12-00144feabdc0.html#axzz39YJSsk5W

Cantillon, B., Collado, D., & Van Mechelen, N. (2015). *The end of decent social
protection for the poor? The dynamics of low wages, minimum income packages
and median household incomes* [ImPRovE Discussion Paper 15/03]. Antwerp,
Belgium: Herman Deleeck Centre for Social Policy, University of Antwerp.

Cantillon, B., Marchal, S., & Luigjes, C. (2015). *Decent income for the poor: Which
role for Europe* [Improve Working Paper 15/20]. Antwerp, Belgium: Herman
Deleeck Centre for Social Policy, University of Antwerp.

Cantillon, B., Van Mechelen, N., Marx, I., & Van den Bosch, K. (2004). *The ev-
olution of minimum income protection in 15 European Countries, 1992–2001*
[CSB-berichten D/2004/6104/02]. Antwerp, Belgium: Herman Deleeck
Centre for Social Policy, University of Antwerp.

Cantillon, B., & Vandenbroucke, F. (2014). *Reconciling work and poverty reduction: How successful are European welfare states?* Oxford, England: Oxford
University Press.

Costamagna, F. (2013). *The European semester in action: Strengthening economic
policy coordination while weakening the social dimension?* [LPF Working
Paper 5]. Torino, Italy: Centro Einaudi—Laboratorio di Politica Comparata
e Filosofia Pubblica.

Council of the European Communities. (1992). Council Recommendation of
24 June 1992 on common criteria concerning sufficient resources and social
assistance in social protection systems. 92/441/EEC, OJ L 245, 26/08/1992.
Brussels: Council of the European Communities.

Council. (2015). Council recommendation of 14 July 2015 on the 2015 national
reform programme of Portugal and delivering a Council opinion on the 2015

Stability Programme of Portugal. Official Journal of the European Union. 2015/C272/25.

Council. (2015). Council Recommendation on the 2015 National Reform Programme of Spain and delivering a Council opinion on the 2015 Stability Programme of Spain. Official Journal of the European Union. 2015/C272/13.

De Wilde, M (forthcoming). *Between legislation and realization comes implementation. The effect of the multi-layered implementation process on social policy outcomes.* PhD Thesis. Antwerp: University of Antwerp.

Eardley, T., Bradshaw, J., Ditch, J., Gough, I., & Whiteford, P. (1996). *Social assistance in OECD countries: Synthesis report* [Research Report 46]. London, England: HMSO Department of Social Security.

Eurofound. (2013). *Developments in collectively agreed pay 2012.* Dublin, Ireland: European Foundation for the Improvement of Living and Working Conditions.

Eurofound. (2014). *Pay in Europe in the 21st century.* Luxembourg: Publications Office of the European Union.

Eurofound. (2015). *Access to social benefits: Reducing non-take-up.* Luxembourg: Publications Office of the European Union.

European Commission. (2008). Commission Recommendation of 3 October 2008 on the active inclusion of people excluded from the labour market 2008/867/EC C.F.R. (2008). Official Journal of the European Union L307. Brussels: European Commission.

European Commission. (2013). *Follow-up on the implementation by the Member States of the 2008 European Commission recommendation on active inclusion of people excluded from the labor market—Towards a social investment approach* [Commission Staff working document]. Brussels, Belgium: European Commission.

European Trade Union Confederation. (2013). ETUC position on the social dimension of the European Union Adopted at the Executive Committee meeting of 23 April 2013. Brussels: ETUC.

Ferrera, M. (2012). Modest beginnings, timid progresses: What's next for social Europe? In B. Cantillon, H. Verschueren, & P. Ploscar (Eds.), *Social inclusion and social protection in the EU: Interactions between law and policy* (pp. 17–40). Antwerp, Belgium: Intersentia.

Frazer, H., & Marlier, E. (2013). *Synthesis report: Assessment of the implementation of the European Commission Recommendation on active inclusion: A study of national policies.* Brussels, Belgium: European Commission, Directorate-General for Employment, Social Affairs and Inclusion.

Gough, I., Bradshaw, J., Ditch, J., Eardley, T., & Whiteford, P. (1996). Social assistance in OECD countries. *Journal of European Social Policy, 7*(1), 17–43.

Immervoll, H. (2009). *Minimum-income benefits in OECD countries: Policy design, effectiveness and challenges* [IZA Discussion Paper 4627]. Bonn, Germany: IZA.

Immervoll, H., Marianna, P., & Mira d'Ercole, M. (2004). *Benefit coverage rates and household typologies: Scope and limitations of tax-benefit indicators* [OECD Social, Employment and Migration Working Papers 20]. Paris, France: OECD.

International Labor Organization. (1956). Social aspects of European economic cooperation. *International Labor Review, 74*(2), 99–123.

International Labor Organization. (2014). *Laborsta.* http://laborsta.ilo.org/

Juncker, J.-C., Tusk, D., Dijsselbloem, J., Draghi, M., & Schulz, M. (2015). *The five presidents' report: Completing Europe's economic and monetary union.* Brussels, Belgium: European Commission.

Leibfried, S. (2010). Social policy: Left to the judges and the markets? In H. Wallace, M. Pollack, & A. Young (Eds.), *Policy-making in the European Union* (pp. 243–278). Oxford, England: Oxford University Press.

Marchal, S., & Van Mechelen, N. (2017). A new kid in town? Active inclusion elements in European minimum income schemes. *Social Policy and Administration, 51*(1), 171–194. doi:10.1111/spol.12177

Marlier, E., Atkinson, A. B., Cantillon, B., & Nolan, B. (2007). *The EU and social inclusion: Facing the challenges.* Bristol, England: The Policy Press.

Marx, I., Marchal, S., & Nolan, B. (2013). Mind the gap: Net incomes of minimum wage workers in the EU and the US. In I. Marx & K. Nelson (Eds.), *Minimum income protection in flux* (pp. 54–80). Houndmills, England: Palgrave-Macmillan.

Nelson, K. (2008). Minimum income protection and European integration: Trends and levels of minimum benefits in comparative perspective, 1990–2005. *International Journal of Health Services, 38*(1), 103–124.

Nolan, B., & Marx, I. (2009). Economic inequality, poverty, and social exclusion. In B. Nolan, W. Salverda, & T. Smeeding (Eds.), *The Oxford handbook of economic inequality* (pp. 315–341). Oxford, England: Oxford University Press.

Schulten, T. (2014). *Contours of a European minimum wage policy.* Berlin, Germany: Friedrich Ebert Stiftung.

Van Lancker, A. (2010). *Working document on a Framework Directive on Minimum Income* Brussels: European Anti-Poverty Network.

Van Mechelen, N., & Marchal, S. (2013). Struggle for life: Social assistance benefits, 1992–2009. In I. Marx & K. Nelson (Eds.), *Minimum income protection in flux* (pp. 28–53). Houndmills, England: Palgrave-Macmillan.

Van Mechelen, N., Marchal, S., Goedemé, T., Marx, I., & Cantillon, B. (2011). *The CSB-Minimum Income Protection Indicators dataset (CSB-MIPI)* [CSB Working Paper Series 11/05]. Antwerp, Belgium: Herman Deleeck Centre for Social Policy, University of Antwerp.

Vandenbroucke, F. (2014). *The case for a European social union: From muddling through to a sense of common purpose.* Leuven, Belgium: KU Leuven, Euroforum.

Vandenbroucke, F. (2018). Social policy in a monetary union: Puzzles, paradoxes and perspectives. In M. Boone, G. Deneckere, & J. Tollebeek (Eds.), *The end of postwar and the future of Europe – Essays on the work of Ian Buruma* (pp. forthcoming). Leuven: Uitgeverij Peeters.

Vandenbroucke, F., Cantillon, B., Van Mechelen, N., Goedemé, T., & Van Lancker, A. (2013). The EU and minimum income protection: Clarifying the policy conundrum. In I. Marx & K. Nelson (Eds.), *Minimum income protection in flux* (pp. 271–317). Houndmills, England: Palgrave-Macmillan.

Vandenbroucke, F., & Vanhercke, B. (2014). *A European Social Union: 10 Tough Nuts to Crack* [Background report for the Friends of Europe High-Level Group on "Social Union"]. Brussels: Friends of Europe.

Verschueren, H. (2015). Preventing "benefit tourism" in the EU: A narrow or broad interpretation of the possibilities offered by the ECJ in DANO? *Common Market Law Review, 52*(2), 363–390.

Zeitlin, J., & Vanhercke, B. (2014). *Socializing the European Semester? Economic governance and social policy coordination in Europe 2020* [SIEPS Report 7]. Stockholm, Sweden: Swedish Institute for European Policy Studies.

# 13

# CONCLUSION

## HOW TO GET THERE?

**Bea Cantillon, Tim Goedemé, and John Hills**

In this book, the contributors present new evidence on what has happened to levels of poverty among the working-age population in the European Union (EU) and analyze what could help policymakers—and those pressing or advising them—to think about approaches that might prove most effective in the future. In this concluding chapter, we reflect on some of the key points the analysis—and the ImPRovE project more generally—reveals, and on what lessons can be drawn from it. Most likely, the ambitious Europe 2020 targets aiming for a reduction of the number of persons living in poverty, jobless households, or material deprivation by 20 million will not be reached in time. However, more than ever, they should firmly remain on the agenda. While it is hard to reduce poverty, the contributions to this book show that it is altogether not impossible. Many examples show that the design of (national) policy packages can have a decisive impact on the poverty-reducing capacity of welfare states, and this extends well beyond raising minimum income floors. As emphasized by the late Tony Atkinson (2015, p. 308), "the solutions . . . lie in our own hands. If we are willing to use today's greater wealth to address these challenges, and accept that resources should be shared less unequally, there are indeed grounds for optimism."

## DECENT INCOMES FOR THE POOR: A WAKE-UP CALL

Ever since adopting the Lisbon Strategy, the European Union has declared poverty reduction one of its main social goals. In 2000, a set of indicators was agreed upon that would enable policymakers to monitor poverty and social ex-clusion in a comparative perspective (Atkinson, Cantillon, Marlier, & Nolan, 2002). Since then, as discussed by Cantillon, Marchal, and Luigjes in Chapter 12, these indicators have silently made their way from the rather peripheral pro-cess of "social coordination" into the European Semester,[1] thereby progressively "socializing" the economic governance of Europe. Yet, notwithstanding meri-torious initiatives like the recent resolution of the European Parliament on a European Pillar of Social Rights, social issues receive very little attention in European policy debates, while progress in terms of poverty reduction has been disappointing in most EU Member States, to say the least.

One of the central indicators used in European social governance is relative income poverty, defined as the proportion of individuals living on an income lower than 60% of the median income in their country. This is also the leading benchmark of most of the analysis presented in this book. Two premises underlie this choice: each household should have at its disposal the minimum income re-quired for participation in its society and, on the national escalators of income growth (or decline), the discrepancy between those at the bottom and those in the middle should decrease if we are to claim success.

Admittedly, the threshold is defined rather arbitrarily, while the indicator builds on the assumption that economies of scale at the household level are proportional to the level of household income and are constant across coun-tries. The context for the thresholds given by the reference budgets presented in Chapter 1 suggests, however, that in many cases the thresholds underestimate the minimum financial resources that a household requires for adequate social participation, especially in the poorest EU Member States. In the ImPRovE proj-ect, several country teams have endeavored to construct, for the first time, cross-nationally comparable reference budgets for seven European cities (Antwerp, Athens, Barcelona, Budapest, Helsinki, Luxembourg, and Milan). These budgets are fully specified in the sense that they cover concrete lists of goods and serv-ices, representing the minimum resources required for adequate social participa-tion. By making more concrete which income is necessary for obtaining a certain living standard, reference budgets help to clarify the actual meaning of being at risk of poverty in countries that vary strongly in their average standard of living. The at-risk-of-poverty line represents very different living standards in terms of the extent to which households have access to essential goods and services, such as adequate food and housing. The approach shows that the at-risk-of-poverty indicator strongly underestimates the needs of households in the poorest EU Member States and suggests that it underestimates poverty among children al-most everywhere.

Such findings amplify the concerns expressed in this book, especially the conclusions related to the inadequacy of the social floor discussed in Chapter 12. Compared to the 60% poverty threshold, even in the most generous national settings, minimum income protection for jobless households falls short, in particular for families with children. However, the inadequacy of minimum income protection differs enormously between EU Member States, ranging from a shortfall of 60% compared to the at-risk-of-poverty threshold for single parents in Romania to (nearly) adequate levels in Denmark. Roughly speaking, the social floor is relatively more generous—although still inadequate—in the richer Member States than in the poorer ones. Moreover, in several EU Member States, the wage floor, too, is inadequate for working-age families, although again with significant variations across countries.

The conclusion is that, in Europe, only a tiny minority of countries are on a "high road" combining adequate income packages for both in-work and out-of-work families. In the large majority of countries, both in-work and out-of-work income protection is inadequate to prevent poverty. This is worrying, especially in the poorest EU Member States, where an income at the level of the poverty threshold is too low for having simultaneous access to adequate housing and adequate food, even if it were spent exclusively on these items.

## EMPLOYMENT INCREASES BY THEMSELVES ARE NOT ENOUGH

Given the importance of income from the labor market for most people of working age, and that in nearly all countries social assistance benefit rates fall short of the relevant national poverty line, employment and unemployment levels are of obvious importance. Indeed, some political actors debate the issue as if increased employment rates are by themselves the solution to poverty.

However, the analysis by Gábos, Branyczki, Binder, and Tóth in Chapter 2 suggests that increasing employment rates is not a sufficient condition for reducing poverty. Before the crisis, there were countries with rising employment levels but where poverty did not decrease. Indeed, employment rates were higher in most member states in 2008 than in 2005, but poverty did not fall substantially in any of them. Relative poverty rates fell in only a minority of countries during the pre-crisis years, remaining roughly constant in many, and they even rose in Greece, Sweden, and Germany.[2] On the other hand, since the crisis, sharper employment falls were accompanied by rising poverty, and there was a clearer "mirror" relationship between the two in many of the countries on the periphery that were hit hardest by the crisis.

There are several reasons why employment gains do not necessarily translate into lowered poverty rates. These include the growth of in-work poverty, when wages are low and in-work benefits or tax credits are not adequate to help people to get out of poverty; the "inefficient allocation" of employment, when the additional jobs go to households that already have paid workers, rather than to poor, low-work-intensity households; and inadequate indexation, when the values of benefits are not increased in line with living standards in good times so that they fall behind rising relative poverty lines. Dealing with all three of these factors is important in any strategy to reduce poverty—but doing so faces conflicts that we discuss further below.

This is not to say that employment rates make no difference, as the experience of the countries hardest hit by the crisis shows. Indeed, looking across all the countries and the whole period from 2005 to 2012, the analysis in Chapter 2 shows that, overall, a 10 percentage point rise in employment would be associated with a 2.9 percentage point drop in poverty rates.[3] Allowing for differences between countries and varying patterns over time reduces the effect to between 1.9 and 2.5 percentage points.

This scale of effect means that employment increases can play an important role in combating poverty, but by themselves they can be only part of the answer. A 10 percentage point rise in employment would be a major success for any country, but a resultant 2 percentage point fall in relative at-risk-of poverty rates would mean that other interventions would still be needed for more substantial progress, given starting rates of between 10% and 20% in nearly all member states.

A further conclusion from the analysis in Chapter 2 is that the effectiveness of social transfers in reducing poverty has declined in many countries, particularly where it was previously having the most effect. More positively, however, there were improvements in some of the previously least effective systems, such as Latvia and Spain. As Chapters 2 and 3 show, this diminished poverty-reducing capacity was not always the consequence of policy changes in themselves (see below). Indeed, broader trends in the population (e.g., changes in employment, incomes, and demography) may also contribute to reducing the effectiveness of policy packages.

The analysis of Notten and Guio in Chapter 4 further amplifies the importance of social transfers in reducing poverty. By simulating the effects of social transfers on material deprivation, Notten and Guio show that social transfers reduce not only monetary poverty but also the extent and depth of material deprivation. The impact of social transfers is substantial, reducing the average number of items for which people are materially deprived by 2.2 in Germany and Greece and by 1.9 and 1.8 in Poland and the United Kingdom. The impact is larger for recipients who are less well off, and it is also significant at higher levels of material deprivation. Changes in social transfers, therefore, have a twofold effect on the Europe 2020 social inclusion target: they reduce both relative income poverty and material deprivation.

The general lesson from these chapters reiterates and reinforces the conclusions of Cantillon and Vandenbroucke in *Reconciling Work and Poverty Reduction* (2014): "Given the persistent trend of demographic aging, a consistent combination of sustainable economic growth, employment-centered social policy, and effective social protection is key." Poverty reduction depends on achieving overall employment growth that reaches low-work-intensity households, coupled with structures of social and fiscal welfare systems that succeed in protecting low-wage earners and those who do not have adequate incomes from work, while doing so in a way that keeps up with rising living standards in good times. The question is whether such an ambitious strategy is feasible at all, and, if it is, how it can be realized.

## THE EXPERIENCE BEFORE AND SINCE THE CRISIS SHOWS THAT POLICY CHOICES CAN MAKE A DIFFERENCE

The analysis by Hills, Paulus, Sutherland, and Tasseva in Chapter 5 amplifies the point that structures of social transfers, and the way they change over time, can moderate or strengthen the effects on poverty of macroeconomic and demographic developments. By isolating in detail the effects of changes in tax and transfer policies in seven EU countries in the Lisbon decade from 2001 to 2011, they also show how policy choices can make a difference.

In particular, they show that it would be a mistake to assume that the generally disappointing trends in poverty outcomes over the period always were the result of policy neglect. In the seven countries analyzed, this was not, in fact, an entirely "lost decade" for poverty reduction: in six of them, indeed, the tax and benefit policy changes considered in the analysis were actually poverty-reducing. Only in Hungary did policy changes result in higher poverty rates than would otherwise have occurred.

However, it is also striking that policies had much more of a poverty-reducing effect in most (but not all) of the seven countries in the "good times" before 2007 than immediately after the crisis. Belgium was the exception, achieving more after 2007 than before it. Some might find this unsurprising—fiscal resources have been constrained, to say the least, as a result of the crisis itself. But the experiences show that there is no simple link between whether policies improve the fiscal balance (or the opposite) and their effects on poverty. For instance, some countries—such as the United Kingdom between 2001 and 2007—implemented policy changes that simultaneously reduced poverty and raised net revenue (when the 2007 system is compared with the initial system with all its key elements, such as benefit levels and tax thresholds, changed in line with growing incomes).

It is also notable that governments made changes to different elements of their tax-transfer policies with different or opposite effects. In other words, to understand policy change, it is essential that policy analysts consider the whole range of policies together, as well as their interactions, when evaluating a policy reform. By the same token, any strategy to address poverty should take into account each element of the full range of benefits, including taxation and social insurance, rather than just one instrument, such as social assistance.

The experiences of these countries also emphasize that one of the often least visible elements of policy change—how the money values of benefits and tax thresholds are adjusted (indexed) each year—can have larger effects than more visible and widely advertised structural reforms. In particular, at times of growth, if benefits are kept fixed in nominal or even real terms, the incomes of those for whom social benefits are the most important source of income will lag behind other people's incomes, and therefore fall compared to relative (floating) poverty lines. If they do not keep up, other types of poverty-reducing policy have to work much harder to make progress. By the same token, where real benefit levels were protected in the wake of the crisis at the time that real earnings were falling, the effect could be a reduction in relative poverty and in inequality.[4]

Even in countries worst hit by the crisis, some austerity measures were "fair by design"—but this depended on national choices. Matsaganis and Leventi expand on this point in Chapter 6. They also use tax–benefit simulation modeling (using the EUROMOD model) to isolate the effects of particular tax–benefit changes from 2009 to 2013 in a different set of seven countries, concentrating on those in many ways worst hit by the economic crisis, countries in the EU's periphery. In these countries, social welfare systems came under considerable stress; they were hit by both rapidly rising needs for social protection and simultaneous declines in the resources available to governments to deal with them.

At the same time, the shape of the crisis changed the compositions of populations most vulnerable to poverty—notably, of course, with younger people affected the worst in many of the countries. This meant that some policies, such as forms of social insurance relying on past formal labor market participation and contributions, were less well designed to protect the new population at risk. As a result, those who were left poor during the crisis, even after government intervention, were considerably poorer than those who made up the poor population before the crisis.

Again, the authors show how different elements of the policy response have had contrasting effects on poverty outcomes. In most of the countries, direct tax and social insurance changes were also generally progressive, but this was notably not so in Greece in 2013. Perhaps surprisingly for some, cuts in public-sector pay as part of austerity policies often had progressive effects, particularly (initially) in Greece, Portugal, and the Baltic countries.

As positive examples, Latvia improved minimum social assistance incomes during the period, while Greece's introduction of more comprehensive child benefits also had positive effects, but cuts in minimum incomes or unemployment benefits increased poverty in Portugal, Lithuania, and Romania.

A positive message from this experience is that, even at a time of crisis, some countries found it possible to structure fiscal retrenchment packages—or at least elements of them—in a progressive form. But, at the same time, such positive policy effects were generally small in comparison to the impact of the crisis itself and the results of falling employment, so poverty rates nevertheless rose sharply, as discussed above.

## THE COST-EFFECTIVENESS OF POLICY RESPONSES
## IN REDUCING POVERTY VARIES WIDELY AMONG INSTRUMENTS
## AND COUNTRIES

Variation in the effect of policy changes among countries is not simply the result of varying national policy choices. Because of differences in underlying income and demographic structures and in their starting points in terms of tax–benefit systems, the same instruments have varying effectiveness in their potential for achieving poverty reduction in each country: one size does not fit all to achieve the same results.

This was examined in detail within the ImPRovE program by Leventi, Sutherland, and Tasseva.[5] They used the tax–benefit simulation model EUROMOD to look at the effect on both poverty headcounts and poverty gaps of increasing (or decreasing) the value of particular instruments, benchmarking their effects by comparing measured effects with the change in their cost as a share of GDP. They compared seven contrasting countries: Belgium, Bulgaria, Estonia, Greece, Hungary, Italy, and the United Kingdom. This was an illustrative exercise, and the modeling does not, for instance, take account of potential behavioral effects. The authors show very clearly, however, how national factors lead to large differences in poverty-reduction effectiveness.

They also show that it matters greatly whether the objective is seen as being simply to reduce the numbers (poverty headcount) below the conventional income poverty threshold, or to reduce the extent to which the incomes of the poor fall short (the poverty gap). For instance, in Estonia, increasing the social assistance rates has very little effect on the headcount measure but a comparatively large effect on the poverty gap. This reflects the starting point, where social assistance rates are well below the poverty line.

Leventi, Sutherland, and Tasseva also show that the relationship between spending increases or decreases and poverty is not linear: as the level of the benefit or other instrument being looked at increases and more people are taken out of poverty, further additions have a declining effect. So, for instance, reducing child allowances in Belgium would have a greater effect in increasing child poverty than increasing them would have in cutting child poverty.

Taken at face value, concentrating available resources to increase social assistance rates would have the greatest effect on poverty reduction in Belgium and the United Kingdom. But, as Chapter 10 in this volume points out, simply raising social assistance rates with high, often 100%, marginal withdrawal rates creates other problems. Avoiding these would increase the cost substantially, leading the chapter's authors to the conclusion that increasing universal child allowances would also be relatively cost-effective in these countries.

Increasing child allowances would in any case be particularly effective in Hungary and Greece, as well as in Bulgaria and Italy (and in Estonia using a poverty gap measure).

By contrast, the poverty-reduction effects of increasing income tax thresholds are generally much weaker than other approaches. This is particularly true in countries where the threshold starts close to or above the poverty line for many households, as in Belgium and the United Kingdom (where the poverty-gap-reducing effects of higher tax allowances are minimal).

In terms of the effects of minimum wages in reducing poverty based on household incomes, increasing minimum wages also has comparatively little effect in most countries (Estonia is an exception). Many beneficiaries of this are in nonpoor households, which increases deadweight costs (although there are other reasons for improving the wage floor along with other policies, as discussed below).

Finally, countries vary in the sensitivity of their poverty rates to failure to maintain indexation of benefit and other values adequately. As Chapter 5 shows, this can be as important as more visible structural reforms. The authors of Chapter 5 show that Estonia and the United Kingdom are particularly vulnerable in this respect.

## THE GLASS CEILING OF POVERTY REDUCTION

Achieving both employment growth, especially among the low-skilled, and social and fiscal welfare systems that succeed in protecting low-wage earners and jobless households requires important efforts in terms of both the budgets involved and the construction of coherent policy packages.

Within the "fabric of the welfare state" there is a hierarchy of incomes: in general terms, politics dictate that the disposable income of low-wage earners should be higher than the minimum incomes for jobless people. Although the relationship between poverty and the level of minimum wages is not that strong overall,[6] minimum wages are indirectly important because minimum wages serve as a "glass ceiling" to the social minimum floor, for reasons of both equity and economic efficiency (Cantillon, Collado, & Van Mechelen, 2015).

Given the inadequacy of the wage floor and further downward pressures on low wages compared to poverty thresholds in many countries, it has become increasingly difficult for welfare states to guarantee adequate income protection for low-wage earners and work-poor households while preserving (or increasing) financial work incentives. This is especially a problem for single-parent families because they rely on a single income while double incomes have become the societal norm, pushing up median household incomes.

Analyzing policy indicators based on simulated income packages of hypothetical households, in Chapter 12 Cantillon, Marchal, and Luigjes observe that many welfare states reacted to the sliding away of the wage floor from the middle by increasing cash transfers and tax credits to people in paid work but with low earnings. In the 2000s, in most cases this helped to support the social floor. However, it appears that increasing financial work incentives was prioritized, while in many cases these additional efforts were not used to raise minimum income packages. The story behind the data is that the persistent and almost general inadequacy of minimum income protection for jobless households is structural—related to the inadequacy of gross low wages. Although most welfare states effectively started to work harder in order to mitigate the impact of the sluggish growth of low wages, efforts to raise the wage and the social floor for single parents and their children need to be increased significantly almost everywhere. This conforms to the findings in Chapter 5 and underscores earlier observations by Cantillon and Vandenbroucke (2014) that, even during the good years before the crisis, not a single EU15 country achieved simultaneous expansion in employment, reduction in poverty, and decreased spending on cash transfers. The lesson to be drawn is that, to achieve the poverty-reduction targets in the future, greater efforts will be required.

## MAKING PROGRESS DOES NOT COME CHEAP

Previous research has calculated the cost of mechanically closing the gap between the incomes of poor families and poverty thresholds (e.g., Cantillon, Van Mechelen, Pintelon, & Van den Heede, 2014; Vandenbroucke, Cantillon, Van Mechelen, Goedemé, & Van Lancker, 2013). These studies usually find that the amounts required to close the poverty gap in the developed welfare states of Northern and Western Europe are sizable, but they seem generally not to be beyond the capacity of these welfare states to generate. However, given that in many European countries the lowest wages are below the at-risk-of-poverty threshold, such a measure in itself would result in considerable "unemployment traps." Therefore, Collado et al. calculated the cost of closing the poverty gap while maintaining average financial participation incentives at the bottom of the income distribution in Belgium, Denmark, and the United Kingdom. The results reported in Chapter 10 show that the cost of closing the poverty gap without worsening average participation incentives at the bottom of the income distribution would be around twice the cost of just lifting all incomes to the level of the poverty threshold. Although the analysis is static and mechanical, the results can be seen as a first minimum estimate of the cost of a targeted strategy to close the poverty gap while balancing social protection and financial work incentives. If, instead of maintaining financial work incentives, policymakers want to increase them, the cost would obviously be considerably higher. Clearly, reconciling work and poverty reduction is not a cheap option.

On a broader level, these results illustrate the magnitude and complexity of countries' mission to simultaneously achieve reductions in poverty and expand employment, with given levels and progressivity of social and fiscal spending. Taken together, the research presented in this book suggests severe structural barriers to reducing poverty in contemporary welfare democracies. At the macro-level, these difficulties point to a social trilemma[7]: as a consequence of mounting pressures on low-production segments of the labor market resulting from skill-biased technological change and increased global competition, it has become difficult to achieve adequate income protection for those out of work while preserving sufficient financial work incentives, without greater efforts in terms of the size and the progressivity of the budgets involved. These findings point to the need to reconnect the discourses about poverty reduction with those on reducing income inequality: necessarily, achieving decent incomes for the poor requires lower income inequality via further measures, such as more progressive income and wealth taxation.

## DIFFICULT TRADE-OFFS

In general, raising the social floor requires:

1. At the least, adjusting social benefits and tax thresholds to changes in prices; from a longer-term perspective, social benefits should also be indexed in line with changes in average living standards.
2. On top of that, increasing the minimum social floor of social assistance and social insurance. In some countries, there is room for doing so without compromising too much on financial work incentives, while in most other countries that space is yet to be created.
3. Raising net income packages for low-wage earning households, through either higher minimum wages, in-work benefits, or increased child benefits and other cost compensations.

The analysis in Chapter 11 by Vandelannoote and Verbist of the effectiveness of alternative forms of employment-conditional earnings subsidies in Belgium illustrates some of the difficult trade-offs policymakers confront when designing such instruments. As explained by Kenworthy in Chapter 7, the attractiveness of earnings subsidies lies in their combination of creating employment incentives for disadvantaged groups and of providing extra income to support their living standards. The effectiveness of in-work benefits in achieving these two aims depends on many factors, notably the size and design of the benefit, as well as the wider policy and socioeconomic context. This wider context refers to the tax–benefit system as a whole, the prevalence and level of a minimum wage, the existence and extent of child-care provisions, and the distribution of incomes and wages. For the first time, Vandelannoote and Verbist studied the impact on both employment incentives and poverty outcomes of various designs of in-work benefits. In Chapter 11 they report hard trade-offs: it is difficult to find the right balance between employment and poverty goals. According to their results, the most appropriate system for the Belgian welfare state would be an individual-based system that uses hourly wages as a threshold. While the current Belgian system of the work bonus resembles this design, Vandelannoote and Verbist find that, in order to generate a significant employment and poverty impact, budgetary efforts should be increased significantly. The authors show how microsimulation techniques can be used to study stylized design changes in a stepwise manner, and they examine which characteristics of an in-work benefit "make it work," in terms of both employment and poverty aims. They find that the details of the design of in-work benefits matter a great deal, as well as the overall budget allocated to them.

The tenacity of trade-offs involved is also illustrated in Chapter 10. There it is shown that raising the social floor while keeping or increasing work incentives at the extensive margin not only comes at a cost, but also inevitably diminishes the marginal gain of working more hours at the intensive margin. The results vary enormously among countries, reflecting the very different nature of current tax–benefit systems in Europe. This reiterates the importance of the details and the coherence of policy reforms, the budgets involved, and the unavoidable link with the overall income distribution.

## SOCIAL INVESTMENT AND INNOVATION

The general lesson from the contributions in this book is important. Anti-poverty strategies are extremely demanding: they come at a considerable cost, they have to deal with difficult trade-offs, and they have to look at the architecture of the welfare state as a whole—the drivers of rising income inequality, the availability of jobs for the low skilled, the pressures on low wages, the issue of adequate work incentives, and the progressivity of taxes and social spending. Clearly, this cannot be achieved with a single measure: significant improvements of the social fabric as a whole are needed. Also, the main focus so far has been on the "mechanics" of the welfare state in terms of taxes and social benefits, with little attention paid to the role of social work, local initiatives focused on social inclusion, publicly provided or subsidized goods and services ( such as housing, child care, and education), and (active) labor-market policies in enhancing peoples' opportunities. This is where the importance of social investment policies and local actions of social innovation comes in.

In finding ways to successfully combine budgetary restraint, employment growth, and poverty reduction, since the second half of the 1990s Member States have been committed to a process of major reorientation toward what has been labeled "the social investment turn." As explained by Cronert and Palme in Chapter 9, the aim of this strategy is not only to promote equality of opportunity but also social inclusion, not least by preparing people to be prepared for, and integrated into, changing labor markets. The social investment perspective underlines the importance of early childhood development, training, educa-tion, lifelong learning, and family reconciliation for the long-term development of human capital. In Europe, the agenda first turned up in the Lisbon Strategy. In 2013, it resurfaced in the Social Investment Package, the aim being to spur Member States to make "investment" part of the social policy reform agenda in order to help reach the Europe 2020 targets (Palme & Cronert, 2015).

By helping to reduce the cost of subsidizing jobs and social protection for the low skilled, social investment strategies should be part and parcel of any coherent anti-poverty program. However, it would be an illusion to believe that poverty reduction and social inclusion could be attained with a one-sided focus on ac-tivation, investment, and promotion alone. To be successful, social investment policies are dependent on decent in-work and out-of-work incomes. Based on the recent Swedish experience of moving toward a "Third Way," away from a bal-anced "Nordic" approach to social investment in which adequate social protec-tion for work-poor households is a crucial complement to an active labor-market policy, Cronert and Palme conclude that an enlightened development path requires serious recasting of the social investment package. Social investment cannot be a substitute for social protection. Instead, the two must be viewed as twin pillars of the modern welfare state.

Meanwhile, in disconcerting circumstances, from the late 1970s onward, a whole range of place-based social innovation policies and actions emerged in the institutional margins of the welfare state. The growing number of local initiatives for civic empowerment inspired the European Commission in the late 2000s to adopt "social innovation" as part of its Renewed Social Agenda. Social in-novation is important because it accords a central role to civil society (whether social movements, NGOs, third-sector organizations, or volunteers), social entrepreneurs, and local governments, thereby strengthening the social fabric of welfare states. It stresses the relational and multidimensional nature of poverty and the crucial role of participation in combating poverty.

The examples shown by Oosterlynck et al. in Chapter 8 point to the potential—but also limits—of local social action. The importance and value of local actions should not be underestimated. They literally feed the hungry, give the thirsty drink, take strangers in, clothe the naked, look after the sick, and visit prisoners.[8] They can help to empower individuals who are insufficiently supported by traditional social policies and improve their capacity to participate in society. However, despite large and meritorious efforts, one should not expect these actions to have a direct and significant impact on at-risk-of-poverty rates. Yet, by alleviating persistent hardship, by forcing public authorities to recognize emerging needs, by strengthening the underlying social fabric, and by fortifying society from the inside out, social innovation can help to create the social and political conditions for more enduring poverty reduction.

## WHICH ROLE FOR EUROPE?

This book focuses on relative income poverty within nations. In Chapter 3, Goedemé, Zardo Trindade, and Vandenbroucke take a different perspective by directly comparing the living standards of EU citizens. This analysis, based on a pan-European low-income threshold, underscores the enormous differences among the living standards of Europeans living at the bottom. When a pan-European benchmark is used, about 40% of those with a low income tend to live in the Member States that have joined the EU since 2004, in spite of their relatively low population share. In past decades, there were clear improvements in living standards in the new EU Member States, most notably in Poland, Slovakia, and Bulgaria, but also strong deterioration of living standards in Greece, and to a lesser extent in Spain and Italy. These trends mark an important change in the composition of the bottom of the pan-European income distribution, with an increasing weight of the old EU Member States at the bottom end, most notably the crisis-hit Southern European countries. The fact that this is related to design failures in the architecture of the eurozone leads the authors of Chapter 3 to a conclusion of utmost importance: that, "whatever the solutions that are proposed to a variety of problems besetting the monetary union (e.g., a banking union, a fiscal capacity at the eurozone level, possibly associated with a re-insurance of national unemployment insurance schemes or a genuine EU unemployment insurance scheme), these solutions always entail the ex ante organization of solidarity mechanisms." (Chapter 3, p. 77)

Solidarity at the EU level also lies at the heart of the question about which role Europe should assume in supporting national anti-poverty strategies. A European guideline on a well-conceived notion of adequate minimum income protection may generate upward pressure, not only on minimum rights in social security and minimum wages, but also on the quality of work for people at the bottom. It may strengthen and render more operational the current processes of Open Coordination on these issues. Moreover, in times of budgetary austerity, an EU-wide concept of adequate minimum incomes would signal to Member States that the most vulnerable must not become the victims of austerity. These ideas already inspired the 2008 recommendation on active inclusion. The need for a better balance between economic and social goals by stronger EU guidance constitutes an important case for an EU framework directive in that field.[9] Recently, this was reaffirmed in a resolution by the European Parliament on the European Pillar of Social Rights, in which "the importance of adequate minimum income schemes for maintaining human dignity and combating poverty and social exclusion, as well as their role as a form of social investment in enabling people to participate in society, and to undertake training and/or look for work" is highlighted, and "the establishment of wage floors in the form of a national minimum wage" is recommended.[10]

Therefore, as a first step, in Chapter 12 Cantillon, Marchal, and Luigjes propose a modest shift from "output governance"—guided by "outcome" goals, such as the reduction of at-risk-of-poverty rates—to "input governance," guided by the identification of policy instruments to be put in place in order to attain the defined outcomes. In order not to violate the—to be cherished—principle of social subsidiarity, they cautiously propose to add policy input indicators regarding minimum income protection—including the wage and the social floor—to the poverty outcome indicators used in the monitoring process of the European Semester.

The principle of adequate minimum incomes for all should serve as a compass for the ethical program of the EU. Incorporating a set of well-thought-out policy indicators would strengthen European social governance. It would help to make more visible and tangible the linkages between commonly defined goals on the one hand and the policies and instruments to meet these goals on the other hand, while pointing to the difficult trade-offs involved. With their recent work on a Minimum Income Benchmarking Framework, the Social Protection Committee made an important step in that direction.

In order to give more bite to social coordination, this benchmarking framework should be strengthened and should be actively used in the European Semester. Later, starting from the 2008 Active Inclusion Recommendation and the European Pillar of Social Rights, a EU framework on minimum incomes should be put in place, not only as a guideline for national governments but also to rebalance the legal asymmetry between economic and social standards. This brings us inevitably back to the aforementioned question of solidarity at the EU level. After all, a European guideline on decent incomes for the poor would require a significantly greater budgetary effort on behalf of some of the poorer Member States in Eastern and Southern Europe (cf. Vandenbroucke, Cantillon, Van Mechelen, Goedemé, & Van Lancker, 2013). Therefore, the eradication of poverty in Europe necessitates substantial additional income redistribution both within and among countries. Ultimately, this raises the question of the meaning of solidarity in Europe.

## NOTES

1 The EU has set up a yearly cycle of economic policy coordination called the European Semester. Each year, the Commission undertakes a detailed analysis of EU Member States' plans for budgetary, macroeconomic, and structural reforms and provides them with country-specific recommendations for the next 12 to 18 months. These recommendations also contribute to the objectives of the EU's long-term strategy for jobs and growth, the Europe 2020 strategy, which is implemented and monitored in the context of the European Semester.

2 Chapter 2, this volume, Tables 2.1 and 2.2.
3 The authors also controlled for the crisis itself in their analysis. They found weak evidence that falling employment through the crisis period had stronger effects on poverty than it would have done in the pre-crisis period.
4 The United Kingdom between 2008 and 2013 is an example of this. See Hills, De Agostini, and Sutherland (2016).
5 Leventi, Sutherland, & Tasseva (2016). See Table 6 of that paper for some of their key comparisons.
6 Marx, Marchal, and Nolan (2013).
7 Discussed in more detail in Cantillon and Vandenbroucke (2014).
8 Matthew 25:35.
9 See, for example, Van Lancker (2010).
10 European Parliament resolution of January 19, 2017, on a European Pillar of Social Rights.

## REFERENCES

Atkinson, A. B. (2015). *Inequality. What can be done?* Cambridge, MA: Harvard University Press.

Atkinson, A. B., Cantillon, B., Marlier, E., & Nolan, B. (2002). *Social indicators: The EU and social inclusion.* Oxford, England: Oxford University Press.

Cantillon, B., & Vandenbroucke, F. (2014). *Reconciling work and poverty reduction: How successful are European welfare states?* Oxford, England: Oxford University Press.

Cantillon, B., Collado, D., & Van Mechelen, N. (2015). *The end of decent social protection for the poor? The dynamics of low wages, minimum income packages and median household incomes* [ImPRovE Working Paper No. 15/03]. Antwerp, Belgium: Herman Deleeck Centre for Social Policy, University of Antwerp.

Cantillon, B., Van Mechelen, N., Pintelon, O., & Van den Heede, A. (2014). Social redistribution, poverty and the adequacy of social protection. In B. Cantillon & F. Vandenbroucke (Eds.), *Reconciling work and poverty reduction: How successful are European welfare states?* (pp. 157–184). Oxford, England: Oxford University Press.

Hills, J., De Agostini, P., & Sutherland, H. (2016). Benefits, pensions, tax credits and direct taxes. In R. Lupton, T. Burchardt, J. Hills, K. Stewart, & P. Vizard (Eds.), *Social policy in a cold climate* (pp. 11–34). Bristol, England: Policy Press.

Leventi, C., Sutherland, H., & Tasseva, I. (2016). *Improving poverty reduction in Europe: What works (best) where?* [ImPRovE Working Paper No. 16/16]. Antwerp, Belgium: Herman Deleeck Centre for Social Policy, University of Antwerp.

Marx, I., Marchal, S., & Nolan, B. (2013). Mind the gap: Net incomes of minimum wage workers in the EU and the US. In I. Marx & K. Nelson (Eds.), *Minimum income protection in flux* (pp. 54–80). Houndmills, England: Palgrave-Macmillan.

Palme, J., & Cronert, A. (2015). *Trends in the Swedish social investment welfare state: "The enlightened path" or "the third way" for "the lions"?* [ImPRovE Working Paper No. 15/12]. Antwerp, Belgium: Herman Deleeck Centre for Social Policy, University of Antwerp.

Vandenbroucke, F., Cantillon, B., Van Mechelen, N., Goedemé, T., & Van Lancker, A. (2013). The EU and minimum income protection: Clarifying the policy conundrum. In I. Marx & K. Nelson (Eds.), *Minimum income protection in flux* (pp. 271–317). Hampshire, England: Palgrave-Macmillan.

Van Lancker, A. (2010). *Working document on a Framework Directive on Minimum Income*. Brussels, Belgium: European Anti-Poverty Network (EAPN).

# INDEX

active labor market policy (ALMP), 203,
209–10, 214
adequate social participation, 18
age group(s). *See also* children
differences in the impact of policy changes
across, 127
effects of policy reforms by, 120–23
ALMP (active labor market policy), 208,
211, 212
AROP indicator, 13–14. *See also* AROP threshold
nature of, xii, 36
qualifications regarding, xii
reasons for contextualizing the, 16
reference budgets and, 13–14, 15 (*see also*
reference budgets)
weaknesses and criticisms of, 14
AROP rate before social transfers (preAROP(a)
rate), 49
AROP rate(s), 17
dynamics in national, 57
employment and, 42–44
reductions in, 102
social cohesion and, 58–59
social transfers and, 36, 48–49, 100–2, 211
in Sweden, 211
AROP threshold, 13–15, 16, 25, 28–29. *See also*
AROP indicator; poverty threshold(s)
calculating, 26
defined, 14
in perspective, 22–24

reference budgets and, 15, 23 (*see also*
reference budgets)
AROP60 (60% at-risk-of-poverty rate), 17
for children, 28
AROP(a) (at-risk-of-poverty rates of active-age
population), 52
AROP(a) rates, 38, 41, 44
employment and, 41, 42–43, 44
nature of, 41
at-risk-of-poverty indicator. *See* AROP indicator
Atkinson, Anthony "Tony" Barnes, ix–x, 1, 2,
209–10, 290. *See also Social Indicators*
austerity, 137, 149, 295
distributional effects, 136–37
and Great Recession, 135
interactions with growth, 134–35
interactions with inequality, 135–36, 138,
146, 149–50
and poverty, 143

benefit policy changes. *See* policy changes
Big Society Initiative, 183
budget standards. *See* reference budgets
budgetary constraints. *See* employment/
poverty/budgetary constraints
trilemma

Cameron, David, 183
cash transfers, 154, 155. *See also* employment-
conditional earning subsidies

307